Char

& CHRISTIAN LIFE

Spirit-Led Reader

The Holy Spirit, My Senior Partner

David Yonggi Cho

The Next Move of God

Fuchsia Pickett

There's a Miracle in Your House

Tommy Barnett

CREATION HOUSE

Charisma's Spirit-Led Reader
Published by Creation House
Strang Communications Company
600 Rinehart Road
Lake Mary, Florida 32746
Web site: http://www.creationhouse.com

Library of Congress Cataloging-in-Publication Data:

Charisma's Spirit-led reader.
p. cm.
Contents: The Holy Spirit, my senior partner / David Yonggi Cho — The next move of God / Fuchsia Pickett — There's a miracle in your house / Tommy Barnett.
ISBN: 0-88419-595-3 (alk. paper)
1. Holy Spirit. 2. Christian life. I. Charisma. II. Led by the Spirit. 1999.
BT121.2C435 1999 98-41148
231'.3—dc21 CIP

9 0 1 2 3 4 5 6 RRD 8 7 6 5 4 3 2 1
Printed in the United States of America

CONTENTS

CHARISMA'S SPIRIT-LED READER

Foreword

FOR NEARLY A quarter century *Charisma* magazine has been reporting on Spirit-led living. From humble beginnings as a church magazine, *Charisma* has grown, by the grace of God, to more than 600,000 monthly readers from all over the world. As *Charisma* has grown, it has become a family of magazines. It also has grown to include Creation House, the publisher of this special book, *Charisma's Spirit-Led Reader.*

All three of the books in this special edition were previously published by Creation House. They are combined into one edition as a special bonus for you the reader.

Charisma magazine has reported about each of these authors. We first reported on David Yonggi Cho in the May/June 1977 issue when his church in Seoul, South Korea, had *only* 40,000 members. Today, it is reported to have 750,000 members. Over the years *Charisma* has reported on his ministry many times, and Dr. Cho has been the author of numerous articles in *Charisma* magazine, including an excerpt from this book, *The Holy Spirit, My Senior Partner,* in May 1989.

I have had the privilege of knowing Dr. Cho since the late 1970s. I have visited his church in Seoul, Korea three times, most recently earlier this year. On numerous occasions, I have had the privilege of interacting with him on a personal basis, so that in many ways I have considered him a mentor. But much more than the one-on-one time I have had the privilege to spend with Dr. Cho, I have been mentored by his books—especially this one on his insight on the Holy Spirit. Dr. Cho, more than anyone else I know, has revelation about the Holy Spirit as a person whom he calls his "senior partner."

I originally read his book many years ago. As I reread it as I prepared to write this foreword, I was deeply moved again by how our lives can be empowered by God, the Holy Spirit.

We wrote about Dr. Fuchsia Pickett in *Charisma* in September 1997. Dr. Pickett is one of the most profound Bible teachers under whose teaching I've ever had the privilege to sit. She and her husband, Leroy, have become close family friends and have been overnight guests in our home many times. This has allowed me to personally delve into many of the topics that she writes about in this book. She has enormous insight, and for those who do not have the privilege as I do to talk to her personally, her books give you the heart of what God has revealed to her about the next move of God.

Finally, *Charisma* has reported many times on Tommy Barnett, especially on his Dream Center in Los Angeles, California, which I have visited twice. Over the years I have cultivated a relationship with Pastor Barnett, visiting his church in Phoenix and spending quality time with him on numerous occasions. He is one of the most positive, upbeat people I have ever known. He has a heart to reach the lost for Christ. He has a purity in his motivation and his ministry that is hard to find these days.

In many ways I look to Pastor Barnett as a mentor. In fact, my wife, Joy, and I have asked him to be a part of a special group of people who give us advice on spiritual matters involving our organization. Dr. Pickett also serves on that small group.

In addition, all three of these authors—Dr. Cho, Dr. Pickett, and Pastor Barnett—serve as editorial advisors for our pastoral magazine, *Ministries Today.* So you can see that I have had a close personal relationship with the authors of these three books, as well as their relationship with our organization.

I hope you are ministered to by these three books, just as I hope you are ministered to every month with *Charisma* magazine. If you haven't read *Charisma* or haven't seen it in a long time, I want to send you a complimentary copy. Just write me a letter and mention that you are responding to the offer I made in the foreword in this book. Write us at:

Charisma Magazine
ATTN: Free Issue Offer
600 Rinehart Rd.
Lake Mary, FL 32746

I have been deeply moved and impacted by these books. I pray that you are as well.

—Stephen Strang

Founder and Publisher, *Charisma* Magazine

Foreword

THE APOSTLE PAUL tells us that each of God's people are "letters of Christ." Because we have all been given the priceless deposit of the Holy Spirit, we each carry a heavenly message—"written not with ink, but with the Spirit of the living God, not on tablets of stone, but on tablets of human hearts" (2 Cor. 3:3, NAS).

But there are some people who have been gifted with the grace to carry a special message to the church. Call them prophets if you wish—they themselves might be too humble to ever describe themselves that way. But the fact is that God has deposited so much of Himself in their hearts that they burn inside with His passionate concerns. They are carriers of His fire, and they spread it each time they communicate with God's people.

During the almost twenty-five years that *Charisma* has been published, dozens of these prophetic voices have been featured in the pages of our magazine. But three of them stand out as having a unique message for the church, and that is why we have compiled some of their best writings in this one volume.

In the decades to come, when church leaders look back on the twentieth century, Dr. David Yonggi Cho will surely stand out as a premier apostolic pioneer. Although most of us know him as the pastor of the largest church in the world, we often forget that he began his ministry with nothing but faith, in a country where missionaries were only recently allowed the freedom to spread the gospel. Cho's message of faith for the impossible—and his assurance that prayer will always prevail—is more applicable to us today as we face the challenges of a new millennium.

Though she is not as well known as Dr. Cho, author and Bible teacher Fuchsia Pickett has stirred the American church to go behind the veil and discover the riches of God's presence. She has called us to forsake the status quo, to abandon our own agendas in order to seek the One who speaks from the secret chamber of the holy of holies. She has called us to make intimacy with the Holy Spirit our chief desire.

Because she made Him her first love, Dr. Pickett also encountered the Spirit's fire in an unusual way—catching a glimpse of what our world will look like in a few more years when Pentecostal revival achieves its most glorious climax in a worldwide outpouring. That glorious vision of a world saturated in the glory of God motivated this dear saint to travel the world in her eighties as a preacher.

Tommy Barnett is another prophet to this generation. Although he is known as a successful pastor and a lively Bible teacher, his most penetrating message to the church is drawn from his motivation to reach the lost. At his core he is an evangelist, and his restlessness over the condition of broken humanity is what stirred him in the early 1990s to launch an ambitious outreach in a troubled Los Angeles neighborhood.

Today, Barnett and his son Matthew have created a prototype of what local church ministry will look like in the early years of the twenty-first century. They have called Christians to leave their comfort zones, to forsake suburban security and to launch out boldly to reclaim Satan's territory in our megacities. I pray their message has not fallen on deaf ears, and that by the end of the next decade hundreds of ministries like The Dream Center in Los Angeles will be operating in places like New York, Atlanta, Philadelphia, Denver, Dallas, Washington, and San Francisco.

It's interesting that all three authors we are featuring in this volume are dreamers. Dr. Cho dreamed of building a megachurch in Korea—a country that had no known Christian converts until the first decade of the 1900s. Fuchsia Pickett read the promise of the Old Testament prophets, which says, "The knowledge of the Lord will fill the earth as the waters cover the sea"—and dared to believe it could happen in our lifetime. Tommy Barnett dreamed that churches could mobilize armies of lay people to go into our cities with love and compassion and see drug addicts, prostitutes, bikers, welfare mothers, and throwaway children rescued and redeemed by the message of Christ.

Let these prophets of God stir you to action. Dream with them—and then let the Holy Spirit plant special dreams in your own heart that will become a reality—as faith gives birth to a miracle.

—J. Lee Grady, publisher
Charisma magazine

The Holy Spirit, My Senior Partner

David Yonggi Cho

THE HOLY SPIRIT, MY SENIOR PARTNER
by David [Paul] Yonggi Cho
Previously published by Creation House

Strang Communications Company
600 Rinehart Road
Lake Mary, Florida 32746
Web site: http://www.creationhouse.com
Library of Congress Catalog Card Number: 88-64193
International Standard Book Number: 0-88419-226-1

Unless otherwise noted, all Scripture quotations are from the King James Version of the Bible.

CONTENTS

The Holy Spirit, My Senior Partner

Introduction

GOD'S DIVINE EXECUTIVE agent in the world today is the Holy Spirit. He is continuing the work that Jesus began. He is moving among millions of believers and unbelievers all over the world—in homes, churches, prisons, behind the walls of communism, and in countries where the gospel has been resisted for centuries. He is moving and working in response to the pleas of God's children everywhere. His work is powerful and continues steadily in the lives of Christians who have sought His help. Christians who have developed a steady and growing prayer life and who communicate and fellowship with the Spirit are those who know Jesus Christ the best.

The Holy Spirit can never be underestimated. He is always in control of situations that have been given to Him in prayer. In split seconds He has intervened to divert disasters, to reveal the right decisions to make, to help Christians through the most critical circumstances. He has alerted believers, even when separated by thousands of miles, to pray or be available to assist Him when necessary. He has asked others to pray for a need weeks before the need surfaced. The busiest executives around the world would pay any price to have a senior partner like Him.

I began pastoring while I was still attending a small Assemblies of God Bible college in Seoul. In the aftermath of the Korean conflict, the despair of the people was so evident I realized that those who desired to minister to them needed a supernatural ability to rise above the problems, sickness, and poverty.

I prayed for an experience with the Holy Spirit about whom I had studied and learned. I asked the Holy Spirit to come and fill me with His power, His ministry, and His message for a sick and hurting world. I realized that by myself I could never find enough uplifting and encouraging sermons to preach unless I lived above my own problems. So daily I prayed for the filling of the Holy Spirit. Other students were also praying for the baptism of the Holy Spirit. We prayed for days, and as fellow students received this experience, I noticed their lives took on a new dimension. They were still poor, but in their poverty they were full of joy and peace with an unexplainable confidence that God was going to help them. Problems did not disturb their peace. As I observed the change in their lives, I knew I had to keep praying until I received this experience also.

And then it happened. One evening while I was asking the Lord for the filling of the Holy Spirit, I felt His presence draw near. It was a wonderful experience. I was worshiping and praising Jesus aloud, telling Him audibly again and again how wonderful it was to know Him and how much I loved Him. Though I could not see anyone, it seemed as if the Holy Spirit stood before me, ready to pour a blessing on me.

As I worshiped, I felt a warm glow touch my face, then my tongue, then my body, and without realizing it I began to speak new words that came to my mind and my tongue at the same time. The more I spoke, the more I felt impressed to speak forth the words that were coming so quickly. I don't know how long I remained in that room worshiping the Lord, and it didn't matter. My heart was overflowing with praise and worship to Jesus in a new language. I was overwhelmed with joy and an awareness of a new power with God that I had not known before.

That was my initial experience when I was baptized with the Holy Spirit. Every day after that, I felt as if I were living in the very presence of Jesus. It was difficult for me to explain it. Each time I prayed, the Holy Spirit came to help me pray, taking my Korean language and substituting for it a heavenly language I had never learned. I knew my spirit had become one with Him, and I could pray for a whole hour or more with greater ease.

After graduating from Bible college, I felt I should start a church. The Holy Spirit impressed upon me where and how to begin, and I recognized His help in those decisions. I purchased a used army tent and pitched it in a slum area among needy families.

Everything did not go perfectly from that day to this, but I began to learn how much the Holy Spirit was interested in helping me develop the ministry that He Himself had given me. No matter how wonderful our experiences with the Lord have been, we are still in the flesh. As long as we seek counsel from the Lord, we will receive it. But it is so easy to evaluate a situation and think, *I can do this myself, so I will not trouble the Lord in prayer or ask the Holy Spirit to help me.*

Without fully realizing what I had done, I formulated my own plans for the new tent church. I wanted the program to be impressive and many people to come, but I struggled to prepare sermons. When my sermons weren't very good, I gathered all the sermons by Billy Graham and Oral Roberts that I could find and preached them. The problem was that I soon ran out of sermons and was right back where I started. At times I became discouraged and wanted to quit. At this point in my young ministry, I returned to prayer and asked the Holy Spirit to help me.

Letting the Holy Spirit direct one's life is not always easy. Self gets in the way even in preparing a sermon; one can choose good Scripture verses and make a sermon—and leave the Holy Spirit completely out of the process. How many times I had to confess my sin of trying to do everything by myself! Then I would invite Him to come again and help me. And each time the Holy Spirit helped me—even to prepare sermons. Sometimes the message was totally different from what I had prepared. He gave me His thoughts and the Scripture verses He wanted me to share, because He knew who would be present in those meetings and their needs.

I returned to the Scriptures often and read that the Holy Spirit came to abide with us forever (John 14:16); to bring all things to our remembrance that He said to us in the Word (John 14:26); to testify of Jesus (John 15:26); to guide us into all truth (John 16:13); to show us things to come (John 16:13); and to glorify Jesus in everything and show that glory to believers (John 16:14).

One day the Holy Spirit spoke to my heart: "If you want your church to grow, you must develop a greater communion and fellowship with Me. Don't preach about the Holy Spirit as an experience only. He is an awesome person! Preach about the person. Develop a communion and fellowship by waiting in My presence after prayer. I want to talk to you also."

After I was married, there was a time when my wife was very unhappy. I had been busy in evangelistic meetings during the week and came home on Saturday to rest and prepare to preach in my church on Sunday. I would bring home a suitcase of dirty clothes and replenish my supply for another week. Every time my wife would try to share something with me or talk about the happenings of her week, I would always apologize that I had to study, or I had to pray, or I had to do something else. I didn't take time to sit and visit as I had when we were dating. "After all," I said without feeling, "God has called me to preach, and I'm very busy preparing sermons. You have a baby to keep you company and a home to take care of. What more do you want?"

One day my mother-in-law came to visit, and she said she wanted to talk with me. In those days I was always afraid when she said she wanted to talk with me because that meant I was not doing something right. "Do you love your wife?" she asked.

"Yes, of course," I answered.

"Then you must spend some time with her as well as with your ministry. She is not a thing. She is a *person.* She is happy when you recognize her and talk with her, and she feels rejected when you don't."

That day I learned a great lesson about love relationships. I began to show my love for my wife in many ways. I took time to talk with her about our home and our baby. We made a plan to take Mondays off together, and she would outline our day. The smile returned to her face. At the evening meal, she presented me with her plans. We were going to the park for our first Monday morning and have lunch out. Those plans developed just as she wanted, and we did the things that made her happy. In no time, my home life turned around. I had a happy and satisfied wife again, which made me happy when I left the following week for more gospel meetings.

Through that experience I learned a tremendous lesson. My understanding of the Holy Spirit changed. He, too, is a person who desires fellowship. Otherwise, He is grieved. Instead of praying and hurrying off to the church, I took time to sit in His presence and let Him talk with me. Since He gave me the ministry I have, and since He desired to lead and guide me into ways to fulfill that ministry, I looked forward to the times of talking with Him. I conversed with Him as a friend talks with a friend, as a husband talks with his wife—talking and listening and remembering.

As the weeks passed, I understood the ministry of the Holy Spirit better than ever. He is a faithful friend who came to do all that the Word declares He would do. I asked Him to be my senior partner in everything that concerned my life and God's work.

Every morning since then, when I awake I say, "Good morning, Holy Spirit. Let's work together today, and I will be Your vessel." Every evening before retiring I say again, "It's been a wonderful day working with You, Holy Spirit. Cover my family and me with Your divine protection as we rest through the night." The next morning again I greet Him as a person and invite Him to go with me through the day and take the lead in all affairs that must be handled, and He does.

When it is time to prepare sermons, He is always present. When I am counseling, He is directing my counsel to each individual. When I am making a decision—which preaching invitations should I accept?—He guides me. Why? Because He watches over the needs and situations of every area of the world, and He knows which area is ready for the words He has prepared me to preach. As I walk to the pulpit, I say, "Let's go, Holy Spirit. You're on!" When the meeting is over and I return home (or to my hotel if I am preaching abroad), I tell Him, "Thank You, Senior Partner. You did a great work in the hearts of people tonight. Keep working. Encourage those pastors through the new converts who found You tonight." And when He has free rein in the service, His presence makes the difference.

Have you ever stood on top of a mountain and observed how small everything seemed below? When you have received the fullness of the Holy Spirit, you will almost immediately notice that life's problems and your personal needs also seem very small—because you are looking at them from a different perspective. You are seeing them as the Holy Spirit does, because He is in control.

As you read this book, I trust you will meet the Holy Spirit personally in its pages. He wants to be your senior partner, too. When you develop that close communion with Him, He will make a difference in your business, your family relationships, your decision making—in every area of your life.

The weeks and months have rolled by, and I have completed nearly forty-five years of ministry. I have seen many miracles of healing, interventions in church situations, and unusual answers to prayer. God has raised up many leaders in our church who have gone on to be outstanding missionaries and pastors. If I were to assess what I have learned since my conversion, I would say meeting the Holy Spirit and learning to know Him in an intimate way has been the greatest experience of my life. My senior partner and I are still very close, and we still fellowship every day!

—DAVID YONGGI CHO
SENIOR PASTOR
YOIDO FULL GOSPEL CHURCH
SEOUL, KOREA

1

Communion With the Holy Spirit—Why?

In 2 Corinthians 13:14, Paul wrote a benediction to the believers in Corinth: "The grace of the Lord Jesus Christ, and the love of God, and the communion of the Holy Ghost, be with you all."

What deep feelings that benediction stirs within me. But I find that's not true with everyone. The countless blessings these words can bestow are disappearing from hearts today. A little later on I'll get to the *why* behind that statement, but first let me describe what the blessings are.

The Grace of Christ

The original meaning of the Greek word for *grace* was "the ultimate in beauty." The Greeks enjoyed the pursuit of beauty—through philosophy and sports, poetry and drama, sculpture and architecture. And of course their land—mountains and streams and coastline—surrounded them with beauty. When the beauty of something gave joy to the viewer or hearer, the Greeks said it was full of grace. Eventually, this meaning developed a broader sense, to include not only the beauty of things but also beautiful works, acts, thoughts, eloquence, and even mankind—all could be considered full of grace.

A second meaning of *grace* was "favor," good will given out of unconditional, overflowing love with no expectation of reward or payment.

A third meaning of *grace* referred to a praiseworthy work, exhibiting virtues far exceeding the common.

In his benediction, the apostle Paul must have felt a surging joy beyond description, knowing the unconditional forgiveness of sins and the many blessings of salvation—full of beauty or grace.

The Love of God

HOW SHOULD WE accept the following benediction, "The love of God . . . be with you all"? Have we become so hardened that we can hear about the love of God without being moved or having a contrite heart? Almost any Christian today can quote John 3:16, yet only the letters remain, the life in them having been forgotten.

There are several kinds of love, including the parental love for children of one's own flesh and blood, the love that longs for and yearns after the opposite sex, and the fraternal love that gives us joy when we fellowship with dear friends. But human love can by no means be compared to the love of God. Parental love is limited to children. The love between the sexes is self-centered. Even the love between friends will falter if one never receives anything in return for care and concern. But the love of God is different.

Divine love in the Greek language refers to a love that wholly sacrifices itself for the object of its love, realizing the precious value of it. For example, man and woman betrayed God and fell into deep sin resulting in an abominable life, which ultimately led to eternal destruction. In spite of this betrayal, God lovingly sacrificed Himself on Calvary to save mankind. Why? Because each individual soul is priceless to Him. This is divine love!

Though in a fallen state of sin, mankind possesses the image of God, and we can become noble creatures if we receive the grace of redemption.

God is love, and His love is true love. He loved the sinners of this world so much that He didn't even spare His only Son but made Him a sacrifice for our sins. Is it not true love that He loved even us who are fallen in sin? Paul was probably moved to tears when he wrote of the love of God, but why have we become so cold?

How can our faith be restored so that we can be deeply moved by the grace of Jesus Christ and the love of God? Where is the path to restoration? Indeed, there is a way to full restoration. There is an answer to the cry of our spirits, and it is found in the communion of the Holy Spirit. The Holy Spirit pours all grace and love into our spirits through His communion with us.

The Communion of the Holy Spirit

COMMUNION MEANS "COMMUNICATING with or traveling together, transporting with." The splendid development of transportation has made the modern world a global town. Through this rapid and convenient transportation, people all over the world share what is needed to meet their cultural, political, economic, military, and scientific needs. It is not an exaggeration to say that you can measure a civilization by the development of its transportation system.

Suppose this global system of transportation were suddenly brought to a standstill. The whole world would become a living hell. Almost every kind of work would ultimately be paralyzed. Cities would suffer from hunger and cold, as food and fuel supplies would stop. Rural areas and factories would become heaped with decaying farm products and commodities, as marketing channels would be clogged. Transportation is no dispensable convenience. It is necessary to human welfare. Likewise, the communion of the Holy Spirit—daily traveling and constant fellowship with the Holy Spirit—is essential for our spiritual well-being.

The measure of our faith is in direct proportion to our communion with the Holy Spirit. Through the communion of the Holy Spirit, we receive spiritual blessings, and we tell Him our earnest desires. Though the grace of Jesus Christ and the love of God may abound immeasurably in heaven, they are useless to us if they do not reach us. Likewise, though our hearts are full of earnest desires, if the Holy Spirit does not help us commune with God through prayer, we cannot pray properly.

The Bible confirms this fact clearly. "The Lord direct your hearts into the love of God, and into the patient waiting for Christ" (2 Thess. 3:5).

In this verse, "the Lord" refers to the Holy Spirit, as He is the One who leads us into the love of God and into the patient waiting for Christ. However abundant the grace of Jesus Christ and the love of God are, if the Holy Spirit does not lead our hearts into such grace and love, our faith is merely the faith of dead words. If the Holy Spirit does not help us commune with God, our prayer will be like that of the Pharisees, totally lacking in life.

The Bible clearly teaches that the Spirit assists us in our praying: "The Spirit also helpeth our infirmities: for we know not what we should pray for as we ought: but the Spirit itself maketh intercession for us with groanings which cannot be uttered" (Rom. 8:26). Jude 20 also points out the Spirit's place in our prayer life: "Beloved, building up yourselves on your most holy faith, praying in the Holy Ghost."

The word *communion*, as used by Paul in his Corinthian benediction, "the communion of the Holy Ghost be with you all," has deep implications. The Greek word has two important meanings.

Fellowship

The first meaning refers to intercourse or fellowship on the basis of intimate friendship. Without fellowship with the Holy Spirit there can be no spiritual life, no faith with power and victory. The early church was abundant with fervent prayer, overflowing passion, rich vitality, and thanksgiving, gushing out like a spring as a result of their fellowship with the Holy Spirit. Why are Christians settling for mere outward formalities of religion, dry ceremonies of worship, seeing the church as a place of social intercourse? This emptiness has left young people sick of the Christian way and its form of godliness. They have become disillusioned—because the church has lost its spiritual life!

John A. Mackey, former dean of Princeton University's theological college and Presbyterian Alliance Theological Seminary, said in a Presbyterian meeting: "It is better to approach religion with natural feelings than to come to it with aesthetic and orderly forms without dynamic power. One of the most important problems the church of today faces is that it regards it lawful to express feelings in every field but religion. What the present church needs is to provide something which will inflame all the human passions. From the very moment the church is completely programized [sic] and depersonalized, it becomes merely a memorial of God instead of the living institution of the power of God."

What is the answer to the problem he points out? Fervent fellowship with the living Holy Spirit. Without it, the church naturally becomes cold; worship becomes mechanical. Faith loses the burning passion that gives a depth to our whole personality. This kind of faith is like a stove with no fire.

Knowing this, the first question the apostle Paul asked some Ephesians who appeared tired and dejected was: "Have ye received the Holy Ghost since ye believed?" (Acts 19:2). When Jesus saw His disciples were in sorrow and despair, He promised the Holy Spirit would come and abide in their spirits: "I will pray the Father, and he shall give you another Comforter, that he may abide with you for ever . . . I will not leave you comfortless: I will come to you" (John 14:16, 18).

That comfort can be ours, but in more cases than we realize, believers today have not even heard about the Holy Spirit.

How do we have fellowship with the Holy Spirit? First, we must acknowledge that He is present in His church and welcome Him, earnestly desiring His guidance and opening our hearts to depend upon Him continually. The love of God and the grace of Jesus can reach our spirits only through fellowship and communion with the Holy Spirit.

Partnership in Evangelism

The second meaning of *communion* is "to do business in partnership" (Luke 5:10) and "to participate in" (2 Cor. 10:16; Phil. 3:10)—to work together as partners for the same purpose and to share joy, sorrow, victory, and trials.

The Holy Spirit was sent to this earth for the very purpose of working in partnership with believers, to quicken dead spirits by witnessing to the grace of Jesus Christ. Before He left this world, Jesus said to His disciples, "When the Comforter is come, whom I will send unto you from the Father, even the Spirit of truth, which proceedeth from the Father, he shall testify of me: And ye also shall bear witness, because ye have been with me from the beginning" (John 15:26–27).

From this, we can understand that the great mission of preaching the gospel was first given to the Holy Spirit and then to the saints who believed in the Lord. But Jesus emphasized here that the work of evangelism should be carried out as a partnership between the Holy Spirit and mankind—with the Holy Spirit participating as the senior partner. We can conclude that the whole reason why evangelism today makes so little progress, why the church is retrograde in the work of winning souls, and why it has been on the brink of bankruptcy is that this partnership with the Holy Spirit has been broken. These days, people neither acknowledge the Holy Spirit nor welcome Him. Since they don't depend on Him, they end up in failure, trying to accomplish the work of God through their own means and efforts.

This tragic failure was clearly pointed out in the Book of Revelation:

> Behold, I stand at the door, and knock: if any man hear my voice, and open the door, I will come in to him, and will sup with him, and he with me.
>
> —Revelation 3:20

If these words had been addressed to the unbelieving world, they would not be surprising. But they were given to the Laodicean church, the believers in the end time of the world. What a horrible revelation!

Think of it. Our Lord said He would be with us forever through the Holy Spirit, yet the church is trying to do the work of God through human-centered worship, driving out the Holy Spirit and leaving Him outside the door!

It was not so in the early church. The first-century saints realized that evangelism should be done from beginning to end in partnership with the Holy Spirit.

When the preaching apostles were taken to be examined before the Jewish council in Jerusalem, Peter answered the council's question thus:

> The God of our fathers raised up Jesus, whom ye slew and hanged on a tree. Him hath God exalted with his right hand to be a Prince and a Saviour, for to give repentance to Israel, and forgiveness of sins. And we are his witnesses of these things; and so is also the Holy Ghost, whom God hath given to them that obey Him.
>
> —ACTS 5:30–32

There Peter confirmed that the apostles' work of evangelism was carried out in partnership with the Holy Spirit.

Jesus did not begin to preach the kingdom of heaven until after He had received the fullness of the Holy Spirit. Only then was He able to complete His ministry in three and a half years with great power and authority. Realizing this, how dare we think we could accomplish the work of God with only human power and wisdom?

A young man named Archibald Brown entered a pastor's college established by the world-renowned preacher C. H. Spurgeon. After Brown graduated from that school, he became a highly successful pastor in London, and thousands of people flocked to hear his preaching. Many admired the tremendous anointing on the young minister and wondered where his great power came from. After he died, the secret was found in the old, well-thumbed Bible he had used. At Acts 15:28 he had penned a footnote: "Ah, how important is a partnership with the senior partner, the Holy Spirit! Without His partnership, no life of faith or evangelical work has value."

The blessing and success in our life of faith and gospel preaching are also in direct proportion to the depth of our fellowship with our senior partner, the Holy Spirit.

After His resurrection and before His ascension, Jesus gathered His disciples about Him and gravely commanded them to preach the gospel to the whole world:

> Go ye therefore, and teach all nations, baptizing them in the name of the Father, and of the Son, and of the Holy Ghost: Teaching them to observe all things whatsoever I have commanded you: and, lo, I am with you alway, even unto the end of the world.
>
> —MATTHEW 28:19–20

But after the Lord said this, He didn't tell them to begin preaching at once. He told them that the preaching of the gospel could not be done without partnership with the Holy Spirit:

> Behold, I send the promise of my Father upon you: but tarry ye in the city of Jerusalem, until ye be endued with power from on high.
>
> —LUKE 24:49

> John truly baptized with water; but ye shall be baptized with the Holy Ghost not many days hence. . . . Ye shall receive power, after that the Holy Ghost is come upon you: and ye shall be witnesses unto me.
>
> —ACTS 1:5, 8

The wonderful victory of the gospel in the early church happened because the disciples wholly obeyed Jesus' commandment. They tarried in Jerusalem until they were filled with the Holy Spirit, and then they preached.

In the Book of Acts, it was written clearly and repeatedly that the gospel was preached in partnership with the Holy Spirit.

In Acts 8, we meet deacon Philip, who went down to Samaria and led revival meetings at which a great multitude of people repented and were saved. Countless people were healed. Great miracles and wonders were performed and joy abounded. In the midst of this great revival, an angel suddenly appeared to Philip and told him to go south, toward Gaza.

How different God's will is from man's. It would *seem* that the devil had tempted Philip with a wrong revelation. Why should he have left those victorious meetings to go to a desolate wilderness? Because Philip did his business in partnership with the Holy Spirit.

He was sure that this order was truly given by the Spirit Himself. In obedience, he left the Samaritan meetings and went out to the wilderness by faith, not knowing where he was going. But the Holy Spirit had planned the deliverance of the whole African continent through the deliverance of one Ethiopian soul whom Philip would encounter!

The Bible described the scene this way:

> And he [Philip] arose and went: and, behold, a man of Ethiopia, an eunuch of great authority under Candace, queen of the Ethiopians, who had the charge of all her treasure, and had come to Jerusalem for to worship, was returning, and sitting in his chariot read Esaias the prophet.
>
> —ACTS 8:27–28

The Holy Spirit sent Philip to the desert to preach the gospel of salvation to one prepared soul. And because this one Ethiopian was saved, Philip came to reap a harvest far greater than he would have reaped had he remained in Samaria leading gospel meetings. We should neither neglect nor despise what seem to be small leadings of the Holy Spirit; we have no idea what He might have planned.

The Holy Spirit's word to Philip became even more specific:

> The Spirit said unto Philip, Go near, and join thyself to this chariot.
>
> —ACTS 8:29

Led by the invisible Holy Spirit, Philip approached the chariot at the right time and place when the Ethiopian eunuch was reading Isaiah 53, the prophecy of Christ's suffering for our atonement. What wonderful guidance and appropriate timing it was. After hearing Philip's preaching, the Ethiopian received Jesus as Savior. When they came upon a place where there was water, he was baptized.

What took place afterward shows how powerful partnership with the Holy Spirit in the work of preaching the gospel can be:

> And when they were come up out of the water, the Spirit of the Lord caught away Philip, that the eunuch saw him no more: and he went on his way rejoicing.
>
> —ACTS 8:39

The Spirit of the Lord "caught away Philip." That's some partnership.

Some might justify their powerlessness with an excuse that the Holy Spirit does not work in such a way today. But Jesus said concerning the Holy Spirit, "He [the Father] shall give you another Comforter, that he may abide with you *for ever*" (John 14:16, italics mine).

The Holy Spirit is the same forever, and He is with us at this moment. If the Holy Spirit is not able to work, it is because believers today betray and deny Him, and they do not depend upon Him and pay heed to Him. Neglect of the Holy Spirit is what makes the powerful gospel become old news, like antiques in a museum.

In Acts 10, we find another scene of partnership. Peter in partnership with the Holy Spirit is sent to preach to a Gentile centurion, named Cornelius, and his entire house:

> Peter went up upon the housetop to pray about the sixth hour: and he became very hungry, and would have eaten: but while they made ready, he fell into a trance, and saw heaven opened, and a certain vessel descending unto him, as it had been a great sheet knit at the four corners, and let down to the earth: Wherein were all manner of fourfooted beasts of the earth, and wild beasts, and creeping things, and fowls of the air. And there came a voice to him, Rise, Peter; kill, and eat. But Peter said, Not so, Lord; for I have never eaten any thing that is common or unclean. And the voice spake unto him again the second time, What God hath cleansed, that call not thou common. This was done thrice; and the vessel was received up again into heaven. Now while Peter doubted in himself what this vision which he had seen should mean, behold, the men which were sent from Cornelius had made inquiry for Simon's house, and stood before the gate, and called and asked whether Simon, which was surnamed Peter, were lodged there. While Peter thought on the vision, the Spirit said unto him, Behold, three men seek thee. Arise therefore, and get thee down, and go with them, doubting nothing: for I have sent them.
>
> —Acts 10:9–20

Here once again, we can understand that the Holy Spirit works for the deliverance of souls. Cornelius, a centurion of the Roman army in Caesarea, was a devout man, but he had not yet received salvation. God's Holy Spirit, through the message of an angel, instructed

Cornelius to send for Peter as the vessel to preach the gospel. Peter, raised a devout Jew, abhorred companionship, even conversation, with Gentiles, who were "unclean" according to Jewish law. But in order to broaden the sphere of Peter's ministry, the Holy Spirit made Peter see a strange vision—three times—and then He ordered Peter not to doubt, but to go to the house of the Gentile Cornelius.

What a wonderful ministry of the Holy Spirit! He had prepared both parties—the messenger and the one who received the message. It is beyond our comprehension how desperately such a ministry of the Holy Spirit is needed today—to send a prepared vessel to a prepared spirit. God is the only one who knows the right timing.

When Peter was preaching the gospel in the house of Cornelius, he said:

> He commanded us to preach unto the people, and to testify that it is he which was ordained of God to be the Judge of quick and dead. To him give all the prophets witness, that through his name whosoever believeth in him shall receive remission of sins.
>
> —ACTS 10:42–43

The account continues:

> While Peter yet spake these words the Holy Ghost fell on all them which heard the word. And they of the circumcision which believed were astonished, as many as came with Peter, because that on the Gentiles also was poured out the gift of the Holy Ghost.
>
> —ACTS 10:44–45

Such a wonderful work as this could take place only in partnership with the Holy Spirit.

Later on in Acts, Luke describes a scene in which a whole congregation worked together with the Holy Spirit.

> Now there were in the church that was at Antioch certain prophets and teachers. . . . As they ministered to the Lord, and fasted, the *Holy Ghost said,* Separate me Barnabas and Saul for the work whereunto I have called them. And when they had fasted and prayed, and laid their hands on them, they sent them away.
>
> —ACTS 13:1–4, ITALICS MINE

From this account we can learn several important lessons concerning the relationship between the work of evangelism and the Holy Spirit. In preaching the gospel, the Holy Spirit is omnipotent, sovereign. Here the Holy Spirit shows that He holds the position of preeminence in the church by using the pronoun *I,* which signifies that the work of the gospel is the work that the Holy Spirit demands. Here the Holy Spirit emphasized that the ambassador extraordinary and plenipotentiary is neither a denomination nor any human person, but the Holy Spirit Himself.

This passage also clearly teaches that those who labored in the gospel could accomplish their mission only through partnership with the Holy Spirit. Without earnestly waiting upon the guidance of the Holy Spirit like this church of Antioch, which ministered to the Lord and prayed with the Spirit, how could one hear the still small voice of the Holy Spirit?

It is sad but true that the church today is filled with plans and programs for human interest; worship is planned and presented for fleshly pleasure through social association. There is little interest in hearing from the Holy Spirit. As a result, the church, which should be taking care of the work of the kingdom of heaven, has become wasted. It is on the brink of bankruptcy and has become an object of ridicule and reproach!

In every city, town, and community there are church buildings, yet the spirits of worshipers have become empty and void. We have discarded the commandment of the Lord that told us that we should become the light of the world. We have stopped up our ears to the calling of the Holy Spirit. The church, like a flock of lost sheep, wanders to and fro, falling prey to the devil who walks about seeking whom he may devour. Heresy and false teachings flourish.

In such a whirlpool, when and how could the prayer meetings of Antioch ever be restored to us? At Antioch, didn't they minister with one accord to the Lord as they waited for their divine orders? Didn't they earnestly fast and pray so they could do the work to which the Holy Spirit, their senior partner, had called them? To evangelize the coming age, we should once again go into the bosom of the Holy Spirit who gives us supernatural power, wisdom, and guidance. We should repent and open our ears to His calling.

The account of the events at Antioch goes on to say that Barnabas and Saul, who were set apart by the Holy Spirit for His work, "being sent forth by the Holy Ghost, departed" (Acts 13:4).

What a thought-provoking dispatch this was. They left, being sent forth neither by any denomination nor by any missionary institution, but by the Holy Spirit! They had no missionary funds and no promise of regular missionary support. Nothing is said about money, yet they were sent forth by the Holy Spirit, the Lord of heaven and earth. With that backing, they had nothing to fear.

Senior Theologian

I REALLY WISH that all of the churches and institutions engaged in evangelizing the world today would be filled with the Holy Spirit—instead of just being filled with people—so that we could experience the divine victory that can be obtained through the pure gospel. Only this—not humanistic, secularized, defeatist preaching—will release the victory of the gospel message to the world.

Behind the scenes, setting up a sound basis for the work of evangelism, the Holy Spirit was also the early church's senior partner in settling theological questions. Like an unseen stage director, He had final authority to supervise, teach, and lead.

In Acts 15, some Gentile Christians were in great confusion because of the false teaching of certain Jewish believers:

> And certain men which came down from Judea taught the brethren, and said, Except ye be circumcised after the manner of Moses, ye cannot be saved. When therefore Paul and Barnabas had no small dissension and disputation with them, they determined that Paul and Barnabas, and certain other of them, should go up to Jerusalem unto the apostles and elders about this question.
>
> —ACTS 15:1–2

As a result, the apostles and the elders held a council in Jerusalem to consider this matter.

The council's discussion and verdict are described later in Acts 15. Reading this leads me to believe that these leaders deeply acknowledged the Holy Spirit, depended on Him, and prayed with a firm faith that He would lead their discussion to arrive at the proper conclusion. Their conclusion was written as a letter to the Gentiles in Antioch, Syria, and Cilicia:

> Forasmuch as we have heard, that certain which went out from us have troubled you with words, subverting your souls, saying, Ye must be circumcised, and keep the law: to whom we gave no such commandment: It seemed good unto us,

> being assembled with one accord, to send chosen men unto you with our beloved Barnabas and Paul, men that have hazarded their lives for the name of our Lord Jesus Christ. . . . For it seemed good *to the Holy Ghost, and to us,* to lay upon you no greater burden than these necessary things.
>
> —Acts 15:24–28, italics mine

Considering that the Holy Spirit was clearly mentioned first—"it seemed good to the Holy Ghost, and to us" instead of "to us, and the Holy Ghost"—should make those who interpret the Bible on the basis of humanistic faith ashamed of themselves. Do they really acknowledge the Holy Spirit in today's religious conferences? We often hear expressions such as "Superintendent So-and-So and the committee have decided. . . . " We rarely hear the sentiment used in the letter sent by the Jerusalem apostles: "With the help of the Holy Spirit we have decided. . . . " Of course, I do not contend that one should follow every statement with the expression "by the help of the Holy Spirit," but it is deplorable that the phrase is never heard.

Depending on His Help

In all we do, we should acknowledge Him, worship Him, give thanks to Him, continuously depending upon Him. And we should surely remember that the Holy Spirit, sent by heaven to be our senior partner in evangelization and teaching, waits to be *invited* to be that partner with us.

The Bible shows us that ignorance is not the only thing that prevents us from having a partnership with the Holy Spirit. Lack of humility in waiting on the Spirit is also a factor.

Acts 16:6–10 shows that Paul worked in partnership with the Holy Spirit. Of course, Paul was the apostle of apostles, whom God used mightily. But we should also realize that even an apostle as sensitive to the Holy Spirit as Paul was capable of rushing recklessly into something because of his great zeal for preaching the gospel. This is what happened:

> Now when they [Paul and Silas] had gone throughout Phrygia and the region of Galatia, and *were forbidden of the Holy Ghost* to preach the word in Asia, after they were come to Mysia, they assayed to go into Bithynia: but *the Spirit suffered them not.*
>
> —Acts 16:6–7, italics mine

When we read this passage, we feel as if we are seeing Jacob wrestling with the angel of God. The expressions "were forbidden of the Holy Ghost" and "the Spirit suffered them not" are combative. Paul was trying to go forth to preach, and the Holy Spirit was pulling him back. Such vivid scenes in the Bible show us that it was the Holy Spirit who was leading Paul.

It is impossible to grasp fully the tremendous lesson this passage teaches. This wonderful scene shows clearly that the Holy Spirit earnestly wants to take part in the work of the gospel as a partner and that the initiator of the work is not man or woman but the Holy Spirit. When they are not led easily, the Holy Spirit even uses force to make His saints obey God's plan for His work. The Holy Spirit commands us to do the work of evangelism, and believers are sent forth as workers for the harvest, but He must be the senior partner.

Even Paul, who possessed an almost spotless and perfect character, had some difficulty being led by the Holy Spirit, because of his burning passion and indomitable will. Maybe the reason God allowed Paul to experience "a thorn in the flesh" was so that he might sense his weakness and depend wholly upon the Lord (2 Cor. 12:7).

From this we learn that we should always seek first the guidance of the Holy Spirit and have an obedient and broken spirit that can be led by Him as easily as sheep are led by a shepherd. Only then can the gospel really be preached—in partnership with the Holy Spirit. If we try to do so without Him, we will sadden the heart of God and oppose His plan and providence to save the world. Such a partnership with the Holy Spirit is indispensable to the church.

2

Who Is the Holy Spirit?

EXACTLY WHO IS this wonderful Holy Spirit of grace? To have fellowship and work together with Him, we must know Him well. Though impersonal metaphors for the Holy Spirit—fire, wind, water, oil, dove, and so forth—have a biblical basis, they have been used to such an extent that some people don't really know who He actually is. Let's look at the bedrock truth.

The Holy Spirit Is God

LIKE GOD THE Father and God the Son, the Holy Spirit is a member of the Godhead. Historically, Arians, Sabellians, and Socinians regarded the Holy Spirit as a power that came from the eternal God, but these groups have always been branded heretics by the orthodox church.

The Bible itself calls the Holy Spirit *God.* Among the things Jesus commanded His disciples to do just before His ascension was: "Go ye therefore, and teach all nations, baptizing them in the name of the Father, and of the Son, and of the Holy Ghost" (Matt. 28:19). Here Jesus clearly set the Holy Spirit in the same position as the Father and the Son. He said that the Spirit had the same authority, power, and glory as the Father and the Son.

Such is the case throughout the Bible. In the Book of Acts, a man named Ananias, along with his wife, Sapphira, sold a possession and brought a certain part of the proceeds to the apostles, pretending that he had brought all. But the apostle Peter, filled with the Holy Spirit, rebuked Ananias: "Why hath Satan filled thine heart to lie to the

Holy Ghost, and to keep back part of the price of the land? . . . Thou hast not lied unto men, but unto God" (Acts 5:3–4). Here Peter gave witness that the Holy Spirit is God by saying that Ananias had lied to God and the Holy Spirit, using the words interchangeably.

Some Old Testament verses spoken by the Lord are referred to in the New Testament as being written by the Holy Spirit. For example, Isaiah 6:9 says, "He [the Lord] said, Go, and tell this people, Hear ye indeed, but understand not; and see ye indeed, but perceive not." When Paul quoted this verse in the New Testament, he credited it to the Holy Spirit: "Well spake the Holy Ghost by Esaias the prophet unto our fathers, saying, Go unto this people, and say, Hearing ye shall hear, and shall not understand; and seeing ye shall see, and not perceive" (Acts 28:25–26).

From Scripture passages such as these I clearly understand that the Holy Spirit is indeed one of the holy Trinity. The word of the Lord God of the Old Testament is the same as the word of the Holy Spirit in the New Testament. (See also Jeremiah 31:33 and Hebrews 10:15–16.)

We can also see that the Holy Spirit is God in that He carried out the work that none but God can do. The Holy Spirit created the heavens and the earth by the will of God (Gen. 1:2; Job 26:13). He raised the dead (Rom. 1:4; 6:11); caused people to be born again (John 3:5–7); reproved the world of sin, of righteousness, and of judgment (John 16:8); and cast out devils (Matt. 12:28).

More than these proofs, the Holy Spirit has all the attributes of God. Only God is eternal, omniscient, omnipotent, and omnipresent—and the Holy Spirit is all these.

Hebrews 9:14 says that the Holy Spirit is eternal: "How much more shall the blood of Christ, who through the eternal Spirit offered himself without spot to God, purge your conscience from dead works to serve the living God?"

The Holy Spirit is omniscient: "But God hath revealed them unto us by his Spirit: for the Spirit searcheth all things, yea, the deep things of God" (1 Cor. 2:10). The Holy Spirit knows *all* things, even the deep things of God.

The Holy Spirit is omnipotent: "And the angel answered and saith unto her [Mary], The Holy Ghost shall come upon thee, and the power of the Highest shall overshadow thee" (Luke 1:35). Clearly, the Holy Ghost is the power of the Highest, and nothing is impossible with God.

Finally, the Holy Spirit is omnipresent. Psalm 139 expresses well the omnipresence of the Holy Spirit. Speaking to the Lord, David says, "Whither shall I go from thy spirit? or whither shall I flee from thy presence? If I ascend up into heaven, thou art there: if I make my bed in hell, behold, thou art there" (vv. 7–8).

So isn't the Holy Spirit—who is eternal, omniscient, omnipotent, and omnipresent—God? The Spirit is also majestic and holy and glorious, as is the Father and the Son.

The Holy Spirit Has a Personality

As soon as we realize that the Holy Spirit is a person—an entity who has a personality, as does the Father and the Son—our postures toward the Holy Spirit completely change. There are several ways the personal nature of the Holy Spirit affects our relationship to Him. In *The Person and Work of the Holy Spirit,* evangelist and Bible scholar R. A. Torrey pointed out the importance of the Holy Spirit's personality. He emphasized that only a being with a personality can understand our problems and give us help.

We cannot have a dialogue with stones, trees, or an impersonal force. But being a divine person, the Holy Spirit can deeply understand our affairs and help us. This allows us to seek His help.

The Korean hymnal includes several hymns of prayer to the Holy Spirit asking for His help. The first line of one such hymn petitions, "Spirit of the living God, fall afresh on me."

What a fervent prayer and song of supplication to the Holy Spirit! Besides this, there are hymns titled "Holy Ghost, the Infinite," "Gracious Spirit," "Come, Gracious Spirit," "Holy Ghost, With Light Divine," "Holy Spirit, Faithful Guide"—all praying to the Holy Spirit. If the Holy Spirit were not a person, how could He know our circumstances and help us? Our hymns of prayer to the Holy Spirit would be foolish.

Biblical Evidence

You might ask how we know that the Holy Spirit is a person. This is made clear throughout the Bible.

People often do not distinguish between personality and corporeality. When we say that any entity is a person, some falsely understand this to mean that this entity must have a fleshly form. But Jesus did not have a fleshly form like ours after He had been resurrected. As the apostle Paul said, "Though we have known Christ after the flesh, yet now henceforth know we him no more" (2 Cor. 5:16), for Jesus now has a spiritual body (1 Cor. 15:44). Does this mean that Jesus lost His personality? Of course not.

I don't know any believers who would disagree with the statement that the Father is a living person—yet no one has ever seen God, for God is a Spirit (John 4:24). An entity is a person regardless of its corporeality, if it has the attributes of a person. Since the Holy Spirit has all the attributes of a person, even though He is not visible, He is a person. Let's look at the biblical proofs of this.

We know the Holy Spirit is a person because the Bible continually uses personal pronouns to refer to the Holy Spirit. "Even the Spirit of truth, which proceedeth from the Father, he shall testify of me" (John 15:26). "If I go not away, the Comforter will not come unto you; but if I depart, I will send him unto you. . . . And when he is come, he will reprove the world of sin, and of righteousness, and of judgment" (John 16:7–8). "Howbeit when he, the Spirit of truth, is come, he will guide you into all truth" (John 16:13).

Many acts that only a person can perform are ascribed to the Holy Spirit. Here is a brief list of these personal actions:

1. The Holy Spirit *speaks:* "He that hath an ear, let him hear what the Spirit saith unto the churches" (Rev. 2:7).
2. The Holy Spirit *helps us in our weakness:* "Likewise the Spirit also helpeth our infirmities" (Rom. 8:26).
3. The Holy Spirit *prays for us:* "The Spirit itself maketh intercession for us" (Rom. 8:26).
4. The Holy Spirit *teaches us:* "But the Comforter, which is the Holy Ghost, whom the Father will send in my name, he shall teach you all things, and bring all things to your remembrance, whatsoever I have said unto you" (John 14:26).
5. The Holy Spirit *testifies of the Lord:* "But when the Comforter is come . . . he shall testify of me" (John 15:26).
6. The Holy Spirit *guides us:* "Howbeit when he, the Spirit of truth, is come, he will guide you into all truth" (John 16:13).
7. The Holy Spirit *commands people* in their service of Jesus Christ: "Now when they . . . were forbidden of the Holy Ghost to preach the word in Asia . . . they assayed to go into Bithynia, but the Spirit suffered them not" (Acts 16:6–7).
8. The Holy Spirit *calls people* to the work of God and

appoints them to office: "The Holy Ghost said, Separate me Barnabas and Saul for the work whereunto I have called them" (Acts 13:2).

9. The Holy Spirit *comforts believers:* "Then had the churches rest . . . and were edified; and walking in the fear of the Lord, and in the comfort of the Holy Ghost, were multiplied" (Acts 9:31).

Actually, whole chapters of the Bible were written about the activities of the Holy Spirit. This list gives only some highlights.

Characteristics of personality are ascribed to the Holy Spirit. To be a person, an entity must have certain attributes: the knowledge of things and facts; feelings such as joy, anger, pleasure, and sorrow; and the will to decide one's attitudes toward these feelings. Does the Holy Spirit have all these attributes?

First, knowledge is ascribed to the Holy Spirit, as shown in these passages: "But God hath revealed them unto us by his Spirit: for the Spirit searcheth all things, yea, the deep things of God" (1 Cor. 2:10); "He that searcheth the hearts knoweth what is the mind of the Spirit" (Rom. 8:27).

Think about it. The Holy Spirit has the intellect to search the deep things of God as well as He searches and understands the human heart.

Let me tell you about my own experience concerning the knowledge of the Holy Spirit. On one sultry summer day, I preached to about thirteen hundred people attending an evening service at my church. About halfway through my sermon, I suddenly was impressed in my spirit by an irresistible prompting of the Holy Spirit. He revealed to me that a person in the congregation had left home to commit suicide, and if that individual was not saved that night, that was the end of the line. After receiving that knowledge, I tried to continue my sermon as if nothing had happened. But I felt too constrained. I finally stopped the sermon for a few minutes and explained the situation to the congregation. "If such a person is present," I asked, "please raise your hand."

A young woman did raise her hand, and after the service, I met her at my office. Though she had left home with the intention of never returning, she had been persuaded by a friend to come to the service. She had nothing in her mind but suicide until she had heard that God was interested in her and wanted to pull her out of her despair.

As we talked, she wept bitterly; she confessed her sins and returned home, saved. A year or so later I received a letter from her saying that she was leading a happy life in the Lord. An experience like that assures me that the Holy Spirit knows all our inner thoughts and our circumstances. Yes, the Holy Spirit has knowledge.

Second, the Holy Spirit has emotions and feelings, as noted in these passages: "And hope maketh not ashamed; because the love of God is shed abroad in our hearts by the Holy Ghost which is given unto us" (Rom. 5:5); "And grieve not the holy Spirit of God" (Eph. 4:30); "The Spirit itself maketh intercession for us with groanings which cannot be uttered" (Rom. 8:26).

Such biblical passages prove that the Holy Spirit possesses a variety of emotions: He pours the love of God into our spirits, He can be grieved, and He groans in earnest prayer in our behalf.

Third, the Holy Spirit has a will, and He works according to His will and plan. "But all things worketh that one and the selfsame Spirit, dividing to every man severally as he will" (1 Cor. 12:11). "Now when they . . . were forbidden of the Holy Ghost to preach the word in Asia . . . they assayed to go into Bithynia: but the Spirit suffered them not" (Acts 16:6–7).

One of the most foolish things people try to do today is use the Holy Spirit for their own purposes. The Holy Spirit is not an impersonal entity, some inanimate object, or an unknown power to be used. He is a real person, and He uses people for His own work according to His will. In the summer of 1964, I keenly experienced this fact.

I had been in California for one week, preaching in several churches. I had just purchased my plane ticket to the state of Washington, when I suddenly felt very uneasy and troubled in my spirit. I tried to calm myself, but I couldn't. I had planned to attend a party given by the Women's Missionary Council before I left town, and after arriving at the party, I asked the president of the women's meeting for a quiet place to pray. I knelt down before the Lord, and immediately the Holy Spirit showed me that it was His will for me to remain in that city a week longer. For a while I enumerated my excuses—why I should leave—but I had no peace. Finally, when I submitted to the Lord and told Him I would obey Him, peace returned and flooded my heart and mind.

Reflecting on that situation, I found that my obedience to the voice of the Lord brought good evangelistic results and fruit for the kingdom of God.

From personal experience I can tell you that the Holy Spirit has a will and a way to make that will known.

Beyond question, the Bible shows that the Holy Spirit is a real person who has knowledge, feeling, and will. He abides and works with and within us. Knowing this, we should expedite our evangelism through His supernatural power by acknowledging, welcoming, and worshiping Him in our personal walks and in our public ministries.

The Holy Spirit's personal nature is the reason our worship of Him is so important. Would we be required to worship an impersonal power? No. But praise His holy name, for He responds as a personality—perfect as He is God.

3

Names and Symbols of the Holy Spirit

The Bible uses at least four significant names in speaking of the Holy Spirit: *the Holy Spirit* (sometimes translated as the Holy Ghost), *the Spirit of God, the Spirit of Christ,* and *the Comforter.* Each name has to do with a particular office of the Holy Spirit. Let's look at the names more closely and then go on to discuss the symbols used to describe Him.

The Holy Spirit

> God hath not called us unto uncleanness, but unto holiness. He therefore that despiseth, despiseth not man, but God, who hath also given unto us his holy Spirit.
>
> —1 Thessalonians 4:7–8

Among the three members of the holy Trinity, the Holy Spirit particularly has the office of holiness and purity, as His name signifies. The Holy Spirit is the power that brings holiness and purity to believers. He sets them apart from the wickedness of this world, in which evil and unclean spirits work in the children of disobedience. It's by the Spirit of holiness that we can distinguish the Spirit that belongs to God from the spirit that belongs to Satan.

The Spirit of God

> Grieve not the holy Spirit of God, whereby ye are sealed unto the day of redemption.
>
> —Ephesians 4:30

In many biblical passages the Holy Spirit is called the Spirit of God. (See Genesis 1:2; 1 Corinthians 2:11.) It is appropriate that the Holy Spirit be called the Spirit of God, as the Spirit is sent by God (John 15:26). The Bible also calls the Holy Spirit the Spirit of God because God works through the Holy Spirit, calling sinners to Jesus the Savior (John 6:44), revealing the truth (Matt. 11:25), and leading believers (Rom. 8:14).

The Spirit of Christ

> Now if any man have not the Spirit of Christ, he is none of his.
>
> —Romans 8:9

The Holy Spirit is called the Spirit of Christ, because Jesus shed upon believers Him whom He had received of the Father (Acts 2:33). Time and time again Jesus said that the Holy Spirit would come in His place and continue His work. He said that the coming of the Holy Spirit to dwell in the hearts of believers would be the coming of Christ Himself (John 14:16–20.) And He said that the Spirit would testify of Jesus' redeeming crucifixion and resurrection (John 15:26).

Some people teach that the Holy Spirit is different from the Spirit of Christ, that one receives the Spirit of Christ when one is born again and the Holy Spirit when baptized by the Holy Spirit. If this is true, should we not pray to receive also the Spirit of the Father? This teaching is not based on the true knowledge of the holy Trinity, but on false theology. The Spirit of Christ is the same as the Holy Spirit.

The Comforter

> But when the Comforter is come, whom I will send unto you from the Father, even the Spirit of truth, which proceedeth from the Father, he shall testify of me.
>
> —John 15:26

Jesus called the Holy Spirit "the Comforter," a name of endless mercy. *Paraclete,* or "Comforter," has its root in two Greek words that mean "at one's side" and "to call." Etymologically this word originated from a court trial. When a defendant was pressed hard by a prosecutor and didn't know how to plead for himself, he looked around, hoping to find someone to help him. Seeing the familiar face of an influential friend, the defendant would beckon to him and the friend would make his way through the crowd to the defendant's side. From that moment, the friend stood by the defendant as his paraclete and helped him to win his case.

The Comforter is the one who gives solace and is called to stand by the side of a person in difficulty. He counsels, pleads, entreats, exhorts, and strengthens so that a person can gain victory over his opponents.

Let's think more deeply about the words of Jesus: "I will pray the Father, and he shall give you another Comforter, that he may abide with you for ever" (John 14:16).

It seems evident that Jesus considered Himself the first Comforter, because He describes the Holy Spirit, who would take His place and work in His name, as "another" Comforter.

The latter half of 1 John 2:1 reads: "If any man sin, we have an advocate with the Father, Jesus Christ the righteous." The Greek word translated "advocate" here is *parakletos,* the same word translated "Comforter" in John 14:16 and 26. This again shows Jesus as the first Comforter (the Holy Spirit being another Comforter).

The adjective *another* in John 14:16 has significant implications in the original Greek. Two different Greek words are used in the Bible to denote *another.* The first one is found in John 14:16, "another Comforter"; the second is found in Galatians 1:6, "another gospel." The *another* of John 14:16 is the Greek word *allos,* which signifies another of the same kind and quality. The word *another* of Galatians 1:6 is the Greek word *heteros,* which denotes another that is different in kind and quality.

Surprisingly, when Jesus referred to "another Comforter," He used the words *allos parakletos.* Why? Because, although the Holy Spirit is a different person from Jesus, He is the same kind of Comforter, of the same divine nature, and with the same purpose as Jesus. He glorifies the name of Jesus instead of Himself, and He works in the place of Jesus. Therefore, the indwelling of our Comforter, the Holy Spirit, is analogous to the same presence of Jesus. When Jesus told about the coming of the Holy Spirit, He said it was like the coming of Jesus Himself: "I will not leave you comfortless: I will come to you" (John 14:18). The abiding of the Holy Spirit is the abiding of Jesus, and the fullness of the Holy Spirit is the fullness of Jesus. Such a wonderful blessing is a supernatural and miraculous experience, quite beyond our description.

Water

The Bible is full of symbols that refer to the Holy Spirit. Now that we've looked at who He is and what He is named, we can also study the properties of the metaphors used to describe Him. Let's start with *water.*

> Jesus stood and cried, saying, If any man thirst, let him come unto me, and drink. He that believeth on me, as the scripture hath said, out of his belly shall flow rivers of living water.
>
> —John 7:37–38

In many places in the Bible water is used as a symbol of the Holy Spirit. Why is this an apt metaphor? By observing the relationship between water and human life we can understand a great deal about the Holy Spirit.

First, water is indispensable to the preservation of life. A human being is composed of 60 percent water. If dehydrated by much vomiting or diarrhea, a person is in danger of losing physical life. Similarly, the Holy Spirit is indispensable to our spiritual life. We are born again of the Holy Spirit (John 3:5); by continuously drinking of the Holy Spirit (1 Cor. 12:13), we can preserve our spiritual life. Through the Holy Spirit we become energetic, enjoying the satisfying life in which we shall never thirst (John 4:13–14).

Water is also indispensable to the cleansing of our bodies. If we had no access to water for a long time, wouldn't the filthiness and corruption eventually make us sick, even to death? Every day we wash our bodies, our clothes, our kitchen counters. So our spiritual lives should be cleansed daily by the Holy Spirit. Of course, we are cleansed from our sins when we believe in the precious blood of Jesus; but the Holy Spirit—as if washing us with water—refreshes us, renewing our hearts so we can lead clean lives (Titus 3:5).

The Holy Spirit is the origin of life to those who are obedient, but He is the Spirit of judgment, a consuming flood, to those who are disobedient. In the days of Noah, God judged the world by the flood for the sins and disobedience of the people (Gen. 7). God judged Pharaoh and his army, destroying them in the Red Sea (Exod. 14:28). In Acts 5, Ananias and Sapphira died by the judgment of the Holy Spirit, whom they lied against. Acts 13 tells the story of Elymas, a sorcerer who became blind by the judgment of the Holy Spirit when he opposed Paul's preaching of the gospel.

Fire

He [Jesus] shall baptize you with the Holy Ghost, and with fire.
—MATTHEW 3:11

Fire is a popular symbol of the Holy Spirit, but the truth the metaphor implies is not so well known. First, fire was used as the symbol of the Holy Spirit because throughout the Old Testament, without exception, the presence of God appeared in fire. Some wonderful historic events show that fire accompanies the presence of God. In the days when Moses kept his father-in-law's flock on Mount Horeb, Moses met with God when he was looking at a flaming bush (Exod. 3:1–5).

In 1 Kings 18 when Elijah contended with the four hundred fifty prophets of Baal on Mount Carmel, he insisted that He who answered by fire before all the people would be God! When Elijah actually received the answer by fire, he destroyed the idolaters.

After the ascension of Jesus, one hundred twenty disciples gathered together in an upper room in Jerusalem. They were encouraging one another amidst much despair and waiting for the promise of the Lord, the Holy Spirit. Then, on the day of Pentecost: "Suddenly there came a sound from heaven as of a rushing mighty wind, and it filled all the house where they were sitting. And there appeared unto them cloven tongues like as of fire, and it sat upon each of them" (Acts 2:2–3).

Here we can see that the Holy Spirit, whom Jesus sent, also appeared in the midst of fire. It is apparent that God works in the flame of the Holy Spirit.

Second, fire burns away that which is unwanted. The most perfect method of purification known to mankind is by fire. All kinds of filthy and ugly things are burned off.

As the Holy Spirit dwells within our lives, He consumes sin in us (Heb. 12:29; Jer. 23:29). Holy and righteous living is not possible unless this consuming work takes place within our hearts.

Third, fire provides us with light, which enlarges the sphere and hours of our activity. Human civilization is called the *civilization of light.* If it were possible to sustain life without the light of the sun, can you imagine how furiously people would resist the lack? How diligently people seek the fire that illumines the physical world while being indifferent to the fire of the Holy Spirit that brightens the eternal soul. The Holy Spirit comes into our hearts, pitch dark with sin and death, and by shedding His divine light of heaven, He helps us realize eternal life and see the secret of heaven.

Fourth, the Holy Spirit is symbolized by fire because fire gives us supernatural zeal. When the Holy Spirit gets hold of our hearts, a love of the Lord and an enthusiasm for the work of the gospel flames like fire within our spirits.

Fifth, fire symbolizes power. The machine power that drives our civilization is obtained primarily by means of combustion. Supersonic jet planes, trucks, trains—all provide convenience for us through the power of a spark, a fire.

Thus the Holy Spirit provides us with the power of heaven, urgently needed for our personal lives of faith and for the ministry of gospel preaching. It is reckless to try to start the work of the gospel without receiving the divine power provided by the fire of the Holy Spirit.

Wind

> The wind bloweth where it listeth, and thou hearest the sound thereof, but canst not tell whence it cometh and whither it goeth: so is every one that is born of the Spirit.
>
> —John 3:8

The Greek word for *wind* and *spirit* is the same—*pneuma.* Therefore, literally translated, the Holy Spirit is the "Holy Wind." There is so much grace in this metaphor of the Holy Spirit. Why do I say that?

First, the wind exists pervasively everywhere on the earth. The air we breathe is there in every empty vessel or in every place, however small it may be. Jesus said that the Holy Spirit would be with us forever; there is no place on the earth where the Holy Spirit is not present. He works all around the earth so that no one can either monopolize or resist Him. As explained in the Bible, we are not deserted like orphans when we acknowledge, welcome, invite, and depend upon the Holy Spirit (John 14:18).

Second, the wind is air in continuous motion. We feel the wind moving when the air flows from high atmospheric pressure to low atmospheric pressure in accordance with weather patterns. So the Holy Spirit is also continually working. It is not true that the Holy Spirit worked in the days of the Old Testament and the early days of the New Testament and then vanished like a mist. The wind blows today just as it did centuries ago, and the Holy Spirit works continuously today.

The Holy Spirit flows into areas of low atmospheric pressure—sin, sickness, sorrow, and despair—and is ever ready to work with the joyful message of forgiveness, healing, and eternal life. As many as come to the Lord with penitent and obedient hearts will experience the regenerating work of the Holy Spirit.

Third, we cannot control the direction of the wind as we wish. Jesus said that the wind blows as it will (John 3:8). Since the Holy Spirit has the supreme will and works according to His own purpose, we should follow the direction of the Holy Spirit obediently as we walk by faith.

Fourth, a blowing wind makes stifling and stagnant air fresh and full of vitality. What wonderful relief the fresh wind gives on a stifling and sultry summer day! The wind blowing into a room full of toxic gas makes the entire atmosphere refreshed and pure.

So it is with the working of the Holy Spirit. When we become depressed and lifeless with the anxieties of living and the temptations of sin, the Holy Spirit comes into our hearts like wind with the new life and vitality of heaven. By pouring it out upon our spirits, He makes us full of the joy of life and the zeal of faith.

Oil

> Then Samuel took the horn of oil, and anointed him in the midst of his brethren: and the Spirit of the LORD came upon David from that day forward.
>
> —1 SAMUEL 16:13

> The anointing which ye have received of him abideth in you.
>
> —1 JOHN 2:27

Throughout the Old and New Testaments the Holy Spirit is symbolized by oil. Again, this symbol can teach us the work of the Holy Spirit.

First, anointed places and persons are holy, set apart unto God. God commanded Moses to sanctify the tabernacle of the congregation, the ark of the testimony, all the instruments, and the altar by anointing them with oil (Exod. 30:25–29). Moses also anointed Aaron and his sons, consecrating them that they might minister unto God in the priest's office (Exod. 30:30). God told Samuel to anoint David as king (1 Sam. 16:13), and Elijah anointed Elisha to be prophet (1 Kings 19:16).

Today God makes those who believe in the Lord Jesus Christ a chosen generation, a royal priesthood, a holy nation, and a peculiar people by the anointing of the Holy Spirit (1 Peter 2:9). No one can receive such grace without being empowered by the Holy Spirit.

We are born again of the Holy Spirit, and we have obtained the office of prophet whereby we preach the Word. We shall one day reign with Christ anointed by the Holy Spirit. How can we help but thank God?

Second, oil was necessary to light the seven candlesticks in the tabernacle of God. In the sanctuary of the Old Testament, the only light came from the golden candlesticks—and the oil. Likewise, only through the bright light of the anointing Holy Spirit can the spiritual world be revealed to us.

Just as no other light was permitted to light the holy place, in the same way, only the light from the oil of the Holy Spirit can illumine the Word of God—the secret of heaven's holy place.

Third, oil prevents wear and tear and breakdown by relieving the friction between moving parts. How could we lubricate the human spirit, strained and torn with endless discord? Why have even churches and Christians been so disruptive? Because we have not been anointed by the Holy Spirit. The lubricating oil of peace, love, and healing comes only when we are filled with the Holy Spirit.

Fourth, oil is a necessary ingredient for the preservation of life. Why have the spirits of some believers become dried up like the bones in the valley of Ezekiel's vision? Why has the church become so emaciated in quality as well as quantity?

Because they have not received the oil of the Holy Spirit, the heavenly nutrition indispensable to our spirits. History and reality prove clearly that churches, as well as individual Christians, that are full of the Holy Spirit are well nourished. It was so in the past, and it will always be so.

Rain

> He shall come down like rain upon the mown grass: as showers that water the earth.
>
> —Psalm 72:6

> Then shall we know, if we follow on to know the Lord: his going forth is prepared as the morning; and he shall come unto us as the rain, as the latter and former rain unto the earth.
>
> —Hosea 6:3

There are two clear reasons for the metaphor of the Holy Spirit as rain. Think about the earth: It can neither bear any fruit nor sustain any kind of life unless it receives rain. In the lifetime of the Old Testament prophet Elijah, when all the herbs and trees were scorched and vegetation died, Elijah prayed earnestly that it might rain. It did, and the earth brought forth fruit. Thus, just as the earth can bear fruit and preserve life only when it receives rain, so a person's spiritual life can bear spiritual fruit and preserve powerful spiritual life only when it receives the rain of the Holy Spirit.

A second reason the Holy Spirit is symbolized as rain watering the earth is a little more complex. In Palestine, farmers expect rain twice during each growing season. The first rain falls in late autumn and is called the "early rain." When the early rain comes, the farmers quickly sow their wheat or barley seed, which absorbs the moisture of that rain. The seed sprouts and comes up, but during the cold winter it barely stays alive. When springtime returns, warm winds from the southeast blow, and the rain falls again, giving new life. The Palestinian farmers call this springtime rain the "latter rain." And after the plants absorb this, the crops grow rapidly until harvest.

This natural cycle is mentioned in relation to the Holy Spirit in the Epistle of James. "Be patient therefore, brethren, unto the coming of the Lord. Behold, the husbandman waiteth for the precious fruit of the earth, and hath long patience for it, until he receive the early and latter rain" (James 5:7).

When the Lord Jesus came to earth, He sowed the seed of the gospel. Ten days after His ascension, on the day of Pentecost, one hundred twenty believers who had received this seed gathered together in Jerusalem. While they were praying, a sound from heaven as of a rushing mighty wind filled the house where they were gathered. Cloven tongues of fire sat upon each of them, and they were filled with the Holy Ghost. At that moment the church of Jesus Christ came into being. This "early rain" of the Holy Spirit was then poured out in Samaria, in a worship service at the home of Cornelius, and on the believers in Ephesus. With the life and power of the Spirit, churches of Jesus Christ were built in place after place, and the Word of life came to be preached vigorously. This work of the Holy Spirit, the early rain, was poured out abundantly until A.D. 300. It then started to diminish, and around A.D. 600 the work of the Holy Spirit almost ceased. The church became ritualistic, and the hard winter of faith approached. The church went through the Dark Ages.

During the Reformation in the sixteenth century, through the efforts of men like Martin Luther, the work of the Holy Spirit revived. Thereafter, through faithful servants of the Lord such as John Wesley, George Whitefield, Charles Finney, and Dwight Moody, the great work of the Holy Spirit reappeared. Around the year 1900 the whole world began once again to receive the Holy Spirit.

Now that the church has received the Holy Spirit in the abundant "latter rain," we are witnessing the work of the Holy Spirit as did the early church. Though some people don't understand the work of God in this present time and oppose this move of the Holy Spirit, no one can resist the work and will of God; His work will be accomplished without fail. We cannot but give thanks, praise, and honor to God who restores to us the power of the early church by pouring out the latter rain of the Holy Spirit.

When I was invited to attend the Eighth World Pentecostal Conference held in Rio de Janeiro, Brazil, I could not help admiring the wonderful work of the Holy Spirit. In that Catholic country rooted in ceremonies and rituals, as many as three million people were said to have received the Holy Spirit according to Acts 2:4.

Now, before the Second Coming of the Lord Jesus, the Holy Spirit is once again awakening the church around the world and pouring out His grace—setting souls free through belief in Jesus Christ. Realizing that now is the opportune time to revitalize our faith by receiving the latter rain of the Spirit, we should pray fervently.

Dove

> And John bare record, saying, I saw the Spirit descending from heaven like a dove, and it abode upon him.
>
> —John 1:32

This verse describes the most prominent occasion when the Holy Spirit was symbolized as a dove: when Jesus was baptized by John the Baptist in the Jordan River. When the heavens were opened, the Spirit of God descended like a dove and lighted upon Jesus. There are deep meanings in the metaphor of a dove symbolizing the Holy Spirit.

First, all over the world the dove is known as an emblem of peace. In Genesis, when God destroyed all flesh by the deluge, Noah and the seven members of his family found grace in the eyes of God. They were saved in the ark. Forty days after the ark rested on Mount

Ararat, Noah released a dove through the window of the ark to see if the waters had abated. The dove returned, and Genesis 8 relates: "And he [Noah] stayed yet other seven days; and again he sent forth the dove out of the ark; and the dove came in to him in the evening; and, lo, in her mouth was an olive leaf plucked off: so Noah knew that the waters were abated from off the earth" (vv. 10–11).

The first evidence to show that peace had returned on the earth and that the judgment and wrath of God had passed away was a dove.

How beautifully this signifies the presence of the Holy Spirit, who never comes to human spirits that are under the judgment and wrath of God. Jesus Christ redeemed us by His death on the cross, thereby paying for the wrath and judgment of God. When we confess our sins and accept Jesus as Savior, the Holy Spirit comes to us because we have the redeeming proof of the precious blood. The Holy Spirit makes us feel the joy of knowing that we "shall not come into condemnation; but . . . passed from death unto life" (John 5:24) and "have peace with God" (Rom. 5:1).

And this is not all! To those who in their sin walk toward hell, opposing and disobeying God, the Holy Spirit keeps preaching the reconciling gospel of peace. The most important thing anyone must decide today is whether to receive salvation and peace—the joyful news the Holy Spirit brings into our hearts—or be destroyed.

The dove is also a symbol of meekness and humility—attributes of the Holy Spirit that He imparts to us. It always puzzles me to see people who profess to having received the Holy Spirit act and speak insultingly. Some behave as if they have been taken by a spirit of evil. But the evidence of the Holy Spirit is a meek and humble spirit.

The dove is also known as a pure and harmless creature. The dove does not kill other animals as does the cat or eagle. In a corresponding vein, note that the Holy Spirit is a *holy* Spirit.

Close relatives of those who are stricken by evil spirits frequently bring their family members to my office, asking me to discern the spiritual state of their loved ones. As I talk with these suffering people, they confess without exception that lewdness, wrong thinking, and abusive language flow through them against their own wills. These are the works of the devil. Such people should determine to stand firmly on the Word of truth and continuously fight against Satan until they drive him out, relying upon the cleansing power of the precious blood of Jesus. If they don't, they will surely become mentally disabled in the end. Fortunately, I can say to those who worry about this that they can be set perfectly free by the precious blood of the Lamb and the power of God's Word.

The Holy Spirit is always a *holy* Spirit. Because there can be no ugliness in Him, we should never allow any spiritual change in us that is not toward holiness. Of course, we do not become holy instantly when we receive the Holy Spirit. Through receiving the Holy Spirit we receive power to grow holy, and we receive a sensitivity that makes us feel guilty when we commit sin. If we heed this, our lives cannot help but become better.

The Holy Spirit has not come to bite, tear, and kill but to save, heal, and bind up. Carefully note Jesus' proclamation at the synagogue of Nazareth concerning what He would do by the help of the Holy Spirit: "The Spirit of the Lord is upon me, because he hath anointed me to preach the gospel to the poor; he hath sent me to heal the brokenhearted, to preach deliverance to the captives, and recovering of sight to the blind, to set at liberty them that are bruised, to preach the acceptable year of the Lord" (Luke 4:18–19).

The fourth reason the Holy Spirit is symbolized as a dove is that the Holy Spirit is easily grieved: The works of the Holy Spirit are quenched by the betrayal of mankind. More than any other animal, the dove is easily frightened. Harassed once or twice, a dove will leave that place forever. To live in harmony with the Holy Spirit in our hearts, we must be very careful to have a reverent attitude toward Him and not grieve Him. Ephesians 4:30 warns us: "Grieve not the holy Spirit of God." If we continually oppose the Holy Spirit, He will leave us like a dove—what a terrible and fearful thing. When repenting, David prayed earnestly, weeping before God after he had sinned: "Cast me not away from thy presence; and take not thy holy spirit from me" (Ps. 51:11).

The Holy Spirit that descended in the form of a beautiful dove and lighted upon Jesus eagerly comes down upon us today to fill our hearts.

Wine

> And be not drunk with wine, wherein is excess; but be filled with the Spirit.
>
> —Ephesians 5:18

> And they were all amazed, and were in doubt saying one to another, what meaneth this? Others mocking said, These men are full of new wine.
>
> —Acts 2:12–13

The Bible contrasts, or in some cases compares, the fullness of the Holy Spirit with drunkenness. Those who have experienced the fullness of the Holy Spirit will well understand what this means.

Like wine, the fullness of the Holy Spirit gives gladness and joy to our hearts. But, though the result of drinking wine is physical harm and dissipation, the fullness of the Holy Spirit brings spiritual joy and the eventual pleasure of heaven. The Spirit-filled life has wonderfully beneficial results: "Speaking to yourselves in psalms and hymns and spiritual songs, singing and making melody in your hearts to the Lord; giving thanks always for all things unto God and the Father in the name of our Lord Jesus Christ; submitting yourselves one to another in the fear of God" (Eph. 5:19–21). The fullness of the Spirit also makes us strong in faith and helps us serve God—not with temporary excitement but with continuous enjoyment.

Wine makes people seem merry, and it also gives temporary peace of mind. It makes one forget anxiety, care, and sorrow for a short time. But such a state is not normal—it's intoxication. The wine that is the Holy Spirit does not anesthetize; it brings about the most normal state of overflowing peace, allowing us to set aside worldly anxieties, cares, and worries as our Creator intended.

A third effect of wine is that it gives unusual boldness, which causes people to take arrogant, wild, unrestrained actions. Life filled with the Holy Spirit is a bold life. The Holy Spirit can change even a timid and shy person into one who is not afraid to give up life itself. The boldness that comes with the fullness of the Holy Spirit enables us to love truth and justice, to be meek and humble, to preach the gospel with authority. The fullness of the Holy Spirit makes us bold to conquer sin and live a victorious life.

Finally, drunken people often do not feel physical pain because the senses have been anesthetized. I once saw a dead-drunk foreign soldier clutching a wire entanglement. He wasn't even aware that his hands were bloody from handling the tearing barbed wires. The Holy Spirit does not dull physical senses, but the power of His love and His strength to persevere can insulate us from personal and spiritual blows. The Holy Spirit gives us the strength to stand firm.

It is true that those who are filled with the Holy Spirit often resemble drunken people. But intoxication with wine is a harmful excess while the fullness of the Holy Spirit makes one perfect.

Seal

[Christ] in whom ye also trusted, after that ye heard the word

> of truth, the gospel of your salvation: in whom also after that ye believed, ye were sealed with that holy Spirit of promise.
>
> —EPHESIANS 1:13

How wonderful that receiving the Holy Spirit is compared to being sealed, for that is how we come to possess the assurance of our salvation. Let's consider for a moment the symbolic meaning in the metaphor of sealing.

First, sealing means to stamp something to guard against its being opened by an unauthorized person. In other words, if something is sealed, no one may touch it without permission. When Pilate sealed the stone that enclosed Jesus' grave, removal of the stone without Pilate's permission was punishable by death. Thus, if we are sealed by the blood of Jesus, God keeps us from falling into sin by the power of the Holy Spirit.

Therefore, we believers—sealed by the Holy Spirit and relying upon His power—should sanctify our minds and lives, so as to defeat sin and the devil.

Second, sealing signifies special ownership—which we experience daily. Think of it this way: No one can draw my money out of the bank without my seal or signature. If I stamp my possessions with my seal, everyone knows that those valuables are mine. Anyone who tried to disregard the seal and take them would infringe on my rights of ownership and incur serious legal consequences.

Likewise, God proves that His people are indeed His by sealing them with the Holy Spirit. If anyone dares oppose or injure the anointed people of God, that person infringes on the ownership of God and brings God's wrath upon himself. When those people who have been sealed by the Holy Spirit humble themselves, obey the will of God, and live for His glory, then the Lord of heaven and earth will be their protector and shelter.

Third, sealing signifies authority. Here in Korea everyone must have a certificate of residence. If it weren't stamped with an official seal, it would be good for nothing; it would have no authority.

Believers, as children of God, have authority. While the disciples were with Jesus, they worked many signs and wonders and acted with authority and power. But after Jesus ascended into heaven they were defeated and miserably incompetent—until they were filled with the Holy Spirit. Then they suddenly had great authority in words. Power followed their words and prayer, giving them courage and boldness. As a result of their own God-given authority, their belief in God's full authority mushroomed.

Guarantee

> Now he which stablisheth us with you in Christ, and hath anointed us, is God: Who hath also sealed us, and given the earnest of the Spirit in our hearts.
>
> —2 CORINTHIANS 1:21–22

Let us understand the wonderful blessing of the Holy Spirit by looking into the full meaning of a guarantee, which is what is meant by the word *earnest.*

First, think of the most ordinary and common guarantee situations. For example, a person who becomes surety makes himself responsible for the conduct or debts of the one he guarantees. The responsibility of a guarantor is serious business.

We can firmly believe that we are saved, yet Satan endlessly shoots arrows of apprehension and doubt at our hearts. He deceives us with many subtle lies: "Do you think that heaven really exists? Forget such foolish thoughts! To have faith is to have religion, and as for religion, it makes no difference which one you have, as all religions are the same!"

At such a time, if it were not for the Holy Spirit who guarantees the validity of the gospel of Jesus, our spirits would go down; in the end we would fail, without faith. But when we are filled with the Holy Spirit—and the Holy Spirit continuously guarantees and assures the truthfulness of the Word—all the arrows of Satan are finally stopped. Thus, the Holy Spirit is with us as our surety, helping us believe without a doubt that God is real and that Jesus is our Savior. Hallelujah!

Second, when we buy goods at a store on the monthly installment plan or sign a contract to purchase a house or a piece of land, we bind our agreement securely by paying earnest money in advance. If I fulfill my obligation in a certain period of time, I know I will eventually possess it and that the property will be mine.

Heaven is just like that. Our being saved by faith and receiving the Holy Spirit is our guarantee. While on this earth, by faith and obedience we should live fervently in accordance with God's Word; otherwise the earnest becomes void. We must be careful that we do not lose our precious deliverance by giving offense to God and falling into sin. If we walk in faith, being sober and vigilant, the Holy Spirit makes us overflow with joy and hope. His continued encouragement that heaven is ours is the earnest of the inheritance that will one day be our possession.

Third, a guarantee has an interesting symbolism in the traditional Middle Eastern bargaining process. When one contracted to purchase a piece of land from another, the buyer returned home with a large bag full of earth from the seller's land. He would place the earth in some corner of his house. When he looked at it, smelled it, and touched it, he had assurance that he had purchased the land. The bag of soil was his guarantee.

What is the spiritual parallel? The Holy Spirit is our guarantee of heaven. We have not yet gone there in person to possess and enjoy it, but we have been given a taste of it in the Holy Spirit.

What is heaven like? While we walk the paths of life, we do not live in mere endless imagination about heaven. Even now we possess part of heaven in our hearts. God permits us to enjoy in advance just a taste of the joy, peace, and everlasting rest of heaven by sending the Holy Spirit to our spirits to satisfy those desires. What wonderful love this is!

By receiving this foretaste of heaven, we more earnestly long for heaven and therefore devote ourselves more fervently to the life of faith to obtain it.

4

Unbelievers and the Holy Spirit

The Bible describes the spiritual state of unbelievers as being "dead in trespasses and sins" (Eph. 2:1). This does not mean that unbelievers don't have souls. Rather, their souls are so far away from heaven and the life of God that they are insensitive to God and His kingdom. If they continue to remain in such a state, when they die physically their souls will fall into hell, which is completely separated from heaven and God.

How can we make such souls in a callous state—"dead in trespasses and sins"—realize their sins and accept the eternal life God gives? There is One who does such a work unceasingly among unbelievers—none other than the Holy Spirit. The Bible teaches: "Eye hath not seen, nor ear heard, neither have entered into the heart of man, the things which God hath prepared for them that love him. But God hath revealed them unto us by his Spirit" (1 Cor. 2:9–10).

In other words, unbelievers cannot understand the salvation of God through their five senses or reason. Only through the power of inward revelation can they receive the light of understanding concerning salvation.

How does the Holy Spirit work when He approaches unbelievers? Concerning this, Jesus Himself gives a good explanation in John 16:8 when He says that the Holy Spirit "will reprove the world of sin."

Reproving the World of Sin

Every person has been born with a sinful nature. Psalm 51:5 reads, "Behold, I was shapen in iniquity, and in sin did my mother conceive me."

Someone may ask, "What does that have to do with me?" When we consider the original meaning of *sin,* we find that we are in a frightful position. We understand that it is impossible for us to contend that we have nothing to do with sin.

People usually call something a sin or unrighteousness when they see outward evidence of sin. But sin is rooted in deeper places than evidenced by specific trespasses. The Bible shows how and why man cannot help but bear sinful fruits.

A person's sinful state involves being separated from God. This sinful state, called *original sin,* is carried corporately: "By one man sin entered into the world, and death by sin... through the offence of one many be dead" (Rom. 5:12, 15).

Adam disobeyed God and was driven out from God's presence; in such a state, Adam produced mankind. As a result, all descendants of Adam—without having time to question it—are born in the state of being separated from God.

As a more familiar example, suppose a certain couple were exiled to a lonely island, and there the wife gives birth to children. The children could not determine their place of birth, far away from their homeland. Even if they choose to blame their father for their isolated circumstances of birth, their circumstances would not change. It's simply the way it happened.

Thus the descendants of Adam have been born in the sinful state of Adam—driven away from the presence of God and placed under Adam's sentence of death. The person who left the God of all righteousness, goodness, and life cannot help but breed unrighteousness and trespasses. In this forsaken condition, mankind would die and go to hell. But here the great love and mercy of God appeared; God delivered us through our Lord, Jesus Christ.

Born of the virgin Mary, Jesus came into this world without original sin. He lived a life of no sin or guile. As a sinless person He became the perfect substitute for sinners. As a righteous person He was crucified for the unrighteous, and after three days He rose from the dead. By His death He paid the total price of our original sin and our self-committed sins. What does that mean? As many as believe in Him and receive the free grace of salvation receive eternal life. They are no longer separated from God.

Since Jesus' resurrection, man does not die eternally for his own sinful acts or for original sin. He is destroyed for not accepting the salvation of Jesus Christ. Because of this, I can't emphasize too much how urgently the gospel message should be preached.

How can we awaken the dead and senseless soul to receive this great gospel message? Who can convince sinners, who often do not realize their desperate state, of the danger to come and prompt them to flee to the shelter of salvation?

Men and women could never do these things. But God promised to carry out this work by sending the Holy Spirit, who is performing this work all over the world through the church's proclamation of the gospel. We cannot but praise Him with all of our hearts.

Reproving the World of Righteousness

THE HOLY SPIRIT also "will reprove the world . . . of righteousness: . . . because I go to my Father, and ye see me no more" (John 16:8, 10).

What is righteousness? When those who live outside the faith of Christ hear the word *righteousness,* they generally think of human behavior. When a person does something legally or morally unblamable, he or she is called righteous.

But what does God say to those who stand before the law of God? "All have sinned, and come short of the glory of God" (Rom. 3:23). "By the deeds of the law there shall no flesh be justified in his sight: for by the law is the knowledge of sin" (Rom. 3:20). Everyone who stands before the law of God is a sinner. Therefore, all not only come short of the glory of God, but they cannot help being driven out of His presence.

Then who can stand before the bright, glorious throne of God with a pure life totally free from sin? Being people who are descended from Adam, we are unable to find such a person—except for Jesus Christ, whom the Holy Spirit conceived in the virgin Mary and of whom He now bears witness. But what is the proof that this very Jesus lived a completely righteous life before God?

The evidence is clear. As previously noted, the apostle Paul said, "All have sinned, and come short of the glory of God." This means that sinners are not qualified to stand before God.

But remember, Jesus said that the Holy Spirit would convict the world of righteousness—"because I go to my Father, and ye see me no more" (John 16:10).

Was such a claim of Jesus really accomplished? Yes. What He said would happen, did come to pass.

Jesus died by crucifixion, bearing all the sins of the world. He was buried, and His tomb was tightly secured by the hands of His enemies. In spite of that, He arose from the dead and later ascended into heaven in the presence of witnesses. His body was never discovered—though people looked for it.

As a surer evidence than this, fifty days after His death, Jesus sent the gift of the Holy Spirit to His disciples to enable them to see and hear clearly.

Peter said this about that experience: "This Jesus hath God raised up, whereof we all are witnesses. Therefore being by the right hand of the Father exalted, and having received of the Father the promise of the Holy Ghost, he hath shed forth this, which ye now see and hear" (Acts 2:32–33).

All flesh, whether saints or sinners, since the beginning of human history eventually died and left behind their physical remains (except Enoch and Elijah who were taken to heaven without seeing death, being counted righteous through their faith). But the empty grave of Jesus Christ silently witnesses that Jesus is alive, that He returned to His Father.

What does Jesus' righteousness mean to us? A sinner can never redeem another's sins. But Jesus' death did redeem our sins. Let me quote Romans 3:23 again—along with verse 24: "All have sinned, and come short of the glory of God; being justified freely by his grace through the redemption that is in Christ Jesus."

Also note these references to what was accomplished by Jesus' death and resurrection: "He [God the Father] hath made him [Jesus] to be sin for us, who knew no sin; that we might be made the righteousness of God in him" (2 Cor. 5:21); "[Jesus] was delivered for our offences, and was raised again for our justification" (Rom. 4:25). Jesus fully paid all the debts of mankind on the cross.

The Holy Spirit now bears witness that through faith in Jesus *anyone* can be counted as if he or she had never committed a sin. That means we can stand before the glory of God without a spot of shame, relying upon the merit of Jesus. What wonderful grace and tremendous blessing this is!

The Holy Spirit works unceasingly to convince the world of such wonderful truth and grace so that everyone may believe in the Savior, Jesus Christ, and be saved from the eternal destruction that comes apart from Christ. Today no flesh can be justified by his or her own works before God, but through the grace of redemption in Christ the abundant gift of justification and entrance into the glorious kingdom of God is available to anyone.

Reproving the World of Judgment

JESUS ALSO SAID the Holy Spirit would "reprove the world . . . of judgment: . . . because the prince of this world is judged" (John 16:8, 11).

What is this *judgment* that the Bible speaks of? And who is "the prince of this world"? Revelation 12:9–11 reads:

> And the great dragon was cast out, that old serpent, called the Devil, and Satan, which deceiveth the whole world: he was cast out into the earth, and his angels were cast out with him. And I heard a loud voice saying in heaven, Now is come salvation, and strength, and the kingdom of our God, and the power of his Christ: for the accuser of our brethren is cast down, which accused them before our God day and night. And they overcame by the blood of the Lamb, and by the word of their testimony; and they loved not their lives unto the death.

As written in this passage, the "prince of this world" refers to "that old serpent, called the Devil, and Satan," who tempted Adam in Eden, who usurped Adam's authority over the world, who eventually deceived the whole world.

Originally, when God created this world, He gave the governing authority to Adam and Eve. In Genesis 1:26 when God created man and woman, He said, "Let us make man in our image, after our likeness: and let them have dominion over the fish of the sea, and over the fowl of the air, and over the cattle, and over all the earth, and over every creeping thing that creepeth upon the earth." Like a king and queen, Adam and Eve were created to rule and govern the world.

Then when was the royal authority usurped and given to the devil? When Adam and Eve disobeyed the commandment of God, listening to the enticing words of the old serpent. As a result of surrendering his will to and obeying the devil, Adam's fellowship with God was broken. He not only became the servant of the devil, but he handed himself and the territory entrusted to him over to the devil.

Since that time "the whole world lieth in wickedness" (1 John 5:19). And from that time on, the devil has made a desperate effort to oppose God and interfere with God's plan.

When the devil tempted Jesus in the wilderness, he took Him up to a high mountain and in a moment of time showed Him all the kingdoms of the world. Satan enticed Him saying, "All this power will I give thee, and the glory of them: for that is delivered unto me; and to whomsoever I will I give it. If thou therefore wilt worship me, all shall be thine" (Luke 4:6–7).

Instead of saying that the power of this world was his from the very beginning, the devil confessed that it had been delivered to him. What a tragic day that was!

Since that day when Satan deceived Adam and Eve, the desperate effort of the devil has been to steal and kill and destroy mankind. But God reached out through Jesus Christ to save the world.

The only possible way to save the human race, enslaved as it was to the devil, was for God to prepare a way through which He could legally forgive the original sin and the willful sins that men and women would commit. But because mankind made the choice to rebel against God and submit to the devil, a person's deliverance must be accepted. You and I must choose to receive the good news of God's forgiveness, made possible through Jesus Christ, His only begotten Son.

Thanks to Jesus' sacrificial death, a way is open for man to come back to God and receive the blessing of forgiveness and grace. Hallelujah! If a person turns his or her back on the devil and chooses God, that person will be saved by the overflowing grace of Jesus Christ, be restored as a child of God, and recover the authority that was lost long ago.

Because of Jesus' death for us, the deceitful wiles of the devil are revealed before the cross; the devil has gone to ruin, and he has been judged. He lost the lawful power to possess man or the world. The devil, who had enslaved the human race and robbed mankind of the world that God had entrusted to them, was judged by the love of God revealed on the cross.

To the devil the cross was a complete defeat—destruction and ruin of his plans with a judgment for final damnation. Through the sacrificial death of Jesus Christ, God has opened the legal way to forgiveness and restoration for all mankind. And the devil is completely incapable of hindering those who are returning to God as they hear the good news of salvation. The devil can only watch in helpless agony.

Then why did Jesus say the Holy Spirit would reprove the world of judgment? There are two meanings in that statement. First, through the sacrifice of Jesus, God forgives the treason of mankind and reproves the devil who enslaved men and women, usurping all the world that God had given to them. Second, it is a touching reproof of God to mankind who, despite the way of salvation that God has prepared, still does not come back to God but continues to forsake the forgiveness freely offered. If anyone persists in this, that person is deprived by the devil of his or her full potential, and that person will go to hell.

Whenever people hear the gospel and are saved from the devil's hand, Satan suffers. It ruins his kingdom; he not only desperately tries to hinder people from hearing this gospel, but he also tries to seduce into destruction those who have already believed. But this will never succeed. The forgiveness and love of the cross do not change, and the Holy Spirit continues to spread the word that the devil has been defeated and judged.

Knowing all this, we ought to pray in this way: "O Lord, the Holy Spirit, call me and fill me with Your power. Let me preach this gospel to the uttermost parts of the earth. Let me preach that the prince of this world was already judged two thousand years ago and has no more dominion over mankind."

So now, through the forgiveness that Jesus provided, men and women can leave Satan's territory, stand again before God, and recover the royal authority that was delivered to Adam and Eve in the beginning. What a wonderful blessing this is to mankind, and what an appalling judgment this is to the devil.

Speaking of His impending death Jesus said, "Now is the judgment of this world: now shall the prince of this world be cast out" (John 12:31). The devil—who through sin and ignorance gained the opportunity to enter the world and has had ruthless dominion over the world—is even now losing ground moment by moment. Why? Because many are receiving salvation after hearing the gospel.

The cross of Jesus was the complete judgment of the devil, the place where his power was totally broken. How can we help but praise our Lord Jesus who has restored us to be "a chosen generation" and "a royal priesthood" (1 Pet. 2:9)? We cannot help but proclaim with the Holy Spirit that the devil has been judged!

Revealing Salvation's Plan

Unbelievers who have been reproved of sin and righteousness and judgment, and who have been guided into all truth, should now turn from their sinful lives and trust Jesus by faith.

But often their human understanding tells them that the Christian walk is too difficult. They see a gulf that they think cannot be spanned. People who interpret the gospel only with human reason fall into this deep gulf, and they never do pass over to the other side of belief.

How can unbelievers pass over this gulf and enter into the wonderful blessing we believers enjoy as we meditate on the Word and preach it? Remember the words of our Lord Jesus: "With men it is impossible, but not with God" (Mark 10:27).

God easily accomplished this miracle, which was impossible for mankind, and He is still working miracles today! The Bible bears witness to the fact that faith cannot be possessed only by human means: "No man can say that Jesus is the Lord, but by the Holy Ghost" (1 Cor. 12:3).

How does the Holy Spirit work to allow unbelievers to accept Jesus as their personal Savior? I must admit that it is only through a miracle. New birth is just as much a miracle as was Jesus' conception without a father of flesh and birth through the virgin Mary. "And the angel answered and said unto her, The Holy Ghost shall come upon thee, and the power of the Highest shall overshadow thee: therefore also that holy thing which shall be born of thee shall be called the Son of God" (Luke 1:35).

The incarnation of Jesus is a sheer miracle. The same miracle is necessary for Jesus to come into the spirit of a person. Without the supernatural power of the Holy Spirit, we could never believe in His redeeming work and grace, which defy understanding and reason.

When anyone confesses Jesus as personal Savior, there may or may not be any immediate signs of outward change. But the change occurring in the spiritual realm is indeed enormous. The Holy Spirit of God comes into the spirit of that person and moves within it mysteriously beyond reason and imagination. The Holy Spirit Himself sheds the divine faith (the faith of salvation) in the heart of that person.

Even though that person's brain is full of doubts and uncertainty, the Holy Spirit helps him believe in his heart. The power to believe gushes out, and he easily passes over the previously unpassable gulf that lies between reason and faith. By the power of the Holy Spirit, that person safely enters the bliss of faith. He then studies the Bible, prays, and hears sermons—always with the help of the Holy Spirit. The foundation of his faith becomes strong and systematized so that he can enter the bright world of truth, which can then be explained to human reason and intellect.

Again, believing faith is not attained through understanding and knowledge, but through a miracle of the Holy Spirit—when man is pricked in his heart after hearing the Word of God. He then cultivates reasonable understanding and knowledge.

As Paul said, "No man can say that Jesus is the Lord, but by the Holy Ghost" (1 Cor. 12:3). Similarly, the preaching of the gospel is impossible without partnership with the Holy Spirit.

Today many churches are losing members and believers are tormented by doubts because man tries to preach the gospel with human effort and calculation. It's impossible! We need the Holy Spirit.

When we try to lead unbelievers to the Lord, we should simply pray earnestly for the miraculous help of the Holy Spirit, becoming His instruments and allowing Him to use us to preach with His fullness.

Not until this is done can unimaginable blessing come before our eyes. We can and will see people flock into the blessed world of faith.

5

Believers and the Holy Spirit

No one can be saved without being empowered with the Word of God and the Holy Spirit. Even after someone is saved, he or she cannot have a steady, victorious life of faith and spiritual growth unless he or she keeps on growing in the Word through the ministry of the Holy Spirit.

Many believers are aware vaguely that salvation comes only when one is born again by receiving the gospel as it is shared in the power of the Holy Spirit. But then they try to continue their life of faith with their own human resolution and effort. They suffer from agony—for the good that they want to do, they don't do, but the evil they don't want to do, they do. In the end they utter sighs and cry like Paul: "O wretched man that I am! Who shall deliver me from the body of this death?" (Rom. 7:24).

Our Lord promised again and again that He would send to believers the Comforter, the Holy Spirit, "that he may abide with you for ever" (John 14:16). The Spirit would come to help "our infirmities" (Rom. 8:26). Just as He promised, seven weeks after He arose from the grave, Jesus sent the Comforter, the Holy Spirit, to this earth.

How does the Holy Spirit take care of the believers who have been born again through the Word and the Spirit?

Bringing Holiness and Helping Our Infirmities

> Likewise the Spirit also helpeth our infirmities: for we know not what we should pray for as we ought: but the Spirit itself

> maketh intercession for us with groanings which cannot be uttered.
>
> —ROMANS 8:26

With agony, every believer will admit that the problem of sin seriously confronts him after he has believed in the Lord Jesus. In times past when we were unbelievers, "we all had our conversation [conduct] . . . in the lusts of our flesh, fulfilling the desires of the flesh and of the mind" (Eph. 2:3). Then we didn't feel guilty, though we lived in sin. Why? Because the soul was dead before God. But when we receive eternal life, sin becomes a problem to us.

We come to ask such questions as: Can I not help but repeatedly fall into sin even after I am saved? Don't I have the power to overcome sin?

Romans 7 and 8 deal with these questions. Romans 6 teaches the fundamental change that occurs when a person believes in Jesus Christ:

> Know ye not, that so many of us as were baptized into Jesus Christ were baptized into his death? Therefore we are buried with him by baptism into death: that like as Christ was raised up from the dead by the glory of the Father, even so we also should walk in newness of life. For if we have been planted together in the likeness of his death, we shall be also in the likeness of his resurrection: Knowing this, that our old man is crucified with him, that the body of sin might be destroyed, that henceforth we should not serve sin. For he that is dead is freed from sin.
>
> —ROMANS 6:3–7

What wonderful and blessed news this is! Yet people ask, "What shall I do to experience this blessing?"

The answer is simple. We all believe and know that we have received remission of sins and salvation by the grace of God.

And what does this grace mean? *Grace* means that God works for us in person. If we try to save ourselves or help God save us, that is not grace. *Grace* means that we receive by faith what God has accomplished for us on His part.

A person who has accepted Jesus Christ as personal Savior is totally different from one who has accepted only the religious system of Christianity, religious rituals, or a moral pattern. Through Christ the old person has been crucified, put to death. The cursed, outcast, corrupt, and fallen man who originated from the first Adam has been buried. But through and with Christ, our last Adam, a new person has risen to a new life.

This truth does not end as a theory. As surely as I was born in this world in the same condition as the first son of Adam, so Jesus, the Son of God, was incarnated into this world where He lived for thirty-three years. Just as He was crucified, I too was crucified and buried. I arose a new creature by the power of His resurrection. All who believe in Jesus Christ have experienced this.

The Bible also commands us to change our attitude and thinking: "Likewise reckon ye also yourselves to be dead indeed unto sin, but alive unto God through Jesus Christ our Lord" (Rom. 6:11). We are to believe that "if any man be in Christ, he is a new creature" (2 Cor. 5:17).

You may wonder why the writer of Romans 7 is still agonizing with the question of sin, when in chapter 6 he died through Christ, was buried, and then resurrected a new, righteous man.

The reason is simple. After the old man died and the new man was resurrected, he depended upon the power and merit of Christ. But because he did not really understand his state of regeneration, he fell back into bondage.

Many believers do not realize that just as we had no power to do that which was righteous when we were in sin, so also, after we are born again, we have no power in ourselves to attain to righteousness and holiness. When we start believing that we can be righteous and holy in our own effort, we taste the bitter cup of defeat.

Adam's descendants have held on to his idea—that he could and would do everything for himself. But actually they have been serving the devil as his slaves, dragged off in defeat. Blind, they do not come out of their delusion and wholly depend upon God. Convinced that they can bring forth salvation and holiness for themselves, they suffer defeat because they simply cannot control their sinful desires.

I can see the believer of Romans 7 fighting a bloody battle against great odds to live a righteous and holy life, trying to keep the law but being deceived by the enticing devil of self. He's so self-centered he uses the word *I* forty times in that chapter. What a proud person! But in the end the Word of God makes us realize an acute truth: No one can possibly overcome sin by himself. The writer finally says, "O wretched man that I am! Who shall deliver me from the body of this death?" (Rom. 7:24).

The answer to this question is simple though it is often understood only after hard trials. As salvation comes only by depending upon the merit of the Lord, so the life of righteousness and holiness comes only by relying upon the indwelling power of the Lord of resurrection.

In Romans 8 the apostle clearly states the answer to his own question, "Who shall deliver me?"

> There is therefore now no condemnation to them which are in Christ Jesus, who walk not after the flesh, but after the Spirit. For the law of the Spirit of life in Christ Jesus hath made me free from the law of sin and death.
>
> —ROMANS 8:1–2

Paul is saying that the victory belongs to those who are not striving in the range of their own efforts. We who have received new life in Jesus—He who trampled sin, death, the devil, and the curse—must be wholly dependent upon Him who is life, righteousness, and holiness. When we make Him our personal righteousness and holiness, the "law of the Spirit of life" that is revealed and given through Him makes us completely free from the "law of sin and death."

When we were born again, our direction in life and purpose for living were converted. The Bible reads, "In that he died, he died unto sin once: but in that he liveth, he liveth unto God" (Rom. 6:10).

We should always bear in mind that the life of Christ is not the life for self. Rather, from beginning to end, it is a life lived "unto God." Remember, Adam lived only unto himself. As a result, he became a servant of the devil, the personification of pride.

The reason why born-again Christians still fall into Satan's delusion is that they insist on continuing to live unto themselves instead of unto God.

As long as we are in this deception, living unto ourselves, we can never escape from lust and sin. But when our first priority is pleasing God in all things and doing His will—when we realize by the Word of God that we are new creatures who are "alive unto God through Jesus Christ" (Rom. 6:11)—the Holy Spirit makes us able to bear the fruit of righteousness and holiness abundantly.

Holiness means being set apart from sin and being in agreement with God. If we depart *from* something, we go *to* something else; if we depart from sin, we should not serve self, but serve God entirely.

While we pass through this process, the selfishness to depend upon one's own efforts and to serve oneself is broken little by little. As a person depends upon the indwelling power of the resurrected Christ and lives only to please and serve God, the Holy Spirit (the Spirit of God's holiness) fills that person with a deeper grace of holiness, making him or her grow more godly.

God comes within us through the Holy Spirit. By working His grace in us, He personally sets us free from the law of sin and death and enables us to keep the law of God. God not only gave us His law, but He empowers us to keep it through the presence of the Holy Spirit within us. This is *grace.*

Therefore the apostle Paul said in Galatians 2:20, "I am crucified with Christ: nevertheless I live; yet not I, but Christ liveth in me."

Now it is not I who live. Christ who is in me lives for me, believes for me, and acts for me through the Holy Spirit. Knowing this, I just trust that He is changing my heart daily. That's it! This is grace! This is what God works for us, and these are the essentials of the gospel!

We can no longer get by with such an excuse as "the spirit indeed is willing, but the flesh is weak" (Matt. 26:41).

We should not only recognize the Holy Spirit and believe Him, but actually welcome Him and allow Him to fill us with Himself so that we automatically keep God's law—not by outward compulsion, but by the power of the Holy Spirit in our inner being. We are not only with the Holy Spirit, but the Holy Spirit is clothed with us. Thus the Holy Spirit helps our infirmities, and He lives the life of faith through us. What a tremendous truth this is!

Teaching Believers

JUST AS A child must receive spiritual, moral, and intellectual teaching to grow into responsible adulthood, so must a born-again Christian be nourished to grow up in the faith. This newly born believer should grow in the likeness of Christ, and the very person who takes charge of teaching believers is the Holy Spirit: "He shall teach you all things" (John 14:26).

We tend to limit this teaching to knowledge of scholarly doctrine. But the Holy Spirit educates the whole personality of a believer.

Before we came into the world of faith, all of our education was humanistic and learned through the senses. But after a person is born again, the ministry of the Holy Spirit is a revelational education through the Word of God.

The teachings of the Holy Spirit always lead believers toward lessons to be learned. He teaches believers to follow Christ. He enables them to serve the Lord of heaven and earth. He leads them to make pleasing the heavenly Father their highest priority, because only in that is the true worth of life received. And only in pleasing the Father does a person find his true identity as well as everlasting faith, hope, and love.

The spiritual teaching of the Holy Spirit is in progress naturally, in every field of our human will, feelings, and intelligence. Through our will and emotions, the Holy Spirit brings us into the likeness of Christ. Through our intellect He works to make us realize the deeper meanings of the Word of God.

Jesus was at the same time perfect God and perfect man. Therefore in the divine nature of Jesus there existed only perfect beauty—but His human nature needed growth. The Bible acknowledges this by saying, "Jesus increased in wisdom and stature, and in favour with God and man" (Luke 2:52).

And the author of Hebrews said this:

> Who in the days of his flesh, when he had offered up prayers and supplications with strong crying and tears unto him that was able to save him from death, and was heard in that he feared; though he were a Son, yet learned he obedience by the things which he suffered; and being made perfect, he became the author of eternal salvation unto all them that obey him.
>
> —HEBREWS 5:7–9

As this passage shows, even Jesus' human nature learned obedience and was made perfect through diverse trials and sufferings according to the will of God. So also we Christians should be taught by the Holy Spirit, growing and learning from Him about the spiritual life.

The Holy Spirit's teaching of believers can be roughly divided into two methods: through the Word of God and through the experiences of life.

Before Jesus left this world, He repeatedly promised that the Holy Spirit would come to teach the whole truth and enable believers to understand and bear it (John 16:13–14). Such promises of the Lord were fulfilled in the lives of the disciples after Pentecost.

Before Pentecost, the disciples did not understand the deeper truths of Jesus' teaching. After Jesus was crucified and resurrected, their bewilderment was beyond description; they were at a loss to know what to do. But after they received the Holy Spirit at Pentecost, their lives changed drastically. They not only remembered the teachings of Jesus concerning the Holy Spirit, but they also came to realize the inner meaning of the Word of God. They digested the truths for their own lives so that they might grow.

And so it is with us. Though we try hard to study and comprehend the Word of God, unless we are filled with the Holy Spirit, who in turn gives birth to a longing for His teachings, we can only cling to words that we do not understand. We remain bewildered and lead a fruitless life, lacking the deep gratitude for God's glory that can be obtained through faithful obedience and service to God. We cannot reach our full potential in Christ unless the Holy Spirit of truth leads us to drink the true milk and honey of the Word, which is spirit and life. Human reason cannot understand the Word. Understanding can come only through the revelation of the Holy Spirit.

The Holy Spirit also teaches us through the trials and experiences of everyday life. We learn to desire God's will and follow the example of Christ. The tests and discipline enable us to claim the truth as our own, and allow us to find and realize the deeper understanding of the Word.

We should not belittle or neglect to live out the teachings of the Holy Spirit that we receive through real-life tests and experiences as well as through the Word.

Being born again and filled with the Holy Spirit can be compared to entering the "school" of the Holy Spirit. This school has neither holiday nor vacation. In every situation of life, the Holy Spirit presents Christ as our model in the study of the Word. The Holy Spirit leads us to imitate and participate in His life. Many times a day He speaks to us through the Word or through an experience, because school is always in session.

The Bible says that when Jesus came up out of the water after being baptized, the heavens were opened and the Holy Spirit descended upon Him like a dove. Then, after Jesus returned from the Jordan filled with the Holy Spirit, He was led by the Spirit into the wilderness to be tempted by the devil for forty days. (See Luke 3:22; 4:1–2.)

Of course the Holy Spirit did not lead Jesus to be tempted so as to destroy Him. This temptation of the devil was only to discipline Him.

Likewise, the Holy Spirit is with us and teaches us—both when we sense the wonderful grace and truth of God and when we feel as if we have been deserted in a wilderness. The Holy Spirit educates us so that our faith—centering on God, depending upon His Word and the love and hope of heaven—may grow.

Under no circumstances should believers who have entered the school of the Holy Spirit be discouraged or move backward. The Bible encourages us by saying, "Count it all joy when ye fall into divers temptations; knowing this, that the trying of your faith worketh patience. But let patience have her perfect work, that ye may be perfect and entire, wanting nothing" (James 1:2–4).

Therefore—if we always live a life that pleases God and centers on Him, if we always depend upon the Lord Jesus—the Holy Spirit, who has come to teach us, will make us grow so that we may lack nothing in the knowledge of the Word and of our faith.

Leading Believers

> For as many as are led by the Spirit of God, they are the sons of God.
>
> —Romans 8:14

The heavenly Father has sent the Holy Spirit to lead born-again believers along the right spiritual paths. The children of God have become people of a spiritual world by regeneration, yet they still live in the physical world in a tabernacle of the flesh. How does one live daily as a child of light in this world of darkness?

It is a difficult problem that cannot be solved by human effort. Yet the Holy Spirit of God easily solves this problem and leads believers into a victorious life. How does this happen?

The big problem believers face today is that of leadership: Is the Holy Spirit their leader, or do they lead themselves?

When believers consult me about problems of faith or when they request prayer, I often look closely into their eyes and find that they really aren't looking for help. They have already monopolized the leadership of their lives. They have already made their own plans and decisions, and now they want to ask the Holy Spirit to come and bless their blueprint. These believers are not allowing the Holy Spirit to lead them; they are leading themselves.

If we are to be led by the Holy Spirit, we need to understand the proper relationship between the Holy Spirit and ourselves. The fundamental sin man committed against God is that he disregarded the cosmic order and usurped the place of God. Man served himself, loved himself, and lived a life of pride. He not only refused to recognize God in his self-centered world, but he rebelled and left Him.

Even many people who have believed in the Lord Jesus and have been born again are still full of pride, that evil root. These people try to take advantage of God and use Him when they need Him—as one who is there for a single purpose, to bless them.

We can never have a satisfactory communication with the Holy Spirit if we have such a misunderstanding of His purpose in the world and in our lives. If we want to be wonderfully led by God, we must not only believe in Jesus and receive the remission of sins, but we must allow the Holy Spirit to cut off the roots of pride with a sharp axe of judgment. Then we should bow down before the throne, surrendering ourselves wholly to God without any condition or reservation (soul, mind, flesh, life—present, past, and future).

We should allow the Holy Spirit to work out through us what God is pleased with instead of what we are pleased with—for His purpose and not for ours. Unless a drastic change comes, the wonderful guidance that the Holy Spirit can give in every area of our lives can be expected only occasionally.

Believers ought to understand that the Creator ordained order in the universe. Why do we creations try to take advantage of our Maker, trying to be equal with Him by exalting ourselves? This pride is sin. It brings sorrow and the curse.

When we come before the presence of God, we should never try to bring Him down to our level. To God, that pride smells like a piece of putrefied meat. Through Christ, God takes hold of me by the power of the Holy Spirit, cleanses and breaks the pride, and then accomplishes His work through me.

That's the secret of being led by the Spirit. The declaration of faith of the apostle Paul—"I live; yet not I, but Christ liveth in me" (Gal. 2:20)—is the foundation of life for sincere and true believers. When we wait upon God, waiting for and serving Him as servants bowing before the Master's feet, God does not endeavor to lead us with humility. He takes possession of us and lives through us. Only in such a life can we have true rest, joy, and a firm belief and hope in life. When we know that God through the Holy Spirit rules and leads in every area of our lives, we can sing joyfully even when our days seem like dark nights.

The Holy Spirit who has come to us works to change our lives in this way. As we surrender to Him, we naturally become the splendid sons of God who are "led by the Spirit of God," as described in Romans 8:14. Moreover, every son and daughter have the qualification and capacity to be led by the Spirit of God. Praise His name!

Comforting Believers

Have you ever felt torn apart by the cares of life? You thought you were about to go under, but then you heard kind words of comfort from dear parents, family, or close friends? Comfort is like oil poured on wounds, and it gives new courage.

Yet there is a limit to human comfort. There is a "bottomless pit" of despair where human comfort cannot reach; there are times when only God can reach us.

Before Jesus left this world, He promised the sorrowing, uneasy, despondent disciples, "I will not leave you comfortless; I will come to you" (John 14:18). While Jesus was with His disciples, He was not only their unfailing Lord; He was a Comforter who took care of them. He provided food for them, healed them, and kept them free from the attacks of the enemy. But when Jesus left them, the disciples felt like comfortless orphans. They didn't understand Jesus' promise: "I will pray the Father, and he shall give you another Comforter, that he may abide with you forever" (John 14:16). Here the Holy Spirit is called the *Comforter*.

On the day of Pentecost, the disciples were all filled with the Holy Spirit and began to speak with other tongues as the Spirit gave them utterance. After they had experienced this wonderful incident, their hearts became full of comfort, peace, and boldness. The Holy Spirit, the Comforter, was within them.

From that day on, their hearts knew neither loneliness nor sorrow, neither oppressed emotions nor despair, though they were slandered, beaten, and put into prison. The Holy Spirit was there, supplying them with the unending comfort of God. They could praise God even in tribulation and affliction.

How could Stephen, the first martyr, possess enough faith to bless his murderers instead of cursing them? Because his heart was full of comfort. How could Paul and Silas in a Philippi prison—beaten, hungry, and bound fast by fetters—begin to sing midnight praises unto God? Because their hearts were overflowing with the comfort of the Holy Spirit.

Do you remember the rest of that story? God responded to the praises and prayers of Paul and Silas and caused an earthquake to shake the foundation of the prison, swinging open all the doors. Their bands were loosed, and they received freedom. By morning, the family of the prison keeper was saved. The Holy Spirit came and gave profound comfort to the torn, hurt, and bleeding souls.

The apostle Paul wrote to the Corinthians concerning God's comfort through the power of the Holy Spirit:

> Blessed be God, even the Father of our Lord Jesus Christ, the Father of mercies, and the God of all comfort; who comforteth us in all our tribulation, that we may be able to comfort them which are in any trouble, by the comfort wherewith we ourselves are comforted of God. For as the

> sufferings of Christ abound in us, so our consolation also aboundeth by Christ.
>
> —2 Corinthians 1:3–5

The comfort coming from God through the Holy Spirit allows us to overcome tribulations and ordeals.

In the first church I pioneered there was an elderly woman who had been widowed when still young. Through much sacrifice and suffering she had brought up a daughter. When this daughter married and started her own family, her mother went to live with her to take care of the house. After childbirth the daughter's heart was weak. The mother prayed earnestly to God for her daughter's healing. The widow experienced the fullness of the Holy Spirit, but the daughter died.

It seemed the mother's world had collapsed. For her daughter she had sacrificed her own desires of life, and now that daughter was gone. What words could comfort this woman in the depths of her despair?

When her daughter's lifeless body was laid out in the house, as is our custom in Korea, I was called to lead the funeral service there. When I walked into that house I knew something had changed. Previously, the woman had been inconsolable. But now the face of that old woman was radiant instead of full of despair. She even comforted me, the servant of the Lord, saying that we didn't have to worry about her daughter for she had already gone to her eternal home in heaven. She assured me that the young woman was in the bosom of God. She sang praises with strength and even danced with joy. Who could have given this wonderful comfort to her?

Only the Holy Spirit of God can and does wonderfully heal painful wounds by pouring oil on them. He gives the power to stand up and march onward, singing a triumphant song.

When we are filled with the Holy Spirit and learn to walk with Him, deep comfort, which the world does not know or understand, overflows in our souls. We can receive new strength to conquer any circumstances. We become believers that can offer solace to all afflicted people.

Confirming That We Are God's Children

> And because ye are sons, God hath sent forth the Spirit of his Son unto your hearts, crying, Abba, Father.
>
> —Galatians 4:6

To be a *father* means to be the author of a child's life and the cause of that child's being. Only one man can be my father in that sense of the word.

But God also is my Father in the faith—the author and cause of my resurrected, or born-again, being. Our Christian faith is not a religion as a lot of people misunderstand it. Can you call the birth of a baby a religion?

The Christian faith is not a *religion* but an *experience* with the Lord Jesus Christ. I experienced the new birth. I was born of God. God became my Father, and I became His own son. All the steps of growth we take in the church (the lessons preceding baptism, baptism itself, church membership, the rites) may be external helps to become better children of God, but they are not the same as being born into God's family by the power of the Holy Spirit.

We read in the Gospel of John: "But as many as received him, to them gave he power to become the sons of God, even to them that believe on his name: which were born, not of blood, nor of the will of the flesh, nor of the will of man, but of God" (John 1:12–13). As this word clearly shows, we cannot become children of God by our blood or the will of flesh or the will of man, however hard we may try. You are born as a child of God only when you are born again by the power of the Holy Spirit. Without the experience of a cleansed heart you cannot obtain the authority to become a child of God.

James 1:18 says, "Of his own will begat he us with the word of truth, that we should be a kind of firstfruits of his creatures." You are born of God when you receive the Word of God by the power of the Holy Spirit.

Even Jesus Himself said to Nicodemus, "Verily, verily, I say unto thee, Except a man be born again, he cannot see the kingdom of God." When Nicodemus asked, "How can a man be born when he is old? Can he enter the second time into his mother's womb, and be born?" Jesus answered, "Verily, verily, I say unto thee, Except a man be born of water and of the Spirit, he cannot enter into the kingdom of God. That which is born of the flesh is flesh; and that which is born of the Spirit is spirit." (See John 3:3–6.)

We are born of God as spiritual children through the Word of God by the power of the Holy Spirit just as we are born of our parents of flesh, receiving physical life.

When we are born again, the Holy Spirit reveals to us our intimate relationship to God, our Father.

A woman with whom I am well acquainted once told me the following story: Because her sister had no children, this woman sent her own daughter to her sister's home for adoption. But the daughter would not call her aunt "Mother." No matter how hard they tried to persuade her to say the word, she would not call her aunt "Mother." She always made an inarticulate utterance when she addressed her foster mother. Refusing to call her aunt "Mother," she could not become her adopted daughter.

That same parent-child bond works in the spiritual world. Through the Word and the Holy Spirit, we come to call God "Abba, Father" out of a tingling instinct in our hearts.

The Bible shows clearly that the Holy Spirit of God is doing this work. In Romans 8 we read: "Ye have not received the spirit of bondage again to fear; but ye have received the Spirit of adoption, whereby we cry, Abba, Father. The Spirit itself beareth witness with our spirit, that we are the children of God" (Rom. 8:15–16). In our hearts by the revelation of the Holy Spirit we know that God has become our Father and we have become His children.

This assurance doesn't come by the rites of any church but by the Holy Spirit Himself, who comes upon our hearts and reveals it to us. Without the work of the Holy Spirit, we could become only religious people, not God's very own children. We could be believers, but not members of the family of God.

Many churches today are cool and have no fervent love toward God because the members come to church merely as religious persons—having no firm belief in their hearts by the revelation of the Spirit that God has become their Father.

Truth dawns in our hearts neither by might nor by power but by the revelation of the Holy Spirit when we are born again by the Spirit of God.

6

The Baptism of the Holy Spirit

REGENERATION IS WHAT Jesus referred to when He told Nicodemus, "Ye must be born again" (John 3:7).

Nicodemus was a ruler of the Pharisees, a group of Jews who kept the strict law and religious rites. Not finding truth and satisfaction in his religion, he came to Jesus at night. In response to a statement by Nicodemus, Jesus made a disturbing declaration: "Except a man be born again, he cannot see the kingdom of God" (John 3:3).

Nicodemus had tried to be admitted to the kingdom of God by keeping the law and religious rites, by cultivating virtue through self-improvement and effort. All his hard work seemed to crumble in a moment.

So Nicodemus asked hastily, "How can a man be born when he is old? Can he enter the second time into his mother's womb, and be born?" (John 3:4).

Jesus answered that question by explaining clearly the law of rebirth:

> Verily, verily, I say unto thee, Except a man be born of water and of the Spirit, he cannot enter into the kingdom of God. That which is born of the flesh is flesh; and that which is born of the Spirit is spirit. Marvel not that I said unto thee, Ye must be born again.
>
> —JOHN 3:5–7

Here Jesus taught that salvation could not be achieved by a person's own effort, self-improvement, or religious celebration.

Rather it takes place when God brings about rebirth at the center of a person's being.

Something new must happen. Think of it this way: However well a monkey imitates man, it cannot become a human being because monkeys are fundamentally different from humans in the level of their existence.

John 1:13 declares that to become children of God we must be born of God: "Which were born, not of blood, nor of the will of the flesh, nor of the will of man, but of God."

Therefore salvation means that a man of flesh is born again through the Holy Spirit by the grace of God and essentially becomes a spiritual being. It is what God does for man. Salvation is possible only by the gift of God.

By that gift we become "partakers of the divine nature" through the grace of God and have the eternal life of God (2 Pet. 1:4).

What then does it mean that God enables sinners to be born again by water and the Holy Spirit?

Some people insist that "born of water" here means the physical baptism of water. But the Bible attaches greater importance to the meaning of this phrase. Of course I do not say that water baptism is a light or unnecessary act. Can it be true that God commands an unnecessary thing?

The meaning of *water* here is, above all, "washing." The Bible elsewhere teaches that we are washed by the Word of God. Jesus said to His disciples, "Now ye are clean through the word which I have spoken unto you" (John 15:3). Paul wrote, "That he might sanctify and cleanse it [the church] with the washing of water by the word" (Eph. 5:26).

When Jesus says we must be "born of water and of the Spirit," He is referring to the Word of God and the Holy Spirit. Who could be the Word of God but Jesus Himself? (See John 1:1–2, 14.)

Further on in His conversation with doubting Nicodemus, Jesus referred to Himself: "As Moses lifted up the serpent in the wilderness, even so must the Son of Man be lifted up: That whosoever believeth in him should not perish, but have eternal life" (John 3:14–15).

Only the precious blood of Jesus, who is the living Word, can make us clean—and that blood is the very word that cleanses us.

But Jesus said we are born again "of water"—or the Word—"and the Spirit." Then what does the Holy Spirit do?

Ezekiel 36:26 describes beautifully how sinners are changed into new creatures by the Spirit of God: "A new heart also will I give you, and a new spirit will I put within you: and I will take away the stony heart out of your flesh, and I will give you a heart of flesh." (See also Ezekiel 11:19.)

Today our Savior Jesus Christ can neither be understood nor explained except through the Holy Spirit, the author of miracles of salvation.

He is the administrative agent of God's salvation, reproving us of our sin through the Word and revealing Christ, who becomes our righteousness and declares the judgment to Satan. (See John 16:8.)

In John 16:14, Jesus showed that He revealed Himself only through the vessel of the Holy Spirit: "He shall glorify me: for he shall receive of mine, and shall shew it unto you."

The Holy Spirit carries out the new creative work that transforms a person by leading him to receive eternal life and the nature of God. But the Holy Spirit goes a step beyond regeneration, and that's what the baptism of the Holy Spirit is all about.

Regeneration is not the same experience as the baptism of (or with) the Holy Spirit. Of course, both regeneration and the baptism of the Holy Spirit can happen at the same time. But in other cases there is an interval of time between the two experiences. Let's take a biblical look at the difference between regeneration and the baptism of the Holy Spirit.

In the Bible there is clear mention of born-again believers who had not received the baptism with the Holy Spirit.

Before Jesus' death His disciples had already received eternal life, for Jesus called them in person and they obeyed Him, believing that He was the Son of God.

Jesus said, "Verily, verily, I say unto you, He that heareth my word, and believeth on him that sent me, hath everlasting life" (John 5:24). Jesus also testified in John 13:10 that His disciples were all clean except Judas Iscariot. And when the seventy disciples returned from preaching and told Jesus how the devils were subject to them, Jesus admitted that the seventy disciples had already received everlasting life. (See Luke 10:20.)

But Jesus did not say that they had received the baptism of the Holy Spirit from the moment they believed (as some theologians today claim). It's quite clear that they hadn't yet received the fullness of the Spirit. Before He ascended into heaven, Jesus told His disciples that they should not depart from Jerusalem yet: "Wait for the promise of the Father, which, saith he, ye have heard of me. For John truly baptized with water; but ye shall be baptized with the Holy Ghost not many days hence" (Acts 1:4–5).

Some people agree that the believing disciples needed the baptism of the Holy Spirit, but they say that was only because they were believers before Pentecost. The argument goes that any believer since that Pentecost when the church was born and the Holy Spirit descended receives the baptism of the Holy Spirit at the time of conversion.

But New Testament accounts show such a theory to be wrong.

Acts 8:5–13 describes the scene of deacon Philip preaching the gospel in Samaria. The people there "with one accord gave heed unto those things which Philip spake, hearing and seeing the miracles which he did." As a result, "unclean spirits, crying with loud voice, came out of many that were possessed with them: and many taken with palsies, and that were lame, were healed. And there was great joy in that city." The account goes on to say that a great number of men and women believed the gospel and were baptized.

But the next passage says that though they believed and were baptized, they were by no means baptized with the Holy Spirit:

> Now when the apostles which were at Jerusalem heard that Samaria had received the word of God, they sent unto them Peter and John: who, when they were come down, prayed for them, that they might receive the Holy Ghost: (for as yet he was fallen upon one of them: only they were baptized in the name of the Lord Jesus.) Then laid they their hands on them, and they received the Holy Ghost.
>
> —Acts 8:14–17

This indicates that to believe and be born again is distinctly different from receiving the Holy Spirit.

Acts 9:5–17 tells a vivid account of Paul's conversion and experience of being filled with the Holy Spirit, which didn't happen simultaneously.

With a letter of authority from the high priests, Saul and his friends went toward Damascus, the capital of Syria, to persecute those who believed in Jesus and bring them into prison.

But when he and his followers came near Damascus, "suddenly there shined round about him a light from heaven," which blinded him. Having heard the voice of the Lord Jesus, Saul fell to the earth and confessed that Jesus was the Lord. He went into Damascus a different man, obeying God.

Saul fasted and prayed for three days. From this we see that he had become a new creature in Christ. Then Ananias put his hands on Saul and prayed that he be filled with the Holy Spirit, which he was.

Another example is the church at Ephesus, which had been established through the eloquent preaching of Apollos. But when Paul visited that church, he found it struggling and weak. The first question Paul asked was this: "Have ye received the Holy Ghost since ye believed?" (Acts 19:2). Paul knew that if they had received the Holy Spirit, they wouldn't have been so powerless and feeble with only twelve or so members.

If Christians always received the Holy Spirit when they believed, why would Paul have deliberately asked the unnecessary question, "Have ye received the Holy Ghost since ye believed?" Faith does not mean that one automatically receives the fullness of the Holy Spirit. It is something a believer should pray and ask for.

In fact, first-century Spirit-filled believers thought that Christians who weren't Spirit-filled lacked a necessary qualification for service. Because of this, new believers as a rule prayed earnestly to receive the Holy Spirit.

Before the believers at Ephesus received the Holy Spirit, the church was miserably weak and sick. But after the people received the fullness of the Holy Spirit through Paul's ministry, a wonderful vitality and power of faith exploded in their midst. After a while it became a famous church that filled all of Asia Minor with the Word of God.

When we take all these accounts into consideration, we can see that regeneration and the baptism with the Holy Spirit are two distinctly different experiences.

Regeneration is the experience of receiving the life of the Lord by being grafted into the body of Christ through the Holy Spirit and the Scriptures. The baptism of the Holy Spirit is the experience in which Jesus fills believers with the power of God for ministry, service, and victorious living.

Regeneration grants a person everlasting life, while the baptism of the Holy Spirit grants regenerate believers the power of God to preach Christ.

Christians today are not powerless, sick, and spiritless because they are not born again, but because they have not received the fullness of the Holy Spirit, the tremendous power of God for service.

Without the baptism of the Holy Spirit the church today can never display God's power as did the early church—a combative, challenging, and victorious power to evangelize a generation. For this reason, we should renounce the foolish, weak, and lethargic excuse that all believers immediately receive the Holy Spirit when they believe. Rather we should pray to receive the fullness of the Holy Spirit.

What Did God Promise?

If a Christian is to have power and authority to carry out the ministry and service of God, he or she must have the baptism of the Holy Spirit.

In Old Testament times God gave the wonderful anointing of the Holy Spirit (which corresponds to today's baptism of the Holy Spirit) to His specially chosen vessels: kings, priests, judges, prophets, and deliverers of the Israelites, whom He used according to His ordained will. But at that time only a few people were anointed with the power of God, so ordinary people could not even dream of such grace.

Yet God prophesied that in the future the call for salvation would come to all people; He would also give the anointing of the Holy Spirit to anyone who answered the call of God.

The most vivid and prominent of many prophecies is written in Joel 2:

> And it shall come to pass afterward, that I will pour out my spirit upon all flesh: and your sons and your daughters shall prophesy, your old men shall dream dreams, your young men shall see visions: and also upon the servants and upon the handmaids in those days will I pour out my spirit.
>
> —Joel 2:28–29

The excellent and wonderful point of this prophecy is that God declared through the prophet Joel that in the future He would provide salvation not only for Israel but for everyone regardless of nation, race, or status; He would give the fullness of the Holy Spirit to all peoples.

Joel was a prophet of Judah who lived some seven hundred seventy years before Christ. Jews of those days were extremely exclusive: God's chosen people were the Israelites. Jehovah God was not the God of the Gentiles; furthermore He could not become the Savior of Gentiles.

In such a climate, this prophecy told that in the future God would give His Spirit not only to Jewish people but to all flesh. There would be no regard for sex and age. God even promised that

He would give His Spirit to humble servants and handmaids, to prisoners taken from foreign countries, to slaves bought with money—people who were ill-treated and despised, in the lowest position of Jewish society.

Yet about eight hundred years later this prophecy was fulfilled literally.

Forty days after Jesus rose from the dead, He commanded His disciples to stay in Jerusalem: "Wait for the promise of the Father, which, saith he, ye have heard of me. For John truly baptized with water, but ye shall be baptized with the Holy Ghost not many days hence" (Acts 1:4–5).

These words make it clear that the prophecy of Joel and the cry of John the Baptist at the Jordan—"I indeed baptize you with water; but one mightier than I cometh, the latchet of whose shoes I am not worthy to unloose: he shall baptize you with the Holy Ghost and with fire" (Luke 3:16)—refer to the life and work of Jesus.

The disciples of Jesus, following the commandment of the Lord, gathered together in the upper room in Jerusalem and continued to pray.

The Jewish calendar tells us how long they prayed. Jesus died at the Passover feast. The Holy Spirit came upon the disciples on the day of Pentecost, a feast celebrated fifty days after Passover. Jesus had shown Himself to His disciples for forty days between His resurrection and ascension. So the disciples gathered together in Jerusalem for prayer for about ten days.

The Bible thus describes the wonderful miracle that came upon the disciples at Pentecost:

> And when the day of Pentecost was fully come, they were all with one accord in one place. And suddenly there came a sound from heaven as of a rushing mighty wind, and it filled all the house where they were sitting. And there appeared unto them cloven tongues like as of fire, and it sat upon each of them. And they were all filled with the Holy Ghost, and began to speak with other tongues, as the Spirit gave them utterance.
>
> —ACTS 2:1–4

Peter, immediately after he had received the baptism of the Holy Spirit, stood before a great multitude of people flocked around him and lifted up his voice. He claimed that this was that which had been spoken of by the prophet Joel eight hundred years before—that God would pour out His Spirit upon all flesh.

In Peter's quotation of the prophecy of Joel, the Holy Spirit clarified the time frame (Joel's "afterward") by saying "in the last days," indicating the last days started when Jesus ascended into heaven; the time had come when God would pour His Spirit out upon all flesh.

Peter gave bigger and more wonderful promises to those who heard him preach and then repented:

> Repent, and be baptized every one of you in the name of Jesus Christ for the remission of sins, and ye shall receive the gift of the Holy Ghost. For the promise is unto you, and to your children, and to all that are afar off, even as many as the Lord our God shall call.
>
> —Acts 2:38–39

Let's examine this passage by dividing it into several parts.

First, this word contains a national promise to Jews: "every one of you" refers to the Jews who were hearing Peter preach.

Second, Peter gives a promise to future generations of Jewish people: "unto you, and to your children."

Third, the promise relates to the whole world: "to all that are afar off." Jewish rabbis of those days used that expression when they spoke of heathens—or foreigners.

Fourth, the promise refers to all times: "as many as" applies not only to everyone regardless of nation, race, sex, age, possessions, or rank—but also to everyone until the end of time, when Christ comes back to earth. What a wonderful promise: God will pour out the Holy Spirit not only in the days of the apostles but throughout the whole age of grace, even now.

Phenomena That Accompany the Spirit

By examining the biblical record of the personal experiences of those who were baptized with the Holy Spirit, we can uncover sound knowledge concerning the phenomena that appear when the Holy Spirit is received.

When Christians want to receive the baptism of the Holy Spirit, many ask a sincere question: What evidence will appear and give me the assurance that I have been baptized with the Holy Spirit?

I know I tried every means and left no stone unturned, earnestly praying to receive the Holy Spirit. During this time I would sometimes enjoy wonderful peace and joy of heart. I could sometimes boldly preach the gospel in marketplaces, in buses, or in streetcars. I often had that experience of feeling that the Word of God was as sweet as honey. In spite of all this, I did not have the assurance in my heart that I had received the fullness of the Holy Spirit, and I did not know why.

Full of questions, I visited many respected servants of the Lord, but I failed to receive a satisfying answer. Finally, I decided to find the answer in the Word of God. But where in the Bible could the teachings concerning the baptism of the Holy Spirit be found?

Material seemed limited. In the Old Testament and in the Gospels "the Holy Ghost was not yet given; because that Jesus was not yet glorified" (John 7:39). In the Epistles the teaching is mainly for believers who had already received the fullness of the Spirit; they contain no direct scenes of the baptism of the Holy Spirit.

Such scenes are recorded only in Acts, and so I decided to study that book with an unprejudiced, honest, and open heart.

As a result of that study, the truth of the Word of God was as clear to me as the bright sunlight, and the fullness of the Holy Spirit I had experienced was accompanied by indisputable evidence. The deep feelings I initially felt at the time I received the fullness of the Holy Spirit became deeper as time went by.

Let's examine the accounts of the saints in Acts who received the baptism of the Holy Spirit.

Pentecost

The most wonderful incident was the baptism of the Holy Spirit of the one hundred twenty disciples on the day of Pentecost.

When they received the fullness of the Holy Spirit, they must have known beyond question that they had received the gift Jesus had told them to wait for. Otherwise, why would they have stopped waiting and gone out into the front lines of gospel preaching? According to the Bible, one hundred twenty disciples without exception stopped waiting for the wonderful experience and had the conviction that they had received the Holy Spirit. How could everyone have had that experience simultaneously? Because the fullness of the Holy Spirit had included not only an outward experience but also an inner assurance.

Let's consider the phenomena that appeared in the upper room when the Holy Spirit came down on Pentecost (Acts 2:2–4).

1. "Suddenly there came a sound from heaven as of a rushing mighty wind."

2. "There appeared unto them cloven tongues like as of fire, and it sat upon each of them."
3. "And they were all filled with the Holy Ghost, and began to speak with other tongues, as the Spirit gave them utterance."

From the above progression we can see that before the disciples experienced the baptism of the Holy Spirit, they heard a sound of wind and saw cloven tongues like as of fire. Then the sign of speaking with other tongues followed the experience of receiving the fullness of the Holy Spirit.

With these signs, the one hundred twenty disciples' experience of receiving the baptism of the Holy Spirit was certain beyond question. Knowing what had happened, their representative, Peter, spoke before the crowd of people gathered together. Speaking of Jesus, Peter said, "Therefore being by the right hand of God exalted, and having received of the Father the promise of the Holy Ghost, he hath shed forth this, which ye now see and hear" (Acts 2:33).

Peter was saying that there was objective proof of the experience of the baptism of the Holy Spirit.

We also should bear witness to our experience of the fullness of the Holy Spirit, not in general terms but like Peter, with that which one can see and hear. If we don't have evident proof—if we continue the spiritual struggle, not being sure whether we have received the Holy Spirit or not—how can we become bold and powerful witnesses?

Samaria

The Book of Acts mentions a second experience of the fullness of the Holy Spirit—in Samaria.

After deacon Stephen was martyred in Jerusalem, great persecution against the church continued. Most of the church, except the apostles, was scattered abroad throughout the regions of Judea and Samaria.

Philip went down to the city of Samaria and preached Christ. As a result many believed in Christ and were baptized in water. Many possessed by unclean spirits were delivered; many lame and many afflicted with palsies were healed (Acts 8:5–8).

Despite these miracles, it seems that Philip did not have the gift of helping people receive the baptism of the Holy Spirit. The Bible goes on to say:

> When the apostles which were at Jerusalem heard that Samaria had received the word of God, they sent unto them Peter and John: who, when they were come down, prayed for them, that they might receive the Holy Ghost: (for as yet he was fallen upon none of them: only they were baptized in the name of the Lord Jesus.) Then laid they their hands on them, and they received the Holy Ghost.
>
> —ACTS 8:14–17

Some readers will ask, "But were there external signs when believers in Samaria received the Holy Spirit?"

When we look more deeply into the Word, we see that some unusual things happened that day.

A sorcerer named Simon attended Philip's big salvation and healing crusade; he was greatly moved as he saw the power of God revealed. He accepted Jesus as his Savior and was even baptized.

Then Peter and John came down from Jerusalem, laying their hands on the believers, who then received the Holy Ghost. Now Simon was so amazed by this that he offered them money, saying "Give me also this power, that on whomsoever I lay hands, he may receive the Holy Ghost" (Acts 8:19).

He was severely rebuked by the apostle Peter when he tried to buy the gift of God with money. But in his behavior there is a tacit lesson that cannot be disregarded. This sorcerer Simon saw all of these things happening: People repenting and confessing their sins were changed and filled with joy. Unclean spirits crying with loud voices came out of many. Many who had been afflicted with palsies or who were lame were totally healed. At the sight of these miracles Simon didn't try to buy such power with money. It was when Peter and John came down and laid hands on believers to receive the Holy Spirit that Simon tried to buy the power.

Why? The answer is very simple: Because a special sign appeared to the Samaritans who received the Holy Spirit through the laying on of hands by Peter and John. Had the Spirit passed calmly and quietly, Simon wouldn't have hurried to offer money.

What did the sorcerer see as a result of the prayer of Peter and John? He must have seen and heard those believers speak with other tongues and praise God.

We cannot help but infer this, because in Philip's crusade all the signs had occurred except one—that of speaking with other tongues.

Don't misunderstand me. Speaking with tongues and the baptism of the Holy Spirit are not synonymous. Some people today mistakenly say that the Pentecostal and charismatic churches teach this. Let me put it this way: In the time of the apostles, whenever God poured out the Holy Spirit upon exemplary churches, He always provided external signs, which both those who received the Holy Spirit and objective spectators could spontaneously feel, see, and hear. Almost without exception, as the final and most common sign, the recipients spoke with other tongues.

It is clear that the Pentecostal experience of Samaria, which occurred about eight years after the apostles were baptized with the Holy Spirit in Jerusalem, was an experience accompanied by wonderful signs.

Cornelius

The third recorded experience of receiving the fullness of the Holy Spirit took place in the house of Cornelius. After leaving Samaria, Peter went down to Joppa and tarried there with Simon, a tanner. One day at the sixth hour Peter went up to the housetop to pray:

> He became very hungry, and would have eaten: but while they made ready, he fell into a trance, and saw heaven opened, and a certain vessel descending unto him, as it had been a great sheet knit at the four corners, and let down to the earth: Wherein were all manner of fourfooted beasts of the earth, and wild beasts, and creeping things, and fowls of the air. And there came a voice to him, Rise, Peter; kill, and eat. But Peter said, Not so, Lord; for I have never eaten any thing that is common or unclean. And the voice spake unto him again the second time, What God hath cleansed, that call not thou common.
>
> —Acts 10:10–15

This happened three times before the vessel was drawn up into heaven. As Peter contemplated what this vision might mean, messengers sent from Cornelius knocked on the door.

It seems God had sent an angel to the Gentile Cornelius in a vision, preparing Cornelius to hear the word of salvation and grace. According to the direction of the angel, Cornelius sent messengers to Peter in Joppa. When Peter heard the story, his own vision made sense to him.

Peter, an obstinate Jew, had always thought it unlawful to keep company with or visit in the home of someone of another nation. If God had not clearly commanded him to go, Peter by no means would have gone to the house of Cornelius.

But God has said clearly that since He would henceforth make Gentiles clean through faith in Christ, Peter should not call common what God had cleansed. That's how the close-minded Jewish thinking of Peter was changed.

Thus God opened a way, the Pentecostal way, for Gentiles, the people gathered together at the house of the heathen centurion Cornelius, to receive salvation and the fullness of the Holy Spirit through faith in Christ.

Let us look carefully into this encounter, when the Holy Spirit came down upon those Gentiles in the home of Cornelius. Peter preached to the people gathered in the house. He started with the prophecy of John the Baptist, then covered the ministry of Jesus, including His death and resurrection. Peter concluded, "To him give all the prophets witness, that through his name whosoever believeth in him shall receive remission of sins" (Acts 10:43).

Just as Peter spoke these words, the Holy Spirit suddenly came down upon all the people who heard it.

> While Peter yet spake these words, the Holy Ghost fell on all them which heard the word. And they of the circumcision which believed were astonished, as many as came with Peter, because that on the Gentiles also was poured out the gift of the Holy Ghost. For they heard them speak with tongues, and magnify God.
>
> —ACTS 10:44–46

As soon as the people there heard the word of truth, that salvation is obtained by believing in Jesus Christ, they believed and uttered *amen* to the amazing power of the Holy Spirit.

How could other people know and testify that the Gentiles in the house of Cornelius had received the Holy Spirit? When we read the biblical account impartially without any prejudice, the proof is evident. Despite the fact that the stubborn Jews tried to believe that salvation and the fullness of the Holy Spirit were not for the Gentiles, the work of God so wonderfully developed that they could not deny it, "for they heard them speak with tongues, and magnify God" (Acts 10:46).

Note again Acts 10:45 and 46. In this passage the Greek word *for* is a casual conjunction, signifying "seeing that" or "since." The circumcised Jewish Christians were astonished, "for [or *because* or *since*] they heard them speak with tongues, and magnify God."

This indicates that early Christians saw tongues as an external, objective sign of the fullness of the Holy Spirit.

Ephesus

The fourth incident in Acts concerning the fullness of the Holy Spirit took place in Ephesus. About forty years had passed since the first outpouring of the Holy Spirit in the upper room in Jerusalem on the day of Pentecost.

The Spirit-filled disciples now preached the gospel with strength, clothed with great power from heaven.

As a result, they endured many persecutions and tribulations, but the persecutions and tribulations could not stop them.

The gospel had shaken Judea; it had swept over Samaria; now it was advancing to the uttermost parts of the earth, largely due to the efforts of the apostle Paul.

Before he became a Christian and an apostle, Paul—then known as Saul—had persecuted the church with a fierce passion. He had bound believers and cast them into prison and even killed some. But he could not forget one scene—the stoning of deacon Stephen. As rocks and abusive language and slander were hurled at Stephen, he showed no expression of resistance or retaliation. Instead, Stephen's face shone as that of an angel. As Stephen died, he was even praying that God would forgive and bless those who stoned him. It was a scene Saul could not then understand.

But Saul's persecution of the church and his oppression of the believers became even more fierce. With special authority from the high priest in Jerusalem, he was on his way to wreak havoc on the church in Damascus when another experience shook him.

The Scripture tells the story in detail. As Saul traveled to Damascus, he was overcome by a light from heaven. Now it is said that the brilliant noon sun in Damascus is like a rain shower. But the light that shone upon Saul was still more brilliant than that, causing him to go blind and fall to the ground. As he fell to the ground he heard the voice of Jesus: "Saul, Saul, why persecutest thou me?" (Acts 9:4). Still blind, Saul had to be led into Damascus. For three days he fasted and prayed for repentance. Later a believer by the name of Ananias prayed for Saul's sight to be restored.

Saul's name was soon changed to *Paul,* and forty years after Pentecost he went to Ephesus to preach. When he met certain believers in that city, they remembered his persecution of the church, and many were fearful of him.

From the standpoint of spiritual life these few believers were lifeless, reduced to a skeleton of rituals and formalism. Figuratively speaking, it was as if they were breathing their last.

What was the first question the great apostle Paul asked these people?

It is a question to which today's churches—bound by ceremonies, formalism, and human-centered ways of thinking—should incline their ears: "Have ye received the Holy Ghost since ye believed?" (Acts 19:2).

Many people who want to hide their powerlessness by justifying their theology are well prepared to answer this question. With ease they quickly say, "Of course, we received the Holy Spirit when we believed." But a little closer look in the Bible reveals the foolishness of this answer. If we automatically received the Holy Spirit when we first believed, why would the apostle Paul have gone to all the trouble of asking the question?

Salvation is received through regeneration by believing in the work of the Holy Spirit, but authority and power can only be received when a born-again Christian receives the fullness of the Holy Spirit after believing. The disciples in Ephesus must have been honest believers. When they were asked by the apostle Paul, they held nothing back from him: "We have not so much as heard whether there be any Holy Ghost" (Acts 19:2).

What a miserable state they were in not to have so much as heard whether there be any Holy Ghost!

As soon as the apostle Paul heard that, he clearly preached the gospel of salvation of Jesus Christ and gave them water baptism in the name of Jesus.

Would Paul have given water baptism to those who were not born again? No. Christians in Ephesus were certainly believers who had accepted Christ Jesus as Savior, but Paul did not regard them as having received the baptism of the Holy Spirit.

Paul then had a prayer meeting for one reason: to ask for the baptism of the Holy Spirit for these people. Does our church today have such a special prayer meeting to receive the baptism of the Holy Spirit?

When Paul laid his hands on them, the Holy Spirit came upon them. The Bible describes that scene in this way: "When Paul had laid his hands upon them, the Holy Ghost came on them; and they spake with tongues, and prophesied" (Acts 19:6).

Summary

Isn't it significant that the gifts of speaking in tongues and prophecy followed right after the coming of the Holy Spirit? The Scripture can neither be broken nor should it be wrestled with. When we study scenes in which the Holy Spirit came down in the early church, filling the lives of believers, we can find one indisputable common sign. What is that?

We saw that wind, fire, and tongues were present in the upper room on the day of Pentecost. It is inferred that these same signs were evident in Samaria also. At the house of Cornelius, believers spoke in tongues as they praised God. Later, people spoke with tongues and prophesied in Ephesus. Probably everyone who observed these biblical incidents in which the fullness of the Holy Spirit was received would say that the believers spoke in other tongues as the Holy Spirit gave utterance.

Of course, I repeat that speaking in tongues in itself is not the fullness of the Spirit; but as confirmed in the Scriptures, tongues is the common external sign that a person has received the fullness of the Holy Spirit.

7

Receiving the Baptism of the Holy Spirit

IF WE ARE to look into how one receives the baptism of the Holy Spirit, we must investigate how the early Christians received the Holy Spirit.

A Look at the Era of the Apostles

AFTER THE DISCIPLES saw Jesus Christ ascend into heaven from Mount Olivet, they obeyed Jesus' command and gathered together and earnestly prayed with one accord (Acts 1:14).

Today, as much as in the past, those who want to receive the promised baptism of the Holy Spirit should have a fervent expectation and a desperate desire to receive.

During my gospel crusades I have seen thousands of believers filled with the Holy Spirit. Almost without exception that blessing has come when the seekers decided, regardless of circumstances or dignity, with tears of determination, that they would receive it without fail.

If those who want to receive the Holy Spirit are half in doubt about their own desire, if they pray with a lukewarm attitude that God will give them the baptism of the Holy Spirit if He wants to, they cannot receive no matter how long they pray. The blessing of the fullness of the Spirit of God always comes when you make up your mind that you will not leave without having the answer to your earnest, desperate need.

In Acts 8, the believers in Samaria received the Holy Spirit when Peter and John laid their hands on them.

The same experience happened to Saul (Paul), who received the Holy Spirit when Ananias laid hands on him (Acts 9:10–18). A dozen believers in Ephesus also received the fullness of the Holy Spirit when hands were laid on them by the apostle Paul (Acts 19:1–7).

Today also, it is well known that you can receive the fullness of the Holy Spirit when hands are laid on you with prayer.

Of course, you cannot receive the Holy Spirit if hands are laid on you when you don't want to receive the baptism of the Holy Spirit or when your heart is not prepared or when you don't have a fervent faith to receive.

On the other hand, if the hands of Spirit-filled servants of God are laid on you, you can receive the fullness of the Holy Spirit when you have a strong desire to receive, even if your own prayer is weak.

Finally, Acts 10:44–48 records the Spirit's filling the Gentiles at Cornelius's house. Verse 44 says, "While Peter yet spake these words, the Holy Ghost fell on them which heard the word."

These people were all filled with the Holy Spirit while they listened to Peter's preaching.

I have seen this happen. While preaching a sermon about the Holy Spirit, I've seen the Holy Spirit Himself poured out like rain upon prepared hearts. They spoke with tongues, magnifying God in a heavenly language, as believers did in the house of Cornelius.

From many pulpits today the true Word of God is not preached faithfully. How can people hear the Word if it is not preached? Though people have worshiped in the church, they do not experience a deep moving or the wonderful grace of the Holy Spirit.

When a servant of the Lord, filled with the Spirit, preaches the anointed Word, listeners will experience a great moving of the Holy Spirit.

Preparing Our Hearts

How do we prepare our hearts to receive the baptism of the Holy Spirit?

First of all, those who want to receive the Holy Spirit should have not only a desire but also a knowledge of and grip on the trustworthy promises of God: He is still giving the same fullness of the Holy Spirit as He did in the era of the apostles. The Scripture concludes: "But let him ask in faith, nothing wavering. For he that wavereth is like a wave of the sea driven with the wind and tossed. For let not that man think that he shall receive any thing of the

Lord. A double minded man is unstable in all his ways" (James 1:6–8).

If you seek to receive the Holy Spirit with an attitude of doubt, not fully trusting the promises of God, you are wasting your time and effort.

The Bible teaches us, "So then faith cometh by hearing, and hearing by the word of God" (Rom. 10:17). We should begin studying the Book of Acts with an open heart, listening to the testimonies of those who have received the fullness of the Holy Spirit; we should remove all human prejudice from our hearts. After we have the conviction that the blessing of the fullness of the Holy Spirit is for us today, we should repent of all unconfessed sins before God and depend upon the precious blood of Christ for a complete cleansing. We must take care of any sin in our lives before we pray for the experience of the baptism of the Spirit.

Peter said in Acts 2:38, "Repent, and be baptized every one of you in the name of Jesus Christ for the remission of sins, and ye shall receive the gift of the Holy Ghost."

Does this command, "Repent, and be baptized every one of you in the name of Jesus Christ for the remission of sins," mean that unless you are baptized with water you will receive neither remission of sins nor the Holy Spirit?

It seems not; when Peter preached the gospel in the house of Cornelius, Gentiles were filled with the Holy Spirit even before they had gone through the process of water baptism.

Needless to say, God cannot give the baptism of the Holy Spirit to those who have not received remission of sins or salvation.

When we repent and believe in the gospel, we receive remission of sins and salvation. We should also try to be baptized with water as soon as possible, as it is the external sign of salvation. But to conclude that unless you are baptized with water you receive neither remission of sins nor baptism of the Holy Spirit is against the teachings of the Bible.

I have seen tens of thousands of people repent and believe in the Lord Jesus Christ as Savior and then be filled with the Holy Spirit before they were baptized with water.

In Acts 10:48, the apostle Peter spoke to Gentiles who had received not only the forgiveness of sins but the fullness of the Holy Spirit and told them, "Be baptized in the name of the Lord."

Most of the believers who lived in the days of the apostles were exhorted to (and did) receive the Holy Spirit as soon as they were saved. But today a great number of believers "have not so much as heard whether there be any Holy Ghost" (Acts 19:2). What a sad commentary.

Although water baptism isn't a prerequisite for baptism with the Spirit, repentance is, because the Holy Spirit will not come to a vessel that conceals sin.

When we pray to receive the baptism of the Holy Spirit, there are generally two kinds of sins we should repent of: Have we knowingly disobeyed the will of God? Have we neglected the duty of believers—believing God's Word concerning being filled with the Holy Spirit?

The first sin is that of disobedience. Before believing in the Lord Jesus, we revolted against God and committed many kinds of sins. When we repented and accepted Jesus Christ as Savior, we received remission of sins. Through our long revolt, however, our hearts had become so hardened that we were not broken easily. Though we have received remission of sins and salvation, when we want to receive the fullness of the Holy Spirit, we must repent bitterly again, asking for His forgiveness and cleansing from our willfulness.

In order to be broken before the Lord and cleansed, we should repent of all the transgressions we can remember.

I remember weeping continually for two years every time I prayed to receive the fullness of the Holy Spirit. Though I cried and prayed hard, I could not receive the baptism. At first I was very thirsty, but later I grew disappointed and frustrated.

Then when I was in the second year of Bible school, I prayed with a resolute determination that I wouldn't leave the place where I was sitting until I had received the Holy Spirit. At the same time I confessed deeply once again all the sins I had committed since childhood. Suddenly my spirit was broken, and the Holy Spirit of God moved upon me and within me with a great infilling. I began to speak with other tongues as the Holy Spirit gave me utterances.

The second sin we must confess is callousness. James 4:17 says, "Therefore to him that knoweth to do good, and doeth it not, to him it is sin." Though we are saved and live as Christians, if we have been lazy we should repent of the sin of laziness. We should repent that we have not lived with God at the center of our lives. If we have not sought the kingdom and His righteousness first, we have not pleased God.

When we repent of all our sins, the power of those sins will be broken. As we pray for the fullness of the Holy Spirit, we will have the right relationship with God—an obedient heart to do God's will.

As far as we have the ability, we need to make amends and repay what we owe to others. We need to ask their forgiveness and make restitution. Unlike repentance in word only, repentance and confession that come out of the inner heart are followed by the fruit of action.

When our hearts have been thus prepared, the Holy Spirit of God always comes down upon us.

Frequently, those who desire to receive the Holy Spirit after hearing someone's moving testimony make up their minds that they will receive the Holy Spirit in just the same manner. But the Holy Spirit does not always come down in accordance with the way we ask. He comes in accordance with the personality of the receiving person. Sometimes He comes calmly like soft rain. At other times He comes tumultuously like rolling thunder. Though the Holy Spirit makes Himself known in different ways, He who comes is still the same—the third person of the Trinity.

A Word of Warning

AFTER WE HAVE confessed sin, how should we pray to receive the Holy Spirit? Let me present a few observations or warnings in this regard.

First, we should not pray to receive the Holy Spirit with a wrong motive. In plain words, you must not cry to God so you can boast or gloat in the special attention that might accompany a great power. People who've asked amiss have sometimes received a different spirit, such as the spirit of covetousness, rather than the Holy Spirit.

But when the motivation of our hearts is pure—when we want to become a more powerful and effective vessel to be used by God, when we want to become by any means a better instrument of God, bearing witness of a Christlike spirit—evil spirits can never come near us.

Jesus spoke of such an assurance in Luke 11:11–13:

> If a son shall ask bread of any of you that is a father, will he give him a stone? or if he ask a fish, will he for a fish give him a serpent? Or if he shall ask an egg, will he offer him a scorpion? If ye then, being evil, know how to give good gifts unto your children: how much more shall your heavenly Father give the Holy Spirit to them that ask him?

Therefore when we pray for the fullness of the Holy Spirit so that the will of God for our lives may be fulfilled (not to satisfy our lust or covetousness), God will surely give us the Holy Spirit.

This second word of warning does not apply to a person who has a cheerful disposition but to the kind of person who is pessimistic and inclined to keep a dark solitude in his or her heart. Since this type of person has been so long oppressed unwittingly by a negative spirit, if he tries to pray hastily for the Spirit of God without first completely cleansing himself of that negative spirit, he can fall into agony and be overtaken by another morbid spirit.

But if this type of person has prepared himself slowly until his inner world, through receiving the Word of God and forgiveness in his heart, has become bright and cheerful and positive, he will receive a wonderful baptism.

When such a person comes to have a cheerful and positive mental attitude, he has already overcome and rid himself of the devil. He can pray for the fullness of the Holy Spirit without anxiety.

Third, a long continuing sickness that wears away the body is often followed by the oppression of the devil. Those who are weak both in mind and body, having been harassed by sickness a long time, should be cleansed by the precious blood of Jesus again; if they are inclined to be oppressed by the devil, when they pray earnestly to receive the Holy Spirit, they could be oppressed again by the devil.

Acts 10:38 teaches that during His ministry Jesus healed all diseases and sickness caused by the oppression of the devil: "God anointed Jesus of Nazareth with the Holy Ghost and with power: who went about doing good, and healing all that were oppressed of the devil; for God was with him."

I have almost always been hindered by the devil when I prayed with those weak in mind and body to receive the Holy Spirit. Knowing this, people who have been oppressed by Satan should pray to receive the Holy Spirit, laying special claim to the precious blood of Jesus.

Fourth, those persons who served the devil long before they came to the Lord should be especially careful. Before these people pray to receive the Holy Spirit, they should bury all the past relationships they had with the devil, repent of their sins fully and have the victory all believers can have over the devil. Then when they pray to receive the Holy Spirit, they can pray for peace and the joy of Christ without any fear and sense of demonic oppression. Occasionally, these people may still be vulnerable subconsciously if they open their hearts.

Fifth, those who pray eagerly to receive the Holy Spirit should not permit just anyone to lay hands on them in prayer. An evil spirit, like an epidemic, is very contagious. I have seen numerous people taken by unclean spirits when someone with evil spirits laid hands on them. When they were seized by that spirit they experienced terrible suffering until they received deliverance. Those who want to have hands laid on them in prayer should always be sure that the person who is going to lay hands on them is a person full of the Spirit of truth.

Sixth, be wary of going alone to a mountain or a cave for prayer. Once in a while those who have heard of other people receiving much grace at a prayer mountain want to visit that place also. But then because their faith was not bold they became frightened and oppressed by evil spirits who took advantage of their moment of fear.

Throughout my ministry, as I have preached about the Holy Spirit, I have seen countless examples of what I've described in this section. Because of my experience, I have received considerable knowledge about how to free people from the bondage of the devil.

Now let us examine how to discriminate between the Holy Spirit and evil spirits.

8

Discerning Evil Spirits in a Person

TWO SPIRITUAL FORCES surround us. Because of Jesus' great love for His redeemed ones, He has sent the Holy Spirit and many angels, commanding them "to minister for them who shall be heirs of salvation" (Heb. 1:14).

Not only is the Holy Spirit with us always, but many angels are also with us always. On the other hand, the enemy, Satan, who is the prince of the power of the air, is continually devising a sinister plot "to steal, and to kill, and to destroy" by sending evil and unclean spirits who walk around in the world (John 10:10). As the apostle John says, "And we know that we are of God, and the whole world lieth in wickedness" (1 John 5:19).

Seeing that these facts are true, I have come to realize that believers should discern these spirits. If you don't have the special gift of discerning of the spirits, discern the work of evil spirits by following the teaching of Christ.

Knowing a Tree by Its Fruit

JESUS TEACHES IN Matthew 7:15–20:

> Beware of false prophets, which come to you in sheep's clothing, but inwardly they are ravening wolves. Ye shall know them by their fruits. Do men gather grapes of thorns, or figs of thistles? Even so every good tree bringeth forth good fruit; but a corrupt tree bringeth forth evil fruit. A good tree cannot bring forth evil fruit, neither can a corrupt tree bring forth

> good fruit. Every tree that bringeth not forth good fruit is hewn down, and cast into the fire. Wherefore by their fruits ye shall know them.

Even though you may have a fantastic, wonderful experience or inspiration, if the fruit you bear is not in line with the Word of God and the fruit of the Holy Spirit, it can never be work that was born of the Spirit of God.

Jesus also warns:

> Many will say to me in that day, Lord, Lord, have we not prophesied in thy name? and in thy name have cast out devils? and in thy name done many wonderful works? And then will I profess unto them, I never knew you: depart from me, ye that work iniquity.
>
> —MATTHEW 7:22–23

You should never assume merely on the basis of its supernatural aspects that any work that is followed by signs and wonders is performed as the work of God. You should always look at the fruit of or the true nature behind the work. Though the devil comes in sheep's clothing, he can neither hide nor falsify his character. Let us examine the fruits of the devil.

The Devil Is Wicked

THE BIBLE TEACHES that "the kingdom of God is . . . righteousness, and peace, and joy in the Holy Ghost" (Rom. 14:17). But when Satan comes in, disguised as the Holy Spirit, he steals away a person's love, joy, and peace.

James 3:14–18 gives us a clear standard of judgment:

> But if ye have bitter envying and strife in your hearts, glory not, and lie not against the truth. This wisdom descendeth not from above, but is earthly, sensual, devilish. For where envying and strife is, there is confusion and every evil work. But the wisdom that is from above is first pure, then peaceable, gentle, and easy to be entreated, full of mercy and good fruits, without partiality, and without hypocrisy. And the fruit of righteousness is sown in peace of them that make peace.

Those who are depressed by the spirit of the devil feel a strong interference in everything. It can be so great that the person begins to wonder, *If this is the Holy Spirit, how can He act so frivolously and prompt such thoughtless action?*

At times, the spirit of the devil tries to give instructions that imitate closely the Holy Spirit. These are not only about petty things but also about problems of faith. The evil spirits also spread negativism and anxiety. In short, evil spirits continue unceasingly to send troublesome prophetic interference.

Clear words in Isaiah teach us about being associated with familiar spirits: "And when they shall say unto you, Seek unto them that have familiar spirits, and unto wizards that peep, and that mutter: should not a people seek unto their God? for the living to the dead?" (Isa. 8:19).

Believers who go around making jabbering and muttering prophecies probably have familiar spirits, and they should be stopped.

Prophecy from the Holy Spirit comes as God needs to speak His message to His people. It comes gently and is divinely accompanied by deep feelings of confirmation and assurance that the message was truly from God.

The Devil Is Unclean

In many places, the Bible calls spirits "unclean." (See Matthew 10:1; Mark 1:27; Luke 6:18.) Unclean spirits, the spirit of the devil, raise ugly imaginations continually against one's own will. They stick like a burr in one's heart, unlike an occasional passing thought. Sometimes unclean spirits cause people to have bad thoughts when they read the Bible. Sometimes they make one feel sick when in the presence of Spirit-filled believers. Those who are oppressed by unclean spirits are in agony, with lewd and filthy imaginations overflowing like a cesspool. When they hear the Word of God, uncontrollable false charges will afflict their hearts, and arrogant thinking will rise as a snake raises its head.

Luke 6:18 says that these unclean spirits can "vex." The Holy Spirit of God brings joy, peace, and a refreshing, but evil spirits bring agony and trouble to mind and body.

Though you may believe that you have received the Holy Spirit, if you are in continual agony, fear, and trouble, if you always feel pressed down by a big burden, this is the sign that you are oppressed by evil spirits.

No matter how deceitfully the devil may disguise himself, when you see such fruit, you can know that his true character is like a ravening wolf.

Discerning a Person's Concept of Christ

THE MOST IMPORTANT question in discerning spirits is, "What does one say about Christ?"

Other discrepancies in doctrine do not reach the point of life and death. But false teaching about the saving grace of Jesus Christ brings eternal destruction to those who preach it and those who hear and follow it.

The apostle John writes in 1 John 4:1–3:

> Beloved, believe not every spirit, but try the spirits whether they are of God: because many false prophets are gone out into the world. Hereby know ye the Spirit of God: Every spirit that confesseth that Jesus Christ is come in the flesh is of God: and every spirit that confesseth not that Jesus Christ is come in the flesh is not of God: and this is that spirit of antichrist, whereof ye have heard that it should come; and even now already is it in the world.

Though someone insists that he has received the fullness of the Holy Spirit, though someone prophesies wonderful things and does mighty acts, if he does not claim that Jesus Christ was born of a virgin and was crucified for the redemption of the whole world, he is not of Christ. If he does not claim that Jesus Christ rose from the grave on the third day, that He ascended into heaven and sits at the right hand of the throne of God, that He will come down in the same appearance as He was resurrected in the flesh, he does not teach by the Holy Spirit but by the spirit of antichrist.

Considering this, in many countries countless religious groups lead a great many people to destruction with completely false doctrines about Christ.

As familiar examples, a person may insist that he is "the Christ" and another may argue that he is "the only lamb," threatening that unless people follow him, they are not saved. Others may contend that there is no need for Jesus to be our mediator because one can communicate directly with the Father. Because there is such a chaotic spirit in the world, we must "believe not every spirit," but strictly "try the spirits whether they are of God."

When I see believers who have latched onto a self-appointed man of grace who shows mysterious power, unconditionally following him and throwing their souls before him, I cannot help but sigh. They have not been cautious enough.

Discerning a Person's Words

A PERSON'S SPEECH transmits character and thought. An angry woman uses angry language. A coarse man uses vulgar language. A merciful man uses merciful language, and a good woman uses good language.

The Bible also teaches this clearly: "No man speaking by the Spirit of God calleth Jesus accursed: and that no man can say that Jesus is the Lord, but by the Holy Ghost" (1 Cor. 12:3).

Therefore, when we hear a person claim to have received grace, we should listen discreetly and carefully. To discern a person's spirit, for what should we listen?

No Praise to Self

When a person who claims to have received the Holy Spirit praises himself whenever possible instead of giving glory to Jesus, he does not speak by the Spirit of Christ; he speaks by the spirit of covetousness.

The devil always shakes and rages like a serpent ready to strike, and all in an effort to show off. If a person's talk honors self instead of Christ, the words are of a spirit of evil, not the Holy Spirit.

Sometimes a person who professes to have received a lot of grace will come to me and say, "Pastor, I have received much grace. The Holy Spirit told me that He loves me particularly and that He will make me a great servant by using me mightily. . . . " If I keep listening, I often grow disgusted, because that person is not speaking words to honor Christ and God; the words are merely self-praise.

The Holy Spirit magnifies God (Acts 10:46). The Holy Spirit reveals the glory of Christ through us by filling us and showing us what He received of Christ (John 16:1–4).

Whether talking privately or speaking publicly, if a person, even a servant of the Lord, shows off his own greatness, not Christ's, he is already taken by the spirit of antichrist.

No Threatening or Hurting Others

When a person who professes to have received the Holy Spirit does nothing but threaten and blackmail others, when he doesn't hesitate to use coarse and hurtful language, we must be careful.

A certain sister who professed that she had received the Holy Spirit carried with her a cloud of terror instead of love and peace. If anyone corrected her, she would call down a curse. How can the personality of the Holy Spirit of God, who is meek and humble, dwell in the life of one who speaks such words?

How can that kind of person (claiming to be speaking by the Holy Spirit and favored with special blessing) knock on believers' doors, whisper slander to church members, and demand hush money unscrupulously?

A Word of Warning

BEFORE WE AFFIRM what wonderful works a person does, we must first notice if he or she praises God and preaches Christ as the Lord. We must see evidence of humility, of a person hidden behind the cross, speaking and acting out the fruit of the Holy Spirit.

The apostle Paul warns us about believers in the latter times: "Now the Spirit speaketh expressly, that in the latter times some shall depart from the faith, giving heed to seducing spirits, and doctrines of devils" (1 Tim. 4:1).

Wherever the real thing exists, there will be counterfeits. Therefore, we should not only always examine our own spiritual experience, but also look to discerning the spirits in order to guide our fellowship with other believers.

9

Gifts of the Holy Spirit

First Corinthians 12:4–11 gives us a classification of the gifts of the Spirit:

> Now there are diversities of gifts, but the same Spirit. And there are differences of administration, but the same Lord. And there are diversities of operations, but it is the same God which worketh all in all. But the manifestation of the Spirit is given to every man to profit withal. For to one is given by the Spirit the word of wisdom; to another the word of knowledge by the same Spirit; to another faith by the same Spirit; to another the gifts of healing by the same Spirit; to another the working of miracles; to another prophecy; to another discerning of spirits; to another divers kinds of tongues; to another the interpretation of tongues; but all these worketh that one and the selfsame Spirit, dividing to every man severally as he will.

The Gifts of God

Let's look at what Paul says: "There are diversities of operations, but it is the same God which worketh all in all" (1 Cor. 12:6).

This word *operation* refers to the *method* used to preach the gospel. To be more specific, it refers to the overall strategic operation used in taking or sending the gospel forth. Effective ways and policies for witnessing of the gospel include pioneering new churches, being used of God to bring revival, and establishing and maintaining schools and hospitals. All these belong to the diverse operations that God uses to further the gospel.

The Gifts of Jesus

PAUL ALSO SAYS, "And there are differences of administrations, but the same Lord" (1 Cor. 12:5). This means that *Jesus Christ* has given the gift of administration to some believers to carry out important leadership and supportive roles within the church. As every organization on earth requires responsible leadership, so does the church, the body of Jesus Christ.

Administration is explained in several places in the Bible. One example, 1 Corinthians 12:27–28 reads, "Now ye are the body of Christ, and members in particular. And God hath set some in the church, first apostles, secondarily prophets, thirdly teachers, after that miracles, then gifts of healing, helps, governments, diversities of tongues."

Concerning this administration, Paul wrote in Ephesians 4:11, "And he [the Lord Jesus Christ] gave some, apostles; and some, prophets; and some, evangelists; and some, pastors and teachers." This verse shows that as believers we cannot choose the type of administration we would like to have within the church. Rather we should each find the gift of Jesus we have received and then serve God faithfully in that place of service.

The Gifts of the Spirit

NOW, FINALLY, GIFTS are given by the Holy Spirit: "Now there are diversities of gifts, but the same Spirit" (1 Cor. 12:4).

Gifts of the Holy Spirit are the means and instruments of power to carry out successfully the operation and administration of God's work in His church.

When a plan has been made to build a big house, and the architect, builder, and specialists have been appointed, then all the tools and materials needed to build the house are brought in and used so that the project is finished successfully as soon as possible.

When there is a great work to do for God, the gifts of the Holy Spirit are given to different believers within the church, His body. These enable believers to accomplish His work and responsibility effectively, and the work grows because of the gifts of the Holy Spirit.

There are nine gifts of the Holy Spirit, and they can be divided roughly into the following three groups:

1. The gifts of revelation
    a. The gift of the word of wisdom
    b. The gift of the word of knowledge
    c. The gift of discerning of spirits

2. The vocal gifts
    a. The gift of tongues
    b. The gift of interpretation of tongues
    c. The gift of prophecy

3. The gifts of power
    a. The gift of faith
    b. The gift of healing
    c. The gift of working of miracles

The gifts of revelation deal with supernatural communication revealed through the Holy Spirit to the heart of one who has received this gift. The knowledge of other people's experiences and situations that is revealed through these gifts is not made known to the public until those who have received any or all of these gifts choose to speak.

The vocal gifts deal with supernatural communication that the Holy Spirit of God reveals by using the human voice. Not only the person using the gifts but others around him or her can hear these gifts; therefore they can be received by the senses.

The gifts of power are mighty gifts in which the power of God appears so as to manifest a miraculous answer through a supernatural, creative intervention. Through these gifts people and their environments are changed.

All of these gifts are distributed to people by the Holy Spirit in accordance with His own will for the benefit and growth of the church, the body of Christ.

The Manifestation of the Holy Spirit

SOMETIMES, BELIEVERS WHO have received the fullness of the Holy Spirit and the accompanying gifts greatly misunderstand these manifestations of the Holy Spirit. (See 1 Corinthians 12:7.)

Some people think that anyone who has received the fullness and various gifts of the Holy Spirit can use the gifts as he or she likes and whenever he or she likes.

For this reason, occasionally we see people who have supposedly received special favor or gifts from God try to use those gifts as if the Holy Spirit were a personal servant. This of course is extremely dangerous because the Holy Spirit in us is the third person of the holy three-in-one God.

When someone has this attitude, the Holy Spirit is grieved. When the Holy Spirit is grieved, the gifts will cease operating through such people. When they sense this in their spirits, these people usually become arrogant. In order to make others believe that the gifts still flow through them, they will operate in the flesh (which is fraud), often speaking lies, which brings disgrace to the church.

The gifts are the possession of the Holy Spirit Himself. Since they are His, they cannot exist independently apart from Him. The gifts of the Holy Spirit can by no means be used at a person's own will. Only the Holy Spirit can possess them absolutely and manifest them through believers in whom He abides.

The truth is not that man uses the gifts of the Holy Spirit. Rather the Holy Spirit, who occupies man and fills him, uses that person and manifests the gifts through him according to His own will, time, and situation.

The apostle Paul wrote clearly about these instructions when he said, "But the manifestation of the Spirit is given to every man to profit withal" (1 Cor. 12:7).

Sometimes arrogant and haughty men have tried to use the Holy Spirit as though He were a clown in a circus. I have felt disillusioned and embarrassed when I have seen them being glorified. They seemed to have no idea that they were standing in the presence of God and the Holy Spirit.

I'm not saying that these people did not receive the gifts of the Holy Spirit. What I am saying is that they greatly misunderstood the purpose of the gifts in their lives. Because they had received certain gifts they thought they could use the Holy Spirit as they desired and when they desired. But the Holy Spirit fills believers to become vessels to manifest the gifts only so the hearers of the gospel will be edified.

What should be the proper attitude of a believer who has experienced the gifts of the Holy Spirit? He should humble himself continually before the presence of God, dedicate himself as a pure vessel, and then wait for the Holy Spirit to manifest the gifts through him at a time and place He chooses.

If the Holy Spirit chooses to manifest diverse gifts through us, we should keep our hearts humble and depend utterly upon Him. This will open the way wider for Him to edify His church through His gifts, through us.

I have had the blessed experience of having diverse gifts operating through me, and I am still praying for even more manifestations of the Holy Spirit. The only reason I was able to build a church of more than five hundred thousand members in less than thirty years was because of the wonderful manifestation of the Holy Spirit flowing through the gifts of revelation, the vocal gifts, or the gifts of power. As this happened we gave all the glory to God for what He was accomplishing.

Even to this day, one thing that makes me tremble with carefulness is the thought that I might resist the Holy Spirit or that when He does move through me—to manifest the many gifts to edify His church—I might be misunderstood to be speaking on my own.

In summary, the gifts belong absolutely to the Holy Spirit. The gifts and the Holy Spirit cannot be separated and the only purpose for the Holy Spirit's manifesting diverse gifts through people is for the edification of His church.

How to Receive the Gifts

HOW CAN WE become the vessel through which the Holy Spirit will manifest His gifts?

The Holy Spirit of God does not distinguish among persons as long as they have received the fullness of the Holy Spirit and manifest the gifts and edify believers. First Corinthians 12:7 reads, "But the manifestation of the Spirit is given to *every man* to profit withal," to clarify that He will use anyone who has received the fullness of the Spirit as a vessel through which He will manifest the gifts.

To say that the Holy Spirit chooses us as the vessels through which He manifests the gifts is more correct than to say that we have received the gifts, for, as I've said, the distribution of the gifts is absolutely up to the will of the Holy Spirit. After listing the gifts Paul says, "But all these worketh that one and the selfsame Spirit, dividing to every man severally as he will" (1 Cor. 12:11).

If you covet the gifts, the proper prayer is not to specify your own desire for specific gifts. You should find which gifts the indwelling Holy Spirit desires to manifest through you according to *His* desire and will for the edification of the church.

Today's childhood educators try to find the nature and temperament of a child and then develop that temperament. In this same way you should observe carefully which gifts the Holy Spirit wants to manifest through you after you've received the fullness of the Holy Spirit. Once you know the gifts He has chosen and given to you, cultivate and develop them by allowing Him to manifest these gifts through you.

When I first received the Holy Spirit, I prayed blindly for more of the gift that was most popular—the gift of healing—and for the gift of the word of wisdom and the gift of the word of knowledge. Though I prayed at length with many tears, the anticipated gifts were not forthcoming. Though it seemed that those gifts appeared for a while, I did not have an outstanding flow of those gifts of the Spirit continually. Instead, gifts I did not ask for or pay much attention to began to appear in my personal life and ministry like new shoots of grass sprouting on the earth.

The gifts I received were none other than the gift of faith and the gift of prophecy. In both my personal life and ministry, supernatural faith captured my heart as if some mysterious power like Samson's had been given to me. Bold confession that could command mountains to be moved into the sea sprang out from my mouth, and the miracles actually happened as I spoke.

Those gifts did not stay with me continuously. The gift of faith does not manifest itself in every situation. When the will of the Holy Spirit was manifested for the glory of God, more faith than I could ever imagine in my situation sprang out of the depths of my heart. The same happened with the gift of prophecy. Frankly, I was never interested in prophecy. Because of the many undesirable results and confusion that some prophecies brought, I would rather have rebuked those who prophesied. To this day I believe the same; yet, out of the blue, the spirit of prophecy began to make my heart flutter with anticipation of His words. When the words of prophecy come, divine wisdom and comfort and direction fill my heart. Needless to say, we should never be boastful of these gifts nor show off indiscriminately.

It is proper that these gifts be used only as a means to prove the eternal, unchanging, infallible, perfect Word of God, not to show off a person's spirituality.

As I have said, once we find out our gift, given according to the Spirit of God, we must develop that gift, letting it manifest itself often. While our gift is blessing the church and God's people, it is also helping us grow and mature as Christians.

When the Holy Spirit wants to manifest some gifts through a person who is afraid to speak out or who, preferring to please other people, refuses to obey the prompting, the Holy Spirit is grieved and quenched. If this happens often, the gifts will disappear. Those who have learned which gift they have received should not be partial to people or organizations. Rather they should simply allow the Holy Spirit to be manifested through them so that those gifts will be permanent, appearing more often to bring blessing to the church and believers.

Also, those who have received the gifts should diligently search the Scriptures and study the circumstances in which the same gifts were used. This study should be accompanied by pruning one's life of wrongdoing.

The gifts can never take the place of the Word of God, our highest authority and our instruction for living. They should always be controlled by the Word of God and be in harmony with the Scriptures. They should be utilized within the boundaries laid down by God's Word.

Can a person possess diverse gifts at the same time?

Needless to say, Jesus used all nine gifts of the Spirit, and we are confident from the Scriptures that the apostles, such as Peter or Paul, also used all nine gifts. How can ordinary believers like you and me today receive all nine gifts?

The Bible states, "But covet earnestly the best gifts" (1 Cor. 12:31). Some people say that love is the best gift, but this understanding is not correct.

First Corinthians 13 says that love is the best way to use the gifts. The verse "But covet earnestly the best gifts: and yet shew I unto you a more excellent way" (12:31) means that the Bible is showing us *the way* to use the gifts. First Corinthians 14:12 also reads, "Even so ye, forasmuch as ye are zealous of spiritual gifts, seek that ye may *excel to the edifying of the church*" (italics mine).

These Scripture passages show that God wants to use to the utmost believers who have received the fullness of the Holy Spirit. When Paul says we should covet the best gifts, he means this: When we desire earnestly that the gifts already being used would be used more, then God, in accordance with His holy will, will give us greater and more abundant gifts. From this we can conclude that Christians can surely possess various gifts at the same time. The gifts of the Spirit are His to give as He wills.

10

The Gifts of Revelation

THE BIBLE REFERS to this gift as "the *word* of knowledge" instead of the *gift* of "knowledge," and there is a reason for this distinction (1 Cor. 12:8). If we were to refer to this gift as the gift of knowledge, it would include all of the knowledge concerning God. But the gift of the word of knowledge refers only to a portion of God's knowledge that God wants to reveal.

Knowledge refers to the condition of knowing something through realization of truth concerning things and matters; today, however, many people greatly misunderstand the gift of the word of knowledge.

Some people act and speak as if they were a walking dictionary because they have received the gift of the word of knowledge, but actually their behavior itself shows that they are very ignorant. Though they have received this gift, it does not mean that they have received the whole knowledge of the omniscient and omnipotent God.

Other people say that they have received the gift of the word of knowledge because their taste for learning has led them to study deeply the Word of God. Because of this, they say, they have received the gift of the word of knowledge.

But the gift of the word of knowledge manifested as one of the gifts of the Holy Spirit is not the knowledge that can be studied and learned. It cannot be investigated or accumulated either. This knowledge, which reveals the hidden truth of things and matters and solves problems at a certain time and place for the glory of God according to His special revelation, comes only by the inspiration of the Holy Spirit.

The manifestation of this kind of knowledge does not mean that one possesses the whole knowledge of omniscient God or has acquired knowledge as a result of research. The word of knowledge is information revealed to one who has this gift when a special need for the kingdom of God and the cause of the gospel of Christ must be uncovered or revealed to the children of God. When there is no human way for us to know the circumstances, God reveals this partial knowledge to believers through the Holy Spirit by revelation, dreams, or visions. This means that the knowledge, given in a supernatural way by the revelation of God, is not gained through human means or efforts.

The Scriptures give us many instances where the gift of the word of knowledge operated supernaturally through God's people by the Holy Spirit.

Let's review some of these instances.

In Joshua 7 after conquering the strong city of Jericho, the children of Israel tried to invade the much smaller city of Ai but were defeated miserably.

At that time, Joshua rent his clothes and fell on his face. With the elders of Israel before the ark of the Lord, he put dust upon his head and prayed. As a result, in the evening the revelation of God came to the children of Israel: Because one person had stolen something in Jericho against the direct command of God not to touch anything, God's anger had been kindled; He was not with them when they attacked Ai.

Joshua received this word of knowledge—the reason why the children of Israel were defeated before their enemy. More than this, through the revelation of the Holy Spirit, Joshua received information that the man who committed the sin was Achan, the son of Carmi, the son of Zabdi, the son of Zerah, of the tribe of Judah.

Such knowledge is neither received by an effort of human study nor by the information secretly transmitted from one person to another. It is only the knowledge that the Holy Spirit reveals to those who have received this gift.

In 1 Samuel 9 there is another scene: Saul and those who were with him went out to search for the lost donkeys of Saul's father. When they couldn't find them, they came near to the seer Samuel to inquire. When Samuel met Saul, Samuel said immediately, "And as for thine asses which were lost three days ago, set not thy mind on them; for they are found" (1 Sam. 9:20).

Even before Samuel talked with Saul, Samuel knew not only that Saul was searching for the asses, but that they had already been found. Such a revelation came by the gift of the word of knowledge.

The gift of the word of knowledge worked greatly in the life of Elisha in 2 Kings 6:8–12:

> Then the king of Syria warred against Israel, and took counsel with his servants, saying, In such and such a place shall be my camp. And the man of God sent unto the king of Israel, saying, Beware that thou pass not such a place; for thither the Syrians are come down. . . . Therefore the heart of the king of Syria was sore troubled for this thing; and he called his servants, and said unto them, Will ye not shew me which of us is for the king of Israel? And one of his servants said, None, my lord, O king: but Elisha, the prophet that is in Israel, telleth the king of Israel the words that thou speakest in thy bedchamber.

Such wonderful knowledge was not obtained by an intelligence network of men, but what God revealed in person to Elisha through the gift of the Holy Spirit.

The gift of the word of knowledge was wonderfully manifested also to the believers of the New Testament. The case of our Lord Jesus Christ goes without saying. So let us look into the experience of the apostle Peter.

In Acts 5 Ananias and his wife, Sapphira, consulted together and sold their possessions. They brought a certain part of the proceeds and laid it at the apostles' feet—as if it were the whole price. They were convinced that no one knew about their lie.

But Peter said, "Ananias, why hath Satan filled thine heart to lie to the Holy Ghost, and to keep back part of the price of the land? While it remained, was it not thine own? and after it was sold, was it not in thine own power? why hast thou conceived this thing in thine heart? thou hast not lied unto men, but unto God" (Acts 5:3–4). God had told Peter what he needed to know in a situation.

I, too, have had similar experiences. One Christmas morning, following the all-night prayer meeting, I led an early morning service at the church. My schedule was heavy, and I was going to go home to sleep a little before I led the regular eleven o'clock service.

When I came back home, I was hungry. I was about to eat breakfast when suddenly there came to my mind an instruction: I was to go immediately to the church; something had happened. In my heart, I didn't want to move my body, but as a servant of the Lord I couldn't help obeying. So I got up right away and went to the church.

In the church everything was quiet. It seemed that nothing had happened. I met only a young janitor hired by the church who was sweeping the trash littered by believers who had attended the all-night prayer meeting.

I couldn't find anything to confirm the Holy Spirit's word to me that something had happened in the church. I craned my neck to check inside the sanctuary. Suddenly there came to my heart a further instruction: I was to go over to the platform. I walked to the platform and searched the pulpit, and there lay a tightly sealed big envelope containing an offering.

I took it in my hand and looked carefully at the sealed part. Thinking that I would return home after I warmed myself a little, I went to the office where there was a stove. With the envelope in my hand, I pulled up a chair near the stove.

Suddenly there was a loud knock on the door. I said, "Come in," and the young man who had been sweeping entered the office. His face was pale, and he knelt down on the floor. To my great surprise he said, "Pastor, today I have come to know that God truly lives. I have committed a terrible crime, but please forgive me."

I was so dumbfounded I couldn't understand what he was saying, but the young janitor kept his eyes downward and continued: "When I was sweeping the inside of the church, I found that big envelope of money on the platform. I looked around, no one was in the church at the moment, and I became covetous of it.

"I took the envelope and ran to my room and opened it with a razor. I took out some money. After putting back the remainder, I pasted it well and put it back on the pulpit before anyone would know. Everything was just as it had been, and I was sure that no one would ever notice. Then, though you had gone home to sleep, you suddenly appeared, nervously looking around to find something. Reassuring myself that you, a human being, couldn't possibly know anything of this, I kept on sweeping the floor.

"I felt uneasy, so I kept looking inside the church to see what you were doing. Then, just as I feared, you stepped on the platform, took the envelope of money, examined the sealed part, and went to the office.

"I knew that all these things were revealed to you by the Holy Spirit, and I was so pricked in my conscience that I came here to confess my sin. Please forgive me."

Hearing the confession of that young man, I shuddered at the thought that I also am so closely searched by the Holy Spirit, who is always with us.

Another incident like this happened to a friend of mine some years ago near the end of the Korean Democratic Party administration.

Mr. Bethel, an American missionary with whom I was well acquainted, moved from the Philippines to Korea for mission work. He and his family came to Korea by plane after sending his household effects securely by ship.

When his goods arrived, he received a consignment list from the Pusan Pier Custom House. He went there to get his belongings, but some of their most valuable things were nowhere to be found. They were included on the consignment list, and everything had been shipped at the same time, yet he was told that these certain items had not arrived at Korea.

Mr. Bethel was very annoyed and kept on asking questions until at last some customs officials grew angry and yelled at him.

Feeling depressed and mistreated, Mr. Bethel prayed to God earnestly right then and there, and in a sudden vision he saw the inside of a warehouse with a small door. It was out of sight but just several feet to the left of where he stood. Inside the door were hidden his valuable things.

Mr. Bethel asked custom officials to allow him to search in person, and they triumphantly said, "OK."

Mr. Bethel walked straight ahead as he had seen in his vision, and, sure enough, there was a hidden hallway. When he turned down that hall, he saw a small door as he had seen in the vision. When he approached the door, the faces of the custom officials turned red. They told him he could not go in that room, but he pushed them aside and opened the door; there were all of his things, hidden just as it had been revealed to him.

The Holy Spirit of God gave Mr. Bethel the necessary knowledge for the moment, and through that supernatural gift of the word of knowledge he was able to solve the problem at hand.

Such a gift of the word of knowledge is never the kind of knowledge that man can possess on his own and use as freely as water, but the Holy Spirit of God possesses it, and through the vessel of His choosing He manifests it as it is needed. He shows the glory of God and solves the problem.

The Gift of the Word of Wisdom

A PERSON MAY be very learned and may have a lot of knowledge, but unless that person has wisdom, he can't use that knowledge.

Wisdom is the function by which we can effectively use knowledge—to solve problems and bring forth blessings and victory. Even if someone has only a small bit of knowledge, if he is equipped with a great amount of wisdom, he can magnify greatly the knowledge he has. On the contrary, if someone has much knowledge, but lacks wisdom, his knowledge can become buried knowledge, which may never be fully known.

Then what is the gift of the word of wisdom?

The gift of the word of wisdom does not refer to any human wisdom. Those who don't understand this sometimes speak of believers who are especially bright and intelligent as people who have received the gift of wisdom, but this is wrong.

The word of wisdom referred to as a gift of the Holy Spirit (1 Cor. 12:8) is given only supernaturally to a believer who through this wisdom wonderfully solves problems in difficult circumstances and thereby gives glory to God.

The Bible urges that those who lack wisdom should ask such wisdom of God. "If any of you lack wisdom, let him ask of God, that giveth to all men liberally, and upbraideth not; and it shall be given him" (James 1:5).

In the Old Testament we can see how God manifested wisdom through King Solomon, the son of David. For example, let us read the incident written in 1 Kings 3:16–28:

> Then came there two women, that were harlots, unto the king, and stood before him. And the one woman said, O my lord, I and this woman dwell in one house; and I was delivered of a child with her in the house. And it came to pass the third day after that I was delivered, that this woman was delivered also: and we were together; there was no stranger with us in the house, save we two in the house. And this woman's child died in the night; because she overlaid it. And she arose at midnight, and took my son from beside me, while thine handmaid slept, and laid it in her bosom, and laid her dead child in my bosom. And when I rose in the morning to give my child suck, behold, it was dead: but when I had considered it in the morning, behold, it was not my son, which I did bear.
>
> And the other woman said, Nay; but the living is my son, and the dead is thy son. And this said, No; but the dead is thy son, and the living is my son. Thus they spake before the king. Then said the king, The one saith, This is my son that liveth, and thy son is the dead: and the other saith, Nay; but thy son is the dead, and my son is the living. And the king said, Bring me a sword. And they brought a sword before the

> king. And the king said, Divide the living child in two, and give half to the one, and half to the other. Then spake the woman whose the living child was unto the king, for her bowels yearned upon her son, and she said, O my lord, give her the living child, and in no wise slay it. But the other said, Let it be neither mine nor thine, but divide it. Then the king answered and said, Give her the living child, and in no wise slay it: she is the mother thereof. And all Israel heard of the judgment which the king had judged; and they feared the king: for they saw that the wisdom of God was in him, to do judgment.

The exact wisdom in this passage was not a natural gift with which Solomon was born. "The wisdom of God was in him" expresses the gift God manifested for the need of that time through the power of the Holy Spirit, which was given to him by God.

Instead of the gift of "wisdom," which would have meant all-round wisdom given at all times, the Bible teaches that it is the gift of the *word* of wisdom. In contrast to the all-round wisdom that humans can use freely as they want, God manifests the word of wisdom in accordance with a specific need and in a time and place for the glory of God and the power of the gospel. God speaks to us in this same manner. Though He is always with us, He does not speak at all times but speaks only in case of need.

In the expression, "I have received the gift of the word of wisdom," we should always put our emphasis on that part: "the word."

The manifestation of the gift of the word of wisdom is wonderfully clear in the life of Jesus. In Matthew 22:15–22, the Pharisees were sure they had found a way to entangle Jesus. In the presence of some Romans they asked Him if it was lawful for a Jew to give tribute to Caesar. If Jesus answered that they should give tribute to Caesar, they were ready to pounce upon Him, judging that He was a tool of Rome and the enemy of the Jewish people. But if He answered that they should not give tribute to Caesar, the Roman governor would charge Him with treason and send Him to prison.

They were confident of their trick, but they were dumbfounded by the words of wisdom with which He answered them. Jesus told them to show Him a coin and, pointing to the image inscribed on it, He asked whose image it was.

"Caesar's," they replied.

He answered, "Render therefore unto Caesar the things which are Caesar's; and unto God the things that are God's." Jesus gave them an answer that couldn't be caught by any noose. It was a word of wisdom, spoken by the power of the Spirit to address the matter at hand.

This happened again when the scribes and Pharisees were tempting Jesus. They brought Him a woman taken in adultery: "Master, this woman was taken in adultery, in the very act. Now Moses in the law commanded us, that such should be stoned: but what sayest thou?" (John 8:4–5).

They invented another trick, hoping to trap Jesus. If Jesus said that the woman should be stoned, they would accuse Him of acting against the law of love that He preached and that His miracles portrayed. But if Jesus opposed the punishment that Moses plainly commanded, they would drag Him off to their court.

How did Jesus answer? Jesus said, "He that is without sin among you, let him first cast a stone at her" (John 8:7). However hardened they might have been, they couldn't help but be pricked in their hearts before this sharp word of wisdom. John says, "They which heard it, being convicted by their own conscience, went out one by one, beginning at the eldest, even unto the last: and Jesus was left alone, and the woman standing in the midst" (John 8:9).

When we see Jesus solving such difficult problems one after another by a word of wisdom, we cannot help but be overwhelmed with respect and love.

Since this same Lord is our living Savior, no matter what difficulty we are confronted with, we should look to Him and not be discouraged. God has promised to give us such a word of wisdom when we are persecuted for our faith in the Lord Jesus Christ and the gospel:

> But before all these, they shall lay their hands on you, and persecute you, delivering you up to the synagogues, and into prisons, being brought before kings and rulers for my name's sake. And it shall turn to you for a testimony. Settle it therefore in your hearts, not to meditate before what ye shall answer: for I will give you a mouth and *wisdom,* which all your adversaries shall not be able to gainsay nor resist.
>
> —LUKE 21:12–15, ITALICS MINE

These wonderful words "mouth and wisdom" mean that the gift of the word of wisdom will be given to us when the need arises. Here again, the promise is that such wisdom will not be given to us by nature. But when we meet an insurmountable barrier, God, by giving the wonderful wisdom of the Holy Spirit, will enable us easily to overcome the difficulty and solve the problem. Jesus' words mean that only the Holy Spirit possesses the gift, and He manifests it from time to time through believers as the vessels.

The Gift of Discerning of Spirits

> . . . to another [is given] discerning of spirits.
>
> —1 CORINTHIANS 12:10

Many people today confuse the gift of discerning of spirits with mind reading. Often those who profess to have received the gift of discerning of spirits create great disturbances in churches, volunteering to take the role of spiritual detective.

The gift is exactly what it says: *the gift that is able to discern spirits.* To put it simply, in this universe there are spirits belonging to God and spirits belonging to the devil; then there are instances when words are spoken by the spirit of man, which is distinguished from the Holy Spirit or the spirit of Satan. We discern the spirits by the manifestation of the Holy Spirit, judging whether the spirit is from God or if someone is speaking by the spirit of man or by the spirit of Satan.

In 1 John 4:1, the apostle John wrote of the importance of discerning of spirits: "Beloved, believe not every spirit, but try the spirits whether they are of God: because many false prophets are gone out into the world."

In these last days, unless you have the gift of discerning of spirits, you are exposed to the danger of being seduced. The apostle Paul said in 1 Timothy 4:1, "Now the Spirit speaketh expressly that in the latter times some shall depart from the faith, giving heed to seducing spirits, and doctrines of devils."

Unless we are quickly able to discern and oppose those who enter our midst with seducing spirits and doctrines of devils, great harm will come to the flock of weak believers.

Like any other gift, the gift of discerning is not that which anyone can possess and use freely at any time. This gift is in the hand of the Holy Spirit, and He manifests it according to His need through the vessel God chooses.

Through my ministry, I have experienced the manifestation of this gift many times, which became opportunities to set the church straight.

Once, a member of my congregation professed that she had

received the wonderful gift of prophecy; in fact her prophecies came true several times. As a result, many weak believers were so carried away by her prophecies that they set aside the practice of personal prayer, Scripture reading, and the life of faith. Their guide was the prophecy from this woman. They flocked to her to hear the so-called message of God about the problems of their daily lives, much as they might consult a fortuneteller.

Since I could not immediately discern whether this was from God or from the devil, I watched as a spectator for a while. But with the passing of time it became clear that the fruit of the woman was not the fruit of the Holy Spirit. The attitude of her prophecy was not only fickle and frivolous; it had no meekness, love, and peace like a dove. Rather her words were cold and fearful and destructive.

When I hinted that the spirit of the woman might not be of the Holy Spirit, not only the woman herself but many of her followers resisted and defied me. They said that a servant of the Lord motivated by jealousy was plotting to injure her.

I was in an awkward situation and became slightly bewildered. What if the woman really were speaking by the Holy Spirit? I didn't want to fall into the sin of resisting the Holy Spirit.

I threw myself down before God and prayed that He would reveal the truth to me by manifesting the gift of discerning of spirits. In a vision He showed me that the spirit in her was an unclean spirit.

With this discernment I had courage to discipline her with conviction. As a result, the church was delivered when it was just on the verge of a tempest. Peace was restored.

Nowadays, in the Korean churches people with seducing spirits and doctrines of devils are eager to beguile numerous ignorant church members to wrong paths. The "self-appointed Jesus," or "righteous" persons by other names, also appear and lift their voices to seduce whomever they can. Now more than ever the Korean church is praying that the gift of discerning of spirits be given to all believers across the country.

Let's consider how this gift was used throughout the Old and New Testaments.

First Kings 22 relates a scene where the gift of discerning of spirits wonderfully appears. Here Ahab, the king of Israel, talked with Jehoshaphat, the king of Judah, to prepare war to take Ramoth in Gilead from Syria's hand.

At this time, Jehoshaphat and Ahab sat majestically on their thrones, having put on their robes at the entrance of the gate of Samaria. Four hundred prophets all prophesied in unison with

Zedekiah the son of Chenaanah saying, "Go up to Ramoth-gilead, and prosper: for the LORD shall deliver it into the king's hand" (v. 12). They also made themselves horns of iron and said, "Thus saith the LORD, With these shalt thou push the Syrians, until thou have consumed them" (v. 11).

Jehoshaphat became a little afraid because all the prophecies were the same, so he asked Ahab whether there was any other prophet of the Lord in the land so that they might inquire of him. King Ahab said that there was yet one man, Micaiah, the son of Imlay, who was a prophet, though Ahab hated him, because he always prophesied evil against him.

But King Jehoshaphat was very persistent and finally Micaiah was called in and asked about the outcome of the crusade. At first Micaiah parrotted the other prophets. But when the king, who thought that Micaiah was insincere, pressed him to speak the truth, he spoke a very negative prophecy: "I saw all Israel scattered upon the hills, as sheep that have not a shepherd: and the LORD said, These have no master: let them return every man to his house in peace" (v. 17). In other words, he said that Ahab would die in the battle. Then, through the wonderful gift of discerning of spirits, God showed Micaiah the hidden things that were happening in the heavens. Micaiah said:

> Hear thou therefore the word of the LORD: I saw the LORD sitting on his throne, and all the host of heaven standing by him on his right hand and on his left. And the LORD said, Who shall persuade Ahab, that he may go up and fall at Ramoth-gilead? And one said on this manner, and another said on that manner. And there came forth a spirit, and stood before the LORD, and said, I will persuade him. And the LORD said unto him, Wherewith? And he said, I will go forth, and I will be a lying spirit in the mouth of all his prophets. And he said, Thou shalt persuade him, and prevail also: go forth, and do so. Now therefore, behold, the LORD hath put a lying spirit in the mouth of all these thy prophets, and the LORD hath spoken evil concerning thee.
>
> —1 KINGS 22:19–23

By clearly revealing in a vision heavenly happenings, God enabled Micaiah, the true prophet of God, to discern the spirits.

Micaiah calmly concluded that the prophecies of the more than four hundred prophets came from the lying spirits.

God decided to allow Ahab to be killed because Ahab had persisted in rebelling and opposing Him. He allowed the evil spirits to enter the prophets of Ahab so that Ahab might be beguiled to destruction.

As we have seen from this, those who don't have the gift of discerning of spirits aren't able to distinguish which prophecy is true. Likewise, we shouldn't believe every prophecy unconditionally but discern whether a prophecy is truly spoken by the Holy Spirit or by evil spirits.

The New Testament also addresses this issue. The apostle Paul wrote of the spiritual depravity of the last times:

> Even him, whose coming is after the working of Satan with all power and signs and lying wonders, and with all deceivableness of unrighteousness in them that perish; because they received not the love of the truth, that they might be saved. And for this cause God shall send them strong delusion, that they should believe a lie: That they all might be damned who believed not the truth, but had pleasure in unrighteousness.
>
> —2 THESSALONIANS 2:9–12

God allows the spirits of delusion to work among those who do not believe the Scripture—the Word of eternal truth of God—because such people insist in indulging in covetousness and delighting in unrighteousness. First Kings 22 bears clear evidence of this.

All the gifts of God should always be tested through and held up to the gift of discerning of spirits, as the more we experience the spiritual gifts, the more we should beware of lying and counterfeit spirits.

The manifestation of discerning of spirits is shown many times in the New Testament.

Since our Lord Jesus Christ is the incarnated God, the gifts of the Holy Spirit given to Him cannot be compared exactly to those given to ordinary Christians. Having said that, we can find evidence that Jesus was very interested in the discerning of spirits during His years of ministry.

In Matthew 16, when Jesus came to the coast of Caesarea Philippi, He asked His disciples, "But whom say ye that I am?" (v. 15).

When Peter answered quickly, "Thou art the Christ, the Son of the living God," Jesus answered, "Blessed art thou, Simon Bar-jona: for flesh and blood hath not revealed it unto thee, but my Father which is in heaven" (vv. 16–17).

One could think that Peter's confession of faith came from his own thoughts and belief, but Jesus made Peter discern that it was not his own thoughts; it was what God in heaven through the Holy Spirit revealed to his heart.

Later, Jesus was showing His disciples that He had to go to Jerusalem and suffer many things, even be killed and then raised again the third day. Peter's reply to this was, "Be it far from thee, Lord: this shall not be unto thee" (v. 22). This time Jesus rebuked Peter severely for what he said.

When we think of this in general terms, this "No, don't say it" of Peter's seemed to stem from his love and faithfulness to the Lord. But the Lord, through the gift of discerning of spirits, penetrated Peter's soul and said, "Get thee behind me, Satan: thou art an offense unto me: for thou savorest not the things that be of God, but those that be of men" (v. 23).

We cannot but wonder why Peter's exhortation (which seemed to be so faithful) was in fact maneuvered behind the scene by Satan. It simply shows again how urgent the need is for the gift of discerning of spirits.

We've described Philip's crusade through Samaria (Acts 8). Many heard the gospel of Christ, received salvation and healing, and were baptized. Eventually, Peter and John were asked to come and pray with these new Christians that they might receive the Holy Spirit. But a sorcerer named Simon tried to buy this gift of the Holy Spirit from Peter.

Now Simon had heard Philip's preaching and had been baptized with water. He had appeared to be a faithful believer. But when Peter saw Simon through the gift of discerning of spirits, Simon's real nature was clearly revealed. Peter said to Simon, "I perceive that thou art in the gall of bitterness, and in the bond of iniquity" (v. 23). Thus, through the gift of discerning of spirits, Simon's true colors were revealed before Peter's eyes.

A similar situation occurred in Acts 16, when Paul and Silas were in Philippi:

> And it came to pass, as we went to prayer, a certain damsel, possessed with a spirit of divination met us, which brought her masters much gain by soothsaying. The same followed Paul and us, and cried, saying, These men are the servants of the most high God, which shew unto us the way of salvation. And this did she many days. But Paul, being grieved, turned and said to the spirit, I command thee in the name of Jesus Christ to come out of her.
>
> —ACTS 16:16–18

Note that when ordinary people saw the girl following Paul, they heard her crying, "These men are the servants of the most high God, which shew unto us the way of salvation." It was natural that they thought that she was really helping the servants of the Lord.

But when the apostle Paul saw through this girl through the gift of discerning of spirits, he knew that she was possessed with a spirit of divination. Only later did Paul find out that she made her living from divination, so it is out of the question that he knew about her occupation through natural means. Outwardly she seemed to enhance the work of the gospel, but Paul was made aware that it was actually the mischief of the devil, so he cast out the spirit of divination. As a result Paul was beaten and imprisoned in Philippi.

The works of the devil are continually trying to spoil the wonderful blessings of God being poured out on today's church. Through the manifestation of the gift of discerning of spirits in us, we should be distinguishing the spirit of truth and the spirit of falsehood so that we may not fall into a snare. We, believing not every spirit, but trying the spirits whether they are of God (1 John 4:1), should participate in the movement of the Holy Spirit who is watchfully furthering our faith.

11

The Vocal Gifts

THE GIFTS MANIFESTED through vocalization are the gift of tongues, the gift of interpretation of tongues, and the gift of prophecy.

The Gift of Tongues

THE LIST OF gifts in 1 Corinthians 12 lists tongues: ". . . to another [is given] divers kinds of tongues" (v. 10).

Tongues should be placed into two categories: as a *sign* and as a *gift*.

The speaking in tongues that we previously discussed—the incidents that occurred at the time of someone's baptism with the Holy Spirit—is called the "tongue of signs," being an external proof of the inward fullness of the Holy Spirit.

To those who read the Bible without a preconceived theology, it is clear that all the instances of tongues recorded in Acts are this external sign of the baptism of the Holy Spirit.

The tongues listed in 1 Corinthians 12 and 14 are essentially the same as the tongues recorded in Acts, but the purpose for which they were used was different. Therefore they are called speaking in tongues "as a gift."

What is the difference? When speaking in tongues is a sign, the tongues cease after the initial baptism of the Holy Spirit. In order to continue speaking in tongues a person would subsequently receive the tongues as a gift, but in many instances people immediately possess the tongues as a gift as well as a sign.

Speaking in tongues as a gift means the tongues continue for the profit of the life of faith. Those who have received the speaking in tongues as a gift can speak in tongues anytime as they pray.

God gives the gift of tongues abundantly to accomplish several goals of faith. Let's summarize some of the reasons the gift is given:

It makes possible a deep spiritual communication with God. "For he that speaketh in an unknown tongue speaketh not unto men, but unto God: for no man understandeth him; howbeit in the spirit he speaketh mysteries" (1 Cor. 14:2). When we speak in tongues we converse directly with God, spirit to Spirit. By using this heavenly language the door is open for us to experience the deep revelations of God.

It brings progress in one's life of faith. "He that speaketh in an unknown tongue edifieth himself" (1 Cor. 14:4). The word *edify* originally meant to lay bricks one by one in building a house. The tongue becomes the instrument by which one's own house of faith is built up.

Along with the gift of the interpretation of tongues, speaking in tongues brings forth the same effect as prophecy. "Wherefore let him that speaketh in an unknown tongue pray that he may interpret" (1 Cor. 14:13). Through the gift of interpretation, the message in tongues is understood and spoken in one's native language so that the people who hear it can be edified. Through this supernatural interpretation, they realize that the living God is with them, and they gain strength in their faith.

This gift is a door to deeper prayer and praise. "What is it then? I will pray with the spirit, and I will pray with the understanding also: I will sing with the spirit, and I will sing with the understanding also" (1 Cor. 14:15). On occasion we are moved with emotion and/or at a loss to know how to pray. At such times praying and praising the Lord in tongues can reach beyond our learned vocabulary and touch the throne of God with the most exacting description of the need or with praise that we may feel but be unable to describe.

A sign to unbelievers. "Wherefore tongues are for a sign, not to them that believe, but to them that believe not" (1 Cor. 14:22).

When the new wave of theology was shouting "God is dead," the miracle of the vocal gifts, speaking in tongues by the Holy Spirit, came as a judgment or challenge to those heretics.

It is no wonder that the person who has received the baptism in the Holy Spirit and speaks in tongues has fervent faith and lives in victory. Summarizing those points, 1 Corinthians 14 tells us the many benefits of speaking in tongues. If we establish proper order and virtue as we use tongues in the church, the gifts will become like a river of grace flowing abundantly into the hearts of believers whose experiences with the Lord have dried up.

The Gift of the Interpretation of Tongues

> . . . to another [is given] the interpretation of tongues.
> —1 CORINTHIANS 12:10

No one can understand a message given in tongues until the meaning is revealed by God through the gift of the interpretation of tongues.

The Bible reads, "For he that speaketh in an unknown tongue speaketh not unto men, but unto God: for no man understandeth him; howbeit in the spirit he speaketh mysteries" (1 Cor. 14:2). Later Paul says, "Wherefore let him that speaketh in an unknown tongue pray that he may interpret" (1 Cor. 14:13).

Interpretation of tongues is different from an ordinary translation. Translation generally gives the word-for-word meaning of a foreign language, while interpretation makes clear the overall meaning of a foreign language. For instance, a message in tongues may be short, while the interpretation is long. At other times the message in tongues is long but the interpretation is short.

Since the interpretation of tongues is a gift of God manifested through man, we should not regard it as being equal with the Bible.

Much caution is needed and the interpretation of tongues should be discerned. The interpretation of tongues largely depends upon the interpreter's condition of faith, prayer life, and depth of spiritual communication with God. There can also be times when the personal thoughts of an interpreter or the interference of the devil influences the interpretation.

Like any other gift, the gift of the interpretation of tongues is manifested through the miracle of the inspiration of the Holy Spirit. No one can interpret messages in tongues continually as he could if he were translating a foreign language.

Interpretation of tongues is possible only when God allows the inspiration of the interpretation. Occasionally, I have seen tongues-speaking people line up to interpret a series of messages, boasting that they can interpret every message given. This is false and very dangerous.

I can best discuss the process of the interpretation of tongues by writing of my own experiences.

After I received the gift of speaking in tongues, in accordance with the teaching of the Scriptures, I kept praying earnestly that I might receive the gift of interpretation.

One day in my room in the dormitory, after having attended an early-morning prayer meeting, I began to pray privately in tongues. Suddenly the whole room seemed brighter. When I opened my eyes the room was still dark, but when I closed them again it seemed as if the sun were shining. Then the interpretation of tongues began to pour out from my lips.

Out of tremendous joy, I abused the gift of the interpretation of tongues in the days ahead and committed many errors. But after graduation from Bible college until now, the interpretation of tongues has become an incomparable treasure in my Christian experience. Like everything else, this gift has improved and settled more and more through the accumulated experiences of time, so that now I possess considerable discernment, for which I thank God.

From my personal experiences as well as those of well-known Spirit-filled leaders, the gift of the interpretation of tongues can be manifested in several ways:

First, a person interpreting a message given in tongues sometimes interprets only by faith through the commandment of the Holy Spirit in his heart, which is like a sudden urging in his spirit. At such a time, the powerful commandment of God fills the heart together with the abundant grace of the Holy Spirit. Then, as Abraham, who in accordance with the calling of God went out of Ur of the Chaldees not knowing where he was to go, the person begins to speak by faith, and mysteriously God provides the ability to interpret the message.

Second, when someone gives a message in tongues there will be times when only the general meaning of it is revealed to a heart. In this case every word of the message is not known. At such a time the person who received the interpretation by the Holy Spirit explains it with his own knowledge and words.

Third, when someone speaks in tongues, sometimes only a part of the message in tongues is revealed. If that part is verbalized, the remaining part is then revealed, like an unwinding spool of thread. As we continue on, the interpretation unfolds.

Fourth, right after a message in tongues is given, the interpretation of it may follow immediately through the same person, flowing as freely as did the message in tongues. In this case, the interpretation is given only to the mouth (the person doesn't mentally form the words) with the interpretation flowing out as long as the inspiration of the Holy Spirit continues.

Finally, there is a case in which a message spoken in a foreign tongue is heard in the vernacular language that everyone can understand. This rarely happens, but I have heard several testimonies of the experience.

The Gift of Prophecy

> . . . to another [is given] prophecy.
>
> —1 CORINTHIANS 12:10

When we say the word *prophecy,* we understand it literally as the revealed word of God about the future.

Through the Old and New Testaments God prophesied of the end of history and of the new heaven and new earth centering on the people of Israel.

All these prophecies written in the Bible are the Word of God handed down to us through the accurate record of the prophets who wrote by the inspiration of the Holy Spirit.

Note what the apostle Peter wrote, "For the prophecy came not in old time by the will of man: but holy men of God spake as they were moved by the Holy Ghost" (2 Pet. 1:21).

By His special providence, God overshadowed the scriptural prophecies and writings so that they were recorded without flaw until the canon (the books of the Bible officially accepted as genuine) was established.

Because the Bible has already been completed, the prophecy given as a gift of the Holy Spirit is different from the scriptural prophecies. The main purpose for the prophecy given under the anointing of the Holy Spirit today is not to foretell future events, but to edify, exhort, and comfort believers. The Bible clearly teaches: "But he that prophesieth speaketh unto men to edification, and exhortation, and comfort" (1 Cor. 14:3).

Concerning this gift of prophecy, I do not mean to say that this gift does not relate to future events. Rather I mean that the word of prophecy resulting from a manifestation of this gift can never be considered equal to or take the place of the written Word of God. Also, even though a prophecy may be spoken by a person who has received this gift, the truthfulness or falseness of the prophecy should be discerned and judged by other believers.

Paul confirmed this in his epistle to the Corinthians, "Let the prophets speak two or three, and let the other judge" (1 Cor. 14:29). Again, the prophecy manifested today as the gift of the Holy Spirit should not be accepted blindly but received with discernment.

This is also clear from Isaiah 8:20: "To the law and to the testimony: if they speak not according to this word, it is because there is no light in them."

Today's prophecy is to confirm that believers can accept the lessons and word of biblical prophecy and receive salvation in accordance with the teachings of the Bible, going into deeper faith.

The apostle Paul wrote concerning prophecy being used in the church: "But if all prophesy, and there come in one that believeth not, or one unlearned, he is convinced of all, he is judged of all: and thus are the secrets of his heart made manifest; and so falling down on his face, he will worship God, and report that God is in you of a truth" (1 Cor. 14:24–25).

Here again the gift of prophecy is described in terms of ministry—convincing of sin, judging a mischievous life, or manifesting the secrets of the heart. As a result, a person's faith will be edified and the church, the body of Jesus Christ, will grow.

Because of such characteristics of prophecy, Paul, of all the gifts, especially emphasized prophecy and said, "Desire spiritual gifts, but rather that ye may prophesy" (1 Cor. 14:1), and "Wherefore, brethren, covet to prophesy, and forbid not to speak with tongues" (1 Cor. 14:39).

Prophecy is the gift that today's ministers and preachers of the gospel of Jesus Christ should especially desire. When the Word is preached through such a gift to a congregation, the invigorating power appears and the fruit of the gospel can be harvested.

Many people today misuse or abuse this gift. Having departed from the teachings of the gospel, they habitually foretell other people's fortunes like a fortuneteller.

Such people have not received the true gift of the Holy Spirit but are possessed by lying spirits and have become prophets of evil spirits of divination. As with all other gifts, the gift of prophecy is given only to preach the gospel of Christ and to edify the church; by no means is it given to fulfill a personal desire or as an instrument of distinction. Those who have received the gift of prophecy, by the inspiration of the Holy Spirit, should use this gift only for the preaching of the gospel and for the saving of lost souls.

12

The Gifts of Power

So far we have studied the gifts of revelation (the word of wisdom, the word of knowledge, and discerning of spirits) and the gifts of vocalization (tongues, the interpretation of tongues, and prophecy). Now let us look into the gifts of power.

The Gift of Faith

> To another [is given] faith by the same Spirit.
>
> —1 Corinthians 12:9

Faith is the treasure without which man cannot live. Suppose you lost your faith even for a moment. You would doubt the faithfulness of your family members. You would not be able to drive your automobile or ride other means of transportation, for you would doubt them. By mistrusting the facilities that are essential to our civilized life—such as banks or post offices—your whole life would be completely paralyzed.

As a person is born with eyes, ears, nose, and mouth, so he or she is born with faith. Some people develop this faith more rapidly than others. With great conviction in life they ceaselessly keep it growing, while others become more shriveled and negative.

But let's think about Christian faith and belief. Nowadays, such expressions as "I don't have any faith" and "I have little faith" often leave the mouths of Christians.

Is there really one who doesn't have any faith? Romans 12:3 says that we are "to think soberly, according as God hath dealt to every man the measure of faith." This verse reveals clearly that God has imparted to every man a measure of faith. If this is true, then why don't people admit that they have received it? God never lies. Therefore, though there may be a difference of degree in faith, no one among those who have accepted Jesus Christ as Savior is totally faithless. So in obedience to the Word of God, we should say, "I have faith as written in the Scripture. I have enough faith to be saved, to receive healing, and to get answers from God."

Moreover, the faith we receive from God in the Lord grows when we hear the Word of God. In Romans 10:17 we read, "So then faith cometh by hearing, and hearing by the word of God." When we hear the Word of God, meditate on it, and digest it, we receive faith. And that faith grows.

Some believers might say, "My faith seems to be so weak." Though God did not praise anyone's weak faith, He never said that weak faith is good for nothing. Jesus said in Matthew 17:20, "For verily I say unto you, If ye have faith as a grain of mustard seed, ye shall say unto this mountain, Remove hence to yonder place; and it shall remove; and nothing shall be impossible unto you."

This word teaches that it is not important whether your faith is strong or weak, great or small, but whether you have a living or a dead faith. Faith as small as a mustard seed—living, working, and believing in the miracles of God—will produce great power beyond human imagination.

So far in this discussion, we have considered general faith, the faith God deals to us according to our measure, and the faith produced by the Word. But how is the *gift* of faith manifested by the Holy Spirit?

The gift of faith given by the Holy Spirit has characteristics very different from the other types of faith mentioned above. Faith given as a gift is itself the direct and immediate work of the Holy Spirit, and it means that divine faith is deposited in the heart of the believer. This strong and keen faith, beyond human imagining, is produced so that great miracles may be performed by God.

This faith is not possessed by a believer permanently but is manifested through the believer when a need arises in accordance with the Holy Spirit's time and place.

I have experienced this particular faith many times. At a time of need the Holy Spirit sheds in my heart the gift of faith to accomplish God's glorious work. Whenever I experience this imparted gift of faith, with supernatural passion and mental concentration I come to believe that God is in control, and as a result the answer to my need follows.

The Gift of Healing

> . . . to another [is given] the gifts of healing by the same Spirit.
>
> —1 Corinthians 12:9

Christian faith and healing are inseparable. Actually, healing is a central part of the gospel of the redeeming grace of the Lord Jesus Christ. In the Old Testament, God is revealed as the healing God. Exodus records God's making a covenant with the children of Israel:

> If thou wilt diligently hearken to the voice of the Lord thy God, and wilt do that which is right in his sight, and wilt give ear to his commandments, and keep all his statutes, I will put none of these diseases upon thee, which I have brought upon the Egyptians: for I am the Lord that healeth thee.
>
> —Exodus 15:26

David, the king chosen by God to lead His people, praised God and said, "Who forgiveth all thine iniquities; who healeth all thy diseases" (Ps. 103:3).

Malachi, the writer of the last book of the Old Testament, prophesied, saying, "But unto you that fear my name shall the Sun of righteousness arise with healing in his wings" (4:2). This showed that the work of evangelism of Jesus Christ would be the work of healing both the spirit and the flesh.

The public ministry of Jesus was truly the life of healing. Nearly two-thirds of Jesus' ministry was filled with the works of healing.

Isaiah, who prophesied about 700 B.C., described the redemption of Jesus. In Isaiah 53, he detailed the redeeming work of Jesus Christ and stressed that sickness and disease were included in the sufferings of the redemptive work: "Surely he hath borne our griefs, and carried our sorrows" (v. 4); "And with his stripes we are healed" (v. 5); "Yet it pleased the Lord to bruise him; he hath put him to grief" (v. 10).

The truths of these prophecies were all verified by the testimonies of Jesus' disciples. Matthew, after recording the wonderful works of healing by Jesus, acknowledged that this was in fact the accomplishment of Isaiah 53:4: "[He] healed all that were sick: that it might be fulfilled which was spoken by Esaias the prophet, saying, Himself took our infirmities, and bare our sicknesses" (Matt. 8:16–17).

Peter, recording the redemption of Jesus, did not fail to include that the healing we receive from Jesus was a part of Jesus' suffering for the redemption of mankind: "By whose stripes ye were healed" (1 Pet. 2:24).

Then the last and greatest commandment of Jesus, given just before ascending into heaven, concerned the casting out of devils and healing. (See Mark 16:15–18.) Here He clearly said that healing was inseparable from the preaching of the gospel.

The Gift of the Working of Miracles

> To another [is given] the working of miracles.
>
> —1 Corinthians 12:10

The word *miracle* refers to a remarkable or surprising event that happens by the direct intervention of God, not following the generally known laws of nature. A miracle is the temporary suspension of the usual laws of nature and the intervention of supernatural and divine power. The Bible contains an extensive record of such miracles.

The Old Testament includes miracles in almost every book. Let us examine some of these recordings.

The most famous example is the miracle God performed in the lives of Abraham and Sarah. When Abraham was about a hundred years old and Sarah was well past the age when she could conceive, God miraculously gave them a son, Isaac, who became the forefather of the Jewish nation.

This miracle was so wonderful that the New Testament describes it thus:

> Who [Abraham] against hope believed in hope. . . . And being not weak in faith, he considered not his own body now dead, when he was about a hundred years old, neither yet the deadness of Sarah's womb: he staggered not at the promise of God through unbelief; but was strong in faith, giving glory to God; and being fully persuaded that, what he had promised, he was able to perform.
>
> —Romans 4:18–22

This faith for the working of miracles was given not only to Abraham but also to Sarah:

> Through faith also Sara herself received strength to conceive seed, and was delivered of a child when she was past age, because she judged him faithful who had promised. Therefore

> sprang there even of one, and him as good as dead, so many as the stars of the sky in multitude, and as the sand which is by the sea shore innumerable.
>
> —HEBREWS 11:11–12

Such an occurrence is not common. It is the miracle that, through the special intervention of God, brought about a conception that was totally impossible by natural laws.

Another miracle occurred when Moses and the children of Israel came to the shores of the Red Sea. They were blocked by the sea to the front and a great army of Egyptian soldiers to the rear. When Moses prayed to God, the answer was given to him. With a rod in his right hand Moses commanded the water of the Red Sea to part and the children of Israel proceeded to walk through the sea as if it were dry ground.

Some opponents insist that this was not a miracle at all. They claim that when Moses came to the Red Sea, the tide subsided so he "luckily" could go into the midst of it.

These people, however, disregard the fact that the Egyptians who pursued Israel all drowned in the water. If the water had been shallow enough for the children of Israel to enter and cross, why were the whole Egyptian army and its horses killed?

By the law of nature the sea could not be divided so the people could cross over on dry ground. Such a phenomenon can happen only by the power of God manifesting itself over the law of nature: a miracle.

Other wonderful manifestations of the gift of the working of miracles took place in the life of Joshua. Joshua was leading the children of Israel in a fierce battle against the Amorites. To win, the Israelites needed time, but the sun began to set. Suddenly Joshua lifted up his voice, looked at the sun and cried: "Sun, stand thou still upon Gibeon; and thou, Moon, in the valley of Ajalon" (Josh. 10:12). The gift of the working of miracles operated through Joshua right there.

From the human viewpoint, what a foolish cry! Yet the Bible records the results: "And the sun stood still, and the moon stayed, until the people had avenged themselves upon their enemies. Is not this written in the book of Jasher? So the sun stood still in the midst of heaven, and hasted not to go down about a whole day" (Josh. 10:13).

Again, God suspended temporarily the operation of natural law to manifest His divine providence.

The New Testament also records numerous cases of the manifestation of the gift of the working of miracles.

The healing that we receive when we come to the Lord falls into two categories: some by the gift of healing and some by the gift of the working of miracles.

When the gift of the working of miracles works, the disease departs in a moment and the person immediately begins to recover health. When the gift of healing works, the cause of the disease is removed slowly and the effect of treatment starts to work, leading to recovery.

Conclusion

When the great work of the Holy Spirit begins to take over, established churches often persecute the work of the Holy Spirit. But Christians must stand firm against wrong doctrines or heresies that arise against or imitate the work of the Holy Spirit. For the Holy Spirit to be free to be manifested more, we must maintain a healthy, strong faith based on the Word of God. And for this a basic understanding of the doctrine of the Holy Spirit is indispensable.

For this purpose, this book was written to enlighten, teach, and encourage believers as they prepare their hearts in prayer for the greatest move of the Holy Spirit—yet to come!

The Next Move of God

Fuchsia Pickett

The Next Move of God by Fuchsia Pickett
Previously published by Creation House

Strang Communications Company
600 Rinehart Road
Lake Mary, FL 32746
Web site: http://www.creationhouse.com
Library of Congress Catalog Card Number: 94-68587
International Standard Book Number: 0-88419-384-5

Dedicated to all the faithful saints
throughout the body of Christ who
have been so supportive of me and my ministry.
I am grateful for their receptivity to the Word and for their
prayers for health, safety, strength and fresh anointing as
I travel so extensively.

CONTENTS

The Next Move of God

Part 1 Personal Revelation of the Next Move of God

Part 2 The Counterattack

Part 3 The Charismatic Renewal and the Next Move of God

Part 4 The New Blessing of the Next Move of God

Part 1

Personal Revelation of the Next Move of God

1

The Proclamation

Revival Is Coming

FOR MORE THAN thirty years I have proclaimed, shouted, and declared, without wavering, that the church is going to experience a great revival before the return of Jesus. I have seen in the Scriptures the promise of the Holy Spirit moving in the earth to bring a wonderful revival to His church and, subsequently, a great harvest of souls. The Lord also gave me a vision in 1963 of some of the things He is going to do in the church world in these last days in which we are living.

I believed the proclamation of a great revival and harvest of souls when I began to preach it. I believe it now more than ever because of the evidences of revival I see. What joy it gives me to see what the Holy Spirit revealed to me in vision form coming to pass more than thirty years later.

A Vision of Revival

IN 1959 I was healed of a genetic bone disease that had taken the lives of several members of my family and was believed to be unto death for me as well.[1] That same day I was baptized in the Holy Spirit. Until then my theology had not accepted either healing or the baptism in the Holy Spirit as biblical. Through these wonderful experiences God "invaded" my life, sending His Holy Spirit to take up residence inside me as my divine teacher. He began to reveal His Word to me as I had never known it, though I had been a professor and minister of the Methodist church for seventeen years.

Four years later, while I was ministering in a church in Klamath Falls, Oregon, God took me "into the Spirit" for two days. The Lord told me that if I would remain in the sanctuary and wait upon Him, He would show me things to come in His church and in the world when He poured out the fullness of His Spirit. As I waited there in prayer He took me into the heavenlies and let me see the revival that is coming. As He wrote it on the screen of my mind and spirit, I saw it more clearly than I see the faces of people.

Hydroelectric Power Plant

THE HOLY SPIRIT used the analogy of a hydroelectric power plant to explain to me what He was going to do. (I knew nothing about electricity; I couldn't have fixed a light switch if my life depended upon it.) Hour after hour He carried me into the revelation of this vision, showing me heaven's *dunamis* power.

The Greek word for the power of the Holy Spirit is *dunamis*, from which we derive our word *dynamo*. The analogy of a hydroelectric power plant was a dramatic word picture to reveal the *dunamis* work of the Holy Spirit.[2] It should not have surprised me that the Holy Spirit would describe His working in the heavenlies using such an analogy.

Above the church, high in the heavenlies, I saw the excavation for the building of a huge hydroelectric power plant. God laid the solid concrete foundation carefully, measuring the sand that went into it exactly. He cleansed everything and placed every screen and tubule in order precisely as it should be. Then He erected the power plant section by section. I saw the pipes, the dam, and all its massive gates, out from which He ran prime lines, primary lines, and secondary lines through great transformers to many points of distribution. After that, He began to fill the reservoirs with water, teaching me that unless a certain level of water was maintained, the high-powered dynamo could not function properly.

As I watched, I saw a church without walls. An awesome divine power was flowing down through the pulpits, out to the people, and then through them to the world. Above this power plant I saw Christ, the head of the church, holding that gigantic power plant in His hands. At the same time, however, it seemed as though He were the One being poured through that power plant, down into the church, and out to the world—a great harvest field, golden and ripe unto harvest.

Networking Churches

SOMEHOW I UNDERSTOOD that He was flowing His living water only to churches where deep wells and reservoirs had been dug. In the vision I saw pipes being placed underground from one fountainhead to another—from church to church. The pipes formed a network of churches, connecting those with deep wells that He had dug and filled with His living water—the living Word.

I wished it was going to all churches, but I realized that many churches could not tap into this living water because they had no reservoir. And I heard the words, "Deep calleth unto deep at the noise of thy waterspouts" (Ps. 42:7).

In 1963 there was little evidence of such networking of churches and ministers. Nevertheless, I understood that He was showing me a network of churches that had been dug out through which He would flow His great flood of truth. The "digging" would happen as pastors and believers obeyed God and allowed the dealings of God to work in their lives. By their yielded obedience to the Holy Spirit and His Word they would become reservoirs of truth. From these churches His power would flow throughout all the world.

Although no specific cities were named, I saw five geographical areas within the United States that would become vital centers for this divine power. When a vast network of churches had been filled with living water, God would pull a great switch and open *all* the gates of truth that have been dammed up by man. I saw the release of stream after stream of truth that God wanted to flow freely in the church, but that truth had been dammed up behind denominational walls erected by man.

Then, as the vision continued to unfold to me, in my spirit I heard the water—His Word—begin to run. Churches that had their reservoirs prepared began to fill up with water. They were ready for God to pull the switch and open the gates of truth from that great dynamo. I remembered Jesus' promise to those who believed on Him. He said: "Out of his belly shall flow rivers of living water" (John 7:38). This verse speaks figuratively of "the effects of the operation of the Holy Spirit in and through the believer."[3]

When God releases His *dunamis* power in this next move of God, rivers of living water will flow out of our innermost beings. Habakkuk's prophecy will become a reality: "For the earth shall be filled with the knowledge of the glory of the Lord, as the waters cover the sea" (Hab. 2:14).

When those gates of truth are finally opened we are going to see an "old-fashioned, heaven-sent, sky-blue, sin-killing, gully-washing revival."

Scientific Documentation

I TRANSCRIBED MY vision of the hydroelectric plant onto paper. Leon McGuire, in whose home I was staying, took the transcript to the Pacific Power Company in Oregon and asked to see the head engineer. He told him he would like to leave a transcript for him to critique, saying, "It is very important to us that we understand this material and know whether or not it is correct. The person who wrote it is deeply concerned as to its accuracy. If you would not mind taking some time to critique it, we would greatly appreciate it." The engineer agreed to do so.

When my host returned to the power company a few days later, the president of the company wanted to see him. A receptionist ushered him into the office of the president. After greeting him kindly, the president asked, "Where did you get this information?"

My host responded, "What would you say if I told you that a little woman who cannot fix a light switch wrote it?"

"I would say she is pulling your leg," the president retorted. "This paper is one of the most scientific I have ever read. There are words and terms in here that only a few master electricians know and understand. Some of these terms are even used by men in the Pentagon. Whoever wrote this paper was a master electrician."

"Please forgive me," my host responded. "I should not have said it was a little lady who wrote it; she just copied it down. The Master Electrician—the Holy Spirit—described it to her."

Construction in Progress

AT THE TIME of my vision, my Father said to me, "I am running the pipes now. And this time, when I pull that great power switch and release all the rivers of my living Word in their fullness, no demon, devil, man, or denomination will ever dam it up again. I will do a quick work; I am going to bring the revival that will result in the ingathering of the great harvest of souls."

God also let me see what the ministry of the local church will be when His Spirit is poured out. The local churches would use the power of the living Word to take care of the needs of the people who gravitated to them. In this way, the vision for the ministry of each local church would develop according to the needs that presented themselves. Whatever type of people—youth, elderly, poor—that gravitated to a local church would receive full pastoral care. I understood that the believers in these churches would also go outside their four walls to take care of the wounded, hurt, lame, rejected, and poor. They would feed the hungry and train disciples. They would teach ministers, raising them up to take the church into her inheritance.

I also saw the printed page rolling, producing Christian literature. I watched the church march into the heavenlies in the Spirit and invade the evil powers of the media. I saw the grainfields of the world ready to be harvested, and my Father said it was going to happen soon.

From October to December of that year, I heard the sound of waters rolling in my ears. Finally I prayed, "Father, if it pleases You, take this sound away from my ears and turn it inside. But let me continue to hear the river of Your living Word."

Since that vision was given thirty years ago I have been to many churches in America where I heard the sound of those waters, confirming that they are reservoirs that are now being connected to the network of pipes. In churches on the isles of Trinidad, the Bahamas, and Hawaii, and in nations in South America I have heard those supernatural waters running. I'm sure they are running as well in places I have not been. God's truth is being stored up, the water levels are rising, and God is getting ready to release His power in the earth in Holy Ghost revival.

Escapist Mentality

People raised their eyebrows in disbelief when I first began to preach what I had seen in that vision. Thirty years ago the church was not focused on revival. Much of the church was caught in the passive, faithless attitude of "hanging on a little while longer." Her theology did not accept the fact of a great harvest of souls. Many were simply waiting to be raptured. Even her hymns reflected her pessimistic philosophy. A line of a favorite hymn sung in those years says: "I'm going through whatever others do... I'll make my way with the Lord's despised few."

Many Christians believed Jesus would steal them away from this world one night as from a fire escape. Then, they believed, the world would be sorry they didn't know who the church was. They thought the media would send reporters throughout the world to discover the facts about the disappearance of the church. My response to that whole idea is, "Jesus does not have to steal me; I'm already His—He bought me."

Christians who were bogged down in this escapist mentality exhorted each other pitifully: "Just hang on, honey. God will get us out of here soon." For many, our infinite, omnipotent God seemed barely able to withstand the onslaught of evil, and the church seemed weak and impotent. Such unbelief denied God's power to establish the glorious church He has promised in His Word.

The more the Holy Spirit taught me from His Book, the more I recognized the fallacy of the church's escapist mentality. The church *is* going to meet Him, but before we do, the world *is* going to know we have been here! We will not have to sneak out onto a smoldering fire escape some night, dressed in smoke-filled, soot-covered tatters to be rescued from the darkness of this world system. God is returning for a glorious church without spot or wrinkle (Eph. 5:27). The reality of a glorious church should convince those who question that revival will be a precursor to His coming. Only revival can establish that glorious church.

Revival or Harvest?

LATER, MY TEACHER told me that I had my terms mixed up, that what I was calling *revival* was actually *harvest*. *Revival* is bringing back to life that which is dying; *harvest* is a reaping of souls. The reviving of the church is necessary before there can be a harvest of souls.

Unless we understand all that is involved in revival we cannot understand what God is doing in the church today. God has the church in His hands and is breathing His resurrection life into her. That is revival. Revival involves repentance and a return to our first love for God. In the process of reviving His church, God is cleansing her, circumcising her, and empowering her. If we misunderstand this sometimes painful work of the Holy Spirit, we may perceive that this pruning process brings defeat and loss—not revival—especially when it results in people leaving our churches.

To the contrary, God's divine pruning process removes dead wood from the vine so the church can bring forth good fruit, fruit that will remain, in preparation for the real harvest that is coming. The life God is giving the church through revival is going to result in a harvest of souls that will reach throughout the world. I believe thousands of souls will be saved in a day.

The great harvest that is yet to come must wait until the church submits to the process of revival. Those who resist the cleansing work of the Holy Spirit may fall away, causing an initial decrease of members in our churches. But after the church has been pruned, circumcised, and revived, harvest will be imminent. In that harvest the church will realize a great ingathering of souls.

The "Third Day" Message

THE MESSAGE OF the significance of the "third day" closely parallels the understanding of revival. Throughout the Bible, the third day represents new beginnings and resurrection life. (See Genesis 22:4; 2 Kings 20:5; Matthew 12:40; Matthew 27:63.) Hosea, the prophet, declared:

> Come, and let us return unto the Lord: for he hath torn, and he will heal us; he hath smitten, and he will bind us up. After two days will he revive us: in the third day he will raise us up, and we shall live in his sight. Then shall we know, if we follow on to know the Lord: his going forth is prepared as the morning; and he shall come unto us as the rain, as the latter and former rain unto the earth.
>
> —HOSEA 6:1–3

I knew God had commanded Joshua to cross the Jordan and to possess the Promised Land on the third day (Josh. 1:11). I declared that this new move of God would bring the church into a land that we had never possessed, just as Israel entered the Promised Land under Joshua's leadership. Joshua is a biblical type of Jesus, our heavenly Joshua, who is going to take His church into the Promised Land.

What is the Promised Land? Some have taught that it is heaven. But it cannot be heaven. There are no giants in heaven and no battles to be won as there were in the Promised Land. Although many of our gospel songs refer to Canaan as heaven, it is a fact that we are going to enter Canaan before we go to heaven.

In my book *God's Dream,* I shared the understanding my Father gave me of how the church would enter into her inheritance—the Promised Land—as it was revealed to the apostle Paul. Paul received a revelation of the fulfillment of God's dream for a *family* conformed to His image, recipients of His character, having the *family* spirit of love. He saw the church filled with transformed people fulfilling God's eternal plan. Paul understood God's eternal purpose to build a glorious church, and he stated:

> Till we all come in the unity of the faith, and of the knowledge of the Son of God, unto a perfect man, unto the measure of the stature of the fulness of Christ.
>
> —EPHESIANS 4:13

Israel, a type of the church, gives us a pattern of what the church must experience to enter the Promised Land. In order to enter their inheritance, Israel had to defeat the Hittites, Amorites, Canaanites, Perizzites, Hivites, and the Jebusites.

For the church to enter into its inheritance, she must defeat the "ites" of the works of the flesh Paul listed for the Galatians (Gal. 5:19–21). She must come into the maturity Paul described throughout his epistles. He taught that the church should be filled with righteousness, peace, and joy in the Holy Ghost, and learn to walk in humility, holiness, and unity.

We will know we have entered the Promised Land when Jesus' high priestly prayer in the seventeenth chapter of John becomes a reality in the church:

> That they all may be one; as thou, Father, art in me, and I in thee, that they also may be one in us: that the world may believe that thou hast sent me.
>
> —JOHN 17:21

This can only be realized through a mighty work of the Holy Spirit yet to come. I believe the purpose of God is to bring His church into the Promised Land on the third day.

Understanding, then, that the Promised Land is a place of maturity in our walk with God as individuals and as the church, some may still be wondering, *What is the third day?* While our purpose here is not to explore fully the significance of the third day as taught in the Scriptures, it is a fact that God chose to intervene in mankind's affairs in special ways on the third day. It is an interesting study to trace through the Bible the promises of the third day.

Although God dwells in eternity, He deals with mankind in time. But His perspective of time is necessarily different from ours. The apostle Peter wrote that "one day is with the Lord as a thousand years, and a thousand years as one day" (2 Pet. 3:8). As we consider that fact, when our calendar turns to A.D. 2000, we will have completed two "days" and will be entering a "third day" era in God's perspective. Because of the biblical pattern of God's intervention into the affairs of men on the "third day," many believe that God is going to do something special in and through His church in the next century.

Evidences of Revival

INDEED, FOR THE last few years as I have traveled throughout our nation and others, I have seen evidences of revival breaking upon the church. I have heard ministers using these phrases: *the new wave, the new revival, the latter rain,* and *the Joshua generation.* These phrases are all synonymous—each a word picture expressing the next move of God.

I heard marvelous reports of revival and manifestations of the harvest in many Third World nations. As I traveled to some of these countries, I saw Holy Ghost revival happening before my eyes. The churches were alive to God; thousands of men, women, youth, and children were swept into the kingdom, and miracles became the norm rather than the exception.

I got excited! I knew the *dunamis* power of God was bringing new life to these Third World churches that would result in a harvest of souls. Yet I realized that although revival also belonged to us in the Western world, events taking place in the American church seemed to contradict the fact that God was ready to pour out His Spirit in a new way in our nation. Many American churches were experiencing losses and painful situations.

I cried out, "Father, where is the church? Why hasn't the American church plugged into your *dunamis* power?"

In His faithfulness He answered me and helped me to see what was happening in many churches. As my eyes opened to His perspective, I was not devastated by what seemed to be contrary reports to what God had promised. God's Word always gives hope in the midst of the most difficult circumstances. In the chapters that follow, I want to share God's eternal plan for the church. That plan unfolds as we identify the present dwelling place for much of the church—crouched in the safety of a cave!

2

Where Is the Church?

Cave Dwellers Anonymous

I TRAVEL EXTENSIVELY THROUGHOUT our nation, teaching in hundreds of churches and at many conferences, and at one time I was shocked and grieved in my spirit by what I saw happening in the body of Christ. All appearances seemed contrary to what God promised and to what was happening in the nations of the Third World.

I also served (and still serve) as one of twenty-nine persons from twenty-five countries who are trustees of the International Third World Revival Fellowship. The wonderful reports of how God was moving among the Third World nations were a sad contrast to the reports of conflict and moral decay in the church in our nation.

The media had begun to defame and slander the church in America—and not without cause. Leaders who had fallen to immorality or misappropriation of funds received daily publicity, and the church became the laughingstock of relentless and merciless media attacks. There was a great falling away of Christians, and many churches suffered division from within.

Many confused and bewildered ministers came to me for counseling because of the turmoil in their churches. These men and women had received revelations of great truths from the Scriptures by the Holy Spirit, filling them with great anticipation for a coming revival. Yet, instead of the move of God they were expecting to see, they were experiencing opposition from the enemy in their churches.

The Cry of the Prophet

THE LAMENT OF the prophet filled our own hearts, and we cried with him: "Revive thy work in the midst of the years" (Hab. 3:2).

We longed for the promise to be fulfilled that God gave to Isaiah: "I dwell on a high and holy place, and also with the contrite and lowly of spirit in order to revive the spirit of the lowly and to revive the heart of the contrite" (Isa. 57:15, NAS). Two prerequisites for revival that are revealed in this verse are *lowliness* or *humility*, and a *contrite spirit. Perhaps,* I mused, *we did not qualify.*

I began to wonder, *Where is the revival? Where is the next move of God so many have believed was on the horizon?* "Why are so many leaders falling," I cried out to my Father, "while others are hurting from wounds inflicted by Christian brothers and sisters? *Where is the church?* What is happening to her?"

The "Hidden" Church

When I refer to the church in this way, I am not speaking of an institution, organization, or denomination. I am referring to the biblical concept of a living organism—the body of Christ. This body is made of true believers who seek God sincerely and desire to do His will. Wherever there are people who are surrendered to the lordship of Jesus, who love and serve Him, God is there to reveal Himself and to build His church.

The answer my Father gave me flooded my heart with understanding and renewed hope. He told me that He had hidden the church away from the eyes of the world today much as He hid David in the cave of Adullam in Saul's day (1 Sam. 22:1).

God had taken the church—the living organism of which Christ is the head—and placed her in a "cave." He was preparing His church, in much the same way that God had prepared David, to reign in the kingdom. In spite of the unpleasant implications of "cave dwelling," my Father's answer brought hope to my heart.

King David's Preparation

During the time of his reign, Saul had a lot going for him. He was a mighty warrior who had been anointed by God and was loved by his people. But he was also impetuous at times and was given to angry fits and jealousies. God allowed a series of trials to test Saul's principles, but Saul failed one test after another.

At Gilgal Saul refused to wait for direction from God and assumed he could choose his own direction (1 Sam. 13:8–9). Soon after this failed test, his greed led him to ignore God's instructions to destroy the Amalekites and their herds, and he kept the best animals for himself, lying to the prophet Samuel about what he had done (1 Sam. 15:3). He fell so far from his pursuit of godliness that ultimately he consulted a witch for advice, having lost the presence of God.

When one is proven unfit for God's service, sooner or later that person is removed from his or her position of authority. King Saul was definitely on his way out. The way David handled this transition of power is worth noting.

David received three separate anointings of God for leadership. As a young lad, years before his cave experience, the great prophet Samuel had anointed David to be king over Israel in Saul's place (1 Sam. 16:11–13).

I wonder who believed this anointing was valid—David? Samuel? His brothers? His father? Perhaps they were the few who did. Knowledge of that anointing did not go much farther for fear of the king's response.

His young life gave evidence that he had been anointed of God. It was after this first anointing that David killed Goliath and found himself enlisted in the service of King Saul. During those years he became a beloved minstrel, his anointing able to dispel the evil spirit that tormented Saul (1 Sam. 16:23). Then he became a great warrior against the Philistines, enjoying such success that he gained recognition throughout the land. The women's songs, as they proclaimed that Saul had slain his thousands but David his tens of thousands, energized Saul's jealousy against him (1 Sam. 18:7–8). During this time, the Bible declares that "David behaved himself wisely in all his ways; and the Lord was with him"(1 Sam. 18:14).

Saul became so jealous of David that he pursued him to kill him, but David escaped and found himself hiding in a cave (1 Sam. 22:1). Four hundred men who were experiencing distress, debt, and discontent defected from King Saul and joined David's army (1 Sam. 22:2). During those years of cave life David trained these desperate men, forging a loyalty of heart and strength of character in them through the many battles they fought together. Later, when David was crowned king, these once desperate men became David's faithful leaders.

On two occasions when Saul was in David's hand, David refused to take his life. He would not touch God's anointed. He had conquered one of the greatest temptations of the human heart—to judge God's anointed. We can observe the godly character that was being formed in David through his responses to these situations.

The demise of Saul continued until his tragic, violent death on the battlefield. David, the pursued, mourned his leader's death, crying: "How are the mighty fallen" (2 Sam. 1:27).

After Saul's death, the men of Judah came to him and anointed him for a second time (2 Sam. 2:1–4). For seven years he reigned over the tribe of Judah while Ishbosheth, Saul's son, reigned over the remaining tribes of Israel. After Ishbosheth was killed in battle, the tribes of Israel came to David and anointed him as king over all of Israel and Judah, thus fulfilling the prophet's word given many years earlier.

Despite David's anointing as a youth and his military feats of heroism, God required him to experience the discipline of the cave before going to the throne.

Perhaps it was the honorable way in which David handled the persecutions of Saul that won the hearts of the men he would one day lead. Or it may have been the victorious, godly character he developed through his cave experiences that prepared him to receive the second and third anointings. Thus his life would follow the pattern of God's dealings with other spiritual leaders such as Joseph, Moses, and even Jesus, who conquered temptation from Satan himself in the wilderness before He began His ministry.

The church has been experiencing the discomfort and trials of the rigors of "cave life"—those circumstances and situations that require our obedience and bring a humbling to our hearts. When we respond correctly, these cave disciplines forge the character of God in our hearts, thus preparing us for sonship, leadership, throneship, and "brideship."

My Father said to me, "My daughter, I am doing a work in the church that the world does not understand. The difficult situations the church is enduring are training and preparing her for the throne. When the church is ready to come out of the cave, she is going to be different. The world will see Jesus in the church, of which He is the head."

The Work of Circumcision

THERE IS A beautiful parallel to the work of the cave in another Old Testament example. Historically, after the death of Moses, God told Joshua to "command the people, saying...within three days ye shall pass over this Jordan, to go in to possess the land" (Josh. 1:11). Thus he led them into the Promised Land on the third day. Joshua is a type of Jesus—as our heavenly Joshua, Jesus will lead His church into the Promised Land.

But there is more revelation in this parallel of Joshua marching the children of Israel into the Promised Land on the third day than we may have understood. As I taught the third day message, the Lord told me that I had left out part of the story. As I read the biblical account again, He said to me: "I told Joshua that before he could take the new generation into the land they had to be circumcised."

In a literal sense, circumcision is an operation performed by a rabbi or skilled physician for the sake of procreation as well as for hygienic purposes. It removes excess flesh that could hinder reproduction. This painful cutting away of flesh represents a covenant of obedience established between God and His people.

In the New Testament, Paul refers to the circumcision of the heart (Rom. 2:29). He explained to the Colossians that we are circumcised "with the circumcision made without hands, in putting off the body of the sins of the flesh by the circumcision of Christ" (Col. 2:11).

With anticipation, we have proclaimed that the Joshua generation is marching into the land to conquer our enemies. But in our excitement, many have not understood that circumcision is necessary before we can enjoy the victory of the Promised Land.

No one considers surgery to be a pleasant experience. But we submit to it because it results in the removal of that which hinders health and life. The Scriptures teach that "the word of God is quick, and powerful, and sharper than any twoedged sword, piercing even to the dividing asunder of soul and spirit, and of the joints and marrow, and is a discerner of the thoughts and intents of the heart" (Heb. 4:12). We cannot receive the Word of God without experiencing the pain of its "dividing" work in our souls. God requires the church to pass through the painful place of circumcision in order to enter into her inheritance.

God is removing the "flesh programs" in our lives and churches, and He is tearing down man's kingdoms in order for the new generation to be what God wants it to be. He is cleansing the church; changing her motivation, attitudes, priorities, and character; and training her to be His army. The enemy's knife cuts for destruction, but the Holy Spirit's knife brings ultimate healing. I believe the church will soon recover from this painful process of circumcision.

Understanding the Types

FROM THESE TWO biblical types—David's preparation in the cave and the process of circumcision—the Holy Spirit showed me the present position of the church in the purposes of God. God's purpose is to cleanse and establish the church in His divine plan—not to destroy it. Today, as in the days of the prophet Isaiah, God's desire is "to revive the spirit of the humble, and to revive the heart of the contrite ones" (Isa. 57:15). As we meet the requirements of humility and contrition of heart, we will be qualified for sonship, leadership, throneship, and "brideship." Our God will dwell with us, and revival will become a reality.

The End of Training

ALTHOUGH DAVID THOUGHT he was fleeing for his life from the pursuit of Saul, his plight was part of God's purpose for his development as a leader. His cave experience prepared him for the leadership the throne would require. The men who followed David also benefitted from the cave experiences, developing godly character as well.

So it is with the church. In order for the church to become "more than conquerors" (Rom. 8:37) and fulfill God's eternal plan, godly character has to be formed in her through divinely ordained "cave" experiences. The church can expect the same kind of triumph David experienced.

David's Mighty Men

THE MEN WHO had come to David in distress, debt, and discontent became "mighty men of valor" (1 Chron. 12:21). They were armed with bows and were able to shoot arrows right- or left-handed (1 Chron. 12:2). This signifies that they were balanced to face any enemy threat, diversified in their skills, and dangerous because of their abilities. The Scriptures admonish believers to "fight the good fight of faith" (1 Tim. 6:12). The cave develops soldiers into great fighters!

The Scriptures tell us also that these brave, battle-ready warriors had "faces...like the faces of lions, and they were as swift as the gazelles on the mountains" (1 Chron. 12:8, NAS). They were bold, poised as a lion stalking its prey, prepared to move quickly and able to adjust to tough situations.The church will arise as a mighty army against the onslaught of the enemy as she emerges from her place of "training."

These men also were united as leaders with their leader, David. The Spirit of God prompted their chief captain, Amasai, to say to David: "Thine are we, David, and on thy side, thou son of Jesse: peace, peace be unto thee, and peace be to thine helpers; for thy God helpeth thee" (1 Chron. 12:18). Leaders must be committed to unity and to their leader's success—not their own agenda. David's mighty men served him with great loyalty, "with an undivided heart" (1 Chron. 12:33, NAS). Such unity, according to the Scriptures, is energized by the Spirit of God.

They kept rank, not moving ahead or lagging behind, not marching in a different direction. We might say they were content with their calling—they knew the importance of maintaining their individual positions. Because they were willing to be tested and trained during the cave season, they would reign with David in his kingdom. Paul understood this process of testing. He told Timothy that "if we suffer, we shall also reign with him" (2 Tim. 2:12).

The church is being tested through hardship and suffering as part of her training. She must be in position to face the enemy—for he is prepared to launch a mighty counterattack against the church.

Part 2

The Counterattack

God showed me five major, divisive, deceptive attacks that Satan has launched against the church. These enemy attacks are real and have caused grief and misery in many churches today. But we will be comforted to know that none of their biblical counterparts, by whose names they are recognized today, won in the end. The end for believers who allow God's character to be formed in them will not be destruction. God is training His church to be more than conquerors and enabling her to fulfill the purpose and plan of God in the earth. His church will reflect His character before He comes again to receive His family unto Himself.

In the following chapters we will expose these attacks of the enemy against the church. Understanding the enemy's purposes will bring hope to those who have been anticipating a move of God but have encountered instead the grievous work of the enemy. One of Satan's first attacks will come from the spirit of Jezebel.

3

The Spirit of Jezebel

Killing the Prophets

THE JEZEBEL SPIRIT has come against the church in a fierce attack, intimidating many and causing much destruction. We call it the "Jezebel spirit" because it has taken the nature of the historical, wicked Queen Jezebel, wife of King Ahab. The Scriptures teach us much about this personality that will help us understand the attack of Satan in this area.

The first time we see Jezebel, it is as a rebellious, manipulative queen who destroyed the prophets of the Lord. As Francis Frangipane writes:

> She was nearly totally responsible for corrupting an entire nation... Jezebel is fiercely independent and intensely ambitious for preeminence and control. It is noteworthy that the name *Jezebel,* literally translated, means "without cohabitation." She refuses to "live together or cohabit" with anyone. Jezebel will not dwell with anyone unless she can control and dominate the relationship. When she seems submissive or "servant-like," it is only for the sake of gaining some strategic advantage. From her heart, she yields to no one. She insists on dominating and controlling every relationship.[1]

No Gender

THIS SPIRIT KNOWS no gender; it can function as well through a male as through a female personality. But, as Frangipane observes:

> The female psyche is often more vulnerable to this spirit because it desires to manipulate and control others without using physical force.[2]

It especially energizes women who are insecure, vain, jealous, and dominating, having a consuming desire to control. Control is this principality's ultimate goal, and to that end it will use even sexual passion as a tool.

It is not difficult to trace the working of this Jezebel spirit in today's culture. It energizes the feminists and is the motivator of abortion. It is especially rampant in the entertainment industry, flaunting itself in its glamour and brazen desire to seduce the minds and affections of a nation. We will limit our discussion, however, to the damage it seeks to inflict on the church.

Jezebel in the Church

The New Testament counterpart of Queen Jezebel was the Jezebel who was exposed in the church of Thyatira, as recorded in the Book of Revelation. She called herself a prophetess while seducing the servants of God to commit fornication (Rev. 2:20).

The Jezebel spirit is most often found in positions of influence and leadership. Because of its supreme desire to control, it maneuvers clandestinely until it can gain the confidence of those it seeks to influence.

In the church, this spirit presents itself as a master of persuasion. It is strong-willed, religious, and often very gifted. It may appear to be extremely loyal and willing to volunteer for special service. It may even be the spouse of a pastor. But make no mistake, the Jezebel spirit is always motivated by a character flaw that desires to control.

If this Jezebel spirit cannot actually attain to a place of leadership, it will often seek to win the confidence of those in leadership in such a way that leaders will bare their hearts to the person, telling the secrets of their lives. Then, because of the ulterior motive ruling the person with the Jezebel spirit, he or she will betray the confidence of those leaders, trying to destroy them with knowledge of their personal lives.

Dick Bernal wrote:

> You can tell the truth about someone and still bring a curse on yourself if your motive is to hurt and discredit that individual.

> Truth is a two-edged sword, like a surgeon's knife. It can cut to heal, or like an enemy's sword, it can cut to kill.[3]

The Jezebel spirit seeks to kill the true servant of God in any way possible.

Our Defense Against Jezebel

JEZEBEL IS NOT comfortable in a church where the Holy Spirit is given preeminence. Jezebel cringes when Jesus is exalted and worshiped. Repentance is greatly feared by one with a Jezebel spirit. He or she may feign repentance, but it is just to protect their influence. The Jezebel spirit knows that true repentance brings the presence of Jesus, cleanses the church, and establishes it in purity and power, thus defeating the usurping control of the Jezebel spirit.

This spirit hates humility, always flaunts itself, and seeks for attention. Though at times it pretends to be a self-sacrificing servant, its ulterior motive is for personal gain—to secure a place of influence and control.

It also hates prayer. Jezebel's control over Christians is ripped out of her hands by true intercessory prayer, setting Christians free while crippling this wicked spirit.

As surely as Jehu's horse trampled Queen Jezebel and destroyed her (2 Kings 9:33), we destroy the spirit of Jezebel as we seek humility and a servant's heart, giving the Holy Spirit His rightful place in our lives and churches. Our greatest corporate and personal defense against the spirit of Jezebel is to cultivate the nature of Jesus in our hearts.

Jezebel and the Prophets

THE SCRIPTURES RECORD that Queen Jezebel destroyed the prophets of the Lord (1 Kings 18:4). The Jezebel spirit hates prophets, for true prophets speak against it. It wars against the prophetic message of God that condemns its rebellion and idolatry. The prophetic anointing brings exposure and defeat to the wickedness of Jezebel.

Ultimately, Jezebel's hatred is against God. The servants of God become the target of its hatred. This spirit hates the grace God lavishes upon His servants—even when they fail. It hates the holiness and purity of heart that God gives to those who serve Him.

By contrasting the Jezebel spirit with the spirit of Elijah, God's true prophet, we can better understand it. Elijah was sent to expose and confront the wickedness of Jezebel and her idolatrous worship of Baal. Again, it is Francis Frangipane who describes these two spiritual counterparts for us:

> Is Elijah bold? Jezebel is brazen. Is Elijah ruthless toward evil? Jezebel is vicious toward righteousness. Does Elijah speak of the ways and words of God? Jezebel is full of systems of witchcraft and words of deceit.[4]

They represent the two kingdoms of light and darkness which cannot coexist. That is the reason Jezebel threatened the life of Elijah. His demonstration of the power of God on Mount Carmel brought fire from heaven and turned a nation to serve the true God (1 Kings 18).

Elijah and Jezebel Today

THE WAR BETWEEN the Elijah spirit and the Jezebel spirit continues to rage today. As God restores true prophetic anointing to the church, and prophets call for righteousness and service to God, we can expect the wicked, idolatrous Jezebel spirit to be exposed. It exalts its rebellion through feminism; the murder of innocent, unborn children; and by causing God's servants to fall to immorality. It demands confrontation with the spirit of Elijah. And it is the spirit of Elijah calling for repentance and raising up prophets that will defeat the spirit of Jezebel.

Restoring Prophecy to the Church

THE GOAL OF this Jezebel spirit is to attack the purpose of God for restoring the true prophetic voice to the church. Historical Jezebel was an idolatrous queen whose intent was to kill the true prophets of God and shut up the voice of prophecy. The Jezebel spirit is trying to do the same thing today. It will use any means to silence the voice of the prophets and to thwart the prophetic anointing to which God is calling the church.

Five Realms of Prophecy in the Church

GOD IS PRESENTLY restoring the true voice of prophecy to the church to strengthen and establish her in His purposes. True prophecy is the divine ability to perceive, predict, proclaim, and prepare for the future. Prophecy in the Old Testament is depicted as both human activity and divine activity. God is the source of the prophetic message. Human vessels become the channel for relating that message to the people for whom the message is given.

In the New Testament, prophecy is further defined by the Greek word *propheteia,* which means "the speaking forth of the mind and counsel of God."[5] It is a declaration from God that could include prediction of the future as well as proclamation of divine realities.

In summary, we can say that *prophecy* is a supernatural utterance by which God communicates to people His mind and purpose, using a Spirit-filled individual as His mouthpiece.

The Scriptures also teach that the "testimony of Jesus is the spirit of prophecy" (Rev. 19:10). That holds much greater significance than a mere pseudo-exhortation that some call prophecy. It refers to the voice of our Lord Jesus Himself being heard in the church. God wants to speak to His people today through the prophetic voice, giving Jesus His proper place in the church.

There are at least five ways that the prophetic voice is expressed in the church.

1. Preaching

Paul declared that "it pleased God by the foolishness of preaching to save them that believe" (1 Cor. 1:21). God has ordained to save the world through prophetic declaration of the truth of the Scriptures. Unfortunately, not everyone who stands behind a pulpit speaks with a prophetic anointing. But God does use human vessels who are yielded to the Holy Spirit to preach the Word with a prophetic anointing. Believers should be able to hear what the Spirit is saying to the church today through the present, freshly anointed, living Word of God.

2. The office of the prophet

The voice of prophecy should be heard through the office of the prophet on whom the mantle of prophecy rests. According to the Scriptures, prophets are placed in the body of Christ to speak forth God's Word (Eph. 4:11). They are a vital part of equipping the church.

3. The gift of prophecy

Prophecy should be heard through believers who are willing to exercise the gift of prophecy, one of the gifts of the Holy Spirit (1 Cor. 12:10). The Scriptures give clear guidelines for the proper use of all the gifts of the Holy Spirit.

4. Music

Prophecy should flow through music. We ought to hear God speak through Spirit-filled musicians worshiping God with their music. Some of the greatest prophecies I have heard came through musicians prophesying on their instruments and singing the song of the Lord. I have heard the Bridegroom sing to the bride, and I also have heard the bride sing back to her heavenly Bridegroom. I am part of a church where music is often a beautiful prophetic expression.

5. Prayer and Bible reading

A fifth realm of prophecy includes praying prophetically and reading the Scriptures with a prophetic anointing that applies them to a present need or situation. Everyone who is filled with the Holy Spirit should learn to become a yielded channel for Him to flow through in prayer and Scripture reading. As we learn to pray according to the will of God and allow the Word of God to live in our hearts, we will walk in revelation under a prophetic anointing.

The more we allow prophetic ministry to develop in our lives and churches, the less place we will give to the Jezebel spirit.

Tolerating Jezebel

A TOLERANCE FOR Jezebel begins in our own inner sanctuary—and it is there it must be defeated. We need to ask God for the zeal of an uncompromising Jehu who cried out: "What peace, so long as the harlotries of…Jezebel and her witchcrafts are so many?" (2 Kings 9:22, NAS). God used Jehu to destroy Jezebel.

We need to be compassionate toward people who are captured by the Jezebel spirit. But, like Jehu, we offer no mercy, no hope for reform, and no sympathy whatsoever to this demonic spirit. We dare not live for our own comfort while her harlotries and witchcraft are rampant in our land. As we stand with God, His judgments will come forth to destroy the Jezebel spirit.

The End of Jezebel's Witchcrafts

IN THE ATTACK of the Jezebel spirit against the church, we have seen people rise up with an idolatrous desire to rule and to shut up the true spirit of prophecy in the church. Satan doesn't want us to hear God's voice; he knows that if we hear it, we will be part of what God is going to do in the earth. So he sent the Jezebel spirit to try to shut the mouths of the prophets.

Many times this spirit works to destroy the credibility of true prophets and to discourage them from a desire to speak for God any longer. Elijah was tormented by Jezebel's witchcraft after his triumph on Mount Carmel. She threatened to take his life, and he found himself in a place of despair and hopelessness, running for his life (1 Kings 19:4). When we war against the Jezebel spirit we have to guard against demonic powers of fear and discouragement. They will cause us to be distracted from the victory God has given us.

The zeal of Jehu will enable us to war against the Jezebel spirit successfully. As we pray for this zeal we do not need to fear Jezebel's onslaught. The historical Jezebel did not win! The spirit of Jezebel was defeated at Calvary! The harlotries and witchcrafts of Jezebel will be destroyed. And as the church puts an end to Jezebel, she will recognize another deceptive spirit of witchcraft poised to strike another blow.

4

The Spirit of Witchcraft

Witchcraft Incognito

THE SECOND GREAT attack against the church is from the spirit of witchcraft, closely related to the Jezebel spirit. The goal of this spirit is to dilute, subjugate, and destroy biblical teaching and subsequently, the Christian life. Because it is a deceptive spirit, many Christians suffer under its bondage without being aware of it.

The apostle Paul warns us to "put on the whole armor of God, that ye may be able to stand against the wiles [or trickery] of the devil" (Eph. 6:11). He warns us that Satan will take advantage of us if we are "ignorant of his devices" (2 Cor. 2:11).

We have no reason to fear our enemy, for the Scriptures teach us that "greater is he that is in you, than he that is in the world" (1 John 4:4). But, the greatest among us is vulnerable to the attack of the enemy if we fail to recognize his tactics. Our ignorance and complacency will defeat us.

Witchcraft Defined

WITCHCRAFT CAN BE simply defined as the "technique of manipulating supernatural forces to attain one's own ends." It may involve the use of psychic powers to project an inner force onto some person or situation. When we try to use emotional power to manipulate others we are engaging in a basic form of witchcraft.

Paul includes witchcraft in his list of the works of the flesh. He wrote:

> Now the works of the flesh are manifest, which are these;

> adultery, fornication, uncleanness, lasciviousness, idolatry, *witchcraft*, hatred, variance, emulations, wrath, strife, seditions, heresies, envyings, murders, drunkenness, revellings, and such like...
>
> —GALATIANS 5:19–21, ITALICS ADDED

The spirit of witchcraft is a counterfeit to true spiritual authority. God gives the believer spiritual authority for the purpose of edifying other believers. But an unholy or evil spirit will counterfeit true spiritual authority by using domination, manipulation, intimidation, and control over other believers. We will only be free from the power of the spirit of witchcraft when we are completely submitted to the power and authority of God.

Sources of Witchcraft

THE OBVIOUS SOURCES of satanic cults or New Age philosophy are not the only sources for the spirit of witchcraft. It can come from well-meaning though deceived Christians. Even prayer, if it is motivated by desire for control or manipulation, is a work of witchcraft, with powers as real as those experienced from black magic. "Charismatic" witchcraft finds its source in gossip, political maneuvering, jealousies, and envyings.

Marriage partners work it on their mates; children on parents; and even businessmen and women on customers as they scheme to make a deal. Any manipulative tactic used in order to reach a selfish end can qualify as a basic form of witchcraft. Using emotional manipulation or hype to enlist the service of others, even for the work of the Lord, is a basic form of witchcraft.

We may recognize these forms of witchcraft and refuse to be manipulated. But if we become resentful or bitter toward the person projecting these tactics toward us, the enemy has gained ground within us. He will bring discouragement, disorientation, and depression as surely as if we had submitted to a controlling spirit. If the enemy can get us to respond negatively in any of these situations, we will be defeated. His strategy is to cause us to depart from exercising the fruit of the Spirit and to combat him on his own terms—fighting anger with anger.

Satan can't cast out Satan; Jezebel can't cast out Jezebel. Fighting on the enemy's terms only increases the enemy's power.

The Scriptures teach us to overcome evil with good (Rom. 12:21). Jesus Himself gave us the divine strategy for overcoming evil: "Love your enemies, bless them that curse you, do good to them that hate you, and pray for them which despitefully use you, and persecute you" (Matt. 5:44). As we pray blessings on our enemies through the power of forgiveness, the evil power of control will be broken. By not returning evil for evil, but overcoming evil with good, we destroy the power of the enemy over our lives.

To forgive does not mean we maintain fellowship with one who is determined to use manipulation and control through the power of witchcraft. Unity will not be restored in our relationship with such people without true repentance on their part. But forgiveness will free us from bitterness and resentment, and our prayers for them will be effective for their deliverance.

Our Defense

OUR GREATEST DEFENSE against counterfeit spiritual authority is to walk in true spiritual authority, establishing our lives on truth. Though we may seem to gain a position of influence through manipulation or self-promotion—forms of counterfeit authority—such gain will ultimately become a stumbling block to receiving a true commission from God. When God establishes us in His purpose for our lives, no man or devil can undo it. But using manipulative tactics to establish and maintain our position amounts to witchcraft.

The Scriptures are clear that we should relate to one another in love. They teach us to "be subject one to another, and be clothed with humility" (1 Pet. 5:5). Such an attitude will protect us from the manipulative work of our flesh that desires to seek its own glory. Anything done through the power of witchcraft is doomed to failure. Though we may even justify our tactics by declaring that our goal is to build the church, God will not bless fleshly manipulation. He will build His church according to the working of His Spirit. Anything else is an affront to the cross and ultimately will oppose the purposes of God.

Hunger for the Supernatural

THE MORE SECULARIZED society becomes, the more magnified the hunger of man for the supernatural. The vacuum created within man for the reality of spiritual life intensifies as society declares, "There is no God." If the spiritual void in every man is not filled with real power and authority from God, as a society we will become subject to witchcraft increasingly as we draw closer to the end of this age.

Some churches that once preached the evangelical message have not followed the move of the Spirit, becoming liberal in their theology and being deceived by New Age philosophy.

We do not have to settle for counterfeit authority or be enslaved by any form of witchcraft. As we submit our lives to God and to one another in love, He will cleanse us and set us free from every evil tendency in our flesh that would thwart the purposes of God. We can be established in God's purposes and rejoice as we see the downfall of the spirits of Jezebel and of witchcraft.

Then we will be prepared to combat still another enemy that has threatened the church through betrayal and disloyalty—the Absalom spirit.

5

Absalom's Betrayal

Unresolved Offense

ABSALOM, KING DAVID'S son, betrayed his father by stealing the hearts of the men of Israel and leading them to revolt against their king (2 Sam. 15:1–6).

The Absalom spirit of betrayal is attacking churches today. This spirit works through discontented or offended spiritual leaders who betray the authority of the senior pastor. They seek to build a following of people who will support their agenda, which is contrary to the purposes and vision of the senior pastor and the majority of the congregation. This "Absalom" will often lead his followers out of the church, causing division and bringing great hurt to God's anointed leadership.

Characteristics of the Absalom Spirit

LIKE THE JEZEBEL spirit, the Absalom spirit likes attention and is consumed with a desire for control. It is independent and bent on self-promotion. Though Absalom feigned genuine concern for the people's problems, his deeper motivation was to undermine his father's authority and to promote himself.

Absalom's Plot

ABSALOM SAT OUTSIDE the city gates declaring his father's neglect of the people and presenting himself as the righteous judge in the land. He received the men of Israel with great affection, kissing their hands and promising them justice. The Scriptures say, "So Absalom stole the hearts of the men of Israel" (2 Sam. 15:6). When he had succeeded in positioning himself in a place of favor with the people, Absalom deceitfully asked permission of his father to let him go to Hebron to make a sacrifice. He intended to proclaim himself king while in Hebron.

The Scriptures declare how deeply this deception affected the people: "And with Absalom went two hundred men out of Jerusalem, that were called; and they went in their simplicity, and they knew not any thing" (2 Sam. 15:11). So complete was his deception that those who followed him did not even realize they were part of a conspiracy against God's anointed leadership.

So today, many naive, innocent, unsuspecting people are seduced into disloyalty to their leadership by this Absalom spirit of betrayal.

The apparent cause of offense between King David and his son Absalom was the earlier murder by Absalom of his half-brother, Amnon. After the murder Absalom lived in exile for several years. Then the king allowed him to return to Jerusalem but refused a face-to-face meeting with his son.

Finally, Absalom persuaded his father to see him. When they met, King David kissed Absalom.

This attempt at reconciliation was not complete, however, for soon after their meeting Absalom began to stand by the palace gates to greet the men of Israel who came to the king with controversies. He maligned his father to them, lamenting that there was no one to hear their matters. He suggested that it would be good if he were appointed to do so—he would bring them justice. Absalom was a prince of flattery and perverted praise, which he used to gain the favor of the people. In this calculating way he gradually stole the hearts of the men of Israel.

Absalom did not undermine his father's authority in one day. There was a long process during which Absalom became openly disloyal and divisive. For forty years he continued to criticize the king and his administration, exalting himself as the righteous man of the hour. He did not bring his disloyalty out into the open until he felt that people were loyal to him and willing to follow him.

His conspiracy was so well thought out and his deception so complete that neither the two hundred men who went with him nor King David suspected any foul play. Perhaps David was blinded by his love for his son. Once he declared himself king at Hebron (2 Sam. 15:10), however, everyone became aware of the dreadful conspiracy that threatened the kingdom. Now the people were forced to make a choice between two leaders: King David, God's anointed leadership, and Absalom, the prince who had deceived them.

Supportive Leadership

THE VERY NATURE of this wicked spirit of betrayal makes church leaders especially vulnerable to its working. Many times this spirit works through associate ministers and other staff members who have served in a church for twenty years or longer. Suddenly these individuals refuse to cooperate with the senior pastor.

Two main causes for their refusal are personal ambition and unresolved offenses. They become discontented in their role as supportive leadership, wanting to be number one, or they fail to resolve little offenses along the way that rise up to become a stronghold in which the enemy can work. Before long they have begun the process of betrayal, spreading their criticism and discontent to those who will listen.

People who are not willing to be led by God's true leadership are vulnerable to this deception. It is easy for an "Absalom" to win their approval of his or her criticism of the leadership. Usually, those who are influenced by the Absalom spirit attempt to usurp the true authority that God has established and set up their own kingdoms. They cannot work alongside God's leadership in a supportive role.

Such wickedness in high places can wreak havoc in the lives of people and in the kingdom of God. Sincere believers must guard against accepting criticism against spiritual leadership, even if it comes from another leader. Do not trust a person simply because of the title or position he or she holds in the church. Be aware of the fruit they produce in their lives and in their relationships. A broken relationship should signal danger, especially when it involves an estrangement from the leader to whom God has given the authority in that church or ministry.

I have sat with pastors who were suffering because of an Absalom betrayal. They lamented: "I trusted him. I would have turned my whole church over to him." This Absalom spirit, energized by unresolved offense and the desire to be number one, has opened many otherwise qualified servants of God to deception. Because they allow themselves to be ruled by the Absalom spirit, their actions bring division and great hurt to the kingdom of God.

Second Fiddle

AN ORCHESTRA LEADER once told me that the hardest chair to fill in the symphony is the second violinist—the "second fiddle." Though it is one of the most important positions in the whole orchestra, having much to do with the precise, harmonious sound of the music, musicians do not appreciate it. They would rather be first chair.

Unfortunately, people in supportive leadership roles in the church sometimes express this sentiment. They plan to stay in their present position only until they get a promotion. The youth pastor, just serving his time while he waits for a better position to come along, wonders why he is not effective with the youth. The young people sense his lack of real concern for them and instinctively do not respect him because of his personal ambition. They want a pastor who cares about them instead of someone who they sense is using them to climb to a higher position.

We need to realize that God appoints people to areas of leadership. He enables them, by His Spirit, to fulfill certain tasks in building His church. If what you are doing now is the will of God for your life, you could do nothing more noble. Whether He has gifted you to be an associate minister, youth pastor, or pianist, you should accept that appointment gratefully and be content in that role. It is a place of anointing and safety.

Some people who hold ministry positions do not want to be accountable to anyone. They refuse to accept counsel or discipline into their lives, intent on having their own ministry. They do not realize that if the ministry is "theirs," it will die and blow away. Ministries that cannot be brought under the leadership of the local church, confirmed by the apostles, prophets, pastors, evangelists, and teachers that God established to guide the church, are not to be trusted. Such so-called ministry may be the result of one person's desire to rule and build his or her own reputation.

I am very grateful for ministers who are comfortable working under another minister's leadership. The test of a true leader is his or her ability to work well with another leader. You cannot truly lead if you are not first willing to be led; you cannot teach if you are not willing to be taught. Those who become offended by serving in supportive roles, or who want to be number one, are vulnerable to deception from the Absalom spirit.

Offense Defined

THE WORD FOR offense in Greek is *skandalon,* from which we derive our word "scandal." It literally means "a trap-stick (bent sapling); a snare; or part of a trap set with bait to catch its victim."[1] Satan uses offense as a bait to trap us and bring us into captivity to the sins of anger, outrage, jealousy, envy, resentment, strife, bitterness, hatred, and even murder. Nursing those offenses produces the fruit of a critical spirit, insulting and wounding attitudes, divisiveness, backsliding, and betrayal.

Offended people can be divided into two categories: those who have been treated unjustly and those who perceive they have been treated unjustly. People in the second category are convinced they have been wronged. Though their conclusions may be drawn from inaccurate information, their misunderstanding brings on the same pangs of offense as are suffered by people who have actually been wronged.

The fruit of unresolved offense develops progressively. It begins with hurt and anger, but soon develops into hatred. It can even express itself ultimately in murder. The violence we are witnessing in the world today is evidence of the fruit of offense. It can be seen in spouse abuse and murder; domestic violence; family violence with sons and daughters killing parents and siblings killing siblings; and even in rape and incest.

Unresolved offense leads to bitterness; bitterness leads to hatred; hatred leads to wrath; and wrath often leads to murder.

Causes of Offense

Too often the cause of offense resides in our own minds. The world's mentality asserts, "My rights!" and desires to get even with those who violate them. Our pride seeks its own exaltation and refuses to forgive those who do not give us the recognition we deserve. That spirit shuts out heaven and brings deception to our hearts. If we indulge those attitudes, it won't be long until we convince ourselves that people are against us and we are justified in our criticism of them.

We also can be offended by the tests and trials of life that God allows. Unless we respond correctly, difficult circumstances that cause pain will offend. God develops His character in us through trials and tests. We will not always like the process that is required to make us Christlike. But as we submit willingly to the dealings of God we will be freed from our offended attitudes. As forgiveness works in us, the love of God will be "shed abroad in our hearts by the Holy Ghost which is given unto us" (Rom. 5:5).

Offense in the Church

Offense may be the strongest weapon the enemy uses to divide the church. According to Jesus, we cannot live in this world without experiencing offense. He declared: "It is impossible but that offenses will come: but woe unto him, through whom they come!" (Luke 17:1). Though we are promised that offenses will come, it is not the offense itself, but our reaction to it, that determines our future.

There are no walls that we can build against offense so that we will never be hurt. God will help us to respond correctly when offenses come. As we put aside our pride, we can humbly forgive those who offend us. God can change hurtful situations into blessings that will result in godly character, making us more humble and less self-centered.

Jesus said, "And blessed is he, whosoever shall not be offended in me" (Luke 7:23). Though we would not admit readily to being offended with Jesus, to nurse offense against His people is to be offended with Him. It is vital to walk in forgiveness with our brothers and sisters in Christ, keeping short accounts, so that we will not be ensnared by the devastating consequences of nursing offense. Jesus lives in the hearts of our brothers and sisters. The Scriptures tell us, "Inasmuch as ye have done it unto one of the least of these my brethren, ye have done it unto me" (Matt. 25:40).

Biblical Response to Offense

THE OLD TESTAMENT records the history of Joseph, the favorite son of Jacob, who was mistreated by his brothers, thrown into a pit, and sold into slavery. He spent some of the best years of his life in exile from his family and country, and then suffered an unjust imprisonment. Yet he did not harbor offense or nurse a grudge against his brothers. He forgave them and declared that it was God who had allowed his "misfortune" so that he could help to save their lives in the end (Gen. 45:5).

He didn't know God was preparing him for rulership. He didn't know that these circumstances were ordained to shape his character. But he submitted to the will of God in every situation and enjoyed the presence of God in his life.

Jesus clearly taught us how to be reconciled to someone who has offended us. (See Matthew 18.) We must be willing to communicate with the offender, going to them in a conciliatory attitude to be reconciled. We dare not suppress hurt feelings, for those feelings will develop into hatred. In our homes, marriage partners need to resolve offenses quickly. The Word of God instructs, "Let not the sun go down upon your wrath" (Eph. 4:26). Following this admonition will keep us from nursing grudges until they grow into hatred and lead to divorce.

The apostle Paul gives a beautiful revelation of love that is free from unresolved offense:

> Love is patient, love is kind, and is not jealous; love does not brag and is not arrogant, does not act unbecomingly; it does not seek its own, is not provoked, does not take into account a wrong suffered.
>
> —1 CORINTHIANS 13:4–5, NAS

According to the Scriptures, the way to get over offense is to show love to the offender. That is why Jesus taught us to love our enemies. He knew the good it would do for us, setting us free from the trap of offense, as well as affecting our enemies' lives for good.[2]

Proper Perspective

A PROPER PERSPECTIVE will enable a believer to walk through a trial victoriously. Proclaim: "Satan, you think you laid a trap for me, but it won't catch me. Without my Father's permission, this trial would not have happened. He permitted it, even if He didn't promote it. He knew I would make it through victoriously if I walked with Him. And He also knew I would be more like Him when the trial was over."

Jesus was rejected, spat upon, and called by evil names. He was forsaken by the men He loved the most. They deserted Him in the time of His greatest trial. Judas betrayed Him, Peter denied Him, and they all forsook Him. If we desire to be like Jesus, we must respond to our painful situations as He did to His. Though He was mistreated, He never became offended.

Only our wrong attitudes, reactions, and refusal to forgive will hinder God's working in our lives. No person or situation can take us out of the will of God.

Absalom in the Church

WE HAVE SEEN how unresolved offense can lead to serious sin. It can open us to the deception of the Absalom spirit of betrayal. As Absalom stole the hearts of the men of Israel, so these flatterers learn to speak in such a way in the church that unsuspecting Christians begin to admire them. This admiration produces a spiritual pride in the deceived "Absaloms," who begin to believe they are more spiritual than their leaders.

Then a competitive spirit takes over, and "Absalom" begins to misrepresent the decisions of the leadership and the direction they are taking. He (or she) sows strife and division and draws a group of people to himself. His followers feed off his critical spirit.

After that, a bold conspiracy arises. The "Absalom" justifies the actions of his group by focusing on the minor issues with which he found fault in the leadership. Usually his accusations are not related to false doctrine or blatant sin within the leadership. Rather he magnifies the imperfections or human traits of the leader.

Soon "Absalom" leads a naive splinter group out to start a new church built on the foundation of offense. Since it is not built on the right foundation it cannot prosper. If the root of a tree is bad, the whole tree will be bad. So it is with every church that is founded on an Absalom spirit. It will be full of rebellion and disloyalty and will suffer continual church splits. God's judgment is on the rebellious church.

Testimony of Fellowship Restored

I KNOW A minister who became the pastor of a church in California that seemed dead to the presence of God. No matter how they changed their worship, or how he preached, the Lord did not move among the people. This pastor determined to find the cause for the lack of God's presence in the church.

One night, while meeting with the board of the church, the pastor asked, "Can you tell me how this church was founded?"

"Why do you need to know that?" the chairman of the board asked.

"I want to know why God's presence is not here. There must be something wrong in the church," he replied. "Do you know how this church was birthed?"

The board replied that the church began as a split from another church more than twenty years earlier. They related that the mother church now had a new pastor, different leadership, and many new members who were not even aware of the history of the church split.

"But we cannot expect to experience the presence of God in our church until we reconcile this long-standing offense," my pastor friend responded.

Taking the board of the church with him, this pastor went to the pastor of the mother church. "You don't know us or our history," he stated. "But our church began as a split off your church. We have come to be reconciled with your church and to forgive the long-standing offenses between these churches."

The pastors and board members of these two churches prayed

together and established a bond of love and fellowship with each other. After that simple confession and act of reconciliation, God's presence returned to my friend's church as the Holy Spirit began to move among the people.

A Warning

GOD SPOKE A startling message to me one night as I was ministering in a church in North Carolina. He declared, "I will not, I will not, I will not allow anyone who touches My plan, My program, My prophets, or My prophecy to be a part of, or participate in, the next move of God."

I immediately recognized the General Epistle of Jude in outline form in that statement. He had mentioned four of the seven steps that led the church into apostasy. I realized that there are sins committed against God that are much worse than sins we commit against our fellowman. It is not a light matter to be involved in criticism or betrayal of an anointed servant of God.

The End of Absalom

WHEN WE TRY to overthrow God's purposes by touching God's anointed leadership we can expect to suffer the consequences. Absalom suffered a humiliating and untimely death, while King David was restored to his throne as the rightful king. God's true anointed leadership, though not perfect, will triumph over the Absalom spirit as these anointed leaders place themselves in God's hands as King David did. As believers and supportive leadership, we need to guard our hearts so that we are not guilty of harboring personal ambition or unresolved offense that will deceive us and make us vulnerable to the Absalom spirit. And we need to guard our relationships, not allowing anyone to undermine God's leadership by criticism. Otherwise, we could become a part of Absalom's tragic end.

We need to be prepared to guard our hearts and relationships against the attack of Absalom. But we must set a guard around our very minds as the enemy offers to open them to freedom and instead causes great harm and emotional bondage to those who fall victim to the spirit of pseudo-counseling.

6

The Spirit of Pseudo-Counseling

Destroying the Believers

A FOURTH ATTACK AGAINST the church came in the form of a pseudo-counseling spirit. This spirit has invaded the church from the secular world and is the most detrimental force I have ever seen claim to be Christian. Raising its head in many of our charismatic churches, as well as in other denominations, it is a humanistic counseling approach for what is called post-traumatic memory syndrome. I have personally witnessed the tragic results of this form of counseling, watching it wreck homes, destroy family relationships, and split churches.

I believe in spiritual counseling. I believe God places people in churches to counsel. A true counselor is one who knows the Counselor—our Lord Jesus—and who is guided by the Holy Spirit. A counselor who knows the Word of God, functions in the spiritual gifts of knowledge and wisdom, and follows the direction of the Holy Spirit will give sound counsel. Any other source of counsel should not be trusted.

Counterfeit Spiritual Counsel

COUNSELING FOR post-traumatic memory syndrome has found its way into the church counseling chamber. I have personally talked with pastors and other people who have been victims of this counseling approach, often perpetrated upon them by unqualified counselors.

Using this approach, someone sitting under the banner of "Christian counselor" suggests false ideas and accusations to the person they are counseling regarding something someone has done to them in the past. These accusations later work on that person's power of recall until he (or she) "remembers" the past negative circumstance the counselor suggested, believing it is coming from his own memory. It is projected to the counselee's memory initially by the counselor, then retrieved from the counselee as fact.

The negative circumstance in his memory is then blamed for his present emotional problems. The counselee is instructed to face his offender, telling that person how the remembered offense has damaged his psyche and caused his present unhappy emotional state.

I understand that there has been much child abuse, molestation, and other evil perpetrated on the young. But I believe this type of counseling is not the answer to help someone cope with those past problems, real or imagined.

When I went to prayer and asked my Father about this extreme counseling approach, He gave me one sentence that satisfied my spirit. He said, "My daughter, if Calvary—the death of My Son—satisfied the heart of God regarding sin, why will it not satisfy the mind of man?"

The power of Jesus' blood is just as real today as it was the day He died. He is the only One who can transform us and heal us from the negative consequences of our sinful nature and past hurts. If the efficacious, vicarious, mediatorial, substitutionary work of Calvary is not enough to redeem us from our sins and heal our psyches, we have no other remedy.

These Christian pseudo-counselors say by their actions that the blood of Calvary isn't the whole answer for redemption. They believe the church does not offer what we need for complete spiritual healing. Though psychology has discovered some principles that can be helpful in understanding problems, my concern is when psychological counseling discovers the problem but denies the remedy found only in Christ. The psyche cannot restore itself. The Scriptures declare that God gives a sound mind, a supernatural work of redemption. Those who defend this extreme form of counseling insist their spiritual counseling can take a person back into the womb or to a childhood experience that is having an emotional effect on that person today. Yet, if they fail to bring that person to the cross of Christ, they are powerless to effect healing in that life.

I know a woman who suffered greatly at the hands of such a counselor. Her counselor said her emotional problems were caused by her father, who had molested her when she was too young to remember. My friend had a godly father who could not have conceived of such wickedness against his daughter. Yet, believing the counselor's conclusion, this woman went to her father's home to "resolve" this offense.

When she told her godly father that she had discovered his molestation of her as a child, he stared at her in disbelief. Shortly after her announcement to him of his "offense," he dropped dead. The shock of such a wicked accusation coming from his daughter had killed him.

That is only one illustration of the destruction this ungodly counseling spirit has caused. Where counseling for post-traumatic memory syndrome has been practiced in churches, it has created divisions and resulted in church splits. I know of a church in Dallas, one of the best churches in this country, where three hundred people walked out as a result of being deceived by this pseudo-counseling. Church leaders taught that the blood of Christ and the cross were not sufficient to cleanse sins of the past.

"Self" Heresy

I ATTENDED A recent conference of pastors and leaders who spent hours sharing the damage this pseudo-counseling spirit had done in their churches. The whole premise for this type of counseling is rooted in the humanistic philosophy that mankind is basically good—it is the bad things that happen to us that make us miserable. Psychologists have done their best to get us to esteem, love, and honor ourselves. The result of this humanistic teaching is a "self" heresy. It has created a doctrine in the church today that is elevating self.

Christians who offer counseling for post-traumatic memory syndrome reject the doctrine of sanctification, which teaches us to bring our self-life to the cross and exchange it for the life of Christ. In this way, they exchange the cross of Christ for the "couch."

Jesus taught us that if we want to follow Him, we must deny self and take up our cross (Matt. 16:24). The Scriptures clearly teach us to exchange our self-life with its carnal thinking, warped emotions, and rebellious wills for the new life we find in Christ. We are to take up our crosses daily so that we can learn to walk in newness of life. Deliverance from the sinful self-life will come by choosing the cross. Just listening to counsel—even godly counsel—won't do it.

It is true that we are to love ourselves, for Jesus taught us to love our neighbors as we love ourselves. But self-absorption—the inevitable result of "self" heresy—keeps us from loving our neighbors. To love ourselves in a godly sense means we will place our carnal self-life on the cross of Calvary. We will seek help from Christians who minister to us through the anointing of the Holy Spirit and the Word of

God. We will find deliverance from our sinfulness through the blood of Jesus. As the Christ-life flows through us it will set us free to love others.

Calvary settles it all. We don't have to go around with bandages on our minds or emotions for fifteen years after we are saved. Children wear bandages to get attention. I believe some immature Christians look for someone else who will agree with their complaint because they think the church doesn't give them enough attention or meet their needs. They are not serious about bringing their need to the cross to find deliverance. Such immature conduct makes them vulnerable targets for the pseudo-counselor.

As we mature in God we will discover that our own needs for attention are met as we learn to meet the needs of others. Growing up in Christ will keep us from being victims of the pseudo-counselor's false pity, which brings destruction rather than healing to our souls.

God Forgets

As I KNELT one night by a little girl who was repenting of her sins and receiving Jesus as her Savior, I said, "Honey, your sins have just been forgiven. Never again will God ever remember your sins."

Then I added one more sentence that the church world often says: "Satan may drag up your sins," I continued, "but God will never remember them against you anymore."

In that moment my heavenly Father rebuked me.

"Daughter," I heard my Father say, "when did the devil become omniscient? How does the devil know what I can't remember? If I forgot it, what makes you think his memory exceeds Mine?" As I listened He continued firmly, "Furthermore, how can he put his hands beneath the precious blood of Jesus? I put the sins of a repentant sinner under the blood, blotting them out forever. The devil cannot touch them—you are in error!"

Recognizing my error, I replied, "Yes, Lord."

"But you have a question?" He continued.

"Yes, I do," I answered. "Why do we remember our own sins?"

"If My people would learn to keep their mouths shut about their past sins," my Father responded, "the devil wouldn't have so much information to feed back to them."

Too often we talk about what we used to do and discuss the past of others. By doing this we inform the devil, giving him a weapon to hurl at us—the memory of our sins. By God's grace we can push the "delete memory" button and replace the past with Paul's admonition:

"Whatsoever things are true, whatsoever things are honest, whatsoever things are just, whatsoever things are pure, whatsoever things are lovely, whatsoever things are of good report; if there be any virtue, and if there be any praise, think on these things" (Phil. 4:8).

The End of the Pseudo-Counseling Spirit

> But when He, the Spirit of truth, comes, He will guide you into all the truth; for He will not speak on His own initiative, but whatever He hears, He will speak; and He will disclose to you what is to come.
>
> —John 16:13, NAS

When He—the blessed Holy Spirit—is come, we have no need for ungodly counselors anymore.

There is a Comforter—a divine Helper, the blessed Holy Spirit—who speaks healing to our past in a moment. It doesn't take Him ten sessions to dig up our past. By yielding to His supernatural work of cleansing, we will be truly delivered, set free to love and serve God. Do not be deceived by the pseudo-counseling spirit. As we yield to the Holy Spirit's work of redemption and to the ministry of a godly counselor when needed, we will find the healing and restoration we need to serve effectively in the body of Christ.

But there remains one more enemy to defeat. And this one has targeted the destruction of the life of Christ within the church.

7

The Pharisaical Spirit

Hostility That Kills

THE LAST ATTACK against the church that we have seen comes through the pharisaical spirit. This spirit is filled with a deadly hostility. The pharisaical spirit killed Abel, crucified Jesus, stoned Stephen, and tried to do away with Paul. Its target is still the life of Christ, and it will try to destroy the Christ-life that dwells within believers today.

By nature the pharisaical spirit hates the grace of God but loves legalism. The Pharisees rejected Jesus as He preached the good news of the gospel to the poor. Though He was the chief cornerstone on which God was building His kingdom, they rejected Him for their own interpretation of the Old Testament and for their religious traditions. Through these traditions, while receiving the praise of men they could manipulate and control the lives of people for their own benefit.

When they tried to judge Jesus according to their traditions, He challenged the legalism they held so dear. Upholding their laws was more important to them than building a relationship with the living Word. Jesus Christ—the only hope for true salvation—became a stumbling block to them. Salvation that was freely given would rob them of the satisfaction of earning their reward through legalistic rituals.

Simeon prophesied of their dilemma when he held the baby Jesus in his arms in the temple: "Behold, this child is set for the fall and rising again of many in Israel; and for a sign which shall be spoken against" (Luke 2:34). The Prince of Peace, sent to reconcile the world to Himself, brought a sword of division to those to whom He was sent—the house of Israel (Matt. 15:24). They loved their darkness and refused to come to the light.

Jesus' miracles threatened the Pharisees' popularity and power with the people, for they could not do what He did. Jesus revealed a gospel of love and forgiveness, but the Pharisees required obedience to rules that superseded the Scriptures and insisted their rules were the only way to righteousness. Theirs was a salvation by works—Jesus offered salvation through repentance, worship, and a personal relationship with Him.

The Pharisee and Worship

THE PHARISAICAL SPIRIT militates against true worship and relationship with God. But Jesus warned them: "Woe unto you . . . Pharisees, hypocrites! For ye shut up the kingdom of heaven against men, for ye neither go in yourselves, neither suffer ye them that are entering to go in" (Matt. 23:13). Worship was the central issue the first time the pharisaical spirit was manifested. Adam's son, Cain, the first murderer in the world, manifested a pharisaical spirit toward his brother, Abel.

Cain became angry with Abel when God accepted Abel's offering of worship but did not accept his own. The New Testament tells us, "By faith Abel offered unto God a more excellent sacrifice than Cain, by which he obtained witness that he was righteous" (Heb. 11:4). Cain hated Abel because his righteousness was accepted by God.

God spoke to Cain, asking him why he was angry and assuring him that if he did well, he would be accepted. He told him also that if he did not do well, sin was lying at the door. (See Genesis 4:3–7.) God gave Cain an opportunity to repent, but Cain persisted in his own way and hated his brother, who had pleased God.

That first murder was typical of the Pharisees' desire to kill Jesus, the Righteous One. The Pharisees hated Jesus because they had made an idol of religion and had rejected the true righteousness of the Scriptures. Jesus said to them: "You search the Scriptures, because you think that in them you have eternal life; and it is these that bear witness of Me; and you are unwilling to come to Me, that you may have life" (John 5:39–40, NAS). They preferred honor from one another and rule by their traditions to the life that Jesus offered them.

Jesus was tolerant of sinners who came to Him, but He had no tolerance for the Pharisee. The Pharisees and doctors of the law were the only ones for whom He did not have one kind word. He didn't bless them—He pronounced woe upon them, calling them whited sepulchres and murderers like their father, the devil (Matt. 23:27; John 8:44). His evaluation proved to be correct, for they were the ones who later crucified Him. Pilate, a pagan ruler, observed "that for envy" they had condemned Jesus to death (Matt. 27:17–18).

Pharisaical Spirit in the Church

PEOPLE WHO ARE ruled by a pharisaical spirit today love the praises of men. They are very concerned about position and honor. They insist on ruling over people with their traditions and laws. They are not impressed with the humble way that Jesus came, healing the sick and feeding the multitudes. They are content to receive glory to themselves for their feigned righteousness.

The pharisaical spirit is one of the greatest abominations that has ever invaded the church. It masquerades as "superspiritual." There is no such thing as superspiritual—for no one can have too much of God. But there are many people who have too much of religion. To be "super-religious" is not the same as being spiritual. Those who allow the nature of Christ to be seen in their lives are truly spiritual.

As with the other five spirits mentioned earlier, people who are ruled by a pharisaical spirit despise authority and true leadership. They are too "spiritual" to be corrected. These religious people do not want to be planted in a local church. They cannot flow in unity with God's anointed leadership. They exalt their own opinions and become bitter, critical, and censorious of others. They live as an island unto themselves, exalting themselves above the humble spirit of our Lord.

The intent of the pharisaical spirit is to kill the Christ-life in each one of us. The first place to look for this spirit is within our own self-life. We resist the idea that our flesh is religious. But without the fullness of the Christ-life in us, it is simply human nature to be religious. But as we humble ourselves to receive the Word of God joyfully, we will learn to guard against the characteristics of the pharisaical spirit we are describing.

In church life, the pharisaical spirit seeks the "chief seats" (Matt. 23:6). This spirit tries to take preeminence, defying the humble Christ-like spirit. It will seek attention one way or another. Although it can't crucify Christ again, it will try to keep Him from living in the church. Its motivation is to put to death the Christ-life wherever it is found. I would rather deal with the most degraded sinner than have someone pharisaical in my church.

"Thy Word Is Truth"

THE ENEMY AND his evil spirits were waging a battle to keep God's truth from the people when the Lord Himself walked the earth. That battle has continued down through history even to this day. Satan's attempt to keep the Word of God out of the hands of the common people was the great spiritual battleground of the Reformation. Satan knows that revelation of God's Word to our hearts will result in his overthrow as the prince of the air. For this reason the Lord declared that the poor would have the gospel preached to them (Matt. 11:5). As they receive Him they are set free from the tyranny of the devil and the power of sin.

Today, many spiritual leaders cannot respond to the Word of God because they are bound by their own doctrines and traditions. Radical obedience to the Word is required in order to release the living waters from which revival springs. True revival is a revolution against the prevailing principalities and powers of the enemy. The pharisaical spirit is Satan's most powerful weapon in this battle, masquerading as the protector of legitimate truth.

The Pharisees were given primary responsibility for maintaining the integrity of the written Word through centuries of copying and recopying. We owe them much for their diligence. But in their zeal to protect the Scriptures from abuse, the Pharisees implemented a system of interpretation based more on their own traditions than on the actual text. Their love of these traditions caused them to reject and even persecute the One who was the personified Word of God.

The pharisaical spirit esteems the written Word above the living Word. It worships the Book of the Lord instead of the Lord of the Book.

The modern counterparts of the Pharisees of Jesus' day still try to protect the Scriptures from doctrinal abuse. In their zeal they have created an intricate system of interpretation that may serve as some protection for the integrity of their doctrine, but it also limits radically any further revelation for those who want to obey the truth. They fight for the truth yet miss the moving of the Holy Spirit during revival because His revelation transcends their doctrinal understanding.

Everyone who loves the truth desires sound doctrine also. Sound doctrine, though important, is not meant to be an end in itself. Adopting such a position results in arguments among brethren and divisions in the body of Christ. Sound doctrine is meant to teach us how to be conformed to the image of Christ. It enables us to determine the will of God so that we can obey Him.

When we stand before the judgment seat of Christ, we will be judged according to our relationship with Jesus and for our service to Him—not according to how accurate our doctrine was. Our motivation, attitudes, and availability to the will of God are the criteria by which we will be judged.

It is possible to memorize the entire Bible and still not know the truth. Truth is a Person. The Pharisees loved the Scriptures more than they loved the God of the Scriptures. Many today fall prey to this same deception. We cannot love God without loving His Word. But it is possible to elevate the written Word above God Himself, making an idol out of the Scriptures. If that happens, we allow the Scriptures to supplant our relationship with God.

Personal relationship—this priceless gift of the Lord to His people—is the truth that will set us free from the bondage of legalism. Christians should search the Scriptures to find the God of the Scriptures. One of the greatest tragedies today is that we read into the Word according to a doctrine or tradition that someone has taught us, instead of reading out what the Holy Spirit wants to reveal to us.

The End of the Pharisee

JESUS HIMSELF DECLARED the end of the Pharisees in the great Magna Carta of the gospel—the Beatitudes. He warned:

> For I say unto you, That except your righteousness shall exceed the righteousness of the scribes and Pharisees, ye shall in no case enter into the kingdom of heaven.
>
> —MATTHEW 5:20

The pharisaical spirit will never enter the kingdom of heaven. We must guard our hearts against this wicked spirit or lose the kingdom of God.

Jesus condemned the Pharisees publicly, crying:

> Woe unto you, scribes and Pharisees, hypocrites! For ye shut up the kingdom of heaven against men: for ye neither go in yourselves, neither suffer ye them that are entering to go in.
>
> —MATTHEW 23:13

It was the pharisaical spirit that killed Jesus. That same spirit is determined to destroy the Christ who lives in you. The church cannot coexist with it. As a Spirit-filled believer, stand and declare boldly, "His house will be a house of prayer, purity, and holiness! I command you, pharisaical spirit, to get out! You will not rule my church. I will not give you a place of leadership here!"

We do not have to be victims of this deception if we choose to submit to the truth of God in obedience to His will.

A Glorious Church

NONE OF THESE deceiving spirits that invade the church will be victorious in the end. That's good news! As we yield to the Spirit of God and refuse to compromise we will not be vulnerable to any of these five marauding spirits at work in our world today. God is faithful to reveal His truth to our hearts and deliver us from these evils.

God will have a glorious church without spot or wrinkle—a beautiful bride for His Son. It is time for the church to come out of the cave, into the light of day. As she emerges, she is going to be different from who she was when she went into the cave. Her heart will have been circumcised from the love of the world and of self and will be filled with love for God alone. The church will fulfill His purposes in the earth as He comes to fill her with His glory.

Set free from her cave experience, the church will then be ready to overcome the external hindrances to revival.

8

Hindering Concepts to Revival

Cleansing the Church

As I HAVE waited expectantly for the revival God showed me in my vision of 1963, the Holy Spirit has deeply impressed upon me that the church needs cleansing from at least five hindering concepts in order to be a part of the coming revival.

Denominationalism

A DENOMINATION IS a class or society of individuals supporting a system of principles and called by the same name. As long as a denomination remains open to the life of Jesus, it is not harmful. It can be an instrument of God. But, when denominational doctrines are taught with dogmatic finality, greater streams of truth that would flow through it are limited.

Elitism, legalism, and judgmental attitudes almost always result from such dogma. Such denominationalism, established upon man's ideologies and dogmas, obscures the true church that Christ is building.

The purpose of a denomination is the same as that of scaffolding that is erected during a building process. But, scaffolding was not designed to obscure permanently the structure being built. When that happens, it has lost its useful purpose and become a hindrance. It needs to be removed in order for the real building to be seen. For the life of Christ to be seen in the church, the scaffolding of denominationalism must be removed.

I recall the words of God during my vision of the hydroelectric plant. When God was ready to pull the switch that would bring revival, He declared, "This time, no man, no devil, no demon, and no denomination will ever dam it up again." We can surely anticipate this wonderful liberty through which the truth of God will flow.

Human Tradition

WEBSTER DEFINES *TRADITION* as "an inherited, established, or customary pattern of thought, action, or behavior; the handing down of information, beliefs, and customs by word of mouth or by example from one generation to another without written instruction."[1]

The Pharisees asked Jesus, "Why do thy disciples transgress the tradition of the elders? For they wash not their hands when they eat bread" (Matt. 15:2). Tradition was more important to them than the Word of God.

Jesus was critical of and even repudiated the oral tradition, concluding that the oral decrees of the elders were wholly of human origin (Mark 7:6–13). And Paul declared that he was more exceedingly zealous of the traditions of his fathers until "it pleased God...to reveal his Son in me" (Gal. 1:14–16). He was delivered from devout loyalty to an intense religious system when Christ was revealed in him.

Because man's carnal mind has interpreted many of the Scriptures in the church today, the Holy Spirit, the divine Teacher who wrote the Book, has not been allowed to reveal truth to our spirits. As a result we have developed religious practices that are "comfort zones" to our church mentality. Failing in "rightly dividing" the Word of God (2 Tim. 2:15), we have instead read it according to the instruction of men.

Peter reminds us that we "were not redeemed with perishable things like silver and gold, from your futile way of life inherited from your forefathers" (1 Pet. 1:18, NAS). Tradition is not the source of our redemption—the Word of God is. The Spirit of Truth will teach us what truth means and will deliver us from religious tradition. God's Word is the final "yea and amen." It alone will be fulfilled to the letter as God intended.

I believe God is creating in the hearts of believers a new hunger and thirst for His Word. As we search the Scriptures and seek God with all our hearts, He has promised to satisfy our hunger and quench our thirst. Revelation will increase as we find Him as our wisdom. Then the true church will emerge, filled with the life-giving waters of the Holy Spirit.

Prejudice

UNREASONABLE BIASES, JUDGMENTS, or opinions, held in disregard of facts, breed suspicion, intolerance, or hatred; they have no place in Christ's church. Whether it is against race, gender, sect, class, or status, prejudice will keep us from hearing and receiving the truth of God as revealed by the Holy Spirit.

Paul declared that "after that faith is come," in Christ our prejudicial distinctions do not exist (Gal. 3:25, 28). He admonished Timothy "that you guard and keep [these rules] without personal prejudice or favor, doing nothing from partiality" (1 Tim 5:21, AMP).

In his christological epistles, Paul teaches us to live in an attitude of humility; esteeming one another above ourselves; loving one another fervently; and looking out for the interests of others.[2] In his great love chapter he defines God's love as longsuffering, kind, and seeking not its own (1 Cor. 13). This is a picture of the true church of Christ, delivered from the destructive power of prejudice.

Culture

PERHAPS NOTHING IS more basic to our natural thinking than culture—the concepts, habits, arts, institutions, and refinements of thought, manners, and taste that characterize our native environment. These traits seem "right" to us. That is why some missionaries have exported more culture than Christ-life as they have attempted to conform others to their own lifestyle.

We have to be delivered from our bondage to culture in order to allow Christ to move in us and through us to any culture. He brings a new and higher way of life that transcends the limitations of culture. He will help us establish a lifestyle within our individual cultures that is free from the sins of those cultures.

Many of Paul's teachings addressed issues of culture. He taught the necessity of moving our spiritual focus from the external cultural issues to the greater moral and ethical issues of our heart attitudes toward God, our fellowman, and ourselves. Living godly lives in a sinful culture was difficult for Christians in Paul's day, as it is in our world. People were often more concerned with externals than with true issues of godly character and motivation.

As we learn to embrace a lifestyle without compromise with the external, we will be able to live a godly life in our sinful cultures. We can learn to live *in* this world without being part *of* it. Then we will be salt and light to those around us.

Purity of heart will establish godly priorities in every area of life as God's kingdom of righteousness, peace, and joy in the Holy Ghost comes to us (Rom. 14:17).

Customs

A CUSTOM IS "a long-established practice considered as unwritten law; a uniform practice by common consent of a society to such an extent that it has taken on the force of the law."[3] Such customs are enforced by social disapproval of any violation.

Christ has freed us from the tyranny of men's external standards of righteousness and has put within us His standard of righteousness through the work of the Holy Spirit. Paul's letter to the Galatian church denounces the Jews who were trying to add their customs as requirements for salvation. They were more comfortable with external codes of living than with faith in Christ, without which there is no salvation.

Today, we often find ourselves caught up in some legalistic custom we believe is necessary to our salvation. Some churches depend on a certain form of dress or religious rite that is performed regularly to ensure their righteousness. Entire religious systems have been developed around external rituals that in effect deny the sacrifice of Jesus. But, to place our trust in these religious customs negates the power of Christ's sacrifice on Calvary to effect our salvation (Gal. 2:21). Unless we place our trust in the death and resurrection of Christ for our salvation, and that of the world, we have no hope of being saved.

The power of that salvation will be nullified if we add anything to it. Wherever the church has inadvertently included demands of custom as criteria for the Christ-life, it must repent and return to complete faith in the work of Calvary.

The Holy Spirit is faithful to speak truth to us as we open our hearts to hear Him. He was sent to guide us into all truth (John 16:13). We need not fear or despair that we will not know how to be delivered from our wrong thinking. As we listen to the Holy Spirit and allow Him to convict and cleanse us, we will be prepared to be a part of the great revival that is coming.

The next move of God will not be like the Charismatic Renewal we have known in the past years. It will restore to the church many things that the Charismatic Renewal did not restore. Yet we need to be grateful for the things that renewal brought, as we allow the Holy Spirit to teach us what is yet to come.

Part 3

The Charismatic Renewal and the Next Move of God

9

The Charismatic Renewal

Blessings Restored

THROUGHOUT CHURCH HISTORY there have been great visitations of the Holy Spirit that have restored wonderful truths to the church, changed thousands of lives, and often spawned new denominations. These supernatural visitations are seasons when God reveals Himself to people with hungry hearts and establishes them in the realities of redemptive truths. As the church learns to walk in new realms of truth, the Holy Spirit enlarges her capacity to receive greater revelation of God. Thus once again He visits His people, bringing still new revelation of Himself.

Our generation received an outpouring of the Holy Spirit that swept through many denominations, baptizing thousands of believers in the Holy Spirit. Some people have called this visitation from God the Charismatic Movement. But it was not a move of God—it was a *renewal.* No significant new truth was restored to the church during the Charismatic Renewal as in other historical moves of God. Truths already present in the church such as the baptism of the Holy Spirit, however, were more firmly established across wider lines of religious thought, which helped to remove denominational barriers for many Christians.

Now, more than thirty years after the Charismatic Renewal began, some are inclined to speak lightly of that visitation of God, and others are even unkind in their attitudes toward it. They point to some negative results they have seen and, instead of evaluating it fairly, denounce it entirely. Though the Charismatic Renewal did sweep up some debris, as is typical of any wave of God, its effect on the church was very positive. It brought blessings to the church that were badly needed.

When a river floods its banks and the waters rush out of control, debris is carried along and washed up on dry ground. Whatever is situated in the middle of the river will experience the exhilaration of being swept along by the power of the flood. But whatever sloshes along in the muck and mire along the edge will end up with mud all over it.

So it is when God visits His people in a way that overwhelms our finite minds—we may not always interpret accurately everything an omnipotent God does. Though we do not understand completely, we may choose to enjoy the sweeping flood of God's presence by staying in the middle of the flowing waters. Or we may choose to concentrate on the debris by becoming critical of the work of God. Every time there has been a visitation of God throughout church history, there also has been some controversial debris surrounding the work of God. The Charismatic Renewal was no exception.

When God showed the prophet Ezekiel the healing waters of revival, he saw waters ankle deep, knee deep, waters to the loins, and waters to swim in. (See Ezekiel 47.) The good swimmer enjoys the deep water and is not concerned with the debris the waters might be sweeping up along the bank. So it is that Christians who choose to seek the deeper things of God will have a different perspective from those who are easily contented close to shore.

Those who enjoyed the waters of the Charismatic Renewal received great benefit from the good things it brought to their lives and to the church.

The Charismatic Renewal was a true visitation of God and came in the timing of God. Thousands were swept into the fullness of the baptism of the Holy Spirit. I was brought in as a Methodist professor and minister along with many other denominational people. I thank God for His visitation during those years of renewal that established the church in important truths. The church would not have been ready for the coming next move of God had we not experienced the waters of the Charismatic Renewal.

There were several areas of truth that were strengthened in the church during the years of the Charismatic Renewal.

Recognition of Spiritual Gifts

BEFORE THE CHARISMATIC Renewal, many denominations, and even some Pentecostal churches, had "muzzled" the mouth of the Holy Spirit, not allowing Him to manifest the gifts of the Spirit in the church. Some churches who professed to be Spirit-filled had relegated the moving of the Spirit to the basement. Not wanting to offend anyone during their liturgical Sunday morning services, they allowed the manifestation of the gifts of tongues or prophecy to be given only in a Wednesday night service in the basement when nobody but the "family" was present. Thus, in essence they were telling the Holy Ghost, "You can't do anything when we have visitors. Wait 'til nobody is here but us."

Since the Charismatic Renewal there has been a greater recognition of spiritual gifts in the church. Even some denominations that have not accepted the gift of tongues are inviting Spirit-filled ministers to teach their congregations about spiritual gifts. As these sincere Christians open their hearts to the working of the Holy Spirit, He may slip in on them—as He did on me—the gift of tongues, also.

The Holy Spirit didn't ask my opinion on tongues. He just baptized me. I found myself speaking in tongues. Then He declared, as Peter declared on the day of Pentecost, "This is that which was spoken by the prophet Joel..." (Acts 2:16).

The day God baptized me in His Holy Spirit with the evidence of speaking in other tongues, He also healed me from a genetic bone disease that the doctors believed to be life threatening. I did not ask for the baptism in the Holy Spirit because I thought I already had it. My theological viewpoint caused me to believe that speaking in tongues was for weak-minded or emotional people. I thought I was too intelligent for such an experience. Frankly, I was too dumb.

So the Lord arranged desperate circumstances that made me cry out to Him. He knew my heart wanted Him, even though my head didn't understand His ways. He baptized me in the Holy Spirit, and I spoke in other tongues even though I hadn't believed in it with my head.

From that experience I realized how little I knew of God's ways. The Holy Spirit became my faithful Teacher. He began to teach me the Word of God by revelation, and He has not stopped to this day. I am one of many sincere denominational believers who received a fullness of the Spirit during the Charismatic Renewal. I thank God that He overruled our theology and brought us to the scriptural recognition of spiritual gifts.

Faith

IT IS UNFORTUNATE that some charismatic teachers have swung the pendulum of faith too far, teaching a hyper-faith doctrine. But the

Charismatic Renewal brought a desperately needed, new dimension of faith to the church. Many Christians had a passive faith. They thought God *could*, but didn't believe He *would*, move through His Spirit in today's world.

Many Christians did not believe that God still uses signs and wonders. They interpreted Paul's statement "When that which is perfect is come, then that which is in part shall be done away" to mean that because the Word of God had come, the gifts of the Spirit were no longer necessary (1 Cor. 13:10). The message of faith came to adjust our incorrect doctrine.

True faith is not given simply to bring us to personal salvation. Faith enables us to understand the eternal plan of God for the church. That plan will be fulfilled sovereignly, as He has determined, to bring many sons to glory. True faith will be required to bring the purposes of God to pass in the earth.

Hebrews 11, the great faith "hall of fame," bears record that those individuals who dare to believe the promises of God receive His blessings and are able to accomplish great things in His name. (See Hebrews 11.)

Much erroneous doctrine concerning faith and unbelief was cleansed from the church during the Charismatic Renewal as people began to believe God for miracles—and received them.

Misplaced Faith

Unfortunately, carnal Christians valued and desired temporal blessings more than eternal ones. The demand of many for material blessings led to what has been called the "prosperity doctrine." I do believe in prosperity, but I can't imagine having the audacity to demand that the almighty, omnipotent, omniscient, omnipresent, sovereign, infinite God do something to satisfy my desire for material things. Be careful to balance the message of faith with the sovereign will of God for His people. God cannot be treated as a Santa Claus. Though He has promised to give material blessings to His children, He expects us to use our faith on a higher plane that will help to effect His eternal purposes in the earth.

The Charismatic Renewal helped the church renew its faith to believe God for miracles and to walk in the promises of the Word of God. Through it our vision has been lifted to expect to receive good things from our God according to His will. God is a good God—not a hard taskmaster. That reality was strengthened in the church through the renewal of our faith.

Authority

THE CHARISMATIC RENEWAL also brought a realization of the authority of the believer. Some Christians did not even know they had power over the devil. The Spirit of God began to reveal the truth that "greater is he that is in you, than he that is in the world" (1 John 4:4). Jesus told us, "In the world ye shall have tribulation." But He continued by saying, "Be of good cheer; I have overcome the world" (John 16:33). Paul taught us to be overcomers in Christ (Rom. 12:21).

Authority in Church Government

THE LINES OF proper authority in the leadership of the church were established during the Charismatic Renewal as well. Unfortunately, some debris was also swept up with the truth about spiritual authority as it became mixed with the carnal desire to rule, causing much grief to the church.

Christ's authority may be defined as the power of attorney that enables one to do legal business for another in their absence (Luke 4:18). It is understood that the one to whom power of attorney has been given will follow the explicit instructions of the one who delegated that authority. In this sense, Jesus exercised His Father's power of attorney perfectly while He lived on the earth. Jesus declared, "The Son can do nothing of Himself, unless it is something He sees the Father doing; for whatever the Father does, these things the Son also does in like manner" (John 5:19, NAS).

Church leaders need to exhibit the same integrity of heart and motivation in order to fulfill God's purpose for His authority in the church. As we allow Christ to be the head of His church, walking humbly as His servants, we can know the true blessing of divine authority in the church.

It is important to remember that Jesus gave His disciples authority over demons and diseases—not over one another (Luke 9:1). He told them not to lord it over each other as the Gentiles did, but to become servants of all (Mark 10:42–44). The Holy Spirit wants to establish true biblical authority in church government.

During the Charismatic Renewal, those who misunderstood divine authority confused it with their own carnal desire to rule. They caused much grief to sincere Christians who were willing to be led. Yet, in spite of the debris this misunderstanding caused, this truth about the authority of God needed to be restored in the church.

An absence of true authority makes us vulnerable to the attacks of the enemy. As our understanding about God's authority is strengthened and we are cleansed from our carnal desire to rule, the church will march triumphantly against all its external or internal foes. God's guidelines for authority protect believers and build a strong church in the earth. We will see a healthy church emerge as we follow them carefully.

The Joy of Giving

THE FRESH REVELATION about giving to the Lord was one of the greatest blessings of the Charismatic Renewal. God has a generous, giving nature. God is love. Because of His nature, He "gave his only begotten Son, that whosoever believeth in him should not perish, but have everlasting life" (John 3:16). The entire Godhead is involved in this lavish giving. The Father gave His best—His only Son—to redeem us. Jesus suffered crucifixion willingly that our relationship with Him might be restored. And the Holy Ghost is giving Himself wholly to reveal Jesus to us.

As children of God, we must experience and demonstrate this "family spirit" of divine love to the world. God's love impelled Him to give. If we love God, we will be impelled to give our best to God joyfully.

For many people, the joy of giving was a spontaneous response to the Charismatic Renewal as we suddenly realized we could invest in so many ways in an eternal kingdom—the kingdom of God.

Peter's Question

PETER ASKED THE Lord, "Behold, we have forsaken all, and followed thee; what shall we have therefore?" (Matt. 19:27). Some may criticize Peter for asking such a question. It may sound too much like: "What do we get out of this?"

I am thankful that Peter asked the question. Jesus' answer reveals the joy of giving and receiving in the kingdom of God: "Every one that hath forsaken houses, or brethren, or sisters, or father, or mother, or wife, or children, or lands, for my name's sake, shall receive a hundredfold, and shall inherit everlasting life" (Matt. 19:29). What a tremendous promise! Our generous God has declared that whatever we give into His kingdom will be returned a hundredfold.

Have you ever tried to fold a sheet of paper a hundred times? A hundredfold is not 100 percent—it is much greater. While pastoring in Plano, Texas, several years ago (before the age of computers), I asked Texas Instruments to calculate a hundredfold. They sent back the message that they had exhausted their largest calculator at fifty-one-fold! A hundredfold increase is an astronomical figure—beyond our ability to imagine. Yet Jesus promised a hundredfold to those who would leave all and follow Him.

According to Jesus' promise, whatever you invest—your time, talents, trusted possessions, or anything else—He will give back to you a hundredfold. Understanding this principle, it wasn't any surprise to me when my Father told me recently that I was not going to die. I know, of course, that my physical body will be buried one day. But I will live on through the lives of people in whom I have invested—preaching to them and seeing them transformed by the power of God. In turn, they will preach to others who will be redeemed for eternity as well.

The precious truths God has revealed to me will also be preserved through books and tapes for the body of Christ to enjoy. The multiplication of my time, talent, testimony, and gifts will continue, and I will enjoy the fruit of its return throughout all eternity.

Recognition of the Church

THE CHARISMATIC RENEWAL also brought a recognition of the body of Christ—the church—as it is described in the New Testament. We have not always had a clear understanding of God's intent for the church. Too often we have viewed it as a social organization with certain religious practices and delegated responsibilities to its constituents. That is not the biblical description of the church.

A Body

ACCORDING TO THE Scriptures, the church is a living organism of which Christ is the head (Eph. 4:15). The apostle Paul declared that the church is a body, "fitly joined together and compacted by that which every joint supplieth, according to the effectual working in the measure of every part" (Eph. 4:16).

Paul told the Corinthians that we are all "baptized into one body" (1 Cor. 12:13). Then he continued by saying, "For the body is not one member, but many" (v. 14). Each member, though different from the others, is necessary and important to the body.

Paul did not use the body as an analogy of the church, as some have taught, for he plainly declares: "Now ye *are* the body of Christ, and members in particular" (1 Cor. 12:27, italics added). An analogy shows a likeness or similarity to something described. Paul declares, however, that in reality we *are* the body of Christ—the church. This mystery of the church being the body of Christ is being revealed more clearly in these days.

Pastor Sue Curran, conference speaker, teacher, and popular author, has observed the blessing of the true church:

> Through the church, the triune Godhead receives distinctive blessings from believers. The Holy Spirit is given a temple to live in, Jesus is given a body, and the Father is given a family to love.[1]

This understanding of the church as the body of Christ is different from the concept of a church as a loose-knit group of people who meet together once or twice a week for "worship."

The Body Functioning

IT TAKES ALL of us to make up the body of Christ. In teaching this reality, the apostle Paul declared that we have some uncomely parts that are just as necessary as the more comely ones. Without them the body dies. As members of Jesus' body, we are responsible to supply what other brothers and sisters need. We do not live for ourselves, nor are we to be secret disciples. You contribute to my life in God, and I contribute to yours.

Perhaps you do not recognize your contribution to the church. You may consider yourself simply an "attender." But your faith, prayers, and love can make a valuable contribution to the spiritual life of others as you give what you have. Knowing that you belong and are needed brings health to your psyche and fulfillment to your life.

One morning as I walked through the sanctuary before the Sunday morning service, I felt discouraged. I prayed, "Jesus, please put Your arms around me this morning. Please hold me. I just want to feel loved. I need someone to hold me."

When the service started, the love of God flowed freely among the people, and the Holy Spirit began to melt hearts. One by one, people moved around, hugging one another and praying together. The children and teenagers ran to the platform to hug me, and many adults followed to show their love. Refreshed in my spirit, I thought, *Isn't this wonderful?*

After a while I heard my Father say to me, "How do you like the love I sent you?" The expressed love of the body of Christ had encouraged my heart and met my need to feel loved that morning.

Every Joint Supplies

TERRY CLARK, A young man in my church, heard me speak one Sunday morning about "every joint supplying" in the body of Christ. He went home for dinner after the service and then lay down to take a nap. That evening, the service was already in progress when this tall young man ran into the church. Excitedly, he said, "I am sorry I am late; I overslept. I have come to be a joint to supply." If everyone realized their responsibility to be a "joint supplier" to the body of Christ, they would be more willing to give joyfully of what they have. And in that joy of giving, they would find themselves receiving as well.

Temporal Blessings

THE CHARISMATIC RENEWAL prepared the church in many ways to receive what God has purposed to give her in His next visitation. The church does not yet have all she needs to become the glorious church God intends. For that to happen, we must look to the next move of God.

Many of the blessings of the Charismatic Renewal, though necessary, are temporal. Though these temporal blessings prepare us for the next move of God, they won't be needed when we get to heaven. We won't need faith, for our faith will become sight as we see Him face to face. There will be no enemies to overcome. Nor will the gifts of the Spirit be necessary for the edifying of the church. Having acknowledged these blessings for the good they have brought, the church is in need of something greater than these temporal blessings to fulfill her destiny.

The church developed charisma during the Charismatic Renewal, but she did not develop character. The mature church described by Paul in his christological epistles has not yet emerged. In fact, the church became self-centered even in the midst of renewal. Seeking for personal satisfaction in spiritual gifts, ministries, and material possessions, many lost sight of valuable qualities that would prepare them to meet the Father.

God has the church hidden in various "caves" of circumstance to cleanse her from selfishness and wrong motivations. He wants her attention to be focused on Jesus and what He is doing. With that change of focus we will be ready to receive everything the next move of God will bring. And we will understand that the temporal blessings derived from the Charismatic Renewal were mere stepping stones. With the next move of God, these temporal blessings will fade away in the revelation of the eternal.

Part 4

The New Blessing of the Next Move of God

WHAT CAN WE expect to happen in the believer's life, and in the church, in the next move of God?

The Scriptures reveal God's intent for the church in the next move of God. They declare plainly what He will do in these last days. The following chapters will make clear the revelation of God's wonderful plan of revival for His people. Allow your faith to rise in anticipation of becoming a partaker of the great blessings that are coming.

> For since the beginning of the world men have not heard, nor perceived by the ear, neither hath the eye seen, O God, besides thee, what he hath prepared for him that waiteth for him.
>
> —ISAIAH 64:4

The revelation that awaits us is so wonderful that none of us will be able to say, "I knew this was coming." We cannot imagine what the great love of God has in store for those who wait for Him.

10

Holiness

The Character of God

ONE OF THE more obvious blessings God will bring to the church in the next move of God is holiness. Both the Old and New Testaments are filled with admonitions to holiness. Our "cave" experiences will bring us to a walk of holiness that we have never known—or even desired—before now. The Scriptures declare that the purpose for God's chastening upon our lives is that we might be "partakers of his holiness" (Heb. 12:10).

Holiness is not who *we* are; it is who *God* is. Holiness is the character of God. The name of the third person of the Godhead—Holy Spirit—reveals that God's nature is holiness. The holiness of God is a wonderful study, its thread running throughout the Bible from beginning to end.

When the Scriptures help us to peer into heaven, we hear the cherubim crying, "Holy, holy, holy" (Isa. 6:3). Perhaps they cry "holy" once for the Father, once for the Son, and once for the Holy Spirit. It will be glorious when they can add a fourth "holy" for the church—the bride of Christ.

God's Plan for Holiness

WHEN GOD MADE mankind He did not give us *eternal* life; He gave us *immortal* life. Immortality simply means we are destined to live somewhere forever. Where we live will be our choice. In order to live forever with God, we have to choose to receive eternal life.

God chose to make man in His own image. Being made in God's image, however, did not automatically give man God's character, His holiness. *Image* was God's choice; *character* was to be mankind's choice. Adam and Eve would have attained holiness of character if they had chosen to obey God in their testings.

God wanted to receive love from mankind. He desired to reproduce Himself in mankind. But, by definition, love is not a response that can be coerced or forced; it is a result of man's free choice. God wanted mankind to respond to His love by choosing to obey Him and walk in fellowship with Him. In that way, the character of God would be formed in man through the process of his right choices.

God offered Adam and his wife the choice of eternal life with Him and placed the tree of life in the garden. They could choose to eat of that tree. He also placed the tree of the knowledge of good and evil in the garden and told them not to eat of that tree. If they ate of it, they would die. It was the only tree they were not to eat (Gen. 2:16–17).

But the serpent deceived Eve, and both Adam and Eve ate of the forbidden tree. Their choice to disobey the command of God caused death to come, not only to them, but to all mankind. In making their choice to disobey God, they severed their relationship with Him, forfeiting eternal life.

In His high priestly prayer (John 17), Jesus defined eternal life for us.

> And this is life eternal, that they might know thee the only true God, and Jesus Christ, whom thou hast sent.
>
> —JOHN 17:3

Enjoying relationship with God is the essence of eternal life. By disobedience, Adam and Eve died to their relationship with God, thus failing to gain eternal life. Instead of allowing His character to be developed in them through obedience to His Word, they condemned all of mankind to disobedience.

Our Plight

THE WORLD HAS been eating from the tree of the knowledge of good and evil ever since Adam's and Eve's fateful choice. From that tree we get all our pagan philosophies: humanism, atheism, skepticism, New Age, and others. Our world is now partaking of that tree more than ever. We partake of that tree almost every time we turn on the TV; public schools feed our children a steady diet of it; and the world's governments face overwhelming problems without remedy because of the fruit of that tree.

God's Remedy

GOD WAS NOT surprised by mankind's treason in the Garden of Eden. From before the foundation of the world, God had initiated His plan of redemption to redeem mankind from his own destructive choices. In the fullness of time, God replanted the tree of life—on the hill of Golgotha—through Jesus' ultimate sacrifice on the cross. Because of that sacrifice, mankind can now choose to receive eternal life, this time by accepting the sacrifice of Christ's blood on the cross.

In mercy, God gave the law of Moses to those who lived before Christ so that by submitting to prescribed sacrificial rituals they could have the hope of eternal life. They looked forward to Christ's perfect sacrifice on the cross; we look back to it. It is the only source of eternal life.

> He that hath the Son hath life; and he that hath not the Son of God hath not life.
>
> —1 JOHN 5:12

To choose Christ is to choose eternal life. Not to choose Christ is to forfeit eternal life. The wonderful miracle of salvation happens as we choose to accept Christ as our Savior. He places an "incorruptible seed" of life in our spirit, and we become alive to God (1 Pet. 1:23). When that happens, not only will we live forever in immortality, but we have made our choice to receive the gift of eternal life.

The Choice of Transformation

IT WAS A powerful revelation when I learned that through the God-given power of choice, I could begin to develop His character after salvation. As we choose to obey the Word of God, our minds are transformed to think the way God thinks. By choosing to walk in obedience, responding correctly to life's trials, we allow God to develop His holiness in us.

God will never force His character on us. He waits for us to choose to exchange self-life for His divine nature. That choice must be made, not once, but in every situation of life where we find our will or nature to be contrary to His. As we learn to yield to the will of God, we can rest in Him, knowing that we cannot produce holiness in ourselves. Holiness is God's character produced in us by the Holy Spirit as a result of our yielding to His working in our lives.

The trees in the garden of Eden were put there to provide for and test mankind. Adam and Eve could have had not only God's image but His character as well. The choice was theirs.

In Christ we can choose to receive God's character. We will be going "home" with the character of the last Adam—Christ—formed in us. We will have the spirit of the family, God's family traits of love, holiness, and integrity, so that we won't be "misfits" in the Father's house.

Sanctification

THE SCRIPTURES DECLARE: "For this is the will of God, even your sanctification" (1 Thess. 4:3). *Sanctification* is the biblical term for the process of becoming holy. Sanctification is not what we do to make ourselves holy, as some have taught. Though it is true that we must cooperate with the Holy Spirit, sanctification is primarily His working in us through the cross.

Holiness is not an external code of living. Holiness is not what clothes or jewelry we wear. Because of a faulty definition of holiness, I spent seventeen years trying to make the part of me look holy that they are going to put in the cemetery—not even wearing a simple gold wedding band. Unfortunately, my external code of holiness did not result in my sanctification. Instead, I lived in bondage and legalism, becoming critical and judgmental of others who did not dress as I did.

A Command

HOLINESS IS A command of God for all believers. Peter admonished believers to "be holy yourselves also in all your behavior; because it is written, You shall be holy, for I am holy" (1 Pet. 1:15–16, NAS). Throughout the Bible holiness is given as a command, not an option. Holiness will continue to be the theme of eternity. "Holiness unto the Lord" is on the priest's crown and engraved on his garments. (See Exodus 28.) That phrase will even be inscribed on the pots and pans in the Millennium (Zech. 14:20–21). Such emphasis on holiness means we are going to have to become holy to be a part of God's kingdom.

Only to the degree that we die to self can we develop the character of God within our lives. We must renounce the humanistic doctrine that man is basically good. We are sinners—lost, undone, aliens to God. Improving our self-image will not eradicate our sin nature.

God's character will become the character of believers. He *will* have a glorious church without spot or wrinkle. We are going home in His holiness. When Lucifer fell from heaven God also kicked out rebellion, selfishness, and independence. He is not going to allow it to enter again. Holiness is not an option; it is a command.

Two Elements of Sanctification

THERE ARE TWO primary elements of sanctification: the Holy Spirit's work, and my cooperation with Him. Sanctification sets the believer apart by God for His use. We cannot be set apart until we are willing to come apart from other pursuits. We have to come out of worldly lifestyles, forsake other interests, and be committed to do His will in order to be set apart.

A second aspect of sanctification is the resultant work by the power of the Spirit of God that literally changes our lives—producing true holiness. The work of sanctification takes us to the cross again and again. It exposes our carnal nature and makes us cry out to be delivered. We realize that we are powerless to deliver ourselves. But as we submit to the testings and dealings of God, we find wonderful deliverance from our self-life and a continual infilling with Himself.

Conquering "Self"

AS LONG AS we love our self-life, we will keep it. We must hate our self-life in order to be delivered from it. When certain Greek men came to see Jesus, He told them: "Except a corn [kernel] of wheat fall into the ground and die, it abideth alone: but if it die, it bringeth forth much fruit" (John 12:24). In this picture of the seed shedding its hard outer shell in death so that new life could come forth, Jesus was showing them the necessity of hating their self-life.

There is a holy cry that is birthed by the Spirit of God in our spirit against everything that is unclean and destructive to body, soul, and spirit. If that holy hatred for sin and self does not come, we will never be cleansed; the life of Christ will not be seen in us.

Isaiah voiced that cry before the throne of God. As he was given a vision of God in His holiness, he recognized his own uncleanness and cried out:

> Woe is me, for I am undone; because I am a man of unclean lips, and I dwell in the midst of a people of unclean lips: for

> mine eyes have seen the King, the LORD of hosts.
>
> —ISAIAH 6:5

Isaiah had to see the holiness of God before he could see his own unclean condition. Then as a coal from the altar was placed on his lips by one of the seraphim, he was cleansed.

I once heard a minister declare that he didn't know the Lord. When I heard him say that, I sat in my self-righteousness and became angry with him. *Why was he in the pulpit preaching if he did not know Jesus? What was he saying?* I was still stewing in my anger when I went to bed that night.

But the Holy Ghost didn't let me sleep. He revealed my own vile self-life. In that awful revelation, I understood what the minister meant when he confessed he didn't know God. He meant that his knowledge of God was very limited in comparison to the reality of who God is. He was declaring, as Paul did, "I count all things but loss for the excellency of the knowledge of Christ Jesus my Lord" (Phil. 3:8).

Until we see our selfishness, "unlove," and pride as God sees it, we will not experience a godly hatred for it. But when we do, we will cry with Isaiah: "Woe is me" (Isa. 6:5). We will wait for the cleansing coal from the altar to purge our iniquity. We will not see our need for sanctification if we use ourselves or others as the standard of holiness. But when we behold God in His righteousness, we see, in contrast, our lack of holiness—and we can then be changed.

Before I go to my Father I will be changed into His image by His grace. By making right choices I can have His character and His holiness. The tree of life—the Christ-life—that is planted within me transforms me into His character as I yield to Him continually. Paul understood this, and wrote: "Christ in you, the hope of glory" (Col. 1:27). The cleansing work of the Holy Spirit releases the life of Christ in us, and as we yield to Him we realize true holiness in our lives and in our churches.

11

Holiness Realized

God's Character in the Church

EVERY CHILD OF God who sincerely desires to grow in the Lord will come to that place of "holy desperation" where our souls cry out with the psalmist, "Wash me thoroughly from mine iniquity, and cleanse me from my sin" (Ps. 51:2).

There are those who are so calloused that they have no sense of guilt and can sin easily. They are no longer sensitive to the sweet convictions of the Holy Spirit! Such souls may drift farther and farther away from the Lord until a devastating, drastic test snaps them out of their apathy and brings them back to God. But the earnest, honest Christian finds no rest or peace until he bows low at the feet of his Lord in open and full confession, seeking forgiveness and cleansing for the stain upon his soul.

Basis for Cleansing

> If we confess our sins, he is faithful and just to forgive us our sins, and to cleanse us from all unrighteousness.
>
> —1 JOHN 1:9

That verse is the basis for our cleansing from the stain of sin. God can never forgive hidden sin. Tears, weeping, or remorse will never bring forgiveness. Only wholehearted confession can bring forgiveness, restore fellowship with God, and bring His blessings into our lives.

In the Greek, *confession* is a poignant word that means "to speak the same thing; to say back to God what His Holy Spirit says to us."[1] When the Holy Spirit convicts us of a mean spirit toward another, it is hypocritical to say, "Yes, Lord, I do lack love for that person." When the Holy Spirit reveals the abomination of our pride, it is quite beside the point to say, "Yeah, Lord, I need a little more humility." God will not receive such confessions.

True Confession

How precious was the confession of God's servant David! After David sent Uriah to the front and gave the command for all others to withdraw so that Uriah would be killed, God spoke to him through the prophet Nathan: "Thou hast killed Uriah the Hittite with the sword, and hast taken his wife to be thy wife" (2 Sam. 12:9). Although David did not throw the spear that killed Uriah, he plotted Uriah's death, and God said: "Thou hast slain him." God laid the guilt right at David's feet.

David cried, "Purge me with hyssop, and I shall be clean: wash me, and I shall be whiter than snow" (Ps. 51:7). In this mighty outpouring of his heart he continued: "Deliver me from bloodguiltiness, O God, thou God of my salvation" (v. 14).

Hyssop was a little shrub that was used to apply the blood and water of purification. Bunches of hyssop were used to sprinkle blood on the doorposts in Egypt and to purify the leper (Exod. 12:22; Lev. 14:4–6). David's confession was real. He was saying back to God what God said to him concerning his sin.

Confessing Only "Sin"

It is our sin that we are to confess. God does not forgive mistakes; He either overlooks them or corrects us for them. God does not forgive doctrinal error—He corrects it. God does not forgive weaknesses; He strengthens us so as to deliver us from them. God forgives sin. When we come to Him for forgiveness, we come with a full consciousness of sin, or we come not at all.

Sin Defined

True, the word *sin* has gone out of vogue in modernistic theology and psychology. It is now defined by such high-sounding and euphemistic phrases as human weakness, negative thinking, maladjustment, or emotional disturbance. It is even rationalized as "upset nerves." But God calls sin, sin, and He forgives only sin!

What, indeed, is sin? We need to come to a renewed and fresh revelation of all that constitutes sin. Sin is the transgression of the law, but it is more. Generally speaking, sin is everything contrary to the nature and will of God. Sin is the opposite of holiness. It is all unrighteousness, all that is ungodly. It is all that is opposed to God or independent from God.

According to the Scriptures, there are sins of commission and sins of omission. There are the sins of the self-life and sins of the spirit. There is manifest sin, and there is hidden, secret sin. One can sin in thought, word, and deed.

Make no mistake about it—God hates all sin. Being a holy God, He could not do otherwise. But because He is a God of love, He loves the sinner. This goodness of God leads us to repentance (Rom. 2:4).

Sin acts as a disease to the soul in the same way that cancer does to the body. It disintegrates personality, affects bodily health adversely, darkens one's mind, and sears the conscience. Furthermore, it always breaks, or makes impossible, one's fellowship with his Maker. It causes untold misery in human relationships. Sin is the cause of all war. It fills our jails, our prisons, and our state hospitals.

We tend to rank sin in our church teachings, thinking that some sins are more wicked than others. We say murder and adultery are gross sins. We may determine others to be minor—such as the proverbial white lie. God does not categorize sin by degrees. Sin is sin if it violates God's law. Anxiety is sin. Unbelief is sin. Selfishness is sin. Worldliness is sin. In these days, above all else, God's people need an acute sense of sin. Anything that separates me from God or from my brother in Christ is sin.

The Scriptures teach only one way to deal with sin: confession. We must always confess our sins to God! And we must confess them to the people against whom we committed the sins. It is important to realize that we cannot get right with God if we do not make things right with men (Matt. 18:15–17, 35).

When we do go to another to be reconciled, we are to confess only our fault. It matters not what fault the other may have had; we commit that to the Lord and pray for that person. God does not ask us to confess another's sin; He asks that we confess our sin.

Let us suppose that we have uttered some unkind remark or some untruth about a person to a third party. To whom do we confess? We go to the one to whom the remark was made; and, if we have any reason to believe that the one spoken about knows of what we said, then we are to go to him also. I believe that if the one wronged does not know of our hurtful remarks about him, then we should hold our peace lest we create further offense.

But having confessed our sin to both God and man, can we be sure that God will always forgive our sins? Yes, hallelujah! We have His promise that He will forgive us:

> If we confess our sins, he is faithful and just to forgive us our sins, and to cleanse us from all unrighteousness.
>
> —1 JOHN 1:9

God is both faithful and just to forgive our sins and to cleanse every stain.

God's outraged holiness against sin has been fully satisfied at Calvary. His wrath is not as man's wrath—it is the awful reaction of His holy nature against sin. The wrath of God has had full expression. When Jesus hung on Calvary's cross, the full force of God's outraged holiness found expression as He turned His face away from His own Son, who was made sin for us that we might be made the righteousness of God in Him (2 Cor. 5:21). Because God's holiness has been vindicated, He can now be "just" in forgiving sinful man.

Oh, with what utter confidence then can we come to God with our sins! How utterly sure we can be of His forgiveness when we confess our sins sincerely. Our sins have already been dealt with, God's holiness has been vindicated, and it is possible for Him to forgive us. What joy fills the soul of him who comes to God in full contrition of heart and brokenness of spirit to confess his sins! What rest and peace is his who *knows* that God has forgiven his sin. The stain of it is wiped out forever, and God remembers it against him no more! What a sense of relief is his whose burden of sin is gone! How quickly then our fellowship with God is restored!

Cleansing From the Power of Sin

CONFESSION DEALS ONLY with sins committed and their stain upon the soul. What about the power of sin that manifests itself in thought, word, or deed? Many of God's children sin and confess their sins over and over again because they do not know the way of true deliverance from the power of sin. They live an up-and-down existence of continual sin and confession.

There is a way to live in continual victory over sin. God wants to bring us into a highway of holiness. He made full provision for breaking the *power* of sin, just as He made provision for cleansing the *stain* of sin.

Walking in the Light

How do we come onto God's highway of holiness so we need not confess the same sins all the time? How can we live in full and unbroken fellowship with God? The Bible declares:

> If we walk in the light, as he is in the light, we have fellowship one with another, and the blood of Jesus Christ his Son cleanseth us from all sin.
>
> —1 John 1:7

God's cleansing from the power of sin is conditional—we must walk in the light. He is that light. His light comes into our souls with revelation from heaven. It is the divine light we receive by being joined to the Lord as a branch to the vine, letting His life become our life. We cannot, in ourselves, overcome the power of sin anymore than we could cleanse away the stain of committed sins. But there is provision for both in Christ.

It would be wonderful if someone could break the power of sin for us by laying hands on us and praying for us. But deliverance from the power of sin does not come that way. Sin's power is broken as we daily walk in the light. Sin's power is conquered as we daily take the cross presented to us in the power of the crucified Christ. The blood of Christ keeps cleansing us from the power of sin as we keep walking in the light.

If we fail or refuse to walk in the light, Satan can again put us under his malicious power. But as we walk in the light, the blood of Jesus Christ remains efficacious to breaking Satan's power over us forever. As we call upon the mighty power of Christ when Satan comes to tempt us, we find that every place of former defeat becomes a place of triumph.

It is one thing to experience the glory and the relief that comes from a deep sense of forgiven sins, but it is quite another thing to experience that greater glory and release that come because the power of sin is broken. We may momentarily stumble as we walk the highway of God's holiness, yet if our faces are steadfastly set toward God, we shall rest upon His everlasting arms. A full confession will bring quick recovery, and we can resume our pilgrimage God-ward.

True holiness characterizes God's people. As the Holy Spirit is poured out in revival we are going to know His convicting and cleansing power. It will bring momentary pain. But we will know great release and victory as His cleansing power breaks our bondage to sin. What joy is in store for the people who will follow their God in holiness! Surely it will be joy unspeakable and full of glory!

12

Revival Through Gladness

Holy Ghost Joy

THERE IS A wonderful supernatural joy spreading throughout the church around the world today. It is both a supernatural sign and an impartation from the Lord. The Scriptures, both Old and New Testaments, are full of the promise of joy for the people of God. Yet we have seen very little joy in the church until this most recent outpouring. Perhaps this fact, more than any other, reflects the backslidden state of the church that so needs to be revived.

The Scriptures declare: "Because you did not serve the Lord your God with joy and a glad heart, for the abundance of all things: therefore you shall serve your enemies" (Deut. 28:47–48, NAS). The children of Israel went into captivity because they did not serve God joyfully. The people of God have submitted to many yokes of bondage simply because they did not cultivate a joyful heart in serving God. The two extremes of bondage—legalism and license—have crippled much of the church today. Legalism is the inordinate regard for rules as a means of salvation. License is the opposite of legalism. It is a disregard for rules and the irresponsible use of freedom. (See 1 Corinthians 8:9.)

God looks upon us with compassion. He wants to return and gather us from all the places where we have been scattered by our disobedience. He longs to turn our captivity so that we experience the reality of joy in our lives and churches (Deut. 30:1–3).

Jesus' Promise of Joy

TO HIS DISCIPLES, Jesus declared the reason for teaching the truths of the kingdom:

> That my joy might remain in you, and that your joy might be full.
>
> —John 15:11

He intended for His followers to be full of joy. The Scriptures declare that God had anointed Jesus with the oil of gladness above His fellows (Heb. 1:9). Joy filled Jesus as He lived on this earth. And joy was the deep motivation that empowered Jesus to go to the cross: "Who for the joy that was set before him endured the cross, despising the shame" (Heb. 12:2).

The Kingdom Is Joy

If we are not experiencing the joy of the Lord, we have not understood the good news of the gospel. The kingdom of God is defined as "righteousness, and peace, and joy in the Holy Ghost" (Rom. 14:17). If we do not experience the joy of the Lord, we have forfeited one third of the kingdom reality. Right relationship with Jesus will result in bringing joy to our lives.

The psalmist David understood that right relationship with God produced great joy. He wrote: "But let all those that put their trust in thee rejoice: let them ever shout for joy, because thou defendest them: let them also that love thy name be joyful in thee" (Ps. 5:11).

Rejoicing and shouting for joy are very energetic emotional responses to the presence of God. When we touch the kingdom of God, we, like David, will respond joyfully to Him.

Joy Defined

Several Greek words can be translated "joy." The word *chara* denotes a sense of physical comfort and well-being. It is an inner gladness, a deep-seated pleasure, delight, relish, enjoyment.[1] The reality of joy brings great comfort and satisfaction to the human heart. Joy also brings a depth of assurance that ignites and overflows from a cheerful heart.[2]

The Holy Spirit produces that kind of joy in our lives as a fruit of the Spirit (Gal. 5:22). It is not a human emotion that can be attained through human effort. Joy is found only through relationship with God. It is an expression of godly emotion that springs from the inner being of one who is moved by love for God.

Another Greek word, *agalliasis,* signifies "exaltation, exuberant joy; an outward demonstration of joy or exaltation, as experienced in public worship."[3] (See Acts 2:6.) David experienced that reality as he shouted for joy because of God's goodness (Ps. 42:4). Joy is more than an emotion; it is a vehicle for expressing what God is doing in the Spirit. It is not a mere display of human feelings, but a spiritual expression of divine happiness that comes as a result of God's wonderful intervention in our lives.

The joy of the Christian is not dependent on circumstances. It is not our environment, the people around us, or the events we are going through that determine our joy or lack of it. The joy of the Holy Ghost causes us to live in trust even in the most trying circumstances. Human happiness looks at things on the earth and is affected by its conditions. Divine joy looks heavenward. It is unaffected by people, events, or surrounding conditions because heaven's benefits are unchanging. As we learn to live in the kingdom of God, we will experience His righteousness, peace, and joy. Our bondages will be broken, and we will be released from our captivity to the enemy's purposes.

Release From Captivity

> When the Lord turned again the captivity of Zion, we were like them that dream. Then was our mouth filled with laughter, and our tongue with singing.
>
> —Psalm 126:1–2

God will do the unusual and unexpected when He begins to revive His people. In some places where revival showers are beginning to break, we are seeing hundreds of people saved, brought into the church, baptized in the Holy Spirit, and healed.

One pastor whose church is in revival said his church had experienced more ministry in the past three months than in all its former years. That is only one example of the phenomenal ways God moves when He turns the captivity of His people.

Two Ways Joy Comes

Sovereign release from captivity is one way God uses to bring great joy to those who have been enslaved and separated from their homeland. The kingdom of Judah experienced this joy after they had been in captivity in Babylon for seventy years, continually dreaming of their homeland. Finally, Cyrus, the Persian king who conquered Babylon, unexpectedly declared the Jews free to return to Palestine

(2 Chron. 36:22–23). Freedom broke in on them as a wild and beautiful dream. Their mouths were filled with laughter, and they were like those who dreamed (Ps. 126:1–2).

Never before had a captive nation been released to return to its homeland. God had done it. Even the pagan nations around were astonished. They declared: "The Lord hath done great things for them" (Ps. 126:2). The Jews acknowledged they had done nothing to bring about this fortuitous turn of events. In gratitude for their sovereign deliverance, they echoed the cry of the heathen, "The Lord hath done great things for us; whereof we are glad" (Ps. 126:3).

Sowing in Tears

When God comes sovereignly to destroy our bondages, it is a source of great joy. In the course of life, however, such events cannot occur continually. The psalmist recognized that. After rehearsing the joy of release from captivity, it is as though we can hear him heave a big sigh. Then he cries, "Turn again our captivity, O Lord, as the streams in the south. They that sow in tears shall reap in joy" (Ps. 126:4–5).

The psalmist is now praying for the remaining exiles in Babylon, for only a few of the exiled Jews had returned to their homeland in the first wave of freedom. He was asking the Lord to bring the rest of them home. His cry is sowing in tears. This second experience will also result ultimately in rejoicing. The psalmist understood that joy can also come as a result of sowing in tears. This source of joy is different from the sovereign intervention of God; it requires our obedience to the principle of sowing.

Jesus gave us the principle of sowing in His parable of the sower who planted seed faithfully in many kinds of soil. Some of the seed fell into places where it could not grow well. But others fell on good ground and brought forth fruit, some an hundredfold, some sixty, and some thirtyfold (Matt. 13:3–9). Jesus explained to His disciples that the seed was the Word of God, and the ground was the hearts of people.

Nothing happens until the sower sows, though not all sowing brings good results. Our tears, in part, are the result of our unrewarded labor. Maybe we have shed tears over an unbelieving co-worker, one who demonstrated an Absalom spirit. Perhaps a neighbor we have been witnessing to for years still shows no receptivity. Maybe our ministry has not been well received and we have little to show for years of heartbreaking work. The process of sowing is often accompanied by tears.

Revival is good news for those faithful servants of God who have invested their time in people with little or no response. Many Christians have poured their lives into a ministry without seeing much fruitfulness. The psalmist declares a wonderful promise for those faithful servants who sow in tears, giving the precious seed of the Word to people who do not respond positively or wholeheartedly to the Lord. There is coming a day when the sower shall come again "with a shout of joy, bringing his sheaves with him" (Ps. 126:6, NAS). The often agonizing labor of sowing will result in a joyful harvest.

That is a fact of life and a promise of God. Though we sow in tears for many years, facing difficulties, disappointments, and even despair, we must keep sowing. If we give up too easily the process shuts down. The Holy Spirit within us is our source of power, but if we do not do our part to keep sowing, the principle fails and there will be no harvest. In the midst of tough times we need to trust God, knowing that the principles of sowing and reaping are in force. It is sowing, though it be done in tears, that is the source of deep, hard-won joy when the harvest is reaped.

A Revival of Joy

IN THE NEXT move of God that is even now upon us, we see Him bringing a fresh anointing of joy to heal and empower His church to go out into the harvest. It seems He is releasing us sovereignly from our captivity and bringing great joy to the church. He is healing the wounds of the church through this baptism of joy.

The Scriptures declare that a joyful heart is good medicine (Prov. 17:22). Medical science provides medicines to fight physical illness and painkillers to provide a temporary sense of well-being. But a heart made merry by God can cure us physically, spiritually, emotionally, and mentally. As the church is healed of her backsliding and wounds and filled with the joy of the Lord, she will be empowered to "go out with joy, and be led forth with peace" (Isa. 55:12). She will be equipped to go out to the harvest with the joy of the Lord as her strength (Neh. 8:10).

Manifestations of Joy

WHEN JESUS SAID, "He that believeth on me, as the scripture hath said, out of his belly shall flow rivers of living water," He was speaking of the Holy Spirit (John 7:38). The Spirit had not yet come to fill His people. As the Holy Spirit visits His people afresh, these rivers of life will bring joy and gladness, rejoicing and laughter.

The time of mourning is over, and God is restoring joy to His people. We cry with the psalmist: "Make us glad according to the days wherein thou hast afflicted us, and the years wherein we have seen evil" (Ps. 90:15). The end of our "cave" experiences will be the joyful celebration of a new anointing to walk in victory with our God.

However the Holy Spirit touches our emotions, the result will be spiritual refreshing, breaking of bondages, and release of His divine life within us. Perhaps our natural reserve or cultural backgrounds make us fearful of entering into the joy of the Lord with abandon. Our part is simply to trust Him and yield to His moving, allowing Him to fill us with Himself.

Real or Counterfeit?

THE FACT OF a counterfeit presupposes the reality of whatever is being counterfeited. There could be no counterfeit money, for example, without the real to copy. In the Spirit's present visitation of joy, the reality of an encounter with God must be experienced before real joy can manifest itself. Anything else will be counterfeit. But the promises of God are sure to those who seek Him sincerely. God will not disappoint those who seek Him with an honest heart.

God is not limited in His methods. Sometimes He allows us to enjoy that which is out of the ordinary, as long as its precedent is scriptural. In this revival of joy that is spreading worldwide, we are hearing of people falling into trances. Even young children are being "slain in the Spirit," experiencing visions and hearing God speak to them. God is visiting His people with a new anointing of joy and using phenomena that are extraordinary, yet biblical.

In both the Old and New Testaments there are recorded incidences of people falling into trances when they experienced a divine encounter with God. God caused a deep sleep to fall on Adam so that he could take a rib from him (Gen. 2:21). A deep sleep fell on Abraham when God came to covenant with him (Gen. 15:12). Daniel sank into a deep sleep when the angel of the Lord talked with him (Dan. 8:18). The apostle Paul fell into a trance when he was praying in the temple (Acts 22:17). Peter was resting on the roof one day when he fell into a trance and had an encounter with God (Acts 10:10).

There are other examples of people in the Scriptures who met God in an extraordinary way and received revelation from Him, such as John on the isle of Patmos.

The trance experiences accompanying this move of God are doing a deeper work in the believer than what occurred when people were slain in the Spirit during the Charismatic Renewal, though the manifestation is the same. In this present anointing, God is communing Spirit to spirit through the trance experience. He is arresting these believers in order to do a deep sovereign work in them that changes their lives.

Though His manifestation in the Charismatic Renewal was anointed, many believers did not seem to experience the deep healing and deliverance that people are giving testimony to now. These are "time outs" with God, during which He speaks to people, gives visions of heaven, and works great deliverance in their lives. Many testify that in these moments with God He has done for them what counseling sessions could not do. The work that is done in His presence is eternal.

New Wine

IN SOME CHURCHES, the Holy Spirit is pouring out a "new wine" anointing that makes people behave as though they were drunk. It is as on the day of Pentecost, when people looking on supposed the disciples were drunk. At a later time Paul admonished Christians: "And be not drunk with wine, wherein is excess; but be filled with the Spirit" (Eph. 5:18). It is significant that he links the state of drunkenness with being filled with the Spirit.

A minister that I know asked the Lord why people were getting drunk in the Spirit.

"I have to get My people drunk in My Spirit because they have been drunk on the world," the Lord responded. "Their minds have been polluted. They have fed their doubts, denying confidence in Me and My power. I have to get them so drunk that I can change their thoughts and their attitudes."

During revival the Holy Spirit comes with power. He has the freedom to move in supernatural ways to do supernatural works in believers. We do not need to fear the supernatural manifestations of the presence of God.

He does that which no man could do. When a believer comes from the presence of the Lord, healing and deliverance have taken place. Grief and sorrow are changed into joy. Coldness of heart is replaced by a fiery love for God.

My Baptism of Joy

THE DAY AFTER I was baptized in the Holy Spirit, a visible, small cloud came into my kitchen. I was a little Methodist woman who had never seen anything like that. Everywhere I went from the thirteenth day of April to the last day of September of 1959, that cloud went with me. It grew larger, blacker, more pregnant. It rode over my grocery basket. It stayed at the foot of my bed at night. I had an awareness that when it broke, my future would be revealed.

I didn't know any pentecostal people in the city where I was living. I didn't have a pentecostal friend or minister to talk to. I was alone in my new walk with God and didn't know what had happened to me. God, in His sovereign mercy, dropped a cloud over me, and it stayed there for weeks.

The night it broke, I was ministering in Atlanta, Georgia. As I left the service and returned to my room the cloud hovered over me. I lay down on my bed and started praising the Lord. As I lay under the cloud it began to burst. Immediately, I began to laugh and continued laughing for some time. I could not stop laughing. I was a guest in a home and didn't want to disturb my hosts, so I stuck a pillow over my mouth. I didn't know there was such a thing as laughter in the Spirit. I didn't know there could be such joy in the Lord.

I was grieving from the recent loss of almost all my family, through the same genetic bone disease I had just been healed of. I had lived for some time at the point of death from that disease. Until Jesus healed me and baptized me with His Spirit, I didn't know you could have joy.

The presence of that cloud permeated the house and woke up my hostess. Sensing the presence of God, she went all over the house trying to "find" it. Finally, she knocked on my door, and said, "Is it in here?"

Laughing and crying at the same time, I answered, "Come on in." I laughed and cried for the rest of the night and all the next day.

The next evening at about six o'clock, my hostess said, "I need to help you get dressed. You are supposed to preach in about an hour." I was still laughing. This Methodist professor had flipped.

As I entered the church, the pastor whispered to his son-in-law, "I knew I was supposed to bring her down here to minister. I knew God was going to do something for her. She is going to be all right now." Then he added, "Revelation will be hers—God has gotten hold of her."

When it was time for me to preach, I started to read the Scriptures. I could not read—all I could do was laugh and cry. But the people rushed to the altar until it was full. I didn't have to preach a sermon; the presence of the Lord as He filled me drew the people to Him.

Power of Joy

I AM TOLD that laughter was a large part of the revival of 1948. It is a part of the move of God today. I know that some people may try to counterfeit this experience. But that doesn't mean that joy and laughter are not real experiences in God.

I preached recently on the joy of the Lord. I had no idea what the response would be. When I finished preaching, we sang a chorus about the joy of the Lord. The glory of God began to breathe through the church. I saw men bending over in laughter. Children were giggling, and teenagers were cackling. I elbowed my husband and said, "It is happening." No one had suggested anything or forced that manifestation of joy to happen. The presence of the Lord was simply filling the people and allowing them to experience His joy without inhibition.

We have lived a sour Christianity long enough. When God brings revival this time, we are going to be so happy that we will harass people with our happiness. They will be provoked to jealousy over our carefree, joyful countenances, attitudes, and actions.

Joy is not found in worldly pursuits. Most people in the world have already discovered that truth. As the world sees our joy in the Holy Spirit, they will be attracted to God. And, as the presence of God reveals the compassionate heart of Jesus, we will be moved with love toward the unsaved.

13

Compassion

The Heart of Jesus

ONE SUNDAY MORNING while we were worshiping in the church I pastored in Dallas, Texas, the Holy Spirit told me we should sing "Where the Healing Waters Flow." At the time, we were in the midst of high praise music, and I knew suggesting this song would bring a drastic change to the mood of the service. But, the impression was so strong I went to my worship leader and whispered, "Lead the people in 'Where the Healing Waters Flow.'" Quickly, he brought the chorus we were singing to an end and directed the orchestra to begin the song I had suggested.

As soon as we started to sing, a young mother ran out of the back door of the sanctuary like an arrow shot out of a bow. Soon she was back, holding her three-year-old son in her arms.

Her story was a sad one. She had married a brilliant young lawyer, and they had two children. He was adamant against the ways of God. In his intelligence he felt that religion was beneath him. As his wife turned to God completely, trying to serve Him faithfully, she suffered the disintegration of her marriage through divorce. Her husband left her, taking most of their financial assets with him. She had little income and was struggling financially but remained faithful to the Lord.

I did not know that earlier in the week she had taken her son to the doctor for tests. He had been diagnosed with a form of muscular dystrophy that progressed rapidly. The doctor had predicted it would cripple him totally within a few weeks. It would take his life ultimately.

After receiving the doctor's report she went home and fell on her knees, crying out to God. She said, "Lord, You promised to be my husband. I have no one else to take care of me. Please tell me what to do for my son."

The Lord spoke to her in that moment: "Doris, on Sunday morning when the church sings, 'Where the Healing Waters Flow,' I will heal your son."

I knew none of this when the Holy Spirit spoke to me to sing that song. But this mother came running up to the platform with her boy and thrust him into my arms. As she did, my heart melted within me, and something like liquid fire ran out of my being, through my arms into that little boy. I felt as if my life had poured into him in that instant. I didn't know what the Lord was doing, but I felt His power flowing from me into that body. I put the boy down and said to him, "Come, Chris, run with Pastor."

Many in the congregation who were aware of his situation began shouting. We ran across the platform and back. As we returned to his mother, she volunteered her story. She told me that a few days ago he could not run like that, and then she informed me of the doctor's diagnosis and the impending prognosis. The compassion of God we experienced that morning brought healing to that little boy.

Recently I received a letter from this family, with a picture of Chris. He is now a professional football player. He is a living testimony to the compassion of God he received that Sunday morning as a little boy.

I have not felt that strong compassion many times in my life, but when I have, it has always had life-changing effects.

Compassion Defined

THERE IS NO other subject more difficult for me to articulate than that of compassion. It is so difficult to find expression in human words for this divine emotion. The Scriptures describe Jesus' response to the needs of people by repeatedly using the phrase "moved with compassion."

The Greek word for *compassion* is *eleeo.* It means "to show kindness or assistance."[1] Far greater than simply feeling a depth of pity or sympathy, it is a divine force expressed in a deep yearning over the suffering of another. In that divine force there is not only desire to help, but the ability to help as well. We could call it "projected love," which is the real meaning of *agape*—God's divine love. It is love that is focused on a specific area of need for a person or group of people.

Godly compassion springs from the deepest part of our beings. The Scriptures refer to "bowels of compassion" (1 John 3:17), speaking of our spirits, or our "inner man." When Paul expressed his love for the Philippians he declared: "For God is my record, how greatly I long after you all in the bowels of Jesus Christ" (Phil. 1:8). Such compassion, flowing out of the deepest recesses of our being, will affect and motivate our lives. The psalmist David referred to his spirit as the "reins" of his life (Ps. 26:2). As the reins on a horse guide his direction and actions, so God's compassion will guide the direction and actions of our lives.

All these pictures place the source of compassion on a deeper plane than a fleeting, momentary feeling of pity or sympathy for another. They refer to the spirit of the believer from which the compassion of the Holy Spirit flows freely.

Compassion is the loving outreach of God to the person who needs His touch. When His agape love touches a person, it sets that person free. Bitterness, past hurts, offenses, emotional scars, physical problems, mental bondages, and relational difficulties are healed when the divine force of His compassion touches a life.

Counterfeit Compassion

SATAN TRIES TO counterfeit everything that God's love does. Many people project a loving attitude toward others with the ulterior motive of gaining their favor. The New Age movement projects a loving face, tolerating everyone's beliefs and opinions, but it refuses to accept God's absolute standards. It is a soulish counterfeit for the love of God.

The counterfeit of compassion originates in the mind and is exercised as mind control. In reality it is witchcraft. Unfortunately, it is found not only in the secular world but is practiced by some Christians in ministry to gain advantage over people.

True compassion is birthed in our spirits by the Holy Spirit. It causes us to reach out to the needy who cannot give anything in return. Struggling in their pain, these hurting people need a touch of God that will bring wholeness to their bodies, souls, and spirits. There is transforming power in the compassion that comes from God, working through a believer.

Compassion and the Anointing

COMPASSION IS NOT the force that completes the healing but that which energizes the miraculous power of God to begin His work. The supernatural power that performs the miracle is the anointing. Jesus declared this fact when He stood in the synagogue to read the Scriptures: "The Spirit of the Lord is upon me, because he hath anointed me to preach the gospel to the poor; he hath sent me to heal the broken-hearted, to preach deliverance to the captives, and recovering of sight to the blind, to set at liberty them that are bruised" (Luke 4:18). The anointing of the Holy Spirit empowered Jesus to perform miracles for men and women as He was moved in compassion for them.

The anointing may be defined simply as the supernatural power of God that is resident in a believer's spirit by the Holy Spirit. It is the source of the actual power to accomplish God's miraculous work. Jesus promised to give the disciples the *dunamis* power of the Holy Spirit after His ascension: "But ye shall receive power, after that the Holy Ghost is come upon you" (Acts 1:8). *Dunamis* means "force, a miraculous power."[2] That is the inherent, divine ability of the Holy Spirit working through us as He fills us with His anointing.

The anointing operates in its fullness when motivated by God's love, though it can flow through us in a measure despite our lack of love. The apostle Paul taught that the energizing force behind faith is love (Gal. 5:6). The catalyst for the *dunamis* power that releases faith is the yearning and caring compassion of God. It releases the power of the grace gifts needed to produce the miracle. Projected love or compassion is the motivation for the tangible, supernatural power—or anointing—that effects the miracle.

Love Motivation

After Paul gives detailed instructions concerning the value and use of spiritual gifts, he declares: "And yet shew I unto you a more excellent way" (1 Cor. 12:31). His famous "love chapter" follows—the New Testament portrait of a Christian. He concludes his description of divine love by repeating that we should desire spiritual gifts, but we are to pursue love above all.

Love purifies our desire for the power of God. There is an inherent desire in human nature to rule, though not for godly reasons. Some Christians have even tapped into the power of God without pure motives, using it to satisfy their personal desires for aggrandizement or control.

So few miracles are being worked through Spirit-filled believers, because the energizing force of compassion is not the motivation for attempting many miracles. One of the primary functions of the Holy Spirit is to shed the love of God abroad in our hearts (Rom. 5:5). If He is working in our hearts, the result will be a divine compassion for others.

Cold Love

AN OVERWHELMING LOVE for God and one another accompanies our initial baptism in the Holy Spirit. That love motivates our words, attitudes, and actions in positive ways. But if we face the trials of life without allowing the Holy Spirit to continue to fill us with Himself, love often grows cold. Cold love is powerless to energize faith. Therefore, we cannot release the anointing that is within.

Jesus warned that cold love would be a sign of the end times: "And because iniquity shall abound, the love of many shall wax cold" (Matt. 24:12). Cold love makes ministers and believers ineffective. We cannot manufacture divine love—it is not a product of soul power. God sheds it abroad in our hearts by the Holy Ghost. As we seek Him in obedience, He will be faithful to fill us with His divine love.

Compassion and Character

AN OVERWHELMING COMPASSION, a baptism of love poured out from Christ Himself to His people, will accompany the last great move of God upon the earth. It shall come in ever-increasing waves—Christ's deep, fulfilling love flowing in us and through us in compassion to others.

How can we show that Jesus lives and walks through us if we don't walk in love? Unfortunately, many charismatic Christians have forsaken the pursuit of character in their pursuit of charisma, anointing, power, and the gifts of the Spirit. They do not walk in love. The love of God is the channel through which the Holy Spirit works. He doesn't work through our giftings alone—He works through love.

Compassion Through Relationship

WHEN WAS THE last time you heard your heavenly Father say, "My child, I love you"?

How long has it been since you crawled onto His lap, looked into

His eyes, and called Him "daddy"? When was your worship so powerful that you knew you were exchanging intimacies of love with the living God? Have you felt His love in such a way that you spoke to Him in the love language of the Shulamite girl in the Song of Solomon? A relationship like that will open our hearts to receive the depths of God's compassion.

Have you ever put your arms around someone to pray for them and felt the love of God well up inside you for them? Have you ever felt the divine force that is an impartation of God into another person? When that happens, the Christ-life within you has reached out, pouring Himself into another and lifting them with His divine presence. That impartation of God's compassion is greater than spiritual gifts. It is the love of God Himself, moving from you to that person.

The alcoholic, the adulterer, and the blasphemer have had enough church rules and restrictions. Nothing will change a person as quickly as pouring the divine compassion of Christ into that person through a loving word or a loving touch in spite of his or her appearance. In that way, the living Word becomes a Person—reaching out to those who can see Him in no other way.

The miracle of salvation won't happen by memorizing verses of Scripture or presenting four spiritual laws. Church programs won't produce change—but projected love will.

As the holiness of God changes our character, we will touch others with the true compassion of God and see lives changed. Everyone that Jesus touched was changed. The church is going to take Jesus to the world and hear people exclaim, "Someone touched me—I'm not the same anymore." The ministry of impartation belongs to the body of Christ.

This next move of God won't bring sinners to us—we will go to them as Jesus taught in His parable of the great supper. When the guests who were first invited to the master's great feast made excuses, the master of the house became angry and told his servant, "Go out quickly into the streets and lanes of the city, and bring in hither the poor, and the maimed, and the halt, and the blind" (Luke 14:21).

The servant obeyed, and still there was room at the table. So the master commanded the servant to "go out into the highways and hedges, and compel them to come in, that my house may be filled" (Luke 14:23). This is a picture of the Father's heart. He has prepared a wonderful banquet and longs for His house to be full.

Do we share His heart? When was the last time we wept over the plight of a homosexual or a drug addict? Are we moved with compassion to help a homeless child or a young girl who is having an abortion? Do we see the child abuser, rapist, or murderer through the compassionate, loving eyes of God? Do we believe God can change completely the lives of people involved in willful, malicious sin?

It is only as God imparts His divine life to us, Spirit to spirit, and impregnates us with His divine life and compassion that we can. When that happens, we will not be content to stay within our church walls. We will be compelled to go to the streets to find those who are hurting and wounded and take the love of God to them. Out of us will flow the divine love of God—the true "agape" force that brought Jesus to the earth to save mankind.

I don't know how long I will live, but above all else I want to leave a legacy of love with the church—a hunger for relationship with Jesus that cannot be satisfied by anyone but Him. When you come to Jesus in prayer, do you always ask for something? Do you ask for your needs to be met? Do you want to display a gift or exercise power? Just come to worship Him. Let Him pour His compassion into your life.

As His compassion fills us we will see the prayer of Jesus fulfilled: "That they may be one, even as we are one" (John 17:22).

14

Unity

Jesus' Prayer Answered

UNITY IS THE greatest challenge facing the church today as we seek to advance God's kingdom in the earth. Yet unity in the church is essential to satisfy the heart of God and to fulfill His purposes in the earth. Jesus prayed that all who would believe on Him would become one. He knew that unity was the priority of the Father's heart.

Unity Defined

UNITY IS THE state of being made one. It means to have "a oneness of mind, or feeling, as when people live in concord, harmony, or agreement."[1] Unity does not preclude diversity, as the Scriptures are careful to explain. Metaphors and allegories in the Bible that describe the redeemed people of God depict a community characterized by unity with diversity and diversity in unity. For example, the Bible describes diversities of manifestations and gifts, but one Spirit (1 Cor. 12:4). Unity is not uniformity, nor is diversity division.

The apostle Paul illustrates the divine purpose for the unity and diversity of Christ's body by referring to the human body. As we mentioned earlier, he explains that the human body has many members with different functions, all necessary to the health of the body. He then exhorts, however, that while the gifts and ministries in the church vary, they must not be allowed to cause division by drawing attention to the gifted person or creating "cliques" within the church.

Paul insists that the redeemed community is one organic whole consisting of diverse members. That diversity is intended to bring a divine variety of ministry to the whole body of Christ for the common good of all. A beautiful picture emerges when we envision a body of people, all variously gifted by the Holy Spirit, ministering in love to one another. As the church leaves the immaturity of competition and manifests maturity of unity in Christian compassion, she will become a witness to the whole world.

The body of Christ cannot endure competition between its members. We need each other if we are going to fulfill God's divine purpose in this earth. When we fail to flow with every other member of the body, we are rebelling against God's purpose for His corporate body and are defeating our own personal destiny. We are injuring other members in the body and withholding the beautiful, corporate Christ that God desires to manifest to the world.

Here is the supreme glory of the Christian man: He is part of the body of Christ on earth. I believe with all my heart that this next move of God is going to bring the church into a greater unity than we have ever known before. The Holy Spirit is going to reveal Jesus Christ to the world through the church: "To Him be the glory in the church" (Eph. 3:21, NAS).

Dashed Hopes of Unity

UNFORTUNATELY, UNITY IS more easily defined than attained, as the history of mankind and the church reveals. During the Charismatic Renewal, many thought unity had come to the church because of the thousands of people from all denominations who were receiving the baptism of the Holy Spirit. Even secular newspapers wrote favorable articles about the "glossolalia movement" bringing together Christians of all denominations.[2]

While I was traveling in Jerusalem during the time of that renewal, I met David du Plessis, who was instrumental in bringing many denominational leaders together, including Catholics. When he found out I was a Methodist minister and professor, he invited me to consider ministering with him. He talked about the formation of an ecumenical movement and felt we would be able to witness to our denominational friends concerning the baptism of the Holy Spirit. Though I was unable to accept his invitation, I shared his enthusiasm for bringing the church together. We both had high hopes for unity in the body of Christ at that time.

But before long we realized that the church had begun not only to split, but to splinter as well, even during the Charismatic Renewal. Some groups followed ministries that had the manifestation of being "slain in the Spirit," while others preferred to follow ministers who "lengthened legs." Though these manifestations were not inherently wrong, they became a means of dividing the church into different camps. Rather than seeing the unity we had hoped for, we saw the church divided over these and other issues.

Shortly after the emphasis on these issues had subsided, the Holy Spirit began to renew praise and worship in the church. He gave many beautiful and anointed songs, and there was a new wave of praise and worship in the church that extended to many nations. International worship symposiums were established to help share the wonderful truths of praise and worship and to train musicians to flow in this fresh anointing.

I was one of the professors invited to teach praise and worship to thousands of believers who attended these symposiums. As I saw people from every denomination, without name tags, worshiping together, I declared joyfully, "This is it! Surely we must be experiencing the unity in the body of Christ that we have all been waiting for. No one is interested in declaring their affiliation; they are all worshiping Jesus together!"

Sadly, however, it was not long before the church was splitting again over new issues—whether or not to carry banners, whether dancing was a true form of worship, whether dancing should be choreographed or spontaneous. Songwriters became "stars" to thousands of enthusiastic followers. Some groups followed one personality while other groups supported another. The unity we had hoped to see come to the church through this wave of praise and worship seemed thwarted once more.

Focus on Jesus

WHEN JESUS STOOD in the synagogue to read the Scriptures, He declared:

> The Spirit of the Lord is upon me, because he hath anointed me to preach the gospel to the poor; he hath sent me to heal the broken-hearted, to preach deliverance to the captives, and recovering of sight to the blind, to set at liberty them that are bruised, to preach the acceptable year of the Lord.
>
> —LUKE 4:18–19

After Jesus finished reading, the Scriptures say:

> And the eyes of all them that were in the synagogue were fastened on him.... And [they] wondered at the gracious words which proceeded out of his mouth.
>
> —LUKE 4:20, 22

Verse 22 reads as follows in the Amplified Bible: "and marveled at the words of grace that came forth from His mouth." The world has not yet heard that message of grace. They didn't hear it in the Charismatic Renewal because we were expounding "our" spiritual gifts and ministries.

In immaturity, some sought to make a name for themselves through spiritual gifts or doctrinal emphasis. Others looked for renown through church government or a program of evangelism. Unity will not come to the church through church programs or forms of government. It will not be a product of human methods or personalities. Unity will come to the body of Christ in this next move of God for one reason—everyone's focus will be on Jesus.

Jesus is going to stand in His church again and declare: "I have come to heal the brokenhearted, to deliver captives, cause the blind to see, and set at liberty them that are bruised." As the church begins to walk in unity, healings and miracles will be an everyday occurrence. But they will seem unremarkable in the revelation of Jesus. We won't worry about "our" ministry any longer. His ministry—healing broken lives and setting captives free—will be all that matters. When that happens, the world will look at the church and exclaim: "Amazing grace!"

The Power of Unity

UNITY CAN BE dangerous. When the Golden Gate Bridge in California was restored a few years ago, the media published a warning to the one million people who planned to walk across it the first night it was open. They warned them that if they walked together in rank—in a unified pattern—the bridge would fall from the impact. Marching bands often break cadence when they cross a bridge. That is a natural example of the power that spiritual unity can bring when the church walks together as one man.

Unity will make the church a powerful force in the earth. Jesus declared that the world would know the Father had sent Him as believers became one in Them (John 17:21). Perhaps He gave us the greatest key to true evangelism in that statement. There is a power in unity that will draw the world to Jesus.

Unity in Type

THE SCRIPTURES ARE filled with admonitions for believers to live in unity, both in the Old and New Testaments.[3] The psalmist, David, extolled the virtues and blessings of a unified people when he wrote:

> Behold, how good and how pleasant it is for brethren to dwell together in unity! It is like the precious ointment upon the head, that ran down upon the beard, even Aaron's beard: that went down to the skirts of his garments; as the dew of Hermon, and as the dew that descended upon the mountains of Zion: for there the Lord commanded the blessing, even life for evermore.
>
> —PSALM 133:1–3

David's analogy of unity here was one the Old Testament saints understood very well. They were familiar with the anointing oil that Moses poured upon Aaron to set him apart for service in the tabernacle. They knew a priest had the responsibility of living in unity with God and man in order to understand and administer holy things.

The holy anointing oil was composed of four major spices: myrrh, cinnamon, cassia, and sweet calamus, all mixed together in a large quantity of olive oil (Exod. 30:22–25). It typifies the Holy Spirit, while each ingredient speaks to us of the bitter and the sweet.[4] Even as we cultivate our relationship with God, we find that life is full of bitter as well as sweet experiences. Jesus, our High Priest, the head of the church, certainly experienced both bitter and sweet in His life. Yet, even in His deepest suffering, He maintained communion with God and companionship with His brothers.[5]

Anointing the Head

THE APPLICATION OF the anointing oil is a biblical type of unity. Following that type, we can understand that unity begins at the head, for the anointing oil was poured upon the head of Aaron. Jesus is the head of the church, and believers are to form the body of Christ. As the church experiences this anointing, it will walk in a spirit of unity that crosses denominational lines, cultural barriers, prejudice, customs, and any other issue that presently causes divisions.

God calls His leaders to unity first. The anointing for unity will begin at the head. As undershepherds of the flock of God, pastors will follow Jesus' example of oneness with the Father and learn to walk in unity with each other before they lead their people to do the same. The spirit of competition must be replaced with a divine spirit of cooperation in order for Jesus' prayer to be answered and for the world to recognize the church as different from them. I thank God for those who are working to bring reconciliation in the church, beginning with the leadership.

Anointing the Beard

CONTINUING WITH THIS biblical type, we see that the next area the anointing oil touched was Aaron's beard. In the Jewish culture, the growing of a beard represents manhood and maturity. When the apostle Paul exhorted the Ephesian church to unity in spirit and in faith, he admonished them: "that we henceforth be no more children, tossed to and fro...but speaking the truth in love, may grow up into him in all things, which is the head, even Christ" (Eph. 4:14–15).

As we mature in Christ we will become seekers of unity, rather than seekers of our own gain. The time is past for believers to seek their own ministries and build their own reputations at the expense of others.

Anointing the Garments

THE ANOINTING OIL fell from Aaron's beard to the borders of his garments. Bells and pomegranates were sewn onto the borders of the priest's garments, side by side and alternating, so that they touched each other (Exod. 39:25). They represent the gifts and fruit of the Holy Spirit as they should be manifested in the church. When the priest entered the inner sanctuary he was hidden from the view of the Israelites gathered in the outer court area. As he walked within the inner court, from the table of shewbread to the golden candlestick and back again, the bells would ring. That sound gave evidence that the priest had not died in the presence of God because of his sin, and that his ministry unto God was acceptable.[6] Each of us needs that anointing to make us acceptable in the presence of God.

The apostle Paul teaches that two things keep us from unity: our carnal natures and the improper use of the gifts of the Holy Spirit. He told the Corinthians: "The testimony of Christ was confirmed in you: so that ye come behind in no gift; waiting for the coming of our Lord Jesus Christ" (1 Cor. 1:6–7). Yet there were attitudes of competition among them that caused them to be divided (1 Cor. 1:10). He said they were carnal and immature, calling them babes (1 Cor. 3:1).

Even today the gifts of the Spirit, given to the church to edify and build us together, too often can become a cause of disunity when we use them to build our own "kingdoms." Like the Corinthians, the very gifts the Spirit gives us to bring us into maturity and unity can be used to separate us as we struggle to become mature. Out of immaturity, we operate in the gifts of the Holy Spirit as if they originated with us, forgetting that all that we have comes from Him and is for Him.

The diversities of gifts and callings given to believers are for the purpose of exalting Christ and building His church. We need the anointing of God to flow to our garments, touch our gifts, and bring death to our carnal nature, that we might bear the fruit of the Spirit.

Place of Refreshing

THE PSALMIST CONTINUES to describe unity as a place of pleasantness and refreshing. He said it was like the dew on Mount Hermon (Ps. 133:3). Dew is that refreshing moisture so welcome after the heat of the sun has subsided. The dew falls at night when all creation is resting and natural elements are at peace. Dew represents restfulness in the kingdom of God that the Holy Spirit came to give.[7]

I wonder if we realize the time and energy consumed by churches as they work to put out "brush fires" caused by carnal competitions. The effort could be put to better use by igniting the flames of the Holy Spirit that would enlighten this darkened world. The enemy energizes our petty differences. He knows the power of unity in the church and fears it exceedingly.

David refers specifically to the dew of Mount Hermon, one of the highest peaks in the mountainous region east of the Jordan River.[8] Is not the church destined to be the highest, most influential place in our society? She is to represent to the world a place of restfulness from competition and division, a place filled with love and cooperation. Only the spirit of unity will exalt the church to her rightful place and cause the world to look to her for refuge.

Unity in Crisis

THE ATTACKS OF the enemy that we have discussed have all hindered the unity of the church in specific ways. Unresolved offense, for example, makes us vulnerable to the Absalom spirit, opening us to the spirit of betrayal against God's anointed leadership. God is cleansing the church of these hindrances to unity, however, and preparing her to reign in the power of that unity that only Christ can bring. Along with these attacks, another internal cause for disunity must be understood so that we can be cleansed from its consequences.

Racism is one of the greatest crises facing the world and affecting the unity of the church today. Racism is not a demon or even a principality—it is a world ruler. This powerful ruling spirit sets itself up in the natural mind of man as an authority on what is right and wrong. It employs even the spirit of death and murder in its verdicts.

The Basis of Racism

RACISM HAS TWO fundamental aspects: pride and fear. Judging that those who are different from us are inferior is the ultimate form of pride. The Scriptures declare that God is opposed to the proud but gives grace to the humble (James 4:6). Fear, the second aspect of racism, is a result of mankind's insecurity because of the fall of man that resulted in his separation from God. The insecure are afraid of those who are different from them, those whom they cannot control. These powerful and deeply interwoven attitudes of pride and fear that permeate all of society make it vulnerable to racism.

The world is about to lose control of its racial problems. In reality, racism is a spiritual problem that no legislation or human authority can control or resolve. If the church does not face the problem of racism and overcome it within herself, the world will soon fall into an abyss of chaos, destruction, and suffering of unprecedented proportions.

God's Remedy for Racism

THE APOSTLE PAUL declared in his day that the greatest racial barrier—the division between Jews and Gentiles—was overcome in Christ. He wrote: "There is neither Jew nor Greek, there is neither bond nor free, there is neither male nor female: for ye are all one in Christ Jesus" (Gal. 3:28). The love of Christ eradicates racial barriers that produce hatred and prejudice, establishing a new standard for right and wrong.

The death of Jesus on the cross broke down the walls between Jews and Gentiles, abolishing enmity and reconciling both groups of people unto God. (See Ephesians 2:11–17.) Only as we accept the sacrifice of the blood of Jesus will we know deliverance from that same kind of enmity between races. The power of the cross deals fundamentally with both the pride of man and his fear.

It is the work of the Holy Spirit to convict the world of sin. Though this convicting work brings a painful revelation of our sins, it causes us to run willingly to the cross to find grace and forgiveness. There our pride is destroyed as we recognize our dependency on the cross. With our intimacy with God restored, we are cleansed from fear, for "perfect love casteth out fear" (1 John 4:18). The deeper the work of the cross in us, the more humble and secure we will be in His love.

When we, who had become so removed from the character of God, are grafted back into Him, receiving His nature, a profound appreciation invades us for those who are different from us. We judge people from a spiritual perspective, not after the flesh or external standards. As Paul stated: "Therefore . . . we recognize no man according to the flesh" (2 Cor. 5:16, NAS). The church, above any other community, should not judge people according to the color of their skin or their cultural background. We must be governed by a biblical perspective and judge all by the Spirit.

Results of Unity

UNITY ATTRACTS PEOPLE. Everyone wants to be on a united team. The world knows that unity is impossible for people who are bent on making a name for themselves. We need only look at the current problems among high-paid, superstar athletes to recognize this fact. The world will recognize the difference unity makes to the chaos of personal ambition and one-upmanship.

Living in unity brings a refreshing, revitalizing force to our lives, in part simply because we have been relieved of the tension created by competing with others. But there is also a refreshing because the Lord has promised to command His blessing in the place of unity. The psalmist ended his description of unity by saying: "For there the Lord commanded the blessing, even life for evermore" (Ps. 133:3). Unity brings the blessing of the Lord to our lives and that gives us a foretaste of heaven.

Jesus ended His prayer with the cry, "that the love wherewith thou hast loved me may be in them, and I in them" (John 17:26). In this prayer He expressed His desire that we enjoy relationship with the Father as He knows it and that we would see His glory. As we learn to walk in unity in the church, we will come to a new revelation of Jesus and, subsequently, of the Father.

15

Jesus in the Church

A Revelation of the Father

WE DO NOT have to wait until heaven to see the glory of God in the church. The glory of God will be seen as Jesus reveals Himself in our human temples of clay. In this next move of God, the glory of God is going to fill the lives of believers, and all the world will see it.

The Scriptures declare that it is the work of the Holy Spirit to reveal Jesus to us and in us. Jesus told His disciples: "When he, the Spirit of truth is come, he will guide you into all truth...He shall glorify me: for he shall receive of mine, and shall shew it unto you" (John 16:13–14). The apostle Paul taught that we are the temple of God and that the Spirit of God dwells in us (1 Cor. 3:16). Without the working of the Holy Spirit in us, we cannot know Jesus, who is Truth. In this next move of God, as the Holy Spirit works to reveal Jesus in us, the church is going to see Jesus as she has not seen Him before. And the glory of God is going to be revealed in the church.

Where Is the Glory?

WHEN GOD MADE mankind, He made him a tripartite being—one with a spirit, a soul, and a body (1 Thess. 5:23; Heb. 4:12). He did not intend for there to be a "veil of flesh" separating man's spirit from his soul. We know that God is a Spirit. Before mankind disobeyed God in the garden, Adam and Eve communed with God, spirit to Spirit. He communicated His words of life through their spirits to their souls. When that communion was broken through deception and disobedience, man's spirit died. This "death" did not destroy the spirit, but it broke man's relationship with God. It was then that man's soul—his mind, emotions, and will—began to rule him apart from relationship with God, under the influence of sin.

When we are born again unto salvation, the Spirit of God restores our spirits so that we can be in communion with Him, and we become temples of the Spirit of God. As it says in Ephesians 2:1, we were "dead in trespasses and sins," and He quickens us. Once again, we are made alive to God. But, because our psyches have been so enslaved to the power of sin, there is a veil of flesh between our recreated spirit, where Jesus dwells, and our carnal mind, emotions, and will. It is as though the veil of the temple that was torn in two when Jesus died must be torn again inside us—His temples—in order to allow Christ free access to them.

Only the Word of God can do the supernatural work required to rend that veil inside us. The Scriptures declare that the "word of God is quick, and powerful, and sharper than any twoedged sword, piercing even to the dividing asunder of soul and spirit, and of the joints and marrow, and is a discerner of the thoughts and intents of the heart" (Heb. 4:12). As we choose to obey the Word of God, it acts as a knife to cut away the veil of flesh that hides the life of Christ within our spirits. Yielding to the working of the Holy Spirit in our lives and allowing our self-life to be crucified through the dealings of God will allow Jesus to fill His temple. When this work of the Holy Spirit is complete, we will see the glory of God in the church, as Paul declared it: "Christ in you, the hope of glory" (Col. 1:27).

Because we have kept the Christ-life in us "locked up" in our spirits, not allowing our self-life to be crucified, we have not known Jesus as we should have known Him. The "cave" dealings of God that bring us to obedience to the Word will cause the life of Christ to develop in us. His glory will fill our temples to the degree that we give up our self-life in exchange for the Christ-life. As that happens, we will become holy and know divine joy and compassion, learning to walk in unity with our fellow believers.

That is not the state of the church at present. Though the incorruptible seed of eternal life has been planted in her, the church has not yet matured to the place of revelation that allows her to know Jesus as God has intended. Some may not even understand the continuing work of revelation, believing the written Word provides the total revelation of Christ. There is much more involved in knowing Jesus than mentally grasping facts about His life or even expounding truths that He taught.

What Is Revelation?

A SIMPLE DEFINITION of revelation is this: disclosing a divine truth that has been hidden. For Christians, it involves the unveiling of the Christ that already lives in our spirits. In my book *Presenting the Holy Spirit, Who Is He?* (vol. 1), I state:

> The Spirit of Truth takes us through a divine learning process to make revelation a reality that changes our lives. That process results in the unveiling of the Christ who is in us...The Word reveals the veil of flesh in our lives that keeps Christ so hidden that we do not know Him as we should. 'Line upon line' the Spirit of Truth works to remove that veil of flesh to reveal Christ in us until His glory, His divine Presence, fills us.
>
> Paul declared that we are the temple of the Holy Spirit (1 Cor. 3:16). As the Holy Spirit fills our temple, the mind of Christ becomes our mind, His emotions become our emotions, and His will becomes our will. Our will becomes His will, and we become the will of God. It is God's desire for His manifest presence to completely fill His temples.
>
> The first step toward revelation in this divine process is to receive *information.* We must first receive a basic truth in our minds in order for the Holy Spirit to bring it to our remembrance.
>
> When that information begins to be a light to our spirits, it becomes *illumination.* We understand, in a way we never understood before, the truth that was once only information to us.
>
> The Holy Spirit (in us) receives the Word with joy, and, as we receive it from Him, it becomes *inspiration* to us. New desires to obey the Word fill our hearts.
>
> When that transcribed Word moves from our heads to our hearts, it becomes a living Word to us as *revelation.* Revelation makes the truth become a living Person to us and in us.
>
> After revelation begins to work in our hearts, the next step in this divine process is *realization,* understanding that we are being changed through our obedience to the revelation that has become a part of our lives.
>
> A consistent walk in greater depth of revelation then brings a gradual *transformation* to our lives. We are changed from glory to glory into the image of the Son through our obedience to that revelation.

> The final step the Spirit of Truth works in us is the *manifestation* of Jesus' character in our lives. Maturity is the beauty of Jesus seen in people who have allowed the Spirit of Truth to touch their lives in every area of their soul and spirit. They, in obedience to God, have continually turned from sin and allowed the nature of Christ to be fully unveiled in them.[1]

Glory Revealed Through Suffering

THE LIFE OF Christ will be revealed in us as we are victorious in the trials we endure. Paul understood this when he wrote, "For I reckon that the sufferings of this present time are not worthy to be compared with the glory which shall be revealed in us" (Rom 8:18). He explained to the Corinthians that believers are changed from glory to glory by the Spirit of the Lord (2 Cor. 3:18). Then he described many difficult trials he was experiencing and declared: "For momentary, light affliction is producing for us an eternal weight of glory far beyond all comparison" (2 Cor. 4:17, NAS).

As Jesus is seen in the church through mature believers, once again the presence of God will fill the temple as He did in the Old Testament. Only this time, the temple will be God's own creation—mankind—as He originally intended when He created Adam. The church will march triumphantly as one man in the world, filled with the glory of the Lord.

The prophet Habakkuk saw clearly the day when "the earth shall be filled with the knowledge of the glory of the Lord, as the waters cover the sea" (Hab. 2:14). He was seeing prophetically the "glorious church, not having spot, or wrinkle, or any such thing; but that it should be holy and without blemish" (Eph. 5:27). And it was Paul who declared that for this reason Christ gave Himself for the church, "that he might sanctify and cleanse it with the washing of water by the word" (Eph. 5:26). In this next move of God, Jesus will be revealed fully in the church as individual believers allow Jesus to be revealed in them. Then we shall experience the greatest revelation of all—a revelation of the Father.

A Revelation of the Father

EVERYTHING THAT JESUS did was for the purpose of revealing the Father to us. Jesus said, "The works which the Father hath given me to finish, the same works that I do, bear witness of me, that the Father hath sent me" (John 5:36). He did nothing of Himself, out of His own will or desire, but only those things He saw the Father doing (John 5:30). Every parable was intended to reveal the love of the Father. Every miracle He performed was to show the Father. When He prayed for Lazarus to be raised from the dead, Jesus said to His Father, "And I knew that thou hearest me always: but because of the people which stand by I said it, that they may believe that thou has sent me" (John 11:42).

Still, while Jesus was on earth, even His disciples failed to grasp the revelation of the Father. When they asked Jesus to show them the Father, Jesus asked poignantly: "Have I been so long with you, and yet hast thou not known me, Philip? He that hath seen me hath seen the Father" (John 14:9). Was Jesus a failure? Did He fail to communicate to His own disciples the reason for His coming? No. Jesus' ministry to those disciples did not end with His ascension into heaven. He instructed them to wait for the day of Pentecost.

After they were baptized in the Holy Spirit, the disciples were empowered to become the church. Though they turned the world upside down with the gospel of Christ, they still did not have a clear revelation of the Father. It was Paul the apostle who first declared: "Ye have received the Spirit of adoption, whereby we cry, Abba, Father" (Rom. 8:15). The other apostles' later writings reveal their revelation of the Father. John wrote: "And truly our fellowship is with the Father, and with his Son Jesus Christ" (1 John 1:3).

The church today needs this same empowering and revelation of the Father. If Jesus were standing before us, would He not ask us the same question: "Have I been so long with you and you have not seen the Father?" How long has He lived in us as born-again believers, without our coming to know Him in revelation and power? We need our eyes opened to the reality of God who dwells in us. We need to experience the fellowship with the Father that the disciples testified about.

That is an awesome prospect to me. When that revelation of the Father comes, we will confess that we have not known God. We say He is our Father, and we know He forgave us. But, in the revelation that is coming, we are going to know the Father's love in its fullness, with all the peace, security, well-being, hope, and comfort that He is. As we focus our eyes on Jesus, we will come to know the Father, for the Scriptures declare that Jesus is the "brightness of his glory, and the express image of his person" (Heb. 1:3).

Jesus will not fail His church; He came to reveal to us the Father. As we receive this revelation, our eyes will no longer be on gifts or ministries or how much faith we have. Our eyes will be fastened on

Jesus. His holiness will be our nature, and the church will be filled with joy that is motivated by compassion. We will march together in unity—in divine fellowship with our Father.

16

The Glorious Church Revealed

The End of the Next Move of God

THIS WORLD IS going to see the church come out of hiding, no longer "cave dwellers" in training. The day will soon dawn when the Spirit will say, "Arise, shine; for thy light is come, and the glory of the Lord is risen upon thee" (Isa. 60:1). It will not matter that darkness covers the earth, and gross darkness the people, for the glory of the Lord will be seen upon us—His church in the earth.

The true church in these days of testing and training is being transformed from pitiful impotence into a powerful influence in the earth as the Holy Spirit reveals Christ in His glory through the lives of believers. The church is going to move in power to bring people to Christ, the living Word.

This glorious church will set the pace, demand respect, and again hold a high reputation for godliness and holiness. It will be a remnant, not in the sense of a small number, but in the sense of being distinctive in character, separate from the false church. *Remnant* refers to a special people, protected from destruction (Zeph. 2:7, 9; Rev. 12:17). As the glory of God shines through Christ's church, protecting her from destruction, she will be God's instrument to speak to the world before Christ's return.

The Breaking Light of Dawn

I HAVE WITNESSED in many churches the attack of the enemy in the form of a Jezebel spirit or the betrayal of an Absalom. I have seen the destruction of the pseudo-counseling spirit in some churches and the tyranny of the pharisaical spirit in others. I have wept and prayed with heartbroken pastors and leaders who felt their lives and ministries were destroyed.

In recent months some of these pastors have called to tell me about the mighty visitation of God they are now experiencing in their churches. They are experiencing the power of God in worship and praise, in fresh revelation of the Word, in renewed zeal in their personal lives and in the lives of their churches, as well as in numerical growth. They are seeing the light of God arise upon them as they walk in repentance and forgiveness. They have allowed God to circumcise their hearts so He could bring them into the promised land.

Beginnings of Revival

WHAT JOY IS filling these ministers and their churches as they open themselves to the fresh visitation of God. Many are experiencing the signs and wonders of laughter and being slain in the Spirit. Believers are giving testimony to emotional and mental healing, restored marriages, a fresh revelation of Jesus and the love of the Father as they lie—sometimes for hours—in the presence of God. Many sense a new compassion for other hurting people.

In my home church in Tennessee, a woman testified that as she lay in the presence of God He showed her that her faith for healing had been shipwrecked. She is a mature intercessor in the church and has offered loyal prayer support for many years. But the enemy had used disappointments to shipwreck her faith in praying for healing for herself and others. She wept as she shared how the Spirit of God had shown her step-by-step how her faith had been hindered, yet He did not leave her with a sense of condemnation. He simply cleansed her and renewed her faith to pray for people's healing. She had never felt the love and compassion of God in such a strong way.

In this same church a middle-aged pharmacist testified that he did not expect ever to have a real relationship with Jesus. He thought he would simply come to church with his family and sit toward the back, hoping to make heaven someday. As he responded to the altar call one Sunday morning, he was standing behind a lady who was slain in the Spirit. He reached out to catch her and found himself falling. For several hours he lay there, unable to get up, as Jesus revealed Himself to him, telling him that He wanted to have a personal relationship with him. That man has been transformed and today is praying for others to receive this fresh anointing of the Holy Spirit.

Children are experiencing supernatural revelations of Jesus and giving testimony of "visiting heaven" as they lie in God's presence. Some have seen angels and express the happiness of heaven. Others have heard God speak to them about His plan for their lives.[1]

Reports are coming from churches across our nation and from around the world of a new outpouring of the Holy Spirit. Recently my pastor, Sue Curran, ministered in the Christ for the Nations Bible School in Germany and experienced a wave of revival as students were being slain in the Spirit, laughing or weeping, or simply having an encounter with God. In England, denominational churches are seeing this same phenomenon of being slain in the Spirit and filled with joy and laughter.[2] The most important characteristic of this fresh outpouring of the Spirit is the consistent report of radically transformed lives and churches, displaying the love and joy and generosity of God.

Many of these believers have withstood the attacks of Jezebel and Absalom. They recognized the enemy's counterattack and have ripped off the disguises of the spirits of witchcraft and pharisaism. Their wholeness is the product of revival—not pseudo-counseling techniques. God has chosen to visit His people once again, as He showed me more than thirty years ago that He would do. What we are seeing now is just a beginning of what God is going to do in the months ahead for those who seek His presence.

Removal of Hindrances

God's remnant is not hindered from revival by denominationalism, human tradition, prejudice, culture, or customs. The Holy Spirit has breathed truth into their hearts, cleansing them from all that would delay the move of God. Cleansed, confident, and prepared, they are actively participating to bring revival to the world.

I was scheduled to speak at the Conference of Third World Revival Churches in Nassau, Bahamas, a few months ago where thousands of leaders and believers were gathered from many nations. As I prepared to go to the platform, I heard the Holy Spirit say to me, "You cannot minister to these people until you repent of the prejudice of your nation against them." I was stunned. How could I address such a sensitive situation? Yet I knew I had heard my Father's voice, and I dared not disobey.

As I was presented to that great congregation, I opened my mouth and told them what God had just spoken to me. I asked their forgiveness for the prejudice of my own heart and that of my nation. A spirit of reconciliation flowed among all those thousands of people. Men and women from different countries began to repent for their own prejudices, weeping and embracing one another. The love of God filled that large auditorium as the body of Christ experienced a new level of unity.

Redemptive Truths Established

THE CHURCH—GOD'S remnant—is established in the realities of the redemptive truths birthed by the Charismatic Renewal. Out of her life flow spiritual gifts, faith, and temporal blessings. Christ Himself has given her His power of attorney, and she carries out His business on earth in that divine authority. That renewal prepared the church for this next move of God, and we are beginning to see evidences of the glorious church—a holy church, cleansed and transformed by the character of God within. Her arms will reach out to all the world with joy, compassion, and unity.

Prophetic Admonition

MAY WE AS God's people hear the word of the Lord. This is a special day. This is the appointed time. This is the year for us to break out of our shells. It is the year of realizing the fulfillment of "It shall come to pass in those days." As it was with Elijah on Mount Carmel, so it will be with us. The day that Elijah should build the altar and pray the prayer that would bring fire from heaven had been appointed in advance. It had been foreordained that the prophets of Baal should be destroyed and that once more the glory of the Lord would come upon His people. To a man, they were cut down—those who had lied to and seduced the people of God, lining up in the name of Baal against the ways of the Lord.

We must be careful not to be deceived into following our usual order of worship, saying that we know how to do it or that we have always done it this way. In this next move of God we will not have "church as usual." God's Jehus are ready to receive a fresh anointing to replace the rule of Ahab and Jezebel. They will be filled with zeal to bring down the rulers of darkness. There is a prophetic word on the lips of the Elijahs of today that will feed the flesh of Jezebel to the dogs. They will share the word of the Lord, and we will hear what the Spirit says to the church.

These are days when God's Spirit will move upon our altars, causing His fire to fall upon them. We must remember that an altar is what we build, not what God builds. It is our task to place our lives on an altar of consecration; it is God's responsibility to let fire fall upon it. Every person is accountable for building his or her own altar, and everyone shall experience his or her own Mount Carmel.

During David's time of preparation, Saul tried to harm him. Today, as the Sauls of this world are going about doing their mischief, seeking their fame and fortune while asking for prophets to stand with them (as Saul said to Samuel, "Stand with me in this sacrifice"), they are trying to cover their sins rather than repent of them. In contrast to that blatant rebellion, the Davids of today are being prepared to enjoy the character of God as they submit to His circumcision of their hearts from the love of the world and bondage to their self-lives.

Resurrection Power in the Church

JESUS TAUGHT THE principle of life coming out of death. As we consecrate our lives on the altars we build, God will send the fire and consume us, our bondages, and our self-lives. But that is not the end of the matter.

Jesus raised Lazarus from the dead after he was buried for four days. The natural evaluation of his condition was that he "stinketh" (John 11:39). There is much death in the church today, much burial of that which is stinking. Many times we have yearned in our hearts, as Martha and Mary did, crying, "Had You been here, our brother would not have died." (See John 11:32.) We lament, "Lord, if You had brought this next move sooner, our brothers would not have died." We grieve over our family members and church members who have fallen away.

The Lord has promised restoration, raising up a mighty army in the earth. You ask, How can that be possible? How can we expect to see such a resurrection? That question reveals that we have not yet understood the magnitude of the coming revival. The prophet saw this overwhelming flood of revival when he declared, "For the earth will be filled with the knowledge of the glory of the LORD, as the waters cover the sea" (Hab. 2:14, NAS).

The Word of God will come alive to our hearts, and preachers will preach as they have never preached before. They will receive revelation even while they are speaking, declaring that they had not understood these truths before. A great wave of divine revelation knowledge is coming in the next move of God. We will "[taste] the good word of God, and the powers of the world to come" (Heb. 6:5).

In Elijah's day there were seven thousand people hidden in caves who had not "attended church" for a long time. They were kept alive on bread and water as they hid from the wicked Jezebel, who was ruling the land. As this current move of God delivers captives, people will be restored to God and will love the Word again. They will love to praise and worship again.

We may have heard this prophesied years ago, but now it is coming to pass. As members of God's church in the earth today, we are part of the present fulfillment of His promise to have a glorious church without spot or wrinkle. We declare with the psalmist: "Thou wilt arise and have compassion on Zion; for it is time to be gracious to her, for the appointed time has come" (Ps. 102:13, NAS). Zion in Scripture represents the church, the people of God, through whom God desires to manifest His presence. It is God's appointed time to favor His people.

National Restoration

WHEN THIS NEXT move of God brings forth resurrection life, it won't just happen in local churches. It will flow into homes, communities, and business places. As it increases, it won't be just droplets of life-giving rain here and there. It will be a flood running to those "in mountains, and in dens and caves of the earth" (Heb. 11:38).

Our government, our church denominations, our social organizations, our school systems, our industries—which have become corrupt, motivated by self-promotion, serving for gold and silver and ruled by covetous practices—will all be changed by the power of God's divine presence. This move of God will be so powerful that throughout our land we will see a return to the great historical foundations of this nation, which declare that in God we trust.

Once more people will talk about God as our fathers did. Their conversations will concern the visitation of God rather than the Emmy awards. They will discuss "the riches of the glory of his inheritance in the saints" (Eph. 1:18), instead of bank accounts, interest rates, and retirement programs.

The Church Triumphant

AS WE BELIEVERS behold Christ in His glory, we will realize that He has not withheld resurrection life from us. It is sin that has prevented it—unbelief, carnal competition, covetousness, and so forth. As we respond to the word of God that is saying, "Build an altar; come in a new surrender of your spirit; come and let Me wash away the cynicism, the criticism, the doubts and unbelief, the fear and weariness of soul," we will hear that sweet sound of heaven as the gates are being raised and the flood begins to pour forth.

I think today I can hear God say, "My people, heaven's windows are opened. The blessings are being poured forth now. They will continue throughout this year, throughout this decade, and into the next century. My glory is going to come forth in a continually greater measure." We won't have to say God is moving in Canada or Florida or California; in England, Germany or Argentina. We will be able to say it is happening right where we are.

God is visiting His people again. The floodgates are about to open, bringing a heaven-sent, gully-washing, sin-killing revival. The Word of God will be fulfilled to us:

> For you will go out with joy, and be led forth with peace; the mountains and the hills will break forth into shouts of joy before you, and all the trees of the field will clap their hands.
>
> —Isaiah 55:12, NAS

The trees of the field are clapping their hands, and the little hills are skipping about. Salvation is come, and deliverance is at hand as the prophecies of God's Word are being fulfilled. There will be such a shout of victory that it will be heard to Saul's kingdom, who will fall on his own sword. We won't have to fight the ungodly leaders of the world. God Himself will take care of them. There will be a great toppling. As the walls of Jericho came down with the sound of the trumpet and a shout (Josh. 6:20), so the walls of wickedness in our country are coming down.

There will be a clamping down on violence and wickedness in the media and an end to the destruction wrought by those who stood against marriage and for abortion. The army of God—His church—is going to march through this nation and bind the powers of darkness, praising the name of our Lord as He releases the spirit of liberty upon our nation.

At present there are little signs of victory here and there as people experience the visitation of God that has caused us to hope again. I believe our hope will increase by leaps and bounds in the days ahead. We will be as the man at the gate Beautiful who came walking and leaping and praising God into the temple (Acts 3:8). We will come in rejoicing in our hearts. As this great move of God breaks forth and the waters I saw in the vision of the hydroelectric plant are released, I believe the church will become a mighty river that floods the earth until the knowledge of the glory of the Lord covers it.

My admonition to the church is that no one decide to stay on the bank and observe the debris that a flood inevitably brings. Those who do will declare that this move is not of God because of some who are not walking in it perfectly. We decide whether we will stay with the debris or lift our eyes above it and plunge into the current of God that is going to run fuller, deeper, and broader until it covers the earth as the waters cover the sea. It is time to behold Jesus and not be distracted by a few people who do not function properly in the new anointing.

As the Holy Spirit works to revive and restore believers, we are going to see the church triumphant rise and face her enemies victoriously. This is the revealed destiny of God's people.

Jesus, the head of the church, declares: "I will build my church; and the gates of hell shall not prevail against it" (Matt. 16:18). Let us end here by shouting together a more literal translation of that cry: "Move back, gates of hell! Here comes the church!"

NOTES

Chapter 1: The Proclamation

1. Fuchsia Pickett, *God's Dream* (Shippensburg, PA: Destiny Image, 1991), 44–49.
2. W. E. Vine, Merrill F. Unger, William White Jr., eds., *Vine's Expository Dictionary of Biblical Words* (Nashville, TN: Thomas Nelson Publishers, 1984), s.v. "power."
3. Ibid., s.v. "river."

Chapter 3: The Spirit of Jezebel

1. Francis Frangipane, *The Three Battlegrounds* (Marion, Iowa, 1989), 98.
2. Ibid., 98.
3. Dick Bernal, *When Lucifer and Jezebel Join Your Church* (Sunnyvale, CA: Patson's Press), 18.
4. Frangipane, *The Three Battlegrounds,* 98.
5. *Vine's Dictionary,* s.v. "prophecy."

Chapter 5: Absalom's Betrayal

1. James Strong, "Greek Dictionary of the New Testament," *The New Strong's Exhaustive Concordance of the Bible* (Nashville, TN: Thomas Nelson Publishers, 1984), s.v. "skandalon."
2. Most of my remarks in the section on offense were drawn from John Bevere, *The Bait of Satan* (Lake Mary, FL: Creation House, 1994), 8–14.

Chapter 8: Hindering Concepts to Revival

1. *Merriam-Webster's Collegiate Dictionary, Tenth Edition* (Springfield, MA: Merriam-Webster, Inc., 1993), s.v. "tradition."
2. Christological epistles emphasize Christ and His life and work in us. They include the books of Ephesians, Philippians, Galatians, and Colossians.

3. *Merriam-Webster's Collegiate Dictionary, Tenth Edition,* s.v. "custom."

Chapter 9:
The Charismatic Renewal

1. Sue Curran is pastor of Shekinah Ministries, Blountsville, TN. She is a conference speaker and teacher, and is the author of *Kingdom Principles, The Praying Church, The Forgiving Church, The Joshua Generation,* and *I Saw Satan Fall Like Lightning.*

Chapter 11:
Holiness Realized

1. *Vine's Dictionary,* s.v. "confess, confession."

Chapter 12:
Revival Through Gladness

1. Strong, *Strong's Concordance*, s.v. "joy."
2. *Vine's Dictionary*, s.v. "joy."
3. Ibid.

Chapter 13:
Compassion

1. *Vine's Dictionary,* s.v. "eleeo."
2. Ibid., s.v. "power."

Chapter 14:
Unity

1. *Merriam-Webster's Collegiate Dictionary, Tenth Edition*, s.v. "unity."
2. Since the word *tongue(s)* in the Greek is *glossa,* the Charismatic Renewal was often labeled the glossolalia movement because so many people spoke in tongues as a result of being baptized by the Spirit. The Greek term *glossai* refers to the gift of speaking in tongues among Spirit-filled believers. For additional information, see *Nelson's Illustrated Bible Dictionary* (Nashville, TN: Thomas Nelson, 1986), s.v. "tongues," and *The Complete Word Study Dictionary New Testament* by Spiros Zodhiates (Chattanooga, TN: AMG Publishers, 1992), 375–377.

3. Scriptures referring to unity include Zechariah 2:11; Judges 20:11; Romans 6:5; Philippians 2:2; John 17:23; Ephesians 4:3, 13, 16; 1 Corinthians 1:10.
4. Fuchsia Pickett, *Holy Anointing Oil,* Outline Study Series available by writing to Fuchsia Pickett, 394 Glory Rd., Blountsville, TN 37617.
5. Allen Cook, pastor of Grace Tabernacle, Brentwood, NH, was a contributor to this study of Aaron's anointing.
6. For more information on the office of the priesthood and the special significance of the priestly garments, see *Vine's Dictionary* or *Nelson's Bible Dictionary.*
7. Fuchsia Pickett, *Presenting the Holy Spirit, Who Is He?,* vol. 1 (Shippensburg, PA: Destiny Image, 1993), 50–51.
8. *Nelson's Bible Dictionary*, s.v. "mount, mountain."

Chapter 15: Jesus in the Church

1. Pickett, *Presenting the Holy Spirit,* 86–89.
2. *Merriam-Webster's Collegiate Dictionary, Tenth Edition*, s.v. "remnant."

Chapter 16: The Glorious Church Revealed

1. Pastor Sue Curran, ministering in Blue Mountain Retreat in Pennsylvania in August 1994; Olen Griffing, at his academy in Dallas, Texas, has documented visions children have had of heaven. Several of them described it in the same way without conferring with each other.
2. Clive Price, "Holy Laughter Hits British Churches," *Charisma,* October 1994, 82.

There's a Miracle in Your House

Tommy Barnett

THERE'S A MIRACLE IN YOUR HOUSE by Tommy Barnett
Previously published by Creation House

Strang Communications Company
600 Rinehart Road
Lake Mary, Florida 32746
Web site: http://wwwcreationhouse.com
Library of Congress Catalog Card Number: 92-75648
International Standard Book Number: 0-88419-330-6

I would like to dedicate this book to:

my staff—people who were miracles in my own congregation and have come to play a very important role in church leadership;

our deacons—they had more vision and daring than I did and stretched me to believe God and trust Him to provide for our financial needs;

the people in my congregation—they helped carry out the dream God gave us;

the miracle in my own house—my wife, Marja; my two sons, Matthew and Luke, who are both powerful evangelists and preachers; and my daughter, Kristi, whose goal has always been to have a family and be a mother, and who's given me three wonderful grandchildren;

and my wonderful heavenly Father, who is the source of all miracles.

Acknowledgments

FOR THE WRITING of this book I am indebted in a tremendous way to the assistance of two men, Ron Hembree and Walter Walker.

Ron Hembree is an outstanding, award-winning author of many well-known books, including *St. Mark of Calcutta;* a TV personality; and a dear friend of many years who knows me as few people do. He took time out of his busy schedule to use his talents on this project, and I thank him.

Walter Walker, former editorial director of Creation House, heard me speak on this subject at the Charismatic Bible Ministries conference in 1991 in Tulsa and challenged me to write this book. Without his encouragement it never would have been written. He hounded me persistently until the dream became a reality. I appreciate his patience with my busy schedule and his helpful insights and teaching.

I would also like to thank the staffs of Creation House and my church for their hard work and patience in seeing this book become a reality.

CONTENTS

There's a Miracle in Your House

Preface

NOTHING BAD EVER happens to you," the radio talk show host blurted out during an on-the-air interview with Tommy Barnett. She was so overwhelmed by the popular preacher's positive attitude she began to think he led some kind of charmed life immune from the petty problems plaguing the rest of us mere mortals.

Of course she was wrong, and Pastor Barnett quickly assured her he was very human and had faced his share of problems. "But," he said, "nothing bad ever does happen to me because our great God takes even the bad and makes it good. So, ultimately, you are right, even though there might be momentary misery and misunderstanding."

Ever since Tommy Barnett started storming through the country on his "special divine mission" over four decades ago, the world has had to sit up and take notice. His life and career have been such a series of miracles that many, like the radio host, wonder if he does lead a charmed existence. Just as a perplexed physician seeks the cause of a mystery disease, many have probed and pondered the reasons for Tommy Barnett's success. Both critics and admirers have offered their opinions, but that is all they are—opinions.

Perhaps the best way to discover the answer to this enigma is to meet the man himself and get to know what lies beneath the polished exterior of this remarkable pastor. In doing so we discover the same flower of faith will bloom for all if we but learn and put into practice the great principles that were forged in the furnace of his life. This ordinary man has become quite extraordinary and insists that we can all grow far beyond ourselves if we really want to. He says, "The miracle is in the house!"

Those of us who have known Tommy Barnett through the years recognize his uniqueness and, at the same time, his "commonness." The thousands of pastors and leaders who attend his annual pastors' school leave far different from when they arrived. For us to touch this man's life is to touch the potential of greatness within ourselves.

This book seeks to capture the passions of this highly successful pastor-preacher. Tommy Barnett is consumed with advancing the kingdom of Jesus Christ through reaching the helpless, homeless, and hurting of our world. He believes in "vicarious" success. That is, he believes all those God permits him to touch can do greater things than he has accomplished. It thrills him to see their success because his single passion is not recognition but that all men might come to know Jesus Christ.

Most want "magical" answers rather than spiritual ones. Not this unique man. Tommy Barnett rejects "pop psychology" and the various fads in the church. Rather he insists there are age-old, available, and viable principles in God's Word giving us information and inspiration so we all can discover and unleash the miracle that is in the house. All those desiring to make the most of their potential would do well to hear and heed: The miracle you need right now is already within your grasp!

—Ron Hembree
Phoenix, Arizona

1

Down and Out in Davenport

There's a miracle in the house! I've said that to myself countless times in the face of discouragement and opposition. As I persevered, the miracle inevitably appeared.

In the midst of impossible situations I have just kept saying, "There's got to be a miracle in the house!" And God comes through—sometimes in ways I could never have imagined.

I've preached it to others in our church here in Phoenix and to the ministers in training in the Master's Commission. The staff and laypersons of our church have presented it to the six thousand Christian leaders who come to Phoenix each year to learn how we discovered that the miracle was in the house. And I've taught it to the more than a hundred businessmen I meet with every Thursday. As a result of this principle, lives, churches, and businesses have exploded into a new dimension of fruitfulness and success. We've built a church with one hundred eighty successful outreach ministries to every group we can think of, from professional athletes to street people and bikers.

The same principles can work for you in your home, your job, your church, or in any situation that calls for a miracle.

When we think of miracles, what comes to mind are the more spectacular brands of divine intervention such as the miracle of healing. Throughout this book I will use the term miracle in a broader sense to include God's protection, provision, or direction.

When I say the miracle is "in the house," I don't necessarily mean in your physical house. In chapter 2 you'll understand why I use that terminology.

To say the miracle is in the house means that the answer to your need begins with something that is already there in your grasp, in your ability, or in your possession.

If God were always to fix our problems in the way we wanted Him to, the skies would be crowded with the provisions that were floating down right out of heaven. Most of the time God's miraculous provision for us in our need comes not so much like manna from heaven but in the multiplication of what we already have—fishes and loaves, for example.

When the challenges become overwhelming, God may say something to you like, "How many fishes and loaves do you have?"

Sometimes the key to miracles is in simply doing what He says even though it goes against conventional wisdom—like casting the net on the other side of the boat.

When you doubt your own power and abilities to do what is required of you, He might ask you, as He did Moses, "What is that in your hand?"

The greatest miracle of your life might just begin with something that is already in the house or already in your hand.

You'll see what I mean by that a little later, but first of all I need to explain how the principle started to work in me. Like most great lessons, the learning experience began in the midst of a difficult situation.

When I arrived in the small Iowa city of Davenport, my self-confidence was low. My dad had wanted me to stay with him in Kansas City as an associate pastor. But I had felt God stirring my heart to pastor my own church. I had been a "successful" evangelist since I was sixteen years old and had assumed that a church would want to grab me up right away. I thought I would be able to pick for myself which one of those large churches I would take.

It didn't hurt to have a successful pastor for a father, a man who had lots of friends and pull in the denomination. I had a lot going for me—so I supposed—as I confidently typed up my "impressive" resumé and sent out copies to all the large churches I heard were looking for a pastor.

But the demand for Tommy Barnett was all in my own imagination.

Not one church called. As the weeks passed I began to feel something must be really wrong. I swallowed my pride and applied for churches not quite as large as I thought I could handle. Surely they would want me, and I knew I could do them good. But they too ignored my gracious offer to become their pastor. Frankly, no one wanted me.

In a state of desperation one day I cried out, "God, no matter what kind of door You open, I promise I will step through it." Within days I heard from Davenport, Iowa. The deacon who called to invite me to try out told me what a great church they had.

I felt I was meant for bigger places than Davenport, a sullen little settlement on the mighty Mississippi River. Nevertheless, I told God I would go through whatever door He opened. So off I went to the tryout in Davenport.

Arriving late Saturday evening, I drove all over town, wanting to take a first look at this great church. But it was nowhere to be found. Early the next morning I went looking again and eventually ended up on the wrong side of the tracks.

There it was—on Elsie Street, right behind A & W Root Beer. In my years as an evangelist I had seen every kind of church, but nothing like this. It was worse than the worst I had ever seen. I was suddenly reminded of my commitment to go through any door God would open.

It was an old, dilapidated building that had been around too long and constructed too cheaply even to pretend to be historical—and it smelled, too. It begged for a bulldozer to come and put it out of its misery.

The little wood-frame building seated fewer than a hundred people and had high, concrete steps that were cracked in the middle. The faded paint was peeling, windows were broken, and the yard was unkempt. As I walked down the aisle, every board creaking under my feet, I noticed that the building was lit by bare light bulbs hanging from wires. The carpet had holes, and the building was heated by an old coal stove.

I remember when I was a kid playing marbles with my friends. If someone made a bad shot and yelled "overs" before he was called or caught, he got a second chance. I wanted to yell "overs" to God. Davenport was not my idea of an open door. But I had made a sacred vow, so I had to say *yes* to the invitation at least to talk with the church board. In my heart I was sure God would not sentence me to such an unlikely place. After all, I had preached to thousands around the world.

If you pray for guidance and look for the open door but are not impressed with what you see (for example, taking a lesser job), *don't be too quick to write it off.* God's miracles are found behind some uninviting doors. We miss the miracles because we don't look in the places where God hides them.

> It is the glory of God to conceal a matter, but the glory of kings is to search out a matter.
>
> —Proverbs 25:2

Sunday morning dawned, and seventy-six people showed up for the service. This was considered an excellent number, apparently pumped up by the curiosity of those who wanted to take a gander at the prospective preacher.

That morning service didn't improve on my first impression. The song service was accompanied by an old, out-of-tune upright piano. The song leader didn't sing well either; on top of that, he led the little group in a chorus that sounded more like a dirge than praise. The people sang listlessly.

I was sure this Sunday in the Quad Cities was equivalent to Abraham's taking Isaac to Mount Moriah. It was only a test, and if I passed it I knew God would open some bright and beautiful door because I had been obedient.

I determined to preach the hardest sermon I knew just to discourage them from even considering me. I stared out at seventy-six of the most negative people I had ever seen and began to hack away at my message on faith. I must admit my heart was not into the subject. I just wanted to get through it and out of town so I could get on with whatever else lay ahead in my life.

The deacons wanted to meet with me that afternoon to interview me for the job. I obliged them because there was little else to do in Davenport but count the hours until I could escape back to the civilization of Kansas City.

That Sunday night I preached my "meanest" sermon and after the altar call set out for the door. I had already checked out of the motel so that I could leave for home immediately. The board stopped me short, saying I could not leave until the voting was over.

Voting?

Now it came to me. I was so preoccupied with my disappointment I had forgotten to tell them I was not going to take the church. They had already gathered the twenty members in the back room to decide my future.

I was stuck.

Pacing the floor, I tried my best to figure out a way to let them know they were wasting their time. I was never coming to Davenport, and that was that. But the board came out before I had time to put a workable plan together. They were all smiles, telling me I had received 100 percent of the votes, and this was the first time in the history of the church such a thing had happened. It must be God!

What they did not tell me was that no pastor had survived the church more than two years before he moved on or was moved by an unceremonious prodding from the same voting body that was so enthusiastically endorsing my candidacy.

It has always been hard for me to say *no* straight out, and the people were so excited I did not want to disappoint them. Therefore, I did the only thing I knew to do—I stalled. I told the church this was a great spiritual matter, and I had to pray it through before responding to their offer. It was indeed a grave spiritual matter, but in all honesty I was buying time so I could let them down easy. They swallowed their disappointment and assured me they understood. In spite of their assurances I knew they did not really understand, and they were wondering why I would not jump at the chance to be their pastor.

Returning to Kansas City I wrestled with God for three weeks telling Him all the reasons why Davenport was not a good idea for me. I had always envisioned myself preaching in New York or Los Angeles. I saw little opportunity in the town or in the church.

After three tormented weeks I called the board and told them I was on my way.

Our first days in Davenport were a struggle. No one came to the altar to accept Christ, and the evangelistic calling within me cried out that something was horribly wrong. I met with the deacons to tell them maybe it was not God's will for me to be there after all. I called my dad and complained. Both the board and my father said I should hold steady. This was especially hard for me after seeing hundreds respond to my altar calls when I was on the evangelistic field. But I stayed and prayed strictly out of sheer obedience rather than any great spiritual desire.

Up until this time everything had gone well with me and my ministry. Now I was stuck in a difficult situation. Perhaps if I could just endure it for a while, I would be out the door and on my way to bigger and better things. But God had another plan, and that was to give me victory in the face of immovable obstacles.

The answer did not come through my mighty sermons or any of the other things I tried in order to bring life into that church. In fact it was at the end of my efforts that I discovered that the miracle had been in the house all along.

I ate lunch with Bobbie Stottlemeyer and her husband, Leon, my first Sunday in Davenport. She had been in the church for several months and had a real concern for the lost, but the seed inside her had never blossomed.

One day after I had exhausted all my ideas she came to me saying, "Brother Barnett, I've been saved for less than a year, and although I've never won anyone to the Lord, I've been going out every Friday for two hours to witness. I believe God has led you to this city to help us win people to Christ."

There was something so sincere in her spirit that I asked if I could accompany her and her partner the next Friday when they went out to witness. She agreed, so I drove them on their rounds. The first week we had no success. But the second week that we went out witnessing I drove around the block after I had dropped the ladies off for their appointment. Not finding a parking place I pulled again in front of the targeted house, and one of the women beckoned to me frantically. I thought something must be desperately wrong because she was so excited and emotional.

"Hurry, Brother Barnett," she cried, as she gestured wildly. "We've got an old man on his knees, and he wants to get saved. What do we do next?" I went inside and helped the ladies lead this dear old man to the Lord.

The next Sunday the excited women brought their brand-new convert to church and put him on the front row. Our people were thrilled when he stood to testify.

Something strange and wonderful happened that very special Sunday so long ago. That little dry and dead Iowa church started to stir to new life. I took advantage of the moment and told the congregation we would go witnessing again the next week and anyone else who wanted to get in on this wonderful joy could join us. Four ladies did, and that week two elderly women came to know the Lord. The following Sunday they showed up in church, and we had them testify. The next Friday we had more people out winning more converts to share what had happened to them. Soon the converts filled the front rows of our church, and the whole congregation caught the soulwinning fever.

So many were being saved and now needed transportation that I began appealing to the congregation for help. The lady who had started it all filled her car each week with new converts and then commandeered her husband's vehicle. They both were making two trips to church every Sunday with our new babes in Christ.

I went to the church board to ask that we buy a bus, but the response was decidedly cool.

"We had a bus before you came," the members told me flatly. "It sat and rusted. No one would ride in it when it would run. We don't want a bus ministry."

"Men, this is not just transportation. This is winning souls," I appealed.

"Let's pray about it," they responded, throwing my own recent delaying ploy back in my face.

"We've prayed long enough," I blurted out. "Let's do something. If the Lord provides the money, will you let me buy a bus?"

They were trapped in the possibility they might just miss God if they gave a flat-out no. Not wanting to discourage their new pastor, the board conceded, "Well, if the Lord provides—but *only* if the Lord provides."

The next Sunday I asked all the people to stand who had been saved in our witnessing program and had to depend on a ride to church. Then I added, "If anyone in the congregation feels inspired to buy a bus, please come to me after church."

Immediately Mrs. Stottlemeyer jumped up and said, "I don't have a thousand dollars to buy a bus, but I do have a house I have been trying to sell for months. If we sell this house, I will give you the money for the bus." We stopped the service right then and prayed.

A miracle occurred.

That week the woman sold her house, and the next Sunday she presented us with a check for our first bus.

We bought our bus, and now the battle was on. All hell wanted to stop this work before it started. Our bus motor burned up the very next week. I stood before the congregation to tell them the news and saw them shake their heads sagely, "We told you so." I did not dare ask for an offering to repair the motor but went to the bank and borrowed the money myself to get the bus back on the road. Within a month the bus was jammed full, and we had to buy another.

One of our excited new members bought the second bus and then a third. "As long as God prospers me and as long as you keep filling them, I will buy you buses," he said. While he could not continue this generous offer for long, God used him to inspire faith that He would provide as long as we continued winning souls.

Soon all our buses were filled, and revival was in full swing with people getting saved and packing out our little building. We had brightened up the place, and excitement was running high. Before long we were forced to new facilities, and the revival had captured the imagination of the whole city.

When revival broke out in Davenport, the news soon made it around the country. Sunday school records were shattered. People poured in from all over, and the media sat up and paid attention. Our church began to battle the porno shops and massage parlors and won, the first time such a victory had happened in the history of Davenport. Hundreds were saved in these special meetings, and lives were changed dramatically.

The remarkable Iowa revival never stopped, and each Sunday new and exciting things happened. Far from damaging my "reputation," Davenport made it. I now look back embarrassed that my faith in God's wise leading was so small. When I left Davenport, forty-seven buses were bringing people to church. Four thousand people were in Sunday school.

Looking back at those years, I am amazed that people perceived I had it all together. How wrong that perception was. When I went to Davenport, God had so humbled me that I did not think even those seventy-six people would stay with me very long. I was so insecure that if I saw someone absent, I would leave the platform during the song service, go to my office, and call that person's home.

It was God's grace, not my dynamics, that made it all happen. At Davenport I learned a lesson that would form the fabric and foundation for the rest of my life and ministry. It was the simple awareness that the miracle is in the house!

Every step of the way and at every obstacle I found that the supply to meet my need began with something God had already put in the house. Pastors need to realize that everything they need to build a great church is already in their congregations. Mrs. Stottlemeyer was the miracle in the house at Davenport, and she has been followed by many more. Almost all of the full-time staff members who have worked with me over the years have come from within the church I was pastoring at the time.

Every businessman needs to recognize that the keys for his success are in his own hand or his own organization. In every child is the potential to become a miracle. In your house or in your life God has already planted the seeds that can blossom and become the answer to your most desperate dilemma.

Today I live in Phoenix, Arizona, a city in the middle of the desert. A seed can lie dormant in the dry sand for months and even years. But when the rain finally does come, the desert blooms like a garden.

That's the way it is with many people's lives. They feel they have been in a dry desert for so long that life appears to be gone. Yet life is everywhere, lying dormant, just waiting to come forth. Tiny seeds waiting to become something great—that's what Jesus said the kingdom of God was like.

> And He said, "How shall we picture the kingdom of God, or by what parable shall we present it? It is like a mustard seed, which, when sown upon the ground, though it is smaller than all the seeds that are upon the ground, yet when it is sown, grows up and becomes larger than all the garden plants and forms large branches; so that the birds of the air can nest under its shade."
>
> —MARK 4:30–32

One pastor said to me, "You seem to have the ability to take nobodies and turn them into somebodies." The key is that I believe in people! I believe everyone has the seed in them to do something great for God. I believe it even when I can't see it. I know there's a miracle in there somewhere.

There was a man in the church in Davenport named Orbie Underwood. Orbie was a hard worker at a factory. He was a rather low-key kind of guy. But he was inspired by Mrs. Stottlemeyer. He took over a bus route, did a great job, and saw his life change.

Not only has Orbie been instrumental in bringing hundreds into the kingdom of God, but he has also become a deacon in the church. Orbie took the principles he learned in church and put them to practice in other areas of his life. Today Orbie Underwood has one of the most successful conversion-van businesses in the quad cities and state.

In the years that followed those early days in Davenport I learned a lesson over and over: Whenever I come to difficult situations in the church or in my personal life, I just need to look for the seed of the miracle that is already in the house. I hope you too can discover that the miracle you need is already in your grasp.

Through the experience in Davenport I discovered the ten commandments for the making of a miracle. That's chapter 2.

2

Tell Me—What Do You Have in the House?

OUT OF MY deep need I learned to lean on God and started to see His sufficiency in each situation. Davenport was a wonderful education. My insecurity was not pleasant at the time, but God used it to teach me things about faith I could not have learned at any other place or time.

In that little Iowa town one vivid Bible story was brought to mind over and over. God was showing me what was to become the key to the series of miracles that would guide my life and give me success beyond anything I had imagined. It was the familiar and simple story of the worried widow with the unpaid bill.

> Now a certain woman of the wives of the sons of the prophets cried out to Elisha, "Your servant my husband is dead, and you know that your servant feared the Lord; and the creditor has come to take my two children to be his slaves." And Elisha said to her, "What shall I do for you? *Tell me, what do you have in the house?*" And she said, *"Your maidservant has nothing in the house except a jar of oil."* Then he said, "Go, borrow vessels at large for yourself from all your neighbors, even empty vessels; do not get a few. And you shall go in and shut the door behind you and your sons, and pour out into all these vessels; and you shall set aside what is full." So she went from him and shut the door behind her and her sons; they were bringing the vessels to her and she poured. And it came about when the vessels were full, that she said to her son, "Bring me another vessel." And he said to her, "There is not one vessel more." And the oil stopped. Then she

> came and told the man of God. And he said, "Go, sell the oil and pay your debt, and you and your sons can live on the rest."
>
> —2 KINGS 4:1–7, ITALICS ADDED

At least ten great principles in this simple story have revolutionized my life. For me, this story speaks of the ten commandments for the making of a miracle. Here they are:

1. Know Where to Go When You Don't Know What to Do

SHE WAS A widow and a single parent in an impossible situation with no food and no means of support. She was being threatened by angry bill collectors. If she did not pay up immediately, she would lose her children.

The only thing going for her was that she knew where to turn. Only God could make a miracle happen in her situation. She went to the prophet with her plight.

Where we place our expectations determines whether we receive a miracle. If we insist on looking to man to supply our needs, we will continue to be disappointed. The major battles of life are spiritual, so there must be spiritual resources if things are to turn around.

We would do well to remember King Asa's downfall. When threatened by hostile forces, this ancient king put his trust in Syria rather than God. His plan of action was to pay King Ben-hadad to send his troops as mercenaries to protect him. The prophet reprimanded him saying:

> The eyes of the LORD search back and forth across the whole earth, looking for people whose hearts are perfect toward him, so that he can show his great power in helping them.
>
> —2 CHRONICLES 16:9, TLB

God wants to show Himself strong on your behalf as well. But going to God means asking, praying, and believing you have received. Paul exhorted the Philippians to worry about nothing and to pray about everything (Phil. 4:6). Our worrying is most often expressed by an ongoing, inner conversation we have with ourselves. We will argue, complain, and moan about the situation just as if someone were actually listening. That's why when someone asks us sincerely how we are doing, that person gets such an earful. The complaint has been well rehearsed.

Looking to God in the midst of your troubles means that you stop rehearsing your complaints and turn that inner conversation into upward prayer. That's when faith begins.

2. Don't Seek an Earthly Messiah

ELISHA GIVES THE widow a surprising answer when she tells him her plight. "What shall I do?" Elisha asked. His reaction to the widow at first seems to suggest frustration that she had come to him. He seemed to be saying, What do you want me to do about it? I believe he was simply refusing to let her put her trust in him, insisting she keep it in the Lord.

Unfortunately, Christianity is very celebrity oriented.

"If I could just talk to Pastor Jones."

"If I could just get Prophet Smith to pray for me, I know God would meet my need."

As Christians we should seek to touch the hem of Jesus' garment—no one else's.

Elisha knew he could not help the widow with his own limited resources. But he did help her keep her faith properly focused.

A man in the church came to me one day in a difficult situation. Before he was saved he had committed a felony and was about to go on trial. He could plead innocent, as his lawyer recommended, and easily get off. Or he could face the consequences of admitting his guilt. He desperately wanted me to make the decision for him. Of course, I could only point him to Jesus.

He got the direction from the Lord firsthand and was shown what to do. He pleaded guilty. But God turned events around so that, instead of spending the next five years in prison, he became one of the most successful businessmen in the church. God's grace and plan were worked out because he heard for himself and obeyed.

Elisha was pointing the needy widow to the source of her miracle. God's wisdom and God's help far surpass anything anyone else can do for you. So always seek Him and put your trust in Him.

3. Find Out What's in the House

LIKE THE NEEDY widow we get so caught up in what we don't have that we do not see the possibilities in what we already have. Elisha, after redirecting the widow's faith, asks, "What do you have in the house?" She did not need a new vision of her need. She was well aware of that. What she needed was to recognize that God had already given her the beginnings for her miracle, even though what she had seemed so small.

When I went to Davenport I had no idea the seeds of a miracle resided in that little, lackluster church. But God had put Mrs. Stottlemeyer there as a seed lying dormant. Finally, He opened my eyes to see that mighty miracles were in that unlikely little house.

4. Don't Be Blinded by Negativism, but Pass On to the Positive

OUR FIRST REACTION to crisis is always negative. Nothing is good or right, and there's no hope. That was the widow's frame of mind when she replied, "Your maidservant has nothing in the house except a jar of oil."

The widow started out in the negative but quickly passed to the positive. Nothing could be more important! When you look to the God of possibilities you suddenly pass from the natural to the supernatural. It would have been very easy and very natural for the woman to have simply said, "Your maidservant has nothing in the house—period, paragraph, and end of story. Now what are you, Mr. Prophet, going to do about it?"

It's easy to say, "I have nothing." But it takes faith to go on and say, "Nothing but a jar of oil, one small possibility, one small asset, one insignificant thing I can offer for God to use and multiply."

Faith does not deny present reality. It just acknowledges that all things are possible with God. It serves no purpose to say a problem does not exist or that the miracle has happened when it has not. You only deceive yourself.

Faith in God does, however, change how you see things.

"Nothing *but* a jar of oil."

"Nevertheless, at Your word we will let down the net."

These statements were made by people who looked the problems square in the face. But it was their faith that enabled them to see beyond the difficulties to the possibilities. Doubt will cause you to say: "We have nothing."

Or maybe: "We've already tried that, and it didn't work."

Miracles begin with faith, and it takes faith to break through the negativism and see the seed you have to cultivate. If you don't look with eyes of faith, small blessings are too little to recognize. So you say, "There's nothing in the house."

During those first few weeks in Davenport when I went to the board and to my dad, suggesting to them that I had missed the will of God, they wisely held my feet to the fire until I passed from the negative to the positive. I shudder to think what would have happened to me and the direction of my life if I had stayed in my negativism, refusing to see the possibilities in that little river town. Thank God for the "Elishas" in my life who helped me move from the natural to the supernatural.

The fact is that we always have far more available to us than we think. Pass on to the positive.

5. Faith Is Not Faith Until You Do Something—Action Is Required

Diagnosis is no cure although it is the first step toward health. There must be follow-up treatment if wellness is to come. Thus, Elisha told the widow she had to take some action to get out of her fix. She was to go out and borrow as many vessels as she could find. Remember two-thirds of the word *God* is *go.* And there is always a *go* in the gospel! She had to get active if she was to experience a miracle.

Most people want God to act on their behalf, but first they must act by faith on their own behalf. Israel wandered forty years in the wilderness because the people failed to take action when God instructed them to move forward.

Unbelief is not expressed so much by what people do as by what they do not do. Every supernatural victory won by Israel when they finally did enter the Promised Land under Joshua was accompanied by some corresponding action on their part—some faith offering of their own resources, which God anointed and blessed.

6. Don't Put Limitations on God's Ability to Provide

"What's that silly widow woman going to do with all of those pots?" her neighbors must have said. "She's finally lost her mind."

Of course, when you are as desperate for a miracle as this woman was, you'll do just about anything. The man of God said to her:

> Go, borrow vessels at large for yourself from all your neighbors, even empty vessels; do not get a few.
>
> —2 Kings 4:3

"Get as many as you can, and get them from everywhere," the prophet was saying. I wonder if the woman had any idea of what was about to happen? In any case she obeyed the prophet.

In the spiritual world we must attempt things so big for God that unless He helps us we will fall flat on our faces. Only then will He get full credit for what is accomplished, and only then will this knowledge keep us humbly aware that but for His blessings we are nothing (John 15:5). It is His work and His success—not ours.

God works through our positive expectations. It seems as if Elisha was dealing regularly with people about this.

> When Elisha became sick with the illness of which he was to die, Joash the king of Israel came down to him and wept over him and said, "My father, my father, the chariots of Israel and its horsemen!" And Elisha said to him, "Take a bow and arrows." So he took a bow and arrows. Then he said to the king of Israel, "Put your hand on the bow." And he put his hand on it, then Elisha laid his hands on the king's hands. And he said, "Open the window toward the east," and he opened it. Then Elisha said, "Shoot!" And he shot. And he said, "The LORD's arrow of victory, even the arrow of victory over Aram; for you shall defeat the Arameans at Aphek until you have destroyed them." Then he said, "Take the arrows," and he took them. And he said to the king of Israel, "Strike the ground," and he struck it three times and stopped. So the man of God was angry with him and said, "You should have struck five or six times, then you would have struck Aram until you would have destroyed it. But now you shall strike Aram only three times."
>
> —2 KINGS 13:14–19

Elisha was angry with Joash because his response lacked faith and passion. You can't do great things if you don't attempt great things. Shooting the arrows was for Joash what collecting the pots was for the widow. Again, God works with us according to our expectations or the lack of them.

When I was in Phoenix years later, the board of elders wanted the new church to seat ten thousand. I felt more comfortable with three thousand. They had much more faith than I. One day one of the deacons and I were watching Pat Robertson's *The 700 Club*.

"You pastors are building your churches too small!" exclaimed Pat. "In fact, there's one pastor listening right now who is planning far too small." The deacon's elbow was planted firmly in my side.

We settled on a sixty-five-hundred-seat auditorium. It was filled as soon as we finished it. The deacons were right. Ten thousand was the right size. God filled the vessel that we brought Him.

7. Shut the Door on Doubt

A KEY FACTOR in this miracle story is what happened after the widow had borrowed the empty pots from her curious neighbors. Elisha told her, "And you shall go in and shut the door behind you and your sons." There will always be plenty of naysayers—those who say, "Precedent is against it." "We've tried before and failed." Or, "We can't afford it." Elisha simply insisted she shut out the skeptics and be deaf to doubt.

The widow's neighbors, who were fully aware of her plight, would think her actions were eccentric and would ridicule what she was doing. They would insist she was foolish to believe in something so impractical as what the prophet proposed. The fact is that many miracles are stillborn because doubt was invited into the delivery room.

Jesus cautioned, "Consider carefully what you hear" (Mark 4:24, NIV). He knew we act on and react to what we hear from those around us. Elisha also knew how quickly seeds of doubt grow in the soil of human depravity and despair. Therefore, he told the widow to go into her house and close the door to doubt. Like Mary, the mother of our Lord, we must ponder some dreams in our hearts rather than see them killed cruelly in casual conversation. Jesus said clearly:

> Do not give dogs what is sacred; do not throw your pearls to pigs. If you do, they may trample them under their feet, and then turn and tear you to pieces.
>
> —MATTHEW 7:6, NIV

8. Pour Until There Is No More

THE WIDOW PROVIDED the effort while God made the miracle. As she poured, the oil flowed. We can only surmise she had borrowed every available empty vessel in her little town. If there had been more vessels, there would have been more oil.

In Davenport where we began, and now in Phoenix, we are continuing to pour because the needs of the whole town have not been met. When all the vessels were full, the miracle ceased. Much of my time is spent looking for empty vessels to fill—hurting people to pour into. And the exciting thing is that provision continues to come as we continue to pour.

This does not mean we do not have money problems. There will always be the constant struggle against the god of this world. But, miraculously, the provision comes as we continue to step out in faith to reach out in love. I believe the oil of anointing will only stop when every empty vessel in our world is filled or when we stop offering up empty vessels. And I do not see that happening soon. We will pour until there is no more! The promise is:

> Now He who supplies seed to the sower and bread for food, will supply and multiply your seed for sowing and increase the harvest of your righteousness.
>
> —2 CORINTHIANS 9:10

9. Move Beyond the Miracle

SADLY, SOME ARE so mystified by the miracle that they get locked in place and fail to move on. A significant part of this story notes:

> Then she came and told the man of God. And he said, "Go, sell the oil and pay your debt, and you and your sons can live on the rest."
>
> —2 KINGS 4:7

It was not enough for her to witness the miracle. There had to be purpose in it.

God gives great miracles for divine purpose—not just for our entertainment. Clearly the widow was not to get so wrapped up in the wonder that she forgot the purpose.

Miracles are so mighty that we often are tempted to glorify them rather than get on with the work of the kingdom. Miracles are meant not to dazzle us but to facilitate the Great Commission of Jesus Christ.

10. Remember: There Will Always Be Enough

ONE OF THE most comforting principles of this great story came when Elisha told the widow, "You and your sons can live on the rest." God had given enough to assure that their family needs would always be met.

After I left Davenport I was to move on to another challenge. At first I thought what had happened in Iowa was a one-time occurrence. I didn't expect that it would ever happen again. But what was to happen next made Davenport look small.

3

Being Led to Your Next Miracle

ONE DAY I finally admitted that I had lost the conscious presence of God. In spite of all the wonderful things I had been learning and the remarkable success of Davenport, the last few months had been deeply disturbing. There was a dryness in my relationship with God, and I couldn't figure out why. There was no great sin in my life or tension in the family or church. Things were going very well, and everyone around me was excited. My needs were all being met, and the church was easy to pastor. I had grown to love these people dearly. But I felt my preaching was mechanical and the spark gone.

I had lost the sense of God's presence. Oh, He was there, but it seemed as if I were just tuned out. I prayed, fasted, and stayed up all night seeking God, but nothing changed.

There I was again, down and out in Davenport.

It was not because of failure but, ironically, because of success. And I did not know what to do to dig out.

I was in this dark mood when the letter came.

The letter was an invitation to be interviewed by the board of First Assembly of God in Phoenix, Arizona. At that point in my life I felt the last thing I needed was another church and another challenge. So I threw the letter in the wastebasket.

Again I was wrong.

Not only did Phoenix need me, but I needed them!

After several torturous days, I returned to the wastebasket. Fortunately, the janitor had not emptied my trash. I dug deep into the office garbage to retrieve the wadded-up paper. Ironing the crumpled letter out on my desk, I leaned over and prayed desperately with my head buried in my hands. Maybe, just maybe, God was speaking to me through my restlessness, and I was not listening.

Could it be that I would sense the nearness of God's presence again only if I followed whatever little lead there seemed to be? Somewhere I had read that while a flashlight shines only a short distance in front, the light extends further as you continue to walk. Maybe this would happen to me if I followed the little light I saw. That little light seemed to be this letter.

Ready to Move When the Brook Dries Up

> Now Elijah the Tishbite, who was of the settlers of Gilead, said to Ahab, "As the LORD, the God of Israel lives, before whom I stand, surely there shall be neither dew nor rain these years, except by my word." And the word of the LORD came to him, saying, "Go away from here and turn eastward, and hide yourself by the brook Cherith, which is east of the Jordan. And it shall be that you shall drink of the brook, and I have commanded the ravens to provide for you there." So he went and did according to the word of the LORD, for he went and lived by the brook Cherith, which is east of the Jordan. And the ravens brought him bread and meat in the morning and bread and meat in the evening, and he would drink from the brook. And it happened after a while, that the brook dried up, because there was no rain in the land. Then the word of the LORD came to him, saying, "Arise, go to Zarephath . . . ."
>
> —1 KINGS 17:1–9

I dialed the church board and made arrangements to fly to Phoenix for the meeting.

When I met with the Phoenix board I immediately knew the reason for my restlessness. Here was where God wanted me, and if I had not experienced such inner agitation I would not have even considered the move. I had everything I wanted in Davenport, and I loved the people dearly. When other churches called asking me to consider their pulpits, I turned them down without even giving them a second thought. God knew that I was a lot like Elijah. I would not listen to His leading unless my river dried up, forcing me to seek hard for His face and will.

The story of Elijah at the brook Cherith is full of surprises. I have come to understand that God's process of miracle making is accompanied by a never-ending series of unusual and unexpected things.

Elijah is a good example of how God leads us into the making of a miracle.

A Surprising Place

ELIJAH DELIVERED DEVASTATING news—the nation of Israel would be crippled by a drought and famine. God knew that wicked King Ahab would be more inclined to kill the messenger than heed the message. The Bible reports:

> And the word of the LORD came to him [Elijah], saying, "Go away from here and turn eastward, and hide yourself by the brook Cherith, which is east of the Jordan."
>
> —1 KINGS 17:2–3

This was a surprising place since Elijah had just announced a famine. In a famine a brook dries up first, and yet it was there God sent Elijah, rather than to a full river where he could survive safely in drought.

In my own life I have always been surprised at where God sends me. I was reluctant when I went to Davenport, and although Phoenix was God's choice for my life, it would not have been my first choice. Even in my daily appointments I discover God often diverts me to surprising places in surprising ways where great things are done for Him.

A casual conversation or a "coincidental" meeting can be life changing. It is exciting and challenging to see what surprising places God will send me in the days ahead. I am learning to follow the Good Shepherd rather than take the lead. I only wish I were a better learner.

After spending a few years in Phoenix I found myself being diverted to another surprising place. I found myself at city hall. It seems the whole town had gathered together at city hall—local television news media, reporters, the city council, representatives from several commissions, the mayor, and hundreds of others assembled. What most of them wanted was to tar and feather Tommy Barnett and run him out of town on a rail. I'll tell you more about that in a later chapter. But what seemed to be a place and a situation I would have avoided at all cost turned into a surprising miracle.

A Surprising Provider

THE SECOND SURPRISE in this story is whom, or what, God told to cater the prophet's food.

> You shall drink of the brook, and I have commanded the ravens to provide for you there.
>
> —1 KINGS 17:4

If we are going to receive "heavenly" food, surely we would expect an angelic catering service. Yet God told Elijah he would be fed by dirty birds.

Eight or more species of ravens are found in Israel. All are considered unclean by Hebrew law and feed on carcasses. Noah used a raven as the first bird to send out after the flood (Gen. 8:7). It did not return, perhaps finding floating carcasses on which to light and feed. The raven and the vulture are grouped in the same disgusting class in Proverbs (Prov. 30:17, NIV). It was probably a shock to Elijah to learn his "angel's food" would be delivered in such suspicious fashion. In fact, it took real faith to eat whatever was brought to him, and only a real saint could see ravens' food as provision from God.

The symbolism in this story is striking. It simply shows how God can and will provide from unusual sources by surprising means. The kingdoms of this world can and will become the kingdoms of our God. Therefore, I fully expect many of the provisions for the church and God's people in these days to come from the world.

One year as we were preparing for our Feed-the-Multitude Thanksgiving celebration, the regional manager of a national fast-food, fried chicken company was touched by what we were doing. He then provided three thousand drumsticks for the meals for our bus children that day and has done so every year since. Incidentally, as he provided, the Lord provided for him, and he married a woman in our church less than a year later.

When the Israelites lived in the land of Canaan, they were threatened constantly. Sometimes the situation looked hopeless. Finally, they turned to God for help. Revival came to Judah after Jehoshaphat turned the nation to God's Word. The writer of Chronicles notes how it affected the surrounding nations.

> Now the dread of the LORD was on all the kingdoms of the lands which were around Judah, so that they did not make war against Jehoshaphat. And some of the Philistines brought gifts and silver as tribute to Jehoshaphat; the Arabians also brought him flocks, 7,700 rams and 7,700 male goats.
>
> —2 CHRONICLES 17:10–11

A Surprising Problem

ELIJAH EXPERIENCED SUCCESS and rest at the little brook. His needs were met, and things were going very well. The great prophet was safe and secure by the brook just as I was in Davenport. He probably had adjusted to his unusual servers and may have even developed a friendly relationship with the accommodating birds. Elijah had no move on his agenda. Then a surprising problem arose—the brook dried up! My brook in Davenport dried up too. It was not some mid-life crisis but simply God nudging me to move on.

One of the hardest lessons in life is to learn that God calls us to a place for a reason and for a season. We want to settle at some comfortable place forever because it is "safe." But life is like a twisting river. Sometimes we stop on a beautiful bank and loll there for some time. But if we do not get back in the stream, we miss the exciting things around the next bend.

If Elijah's supply had not dried up, he might have missed the mighty miracles that lay ahead. He would not have had the dramatic encounter on Mount Carmel in which the fire of God descended (1 Kings 18:38). He would have missed the supernatural end of the famine, the angel's touch, and his final fantastic ride to heaven in the whirlwind (1 Kings 18:45; 19:5; 2 Kings 2:11).

Most of all, he would have missed his role in God's plan to save a precious widow and her son from starvation. Elijah's surprising problem was only a prod to move him on to another area of ministry.

We live in a transient society, largely as a result of the job market. Often when Christians go into a new job, a door has opened miraculously. And when they leave a job, it is almost always because of an accumulation of problems. Going in is filled with excitement and new possibilities. Going out is usually accompanied with stress and tension, that is, until the next door opens.

That's how it is in life and in business. That's also how it was with Elijah. If it hadn't been for the accumulation of things leading up to his departure, he may have missed God's leading to his next miracle.

A Surprising Directive

> Then the word of the LORD came to him, saying, "Arise, go to Zarephath, which belongs to Sidon, and stay there; behold, I have commanded a widow there to provide for you." So he arose and went to Zarephath, and when he came to the gate of

> the city, behold, a widow was there gathering sticks; and he called to her and said, "Please get me a little water in a jar, that I may drink." And as she was going to get it, he called to her and said, "Please bring me a piece of bread in your hand." But she said, "As the Lord your God lives, I have no bread, only a handful of flour in the bowl and a little oil in the jar; and behold, I am gathering a few sticks that I may go in and prepare for me and my son, that we may eat it and die."
>
> —1 KINGS 17:8–12

Again, the instructions of God are surprising from a human standpoint. Why did He call on a widow to feed Elijah? Widows had no means of support, especially this widow.

The story of Elijah and the Sidonian widow of Zarephath is similar to the encounter that Elijah's successor, Elisha, had with a widow. Both widows were despairing for their lives and the lives of their children. They both also found out that the miracle they needed was already in the house. They only had to recognize it and activate it.

At the beginning of His public ministry in Galilee, Jesus highlighted how improbable it was for God to send Elijah to this widow. After having read from the scroll on the Sabbath, Jesus was teaching those who had come that day to the synagogue. Luke's Gospel says that they were all speaking well of Him and wondering at His gracious words—that is, until He mentioned Elijah and the widow of Zarephath.

> And He said, "Truly I say to you, no prophet is welcome in his home town. But I say to you in truth, there were many widows in Israel in the days of Elijah, when the sky was shut up for three years and six months, when a great famine came over all the land; and yet Elijah was sent to none of them, but only to Zarephath, in the land of Sidon, to a woman who was a widow."
>
> —LUKE 4:24–26

How did those in the synagogue react to this? Luke goes on to say that they were all filled with rage when they heard these words and immediately tried to kill Jesus by casting Him off a cliff!

Being sent to the widow of Zarephath was more than an unconventional surprise. It was unthinkable.

God's plan for Elijah was a surprise not only because the Sidonians were considered pagans and idol worshipers. Why would a man of Elijah's stature and anointing have to be supplied by one in such need herself? God asked the prophet to go to a place of want and put a heavier burden on that household. It just didn't make sense.

Whatever you need, give that away to someone else. Every Sunday I stand at the front door to shake hands and hug everybody who will let me.

One person said to me, "Pastor Barnett, you sure are a loving person."

"No," I replied, "it's just that I need to be loved so much myself. So I'm just giving away what I need!" The opportunity to give turned out to be a blessing for the widow. It was also the beginning of her miracle.

God had already told the widow that the man of God was coming, and she would be the supply for his need (1 Kings 17:9). By acting in accordance with God's surprise directive, she reaped what she sowed many times over.

A Surprising Request

> Then Elijah said to her, "Do not fear; go, do as you have said, but make me a little bread cake from it first, and bring it out to me, and afterward you may make one for yourself and for your son. For thus says the LORD God of Israel, 'The bowl of flour shall not be exhausted, nor shall the jar of oil be empty, until the day that the LORD sends rain on the face of the earth.'"
>
> —1 KINGS 17:13–14

The prophet made a startling request. One might expect sympathy from this man of God, but all the woman received was what seemed to be a selfish demand: "Use your last oil and flour to feed me first."

What do you suppose went through the widow's mind? Maybe she thought sarcastically, *Great, give the preacher our last meal—then we can eat.*

Maybe she said to herself, *Well, we're going to die anyway. What difference is one last meal? We might as well give it to the prophet and see what happens.*

There's no way of knowing what the widow was thinking. We do know that the Scriptures say that God had commanded her to provide for the prophet. What she had was a command from God and a promise from the prophet.

As the old hymn says, "Trust and obey, for there's no other way. . . . "[1]

A Surprising Miracle

> So she went and did according to the word of Elijah, and she and he and her household ate for many days. The bowl of flour was not exhausted nor did the jar of oil become empty, according to the word of the LORD which He spoke through Elijah.
>
> —1 KINGS 17:15–16

The answer to a desperate need came from a "miracle in the house." Miracles are not magic—but multiplication. Obedience to His Word and faith in His promise put what we have into the Lord's hands so it can be multiplied. Then the miracle occurs. Just as a farmer must not eat the seed, so we must sow the seed and look for Him to multiply it.

Bringing what we have to the Lord to use and multiply is as true for us today as it was for the two widows. This is a law of the kingdom. Jesus said:

> Give, and it will be given to you; good measure, pressed down, shaken together, running over, they will pour into your lap. For whatever measure you deal out to others, it will be dealt to you in return.
>
> —LUKE 6:38

What do we give? That which we have. Where do we find it? Somewhere in our house.

4

What's That in Your Hand?

Moses cringed every time a whip cracked against a trembling Hebrew slave's back. Growing up in the house of Pharaoh's daughter, he never knew the cruelty of the slave drivers, but he was tormented inside. Why did his people have to suffer so much?

A botched attempt at revenge on a slave driver sent him running for his life, and he ended up tending livestock on the back side of the desert. One question haunted him continually: "God, why don't You help them?"

Finally God said to Moses, via the burning bush, "Why don't *you* deliver them, Moses?" But Moses wasn't eager to be a part of that plan.

> "Who am I that I should go to Pharaoh, and that I should bring the sons of Israel out of Egypt? . . . What if they will not believe me, or listen to what I say? For they may say, 'The Lord has not appeared to you.'" And the Lord said to him, *"What is that in your hand?"*
>
> —Exodus 3:11, 4:1–2, italics added

Some people, like Moses, see a need and ask, "What do I have to offer in the face of such a challenge?" These people do nothing. But God said to Moses: "Look at what you have in your hand right now. You can take what you have and use it to meet the need—if you let Me help you."

The key to greatness is seeing the need and letting God use what is in your hand. There has been no better example of this to me than my own mother.

The Barnetts came from a strong and sturdy stock of old-fashioned Pentecostals and hard-shelled Baptists. Dad's mother was proud that she was a first cousin to President Woodrow Wilson's second wife, Edith Boling Galt. Mrs. Galt had been the widow of a Washington, D.C., jeweler when she and the president married following the death of his first wife. Later, when Wilson was struck down by a debilitating stroke, Edith "ran the government," guiding the ailing president's hand as he signed official documents.

Dad had inherited all the grit and gumption from the Barnetts and used these traits well during his long and prosperous ministry. My mother's fine family hailed from England. Her grandfather had been the pastor of a large and historic Presbyterian church. Mom's life was all joy, just like her name, until her adored father died of double pneumonia when she was just eleven years old. From that day until she met and married my dad, she felt cheated because such a huge part of her life was grabbed away. To make matters worse, Mom was shunted off to a Bible school by her new stepfather who wanted her out of the way. While the pain of this rejection was intense and the sorrow deep, it was at that school she met my dad.

Enid, Oklahoma, sits glumly in the middle of the great Red Beds Plains that extend from Kansas to Texas. Here the soft red sandstone and shale lie shallow under the grassy soil. And it was here, at Southwestern Bible School, that love and destiny awaited young Herschel Barnett and lovely Joy Patten.

On the special day that Mom and Dad met, the boys of the Bible school were playing baseball while the girls strolled over the tiny campus of the struggling institution. The rules of this "holiness" Bible school were so strict that the faculty forbade any contact between the sexes. Boys and girls were even instructed to walk in opposite directions and could only speak while passing. They were severely reprimanded if they stopped to talk, much less date or hold hands.

Then it happened.

Suddenly a baseball smashed across the playing field onto the sidewalk and slammed into a pretty young girl. The ball struck so sharply that she doubled over with pain and crumpled onto the sidewalk. The ball hit the precise location where a still tender incision from an appendectomy was healing slowly. Girlfriends hovered over the fallen girl, and a young, handsome ball player dashed off the field to help.

Their eyes met.

Love was born in that moment.

Both Herschel and Joy knew—and both would express later—that something fateful and wonderful had happened in that first brief encounter. The boy walked away in a daze after making sure she was OK. He told his buddies, "That's the girl I'm going to marry." Later on he learned she left saying to her girlfriends, "That's the man I'm going to marry." The pain from the baseball soon faded, but the memory of that special encounter lingered.

Romance had little chance to blossom under the sharp eyes of the fussy faculty. Students were told young preachers must prioritize their Bs. First, they must get their books, then a Buick, and finally a bride. If they ever got these out of order, there would be trouble, so said the older and "wiser" heads.

That first year after their brief encounter Herschel and Joy had little chance to speak to each other, but both harbored a secret inside: "This is the person I will marry." That awesome, unspoken awareness never left, even though there were the usual teenage fleeting flirtations and fantasies with others. And, in spite of the strict Bible school rules, young men and women will still be young men and women. There are always creative ways to communicate and circumvent unreasonable laws when a couple is in love. These Bible school kids had discovered such a way.

One day as the girls marched into the dining room, Joy felt a hand reach over her shoulder to take her fancy handkerchief. The drab school uniforms permitted only one accessory, and that was a fancy handkerchief fluffed out of the blouse pocket. Herschel grinned sheepishly and neatly tucked the feminine handkerchief into his own jacket pocket, arranging the tatted edges so they would show. This "mating rite" was commonly recognized among the students at the strict school. It meant Joy was now his girl if she did not grab the handkerchief back.

She did not.

The one time that afforded an approved way to talk to the opposite sex was at meals. The boys and girls had the luxury of sitting at the same tables, though the assigned seating arrangements were changed monthly. This gave the two young lovers opportunities to get to know each other and spend time conversing. They would make the most of each meal together, lingering so long that they drew disapproving glances from the faculty.

By the time graduation came, Herschel and Joy had grown strong in their commitment to each other even though they had not had the opportunity to date. As school closed, Joy wrote her first poem:

After I think and think of you,
Wondering just how or what to do,
To make our love a lasting song,
One that will last for years to come,
Something whispers softly to me,
"God is the Author of things to be."

Summer came, and school was finally out. Joy reluctantly returned home to Ponca City, Oklahoma, while Texan Barnett went back to Electra. The two kept in touch by letter, with Joy writing at the bottom, "Delight thyself also in the LORD; and he shall give thee the desires of thine heart" (Ps. 37:4, KJV). She admits, "I was hoping, of course, I was that desire."

She was.

On March 21, 1935, Herschel Barnett and Joy Patten were married.

Through the years Dad and Mom made a powerful team. There were many successes and some failures, but this dynamic duo always plunged ahead—innovating, invigorating, and inciting passion for God wherever they went. It was in a little town in Texas that my mother discovered the positive power of pain.

The young evangelist and his new wife were seeing phenomenal results. Crowds jammed the little church. Many souls were being saved and blessed. On the last night of this great meeting, the district superintendent of the Assemblies of God and the presbyter of the local section came calling. These were the men who had the power and influence to open and close doors for a young evangelist.

The word got around that Herschel Barnett was a rising star in the evangelistic circuit. Naturally, the church leaders were curious, so they came to see for themselves.

After a fantastic final service, Mom slipped across the street to the parsonage while Dad continued praying and talking with the people. There was no air conditioning in those days, so she opened her window to the warm Texas night and started to settle into sleep when faint, but familiar, voices filtered into her room. The district superintendent and the presbyter were talking about what they had witnessed that night and about the rising young evangelist.

"Well, what did you think about him?" the presbyter asked, alluding to young Herschel Barnett.

"He's a good preacher," the official noted. "I believe he can go far."

"But," interjected the presbyter, "what will he ever do with that wife of his? She can't even play the guitar or sing. She can't do anything. She will hurt his ministry."

Those cold, condemning words stabbed my mother's young and tender heart. She sobbed into the pillow, fearful that the leaders were right. She would be a drag on Herschel's ministry because she was so shy and "untalented." She felt she had been selfish in wanting Dad so much, and if he had only chosen a more gifted wife, he could reach his potential. The overheard conversation had shaken her to the soul, letting loose all the normal misgivings of a young bride. When my father came to bed, Mom pretended to be asleep so he would not know her hurt or see her crying.

Joy Barnett understood the ministry to which God had called her. She was also aware of her own inadequacies. She was in many ways like Moses when God spoke to him out of a burning bush. Moses was told about the promise to give them the land of Canaan and that he was going to be the one to deliver them.

Questions were running through Moses' mind: *Who, me? Why me? I can't do it!*

That's when God asked him, "What is that in your hand?"

Completely confused, Moses replied, "A staff," probably thinking to himself, *The only thing I can deliver from Egypt with this is sheep* (Exod. 4:2).

But the staff of Moses, a simple shepherd's stick, became the staff of God. With it Moses performed miracles before Pharaoh, turned the waters of the Nile into blood and brought forth frogs, gnats, locusts, thunder, and hail upon the land of Egypt. He lifted up the staff and stretched it over the Red Sea, and it parted. He struck the rock at Meribah, and water flowed out. (See Exodus 17.)

God can take our limited abilities and use them for great purposes. The key is offering up those abilities, feeble as they may be, to God. Then that insignificant thing in our hands becomes the staff of God.

Mom did not sleep much that night. But when dawn came she had made a decision. She would not give up in defeat. She would not prove those men right. From the pain she felt, a righteous anger and determination rose. Like Moses she seemed to hear God say, "What is that in your hand?"

Joy Patten Barnett searched her soul and took inventory of her potentials. Although she was too shy to stand before an audience, she decided she could write scripts and produce pageants, plays, and skits. She could design costumes, paint backdrops, organize drama. The ideas kept coming.

She would take music lessons. She would do everything she

could to polish what little she had and become an asset to her husband rather than a liability.

It was as if God said to her, "Joy, what is that in your hand?" The first thing the two Old Testament widows had to do was recognize the miracle that was already in their houses. For Mom she had to recognize the staff in her hand.

Neither the widows' provisions, the staff of Moses, nor Mom's talent amounted to much in themselves. But God's plan was to use what they had.

The pain of that warm Texas night changed and challenged my dear mother. She refused to cave in to the negative expectations of others and determined to be the very best. And, in my opinion, she became just that.

Mom developed into one of the most dynamic of pastors' wives, pioneering pageants and dramatic productions in churches. Her original plays were performed nationally, and she became a highly sought-after speaker. People came to her and called her from all over the world for her counsel.

Years later those who saw and knew my mother would have been shocked that anyone would have uttered such cruelties that painful night so long ago.

I am learning to make troubles my servant. I am also learning to see situations that challenge my ability as opportunities to see God empower my feeble efforts. God doesn't allow us to be tempted beyond that which we are able to endure. Neither does He challenge us without supplying His help.

Look at what Paul learned through facing insurmountable obstacles with limited ability:

> And He has said to me, "My grace is sufficient for you, for power is perfected in weakness." Most gladly, therefore, I will rather boast about my weaknesses, that the power of Christ may dwell in me.
>
> —2 CORINTHIANS 12:9

God often picks for a job a person who lacks the ability to accomplish it. One of the prerequisites of tapping into God's grace and power is the realization of your own inability. James wrote:

> But He gives a greater grace. Therefore it says, "God is opposed to the proud, but gives grace to the humble."
>
> —JAMES 4:6

We receive grace to accomplish great things through God's power in the same way we receive grace for salvation. In order to be saved, a person must first humble himself and admit that he has no ability to save himself. Then he receives the grace for salvation.

When you realize that by your ability you can't accomplish the task God has placed before you, you are only one step away from finding that through His power you can do all things. As we grow in faith we learn to look to God for His grace and not to our own abilities.

Many times God will use needs to show you both His power and part of His plan for your life. I often tell people, "If you don't know what to do, find the need and fill it. And if you don't think you have the ability, just trust God, use what you have, and do what you can."

We needed someone to work the wheelchair ministry. We had about thirty people to whom we were reaching out. Sharon Henning had been helping, so I asked her to take over for a few weeks until we found someone else. I was amazed to find that she started bringing twice as many people as we had before. Nevertheless, at the end of a few weeks she came to me and said, "I don't feel God's called me to this. Please hurry up and find someone else to take over."

I told her that I understood how she felt, but because the need was there and she was having such success, I wanted her to continue for a little while until I got someone.

That ministry grew to the point that on one Sunday at church she had four hundred people who were in wheelchairs or were disabled.

Finally she came to me and said, "Pastor, I've got to take back what I said earlier. I feel that God has called me to do this."

Today Sharon Henning is a wonderful ambassador for Christ and one of the greatest Christian workers I have ever seen do anything. It began with a need, and she took what she had in her hand to meet it. Before that, Sharon had not established any great ministry nor commanded a great following. She was not a dynamic speaker but simply had a heart for hurting people and a real love for God.

You can take a job nobody else wants and make it so great that they'll have to hire you because they won't be able to do without it. That's how most people came to be on my staff.

Now Sharon Henning is a part of our church's paid staff and has become the leading authority in the city—and maybe in the world—on reaching hurting people in wheelchairs. At our last Fourth of July rally she brought over eight hundred people to church. Even though she is scared to death to stand up and speak, Sharon receives invitations to speak from all over the nation.

Trouble can be a stumbling block—or it can become your servant and be a stepping stone. The same is true when you face insurmountable obstacles and feel totally inadequate. It is the chance of a lifetime. Whether they are forced upon you or you simply accept the challenge to meet a need, you'll discover how God can use the gifts and talents you possess when they are placed at His disposal. Troubles and need bring out the best in you, and when the best of you is brought out, you discover the special talent God has planted in you.

Most of us would jump at the chance to have a burning bush or Damascus road experience with God. But if you get that close to God, He might just say something like, "Go and deliver My people from Pharaoh's hand" or "I have called you as an apostle to the Gentiles."

God takes no account of your abilities or lack thereof. He only sees your possibilities. What He looks for is people who are willing to accept the challenge to meet the need.

When faced with desperate needs and overwhelming challenges, look to God and ask Him to help you see if the seed of your miracle is already in your hand. When you recognize it, offer it to God in faith that the works of God will be displayed through you.

5

Finding the Miracle Within

INSIDE EVERY HUMAN being is a miracle waiting to be discovered and released. Pastors ask me over and over how I seem to be able to motivate and develop the potential in all the great people I serve. There are two simple answers to that question. First of all, I am convinced that every Christian has the innate desire to do something great for God, to lay down at the foot of the cross the biggest gift he or she possibly can. All the needed motivation already exists inside that person.

Second, and most important, I believe in people. That is the key to leadership. I believe there's a special calling, purpose, and gift waiting to be manifested through every person. As a pastor, one of my primary concerns is helping people discover the special measure of grace God has put in them.

We live in a society where kids are so often told that they can't do anything right, that they're no good, and that they're not really wanted. I've had so many people tell me, "Pastor Tommy, you are the only person who has ever believed in me." Even when a person shows no outward signs of potential at all, I just believe it's there. Each person has a special grace and calling.

Of course, there are people who attend Phoenix First Assembly who at first have a hard time believing God can use them to do anything. Believing in yourself, however, can become contagious. These members see many people with no more ability than they have stepping out in faith, pouring into empty vessels, and seeing miracles happen. As a result, they begin to believe they can do great things too.

Hundreds of Christian conferences are held each year in every part of the country. In order to get people to come, the biggest and the best speakers are invited and advertised. Each year we have more than six thousand pastors and church leaders attend a conference at our church. But we do little advertising, and we don't have any guest speakers. All the sessions and workshops are taught by our staff and laypeople.

So many keep coming each year because each person walks away with the idea, *If these people can do it, certainly I can, too.* We have created an atmosphere that causes people to begin to believe in themselves. Now we're having to expand to two conferences a year.

When the people find their grace and calling, it's like striking oil. The searching process is sometimes long and hard, but the returns are overwhelming.

One of the best ways to discern the calling of God is to discover the special measure of grace that is your gift from God. Many people labor to fulfill some occupation or calling that is not theirs. Their ministry or occupation is a burden because the grace of God is not working with them. This often happens when people try to be what others expect of them. At other times people fail to discover their gifts because their priorities are wrong. They consider one calling more socially esteemed and are determined to do that, with or without the grace of God.

I have noticed that when people operate in their giftings, they feel a sense of power, grace, and fulfillment. I used to have an old Plymouth. When I would crank it up on a cold morning, it would cough and sputter. I would start off to the church running on about five cylinders. Even with the accelerator pushed to the floor, the car would barely move. But when that old engine warmed up and all eight cylinders kicked in, I could feel a surge of power.

That's the way it feels when you serve in an area that uses the gifts God has given you. You feel the grace of God kick in. Sharon Henning found that grace and gifting when she reluctantly took over the wheelchair ministry.

It is no wonder that the Bible so often mentions grace and the calling of God together. In each of the following examples, Paul refers to his calling as an apostle or to the ministry gifts of Ephesians 4 as a function of the graces and abilities given by the Holy Spirit.

> But to each one of us grace was given according to the measure of Christ's gift. Therefore it says, "When He ascended on high, He led captive a host of captives, and He gave gifts to

> men." . . . And He gave some as apostles, and some as prophets, and some as evangelists, and some as pastors and teachers.
>
> —Ephesians 4:7–8, 11

> I was made a minister, according to the gift of God's grace which was given to me according to the working of His power. To me, the very least of all saints, this grace was given, to preach to the Gentiles the unfathomable riches of Christ.
>
> —Ephesians 3:7–8

> Through whom we [the apostles] have received grace and apostleship [the calling to be an apostle] . . . .
>
> —Romans 1:5

> And since we have gifts that differ according to the grace given to us, let each exercise them accordingly: if prophecy, according to the proportion of his faith; if service, in his serving; or he who teaches, in his teaching.
>
> —Romans 12:6–7

When you find yourself serving with the gifts and in the calling God has given you, the power of His grace becomes a reality. Grace is not just forgiveness and unmerited favor. Grace is God's strength and power enabling you to do more and be more than you ever could in your own strength. Listen to what the apostle Paul said about working with the help of grace.

> But by the grace of God I am what I am, and His grace toward me did not prove vain; but I labored even more than all of them, yet not I, but the grace of God with me.
>
> —1 Corinthians 15:10

God has graced so many people in our church with ministries any of which would exhaust me in a very short period of time: Larry Kerychuk and his great ministry to college and professional athletes; Lloyd Zeigler and his tireless work leading the Master's Commission; Leo Godzich and his ministry to AIDS patients; Jeff Allaway and his persistence in inner-city bus ministry in over 100 degree temperatures; Lorna Gail, who selflessly directs ten ministries related to women; Diana Nutt, who directs the largest totally volunteer nursery and early childhood ministry that I know of; Walt Ratray, who ministers each week to over two thousand transients, homeless, and prisoners with seven homes to house them in and a mission. The list goes on to include hundreds of deacons and deaconesses and over 180 ministries to the hurting.

Each of us has learned that when we work long and hard, we feel physically tired, but inside we feel invigorated because we are working in the calling and by the grace God has given.

Be Careful What You Do With That Gift

THE WORD *BURDEN* is often used by people to describe God's guidance and direction. "I've got the burden for China," says one, while another says, "My burden is for Africa."

What people mean by *burden* is that they feel a desire or compassion to help a certain group of people. I feel compassion for lots of people groups. Nevertheless, I am not led by my burden as much as I am by my calling. I have found that burdens come and go, but the sense of calling remains. For example, I don't feel a great burden to get up at 5:00 A.M. to pray, but I feel called to it. So I'm up.

The word *burden* is found in its Hebrew and Greek forms throughout the Bible, but in almost every case it has a negative connotation, implying that a burden is something you don't want to have. The most notable reference in the New Testament is when Jesus said, "My yoke is easy, and my burden is light" (Matt. 11:30, KJV).

On several occasions in the Old Testament, a reference is made to the "burden of the word of the Lord," but in no case did the burden refer to the prophet's compassion for the people to whom he was called. (See Zechariah 9:1; 12:1; Malachi 1:1.) It was more a sense of obligation to be faithful as God's messenger.

As I have said, each one of us has a special calling and gift of grace to use in serving the Lord. But just as there was the burden of the word of the Lord, there is the burden of the gift of God. In other words, we are stewards of our gifts and graces. What shall we do with what we have been given?

Notice how Peter understands our accountability as stewards for the grace we have received.

> As each one has received a special gift, employ it in serving one another, as good stewards of the manifold grace of God.
> —1 PETER 4:10

Listen to what the apostle Paul says:

> Indeed you have heard of the stewardship of God's grace which was given to me for you.
>
> —Ephesians 3:2

Every person has a gift and measure of special grace, but many people never discover it because they are unwilling to let it operate. Others recognize the potential miracle within them, but if they never use it, they will never feel the power of God working in and through them. Even though the grace and potential existed, if the widow had not poured into the empty vessels, no miracle would have occurred.

In the parable of the talents, one of the servants took the talent he had been given and hid it because of his fear. The talent was taken from him and given to the one who had many. The parable ended with these words:

> For to everyone who has shall more be given, and he shall have an abundance; but from the one who does not have, even what he does have shall be taken away.
>
> —Matthew 25:29

We have found that if we pour, we get more! What motivates us to serve is not the fear of judgment if we don't use our gifts, but the desire to feel the grace of God working through us. The greatest joy you can have in life is to find a gift of grace and use it to serve others. When you discover that, you want to serve more and more.

One man said to me, "Pastor, if you said we needed to provide a steak dinner for five thousand hurting, homeless people, the members of this church would drive a herd of steers right through the auditorium to try to provide that food."

Why do people respond so enthusiastically when I give them a chance to serve by pouring into empty vessels? They've learned that the greatest joy in living is giving.

See the Need and Take the Lead

Shortly after our bus ministry had fueled dramatic growth in the church, a jolly young man flew to Phoenix to meet with me.

"Pastor, I saw you on television the other day. You said the way to grow a church is to find a need and fill it. I heard you talk about how you started with one old bus, and as soon as it was filled you bought another and then another, until six months later you had forty buses."

He went on to tell me everything that I, of course, already knew: how one ministry after another had been started.

Then he said, "Pastor, there are over four hundred thousand senior citizens in Phoenix. Nobody is reaching them, but God has laid it on my heart to help you reach them. Pastor Barnett, if you'll hire me, I'll reach 'em."

My initial response almost made me miss the miracle God had for me. "I can't afford it," I said.

"Then I'll work for free," said Keith Buchanan.

Well, it was hard to pass on that deal. During the next several years, Keith became phenomenally successful and developed a great ministry. Because of Keith, I have found myself going to the board again and again, asking them to buy more buses.

The same is true in business. Tom Peters and Robert Waterman in their best-selling book *In Search of Excellence: Lessons From America's Best Run Companies* reveal that success in business comes from recognizing needs.

An engineer at 3M corporation sang in the choir at his church and needed a bookmark that would not fall out of his hymnal. He fooled around for months trying to solve his problem. As a result, today we have 3M's Post-it note pads, and those who work in offices feel they cannot do without them. Virtually without exception, the last few chairmen and all the key executives at 3M were people who recognized needs and championed products to meet those needs.[1]

Some people want to do something great for God, yet they have not responded to the needs He has placed before them. Whether in ministry or in business, success and position are not going to be handed to you. No one's preparing an invitation for you to be the head of a great ministry or the president of a big corporation.

Some people think if they just had a certain position, they could do great things. But the position won't make you great. You can take any job or any ministry and make it explode, if you will only find the need and meet it.

You will see a marvelous work in your life if you simply practice this principle. Don't worry about how to meet the need. Just step out in faith, and God will show you how. Find the need and take the lead!

Find Yourself: You're in There Somewhere

I DON'T LIKE using the phrases "called into the ministry" or "called to preach." They seem to imply that ministry or preaching is some kind of special position for only a selected few. We are all called in one way or another to be ministers of Jesus Christ and to tell others about the good news.

You are not an accidental person. God has a unique purpose for you that only you can fulfill. No one else can do it, and if you don't fulfill that purpose, no one else will.

Of course there may be someone else who will take that job, marry that man, or share the gospel with that hurting person. But even if someone does replace you, he or she will neither be able nor inclined to carry out that purpose in the same way you would have done it.

I have a wife and three children, and each one of them loves me differently. Each one encourages me, challenges me, and delights me in a special way that no one else in the world can.

If you don't praise God and love Him, someone else will. But not exactly as you would.

God has a task on which He desires to see your special touch. Others could do it, but not with your unique touch.

Years ago in a little Southern town a man was carving a bust out of a large piece of wood. Eventually that log became a statue of Abraham Lincoln. One little boy who had seen the beginning of the project looked in amazement at the figure and said, "Wow, I didn't know Abraham Lincoln was in that log!" Yes, Lincoln was in there all along. He just had not been discovered.

A lot of people are like the prophet Jeremiah, needing to discover who they are.

> Now the word of the LORD came to me saying, "Before I formed you in the womb I knew you, and before you were born I consecrated you; I have appointed you a prophet to the nations."
>
> —JEREMIAH 1:4–5

God revealed to Jeremiah that his life purpose was to be the prophet to the nation. That had been determined even before Jeremiah had been conceived in the womb.

From birth, Jeremiah was who God had made him to be. Now it was time for Jeremiah to find out who he really was, to discover who he had always been.

Each one of you was made with a special purpose in mind. You're a lot like that log with the bust of Lincoln in it. Somewhere in there is the real you. It's up to you to make the discovery.

I have often said that on a Wednesday night over forty years ago at Victoria Tabernacle in Kansas City, Missouri, I was called to preach. It is more accurate, I am now sure, to say that on that night I simply found myself. I realized who I was and what I was meant to be. I found that inside that little boy was a preacher. And once I realized who I was, things that were not truly who I was began to fall away.

You see, the devil's plan for you is to make you into someone or something that you're not. He wants to distort your understanding of who you are. To create the statue, the woodcarver simply needed to chip away the things that didn't look like Lincoln. That's the last thing Satan wants us to do—allow God to chip away the excess in our lives and reveal who we are and His plan and purpose for us. So the more sin we can be tempted to live with, the less likely we are to discover who we really are and what God's purpose for our lives is.

You should not think of the two paths before you as God's plan or the devil's plan. The choice is between who you are and who you are not.

People who are living in sin and selfishness are lost—lost in the sense that they haven't yet found themselves. The literal definition of the Greek word for *sin* is "to miss the mark."[2] To live in sin is to be walking down the wrong road on the way to being someone you are not.

Even before you were in your mother's womb, God consecrated you—that is, set you apart—to do and be something for Him. The real joy, peace, and fulfillment are in being who you are.

You're in there somewhere. Find yourself!

6

How Many Loaves Do You Have?

WHEN I ARRIVED in Phoenix, two hundred people were meeting every Sunday in a twelve-hundred-seat auditorium. To say the least, nobody was crowded in the pews.

After ten months fifteen hundred were attending, and we had gone to two Sunday morning services. That's significant growth by any standard, but I still felt that the church needed something to get it off dead center. This had been a church that spent most of its time reaching inward to feed itself.

With the Thanksgiving holidays approaching, I stood before the church on Sunday morning and announced, "We're going to do what Jesus did. We're going to feed five thousand people. I want you all to come tonight, and I'm going to tell you how it is going to happen."

One of the new converts met me on the way out of church and asked, "Pastor Tommy, where are you going to get all of that food?"

"Well," I said, "I'm going to take a few loaves and a few fishes. I'm going to pray over them and break them, and we're going to feed the multitude."

With wide eyes the young convert said, "Wow, are you really going to do it that way, pastor?"

"No, not literally," I had to explain quickly, "but you come tonight, and you're going to see a miracle."

A great multitude followed Jesus as He went far away from the city seeking a remote and secluded place to rest. He taught many things to those who had come so far with Him. But at the end of the day the disciples were telling Jesus that something needed to be done about all these people and their need for food.

> But He answered and said to them, "You give them something to eat!" And they said to Him, "Shall we go and spend two hundred denarii on bread and give them something to eat?" And He said to them, "How many loaves do you have? Go look!" And when they found out, they said, "Five and two fish." And He commanded them all to recline by groups on the green grass. And they reclined in companies of hundreds and of fifties. And He took the five loaves and the two fish, and looking up toward heaven, He blessed the food and broke the loaves and He kept giving them to the disciples to set before them; and He divided up the two fish among them all. And they all ate and were satisfied. And they picked up twelve full baskets of the broken pieces, and also of the fish. And there were five thousand men who ate the loaves.
>
> —MARK 6:37–44

Almost everybody came to church that night. I told them we wanted to feed everybody as Jesus had, but in our case the menu would be turkey, dressing, and all the trimmings—everything we needed to feed the multitude, and we would do it free of charge.

"We'll need one hundred sixty people to bring baked turkeys, sliced and prepared and ready to serve, and have them in the kitchen by 6:00 A.M." One hundred sixty stood. We did the same for the ham, dressing, desserts, and so on.

Then I said, "The Bible says that when you have a feast, you don't just bring those who are full. You bring those who are hungry. Where can we go to get these people?"

Different ones began to suggest that we go to the welfare lines, food kitchens, orphanages, and convalescent homes. So we had our plan. We would invite our guests to a Sunday morning service and feed them in the afternoon.

Sunday morning came. When I walked into the 8:00 A.M. service, a smell hit me that I had never encountered at Phoenix First Assembly. But it was not the smell of turkey. It was the stench of dirty humanity.

The auditorium was jam-packed that morning. The balcony was crowded with four to five hundred of the dirtiest, filthiest people I had ever seen. They had their backpacks and bed rolls with them. Some of them even brought their dogs.

I could just hear some of the class-conscious members of our church saying, "Since Barnett's been here, the church has gone to the dogs."

That morning I preached on how the King has paved the way back with love. I told them the food that day was prepared with love, the buses ran with love, and the way back to God was paved with love. There was a tremendous response.

I was amazed by the visitors in our church that morning. I had never seen people who were dirtier. The regular church attenders were in shock, too. Some would consider these to be the scourge and plague of the city, but not God. And the next service had so many people that they couldn't get them in.

I didn't realize it, but right around our church the parks were full of transients who had come to Arizona for the winter. Our people had gone out and invited the transients, and they had overrun the church that day.

Since we couldn't get them all in, I sent many of the men into the parking lots to preach to the people in small groups. Then they went through the food line. There were sixty-seven hundred people in church that day.

It became such an event that it made the front page of the local newspaper. Soon after seeing what a tremendous thing had happened, some other churches got together and decided they were going to have the world's greatest Feed-the-Multitude Sunday. The dinner would be so big that it would be put in the *Guinness Book of World Records.*

They rented a football field and got all the major hotels to donate chefs, food, and equipment. That Thanksgiving the local media gave all the publicity to the Feed-the-Multitude Sunday, which was OK with us. We still fed our ill-smelling mob.

But they ended up having only about three thousand people. Why? They were trying to feed the people that had already been fed, while we were feeding empty vessels. They ended up giving us their food.

We've kept on feeding the multitudes every year since then. At our last Thanksgiving dinner we had over seventeen thousand people feast on the meal and hear about the love of Jesus Christ. Every year we have more than we need. The church members bring so much. We take all the leftovers to soup kitchens. Those who get the meal appreciate it, but it is the church that always gets the biggest blessing.

In the next ten years there is going to be an abundance of needy people in our society—and not just with financial needs. There will be divorce; broken homes; incurable diseases like AIDS; all kinds of abuse, addictions, and emotional problems; a growing number of older people who need help; and many with a general emptiness from not knowing Jesus Christ as their Savior. What a great time and a great opportunity for the church. That's our mission—to show the love, grace, and power of Jesus to a hurting world.

Some look at the growing critical needs, however, and conclude that they are more than the church can handle. The church says we don't have enough to feed the multitude of problems.

But that's not so. We have all we need already, and it's in our house. The church has all the resources it needs to show the love of Christ to the world, and those resources are already sitting in the pews. Maybe there aren't many sitting in the pews in some places, but if those who are there begin to pour, God will miraculously multiply your pouring and your pourers.

We were instructed to pray for God to send laborers, but it is our responsibility to compel the hungry guests to come in. It was the widow's responsibility to gather the empty vessels, and it was the Lord who multiplied what she had to pour into them.

When faced with an overwhelming need and a limited supply, the disciples went to Jesus and recommended He do something. Their suggestion was to send the hungry crowd away. Their needs were too great. Jesus' response to them was, "You give them something to eat!"

How could they? There were only twelve of them. Jesus continued:"How many loaves do you have? Go look!" All they could find was a little lunch, and that was borrowed. What good would that do when the needs were so great?

Constantly people talk to me about "what the church ought to do."

"But there's nothing more I can do," I say to them. And like Jesus I frequently tell them, "*You* do something!" or "*You* give them something to eat." Many times they have accepted the challenge and offered what little they had, and the miracle of multiplication occurred. That's how all those ministries in our church began.

One night we were to have a communion service. As is our custom on those occasions, spotlights shone on only the front of the church while the houselights were dimmed. After the elements had been distributed, I said as I usually do, "Has everyone been served?"

I had prearranged for three or four people to respond to my question. The first one stood and said, "Pastor Barnett, the people who live in the park—they have not been served."

Then someone from the wheelchair ministry said, "There are those hurting people in wheelchairs; they have not been served."

After the few I had prearranged stood and spoke, others in the congregation began to stand and identify those who had not been served.

Several new ministries were birthed that night out of the realization that hurting people were out there who had not been served by the church. Some of these ministries are highlighted in a later chapter.

Ellen Dodge stood and said the victims of crime were not being served. I really didn't think there would be many people in that category. So I asked the congregation, "How many of you have been a victim of crime in the last year?" Over half of the people raised their hands. A large segment of our society has been victimized, and it leaves a mark on them.

Today Ellen has a ministry to victims of crime and to those who have suffered great losses. She sends out letters to people who have been in serious accidents, to those who are getting divorces, or those dealing with a death in the family. We check the newspapers for those who have been through tragedies, and we let them know we feel for their hurts and would like to do anything we can to help.

Are there people in your community who have not been served? Go and see what you have, even if it seems insignificant, and then give them something. That's how miracles begin.

Is there anyone out there who feels as if he has dried up as a Christian? Is there anyone who has lost the joy of salvation and whose worship has become rote? Are there people who feel deep in their hearts that they are slipping away from God and realize they have become at best only lukewarm Christians but don't know how to be hot again?

Yes, there are millions.

The world we live in exerts a constant downward pull on every Christian. And we all to one degree or another have the same problem. Paul wrote in his letter to the Corinthians that these temptations were common to all people, but that certainly God would provide a way of escape for us (1 Cor. 10:13).

The most discouraging part for some is the thought that having lost their first love, they can never find it again. But the Scripture passage doesn't say they "lost" their first love. It says they "left" their first love (Rev. 2:4). When you lose things, sometimes they can never be found again. If you've left something, you can always go back for it—that is, if you can just remember the way.

As Christians we all long to have the abundant life that Jesus talked about flowing constantly out of us. Jesus explained this abundant life to a Samaritan woman at a well where she was drawing water. John records His conversation with her:

> Everyone who drinks of this water shall thirst again; but whoever drinks of the water that I shall give him shall never thirst; but the water that I shall give him shall become in him a well of water springing up to eternal life.
>
> —JOHN 4:13–14

Sounds great, right? But you may ask, "Where is it in my life?" If you have put your faith in the blood of Christ, which was shed on the cross for your sins, and you have accepted Jesus Christ as your Savior, then the Holy Spirit has come to live inside you. He is that living water that springs up. That's good news—because you don't have to look anywhere but inside to find the source of your spiritual renewal.

If the well has ceased to flow, it's not because the living water has run out. It's only that the well is clogged, and you need to clean out the pipes.

Many factors can cause spiritual dryness—more than we can talk about here. But there are a few simple overriding principles of the kingdom that, when discovered and acted upon, will enable you to deal effectively with many of the other problems.

I know this is not a new concept. It's simple, it's central to kingdom living, and it is essential to keeping the living waters flowing. It is, however, contrary to our natural way of thinking. Jesus expressed this principle in several different ways:

- If you want to live, you must die (Matt. 10:39).
- If you want to be great, become the servant of all (Matt. 23:11).
- If you want to be exalted, humble yourself (Matt. 23:12).
- It is more blessed to give than to receive (Acts 20:35).

A few chapters later John records more of Jesus' teaching about that living water.

> If any man is thirsty, let him come to Me and drink. He who believes in Me, as the Scripture said, "From his innermost being shall flow rivers of living water."
>
> —JOHN 7:37–38

Take one drink, and it becomes a well! That's miracle talk. The miracle of the widow and the empty vessels caused the widow's oil to flow as long as she kept pouring. It is the lack of pouring that clogs the well. When you save your life instead of losing it, hoard instead of giving, expect service instead of serving, the oil of joy in your life dries up.

The remedy for your dryness? Start to serve and start to give. Find some empty vessels and start to pour. You may think that you have so little to give and that you must save that for yourself and your family. The widow at Zarephath faced the same situation. She had only enough for her son and herself to prepare their last meal and die. But she gave in faith, and the miracle occurred in her house.

Take a step of faith. Find some empty vessels and begin to pour. Perhaps you will discover why the well has been clogged all along. You will discover that there's a miracle in your house too—it's a well that won't run dry.

7

Miracles on My Doorstep

I HAD COME TO preach a crusade in a city that sits like a running sore on the bloated underbelly of India. It was this experience that took the blinders off my eyes and enabled me to see the incredible miracles that were sitting right at my doorstep. In the years that followed, God has used and multiplied these "miracles in waiting." Much of the success in Phoenix began in Calcutta, India.

It was there I met the famous missionary Mark Buntain, one of the great saints of this century. He had gone to Calcutta years before and had singlehandedly turned on a light on what some call the front porch of hell. Books, movies, and documentaries have been written about his remarkable work. He built hospitals, schools, and churches and fed hundreds of thousands of starving people.

Only Mother Teresa has received more accolades and recognition than this great missionary who literally created an island of hope in a sea of despair. Even though Mark has now been graduated to heaven, his great work continues to touch tens of thousands of Indians every day in that lost land.

That night thousands of hungry, hurting Indians poured into the public racetrack to hear me preach. Mark Buntain had arranged the meeting, and as the crowds came in wearing their baggy, dirty wraps, my heart broke. Their dark eyes were like circles of black fire boring silently into me, pleading for help. I tried to let them know there was a God who loved them and would give them life even here.

While many precious Indians responded to the altar call, I did not feel the meeting was much of a success. Perhaps I was too emotionally moved by the horror of what I had seen around me. Maybe I was in culture shock. One thing was for sure: What I had witnessed would haunt me forever, and I would lie awake many nights weeping for their great sorrow.

As my plane swept down the runway and rose high over the sordid city of Calcutta, part of me was left there forever. I had not changed the city much, but it had changed me.

Winging away from that sorrowful city I determined the poor and powerless of our world deserve better than what they now know. I determined to do all I could to help them break the awful, gripping, grinding cycle of poverty and pain. I would help them find life through the Life-Giver.

As the years passed, the memories of those Calcutta scenes faded. But in Phoenix God again gave me a firsthand vision of His love and concern for hurting people, and all the memories of Calcutta returned. I determined again to give myself to those who had no one else to care. Like Isaiah I had heard God ask:

> Whom shall I send as a messenger to my people? Who will go?" And I said, "Lord, I'll go! Send me."
>
> —Isaiah 6:8, tlb

Many times when people come to the place of saying, "God, I'll go wherever You send me," they usually think of some place like Calcutta. I was willing to go, but for me the job began at home.

At the beginning I only thought that God's purpose was for me to meet the needs of hurting people. As time went on I realized that God was not just sending me to the poor; He was sending the poor to me to meet my needs. They were to become the answer to my prayers—just as it was with King David.

> So David departed from there and escaped to the cave of Adullam; and when his brothers and all his father's household heard of it, they went down there to him. And everyone who was in distress, and everyone who was in debt, and everyone who was discontented, gathered to him; and he became captain over them. Now there were about four hundred men with him.
>
> —1 Samuel 22:1–2

Assembling an Army of Ragtags

Caring for the poor and powerless was neither new nor strange to me. I had seen my dad live out this passion. Although he had many church buses, he always also used his own car to pick up the poor to bring them to church. Every Sunday after services our family waited at the church while Dad delivered his many riders back home. I once asked him why he did this, and he replied, "Son, I will never ask my people to do something that I will not do. This is our ministry. This is our calling."

People often laughed at my dad, saying all he had in his church was a bunch of poor bus kids. But those poor bus kids grew up, and they never forgot the love my dad had shown.

When my dad died, the church was filled with people from all walks of life. Senator Bob Dole, the mayor of the city, city council members, prominent business people, and social leaders were all there. Herschel Barnett pastored Victoria Tabernacle in Kansas City for forty years, and during that time it became one of the largest churches in the denomination.

I stood at the head of my dad's casket and watched the people pass by to pay their final respects. Along with the high and mighty, an old, tattered street alcoholic brought his little, ragged mongrel dog to say good-bye.

Almost daily my dad would stop and talk to this street dweller, often giving him a little money and a piece of candy for his dog. Before the undertaker could stop him, the teary-eyed old alcoholic patted my dad, mumbling words of appreciation because this preacher had always treated him with respect regardless of how others had viewed him. Clutching his little dog, he leaned over the casket for a last look. The little mutt lovingly licked my dad on the nose. This was "their" pastor.

Some of the poor bus kids to whom my dad reached out developed into wonderful pastors and prominent leaders, great pastors like Bill Baker and Ray Thomas who had come to dad's church on the buses from families who never attended church. They were not just bus kids. They were miracles in the house.

Elisha told the widow to go out and bring back as many pots as she could. As she began to pour what little oil she had into empty vessels, the miracle occurred.

The greatest revival is always among empty vessels. Those who consider themselves to be filled don't thirst for more. In most churches Christians spend too much time filling themselves. We must be careful not to become addicted to the self-gratification of our senses when there are so many empty vessels waiting to be filled.

In our church the greatest miracles are taking place among street people, bikers, drug addicts, and prison inmates. Revival is where the hurting people are.

Jesus told a story about a man who was giving a big dinner. He invited many people, but most were preoccupied with other things. The man finally said to his servant:

> "Go out at once into the streets and lanes of the city and bring in here the poor and crippled and blind and lame." And the slave said, "Master, what you commanded has been done, and still there is room." And the master said to the slave, "Go out into the highways and along the hedges, and compel them to come in, that my house may be filled."
>
> —LUKE 14:21–23

People without a need won't come to the feast. They're not hungry.

I was worrying that our church ministry was getting a little stale. We had at that time eighty outreach ministries, but I knew there were more empty vessels to fill. We needed to find them. I remembered that when the widow had no more vessels to fill, the miracle was over.

So I asked the church one night, "What else can we do?"

One by one people stood up. One lady said, "We need to start a ministry to reach prostitutes. I used to be a prostitute, and no one is doing anything to help them."

I then said to her, "I now make you the head of the prostitute ministry."

Another stood, "Only Salt Lake City has a larger Mormon population than Phoenix."

"I now make you the head of the Mormon ministry."

And that man started a church within our church to reach out to Mormons.

"We have a city full of Jews," another said.

"I now put you in charge of the ministry to the Jews."

Gene Johnson stood and said, "What about young girls who have gotten pregnant and don't want to abort their babies?"

Gene and Carolyn opened their home to some young unwed mothers. Soon it was filled with young girls. But, the man who owned the house next door didn't approve of what they were doing. So when the house was available, they rented it and filled it with empty vessels, and the ministry has continued ever since. Today the Johnsons have a dynamic ministry of pouring into teenage girls, and miracles are happening in their lives.

"I think we need to do something for the throwaway kids," one young man said—and he did it. He took in the little throwaway kids on his bus route until he had a total of thirty-four living in his home over a period of several years.

This meeting came during the time when the AIDS epidemic was first getting national attention. In those days when much less was known about how the disease could and could not be spread, Leo Godzich stood and said, "Pastor Tommy, we've got to do something for the victims of AIDS." Today Leo has led more than a hundred AIDS patients to the Lord and is a national spokesperson to churches on reaching out to these people with such great needs.

After the service was over, Mike Weymouth came up to me and said, "Pastor, I think God has called me to reach out to the motorcycle people. I used to ride with that bunch, and they need to hear about Jesus Christ."

So Mike became the leader of our new motorcycle church. Of course, it had no members—at least not yet. Mike used to be a drug dealer before he became a Christian. At first he was very apprehensive about knocking on doors. But he decided he would put away his hesitations and trust God to take care of all that. It's not that Mike was ashamed of Christ. He just knew that behind one of those doors might be someone out to kill him over a past drug deal.

I was totally in support of all these new ministries to hurting people. But the motorcycle church worried me a little. I'm a pretty straight guy and not used to people in black leather, chains, and tattoos. Who knew what kinds of weapons they were carrying with them? I had to enlarge my circle of love to include them too.

I will never forget the first time I saw them come into the parking lot. Their Harleys were popping as they rolled in like Hell's Angels. *Oh, no,* I thought, *what will the deacons say?* The church members had been careful to remind me that Phoenix is a white-collar city.

We bought a bar on the edge of our property and started the Church in the Wind. Ten months later more than three hundred bikers were filling it every Sunday morning. Soon Mike had to have two services.

Pork Chop was a four-hundred-pound biker whom Mike led to Christ. He was well-known to motorcycle people and became a dedicated missionary to his old friends. One day, while on an outreach, Pork Chop had a heart attack and died. Mike was right there, giving CPR and mouth-to-mouth resuscitation.

Mike Weymouth's dedication to Christ and his love for these people are becoming legendary. Every week more bikers are getting saved, and they follow Mike as if he were the Pied Piper.

Why? Because he was willing to pour himself into empty vessels.

Walt Ratray came to me from another church during the first year I was in Phoenix. His previous church had asked him to leave because he kept bringing so many street people to their meetings.

"The other church didn't want me," Walt said. "Do you?"

"Walt, I want you more than anything in the world," I replied. "I not only *want* you; I *need* you!"

I told Walt he could use one of our buses, and on the first Wednesday night he brought a bus load of street people into that very class-conscious church. One man who came with Walt had had a little too much to drink. Before I even got into the service, this man was in the pulpit, wanting to preach. As he was being escorted back to his seat, I came into the meeting and ran right into Walt.

"Oh, pastor, I'm so sorry. I won't bring any more if you don't want me to."

"I want you to bring even more next week," I told Walt. And he did.

We didn't let that stop us. The Church on the Street, as we started calling it, increased to the point that he was bringing five bus loads to church.

One of these was Richard Hudalla, who was found drunk on a cot in a shelter. Every week Walt would invite him to come to church, but he was always too drunk. All he gave were promises until one day Walt caught him when he was sober, and he came. Richard had been a very successful accountant before his life was destroyed by alcohol. He came to the altar, was saved, and was instantly delivered from alcohol and cigarettes. Now Richard is again a respected businessman and has a beautiful family. He is the business manager of the Church on the Street and Walt's right-hand man.

For a long time Walt's dream was to have his own church for these people with a home to put them in. Today he has the church, a mission, and seven homes. Walt Ratray runs perhaps the nation's greatest outreach to street people.

Last week the Church on the Street reached out to twenty-five hundred hurting and homeless people. So many people are getting saved in the prisons that in one the officials even let us put in a baptismal tank.

One section of our church is filled with two hundred people from the park every Sunday evening. After church we feed them and provide them with showers, haircuts, and new clothes.

Sunday afternoon the buses leave about 4:30 and go wherever they can find empty vessels—apartment houses, the battered women's home, shelters, and so on. We pick up anyone who will come.

Every Sunday night many are led to Christ. Why? Because they are empty vessels. The revival is where people feel they have a need.

Fred Boulineau, an executive for the Marriott corporation, agreed to be a part of our bus ministry. The first week that he drove a bus route he came back without picking up anyone. I knew that his bus route was in a Spanish-speaking neighborhood, and he didn't know a word of Spanish.

"Why don't you try a different route next week, Fred?" I asked him. "An English-speaking neighborhood would be less difficult."

"No, I am not going to accept defeat," he replied.

Fred went home and created a Spanish tract. He went out on the route with the tract, showed it to the people, and invited them to come to church on Sunday night.

Last year more than six hundred people were saved through his bus ministry. He is believing God to double that number this year and is well on his way to reaching his goal of twelve hundred.

When we care for the poor and powerless, God blesses us with the prominent and powerful. I've heard it said many times by so-called experts that if you spend too much time reaching out to lower-class people, the middle and upper classes will never come. I never believed that, and I never will. The New Testament church had all kinds of people: Palestinian Jews, Hellenistic Jews from all over the Roman Empire, Galilean fishermen, pharisaical scholars, rich, poor. Everyone was there, and they were in one accord and had all things in common. I don't know of a church that has more upper-class, successful people than Phoenix First Assembly. Professional athletes, movie stars, city officials, and Fortune 500 CEOs are regularly in our church.

When we love those God loves, He gives us an abundance that others will never know. For example, I think of former United States senator Roger Jepsen. He had come to our Davenport, Iowa, church where he accepted Christ as his personal Savior and went on to become a powerful leader in Washington, D.C., for many years. His wife became a famed leader of women during the Reagan years, and they were faithful members of our church. Because we cared for the poor and powerless in Davenport, God gave us much more.

Mighty Messes to Mighty Men

DAVID'S MIGHTY MEN started out as poor, disgruntled refugees (1 Sam. 22:2). But David wasn't doing them a favor by giving them a chance to join his army. They were his only hope.

God didn't send me to help the hurting. He sent the hurting to help me.

My church in Phoenix is filled with wonderful, respectable, successful, and dedicated people. But many of them first came to church as drug addicts, street people, or bikers.

One woman came to our church and sat on the front row for many months. She didn't attract much attention until someone saw her going into the men's rest room. She—or rather, he—was actually a man dressed up like a woman. He was a broken and distressed individual looking for help. Leo Godzich, who is in charge of our AIDS ministry and who had some understanding of his situation, ministered to him.

This man was saved and over time experienced a tremendous and thorough emotional healing. Today that man, who came dressed as a woman and was one week away from having a sex-change operation, serves alongside me as a visitation deacon in our church and is committed to the cause of Christ!

The bravery and dedication with which David was served by his mighty men are unparalleled. The men's loyalty went beyond obedience to commands. They were intensely devoted to him as friends.

> Then three of the thirty chief men went down and came to David in the harvest time to the cave of Adullam, while the troop of the Philistines was camping in the valley of Rephaim. And David was then in the stronghold, while the garrison of the Philistines was then in Bethlehem. And David had a craving and said, "Oh that someone would give me water to drink from the well of Bethlehem which is by the gate!" So the three mighty men broke through the camp of the Philistines, and drew water from the well of Bethlehem which was by the gate, and took it and brought it to David. Nevertheless he would not drink it, but poured it out to the LORD; and he said, "Be it far from me, O LORD, that I should do this. Shall I drink the blood of the men who went in jeopardy of their lives?" Therefore he would not drink it. These things the three mighty men did.
>
> —2 SAMUEL 23:13–17

I could never say enough about the mighty men and women whom God has put around me. They protect me, they encourage me, and they never cease to amaze me. I haven't done so much for them. I only believe in them, that each one has the seeds for greatness within. People say, "Look at what a church Tommy Barnett has built." But other men and women did it. I was just a cheerleader. I just believed in people.

Jesus believed in people, too. He placed the proclamation of the good news in the hands of twelve men. If they had failed, the gospel would not have gotten out!

In 1971 God sent a young couple, Dale and Lynn Lane, to my church in Davenport, Iowa. They had a heart to serve God. Their lives were challenged. They devoted themselves, their time, their family, and their finances to the work of God.

Dale started as a bus driver but was always looking for greater needs to fill. Early one very cold winter morning, I was trying to start the engines of the fleet of buses (not an easy thing to do at that time of year). I was getting very frustrated. Dale stepped in and said, "Pastor, go study and prepare for preaching. You don't need to be out here. From now on, I will come early every Sunday morning and make sure they are all started."

It was about that same time that Lynn became my secretary. She devoted her life to serving. Her good spirit, faithfulness, dedication, skills, and attention to details have literally added years to my life.

Dale is now my associate pastor, and I believe he is the most noted associate in America. I consider him my "Aaron." He is my arms, my legs, my hands extended. I can always count on him. We are of like heart and like mind, both devoted to winning souls and meeting needs.

You see, in the early years I poured my life into Dale and Lynn. Now they live their lives pouring back into not only Phoenix First Assembly, but into people all over America. They could be building a great church themselves anywhere in America, but I am glad they felt more could be accomplished for God by working as a team with me and the staff of our church.

It was a few months before Marja and I were to celebrate my fortieth anniversary in the ministry when I got wind of their plan. At first I thought it was a joke, but then I realized they were serious. These people were going to rent out the America West Arena where the Phoenix Suns play basketball, have people fly in from all over the country, and put on the biggest anniversary party anyone had ever seen.

They were inviting celebrities, sports figures, politicians, and so on. People from Davenport and individuals who were saved when I was in evangelistic ministry were coming, as well as a long list of pastors whose lives and ministries had been touched at our annual pastors' school. It was to be the grandest of all pastors' anniversary celebrations.

No one was risking his life for this project, but I did feel a little bit like David in the cave of Adullam. He couldn't accept the gift, and neither could we. Marja and I put a stop to it. It didn't matter so much to us whether or not we had that great party. What really mattered was that they wanted to do it.

If I have learned anything in Phoenix, it is this: If you pour into empty vessels when you are feeling empty yourself, they'll pour much more back into you.

The Shoes of Happiness

FAMED PREACHER-POET Edwin Markham captured the essence of Christlike living and giving in relating the story of Conrad the Cobbler. In his classic work "The Shoes of Happiness," Markham states that saintly Conrad had a vivid dream in which he was told Christ would visit his humble cobbler shop on a certain day.[1] The dream was so real that Conrad was certain Jesus would indeed come. So he decorated his simple shop with boughs of green and prepared breads and cakes to serve the Master.

Early on the morning that Jesus was to visit, two of Conrad's friends came by, and Conrad shared the dramatic dream with them. They wanted to wait for the Master with him because they knew that if anyone in the village would ever have a visit from Jesus it would be kindly Conrad. But, Conrad told them the Lord had said specifically that He wanted to visit with the cobbler alone. Markham wrote:

His friends went home; and his face grew still
As he watched for the shadow across the sill;
He lived all the moments o'er and o'er,
When the Lord should enter the lowly door.
The knock, the call, the latch pulled up,
The lighted face, the offered cup.
He would wash the feet where the spikes had been;
He would kiss the hands where the nails went in;
And then at last he would sit with Him
And break the bread as the day grew dim.

But the Master did not come. Instead a beggar knocked on the door and asked for a pair of shoes. Conrad was irritated by the interruption, but his kindly heart would not let him ignore the need of the old man. He hurriedly made the shoes and gave them to the poor beggar, rushing him off so he would not interrupt or prevent the visit of the Great Guest.

A little later another knock sounded, and Conrad was sure this was the Master. But it was only a hungry old woman carrying a heavy load of sticks. She asked for food, which Conrad reluctantly gave her. The only food he had was what he had prepared for the Master. With each bite Conrad's heart sank. He feared he would have nothing left for his Lord, and he secretly hoped she would leave a little. But, she devoured every crumb. Then the old woman asked if Conrad would help her to the edge of the village because her load was so heavy. He did not want to leave the shop, but again the cobbler could not turn down the frail old woman. He wrote a hasty note and put it on the door, hoping the Master would not miss it and leave. When Conrad returned, the note was still there, undisturbed, so he knew the Master had not yet come.

Late in the evening there was a final knock on the cobbler's door. Conrad's heart leapt within him, knowing at last this would be the Master. But when he opened the door he found a lost and crying child.

"Mister, I'm lost," the little lad cried. "Will you please help me find my home?"

Conrad sighed, gathered the little tot in his arms, retrieved his note from the wastebasket and again placed it on his shop door. He took the lost lad far across the village to his worried mother. Rushing back, he hoped he had not missed the Master and then saw the well-used note still unmoved. Conrad knew Jesus had not yet made His visit.

As the midnight hour approached Conrad knew now the Master would not appear at his door. It really had only been a dream.

The kind cobbler's heart was broken, and in his crushing sadness Conrad fell to his knees crying:

"Why is it, Lord, that your feet delay?
"Did you forget that this was the day?"
Then, soft in the silence, a voice he heard:
"Lift up your heart, for I have kept my word.
"Three times I came to your friendly door;
"Three times my shadow was on your floor.
"I was the beggar with the bruised feet;

"I was the woman you gave to eat;
"I was the child on the homeless street."

Poet Markham caught the passion of our Lord for the poor. Jesus says:

> For I was hungry, and you gave Me something to eat; I was thirsty, and you gave Me drink; I was a stranger, and you invited Me in; naked, and you clothed Me; I was sick, and you visited Me; I was in prison, and you came to Me. Then the righteous will answer Him, saying, "Lord, when did we see You hungry, and feed You, or thirsty, and give You drink? And when did we see You a stranger, and invite You in, or naked, and clothe You? And when did we see You sick, or in prison, and come to You?" And the King will answer and say to them, "Truly I say to you, to the extent that you did it to one of these brothers of Mine, even the least of them, you did it to Me."
>
> —Matthew 25:35–40

God's Word demands we see the poor as people rather than cold statistics or despised parasites of society. Clearly, God insists that a person's worth has nothing to do with what he does or does not possess.

I have found that as we reach out to hurting people and continue to pour into empty vessels, the miracle God has been working in our midst continues. The fresh oil keeps multiplying, and the hurting people become the miracle in the house.

8

Don't Let Troubles Keep You From the Making of a Miracle

THE TOWN TORE me apart! Front-page news stories, harsh editorials, caustic radio commentators, and blistering editorial cartoons all threw their best punches, knocking me to my knees.

There was a lot at stake—really more than I realized. But I knew there was a miracle to be found in every situation. I just had to be careful not to let my troubles cause me to miss it. I see now that if I had responded according to my feelings, the blessing would have passed me by, and I would have lost the miracle.

I felt somewhat alone in the midst of the battle. Have you ever noticed that when you get in big trouble, people shy away from you? Well, I was in big trouble.

And it all started over a hill.

Back in the midwest we called them hills although they were reverently elevated to mountains out here in the desert. This mammoth mound of desert dirt was appropriately named Shadow Mountain, and it certainly cast a long, dark shadow over my life for many months. The firestorm had its spark in a dream.

Built at the base of Shadow Mountain, our church was carefully designed to snuggle into the rugged desert terrain. Ever conscious of the raw natural beauty, we sought to enhance and embrace our environment, providing an awe-inspiring structure for our people and the whole community.

We believe architecture is "frozen music," and we wanted to orchestrate the best for the Lord. Part of our master plan called for a simple prayer chapel to hug the steep slope of Shadow Mountain. It would provide a sanctuary of solace and spiritual refreshing for all.

The idea for a mountain prayer chapel was not new or unique. In fact, one of Arizona's most popular attractions is the magnificent Chapel of the Holy Cross in Sedona. Designed by famed architect Frank Lloyd Wright, this beautiful Catholic chapel has served as a great spiritual inspiration for people all over the world. I knew the value of such a structure and pictured a similar site for our busy and needy city.

In this small chapel I envisioned a dozen telephone prayer lines to be manned around the clock by compassionate workers caring for and helping hurting people. There would be facilities for those hikers who trudged the trails of the majestic mountain. Most important, the chapel would be a warm and loving place where all could come in privacy and pray for their unique needs, regardless of their denominational background.

Knowing we should be responsible citizens of our community, we did not make our plans clandestinely. In fact, we had discussed the chapel with Phoenix mayor Terry Goddard and received his enthusiastic approval. Then the Phoenix Mountains Preservation Council got wind of our proposal and launched an emotional campaign against the project, rejecting reason or compromise.

We became the talk of the town with a few even suggesting I was some wild cult leader with Jim Jones-like persuasion and a pocketful of money gleaned from foolish and duped attenders. Radio talk shows had a field day at our expense, and it seemed everyone wanted to go public with their comments, whether they were based on facts or not.

A flurry of newspaper articles reported that our intention was to deface the mountain and rape the environment. Editorials soon followed. They demanded that the city council condemn our property so we would be forced to sell it to the city. Then, they noted, nothing could ever be built there on the mountain. I called the newspaper editor, but he refused to present my side of the issue or even publish the architectural plans of our proposed chapel. He said flatly he would print what he wished, when he wished.

I knew we were in for trouble.

Editorial cartoonists jumped on the bandwagon with delight, portraying me in less than complimentary fashion.[1]

An editorial two days earlier had flogged our plans for a chapel. Taking liberties with both facts and issue, the editorial stated:

> Of course, the edifice the Rev. Tommy Barnett is hoping to build atop Shadow Mountain will stick out like a sore thumb.

> It is intended to stick out like a sore thumb.
>
> In Mr. Barnett's view, the prayer chapel he hopes to plop down in north Phoenix—on land the city ought to buy up and safely incorporate into the Phoenix Mountains Preserve—has to be located there "to be inspirational" . . .
>
> What makes Mr. Barnett's proposed structure objectionable is its intrusive nature—a 70-foot tower assaulting the sensibilities in an awesomely beautiful corner of God's wilderness.

It did not seem to matter to the editors that such a tower was never in our plans. We had considered a small spire, but the newspaper somehow concluded that we wanted to build a structure similar to the Oral Roberts prayer tower. The editorial writer went on:

> Whereas others view the project as religious graffiti, Mr. Barnett sees it as outdoor advertising for the faith.[2]

Unwilling to leave the issue alone, the newspaper attacked again with another dramatic editorial a month later.

> Surely Mr. Barnett and his parishioners are among a microscopic minority who hold to the belief that a mountainside edifice of 8,000 square feet with a 70-foot-high spire thrusting heavenward is "natural" for a rugged, relatively unspoiled piece of God's handiwork. Others, alarmed at the degree to which the city's outskirts already have been defiled, think of Mr. Barnett's proposal as something close to vandalism.[3]

The editorial was accompanied by another cartoon.[4]

Never-ending radio talk shows kept the controversy going, and a biting, bylined article added to the furor. Journalist Dee J. Hall stirred up the brewing caldron by reporting:

> Some neighbors say the chapel controversy is just the latest in a series of squabbles they've had with the church at 13613 N. Cave Creek.
>
> They say dozens of buses and thousands of parishioners clog their streets each Sunday, flocking to one of Phoenix's largest churches.[5]

The reporter claimed some neighbors accused us of being insensitive to their needs, blocking their views of the mountain with our buses and "blockbusting"—that is, buying a large number of the lots and homes in an area so that the remaining residents will sell their property at bargain prices.

She concluded by insisting I had been dishonest about buying residential properties near the church and had also lied about the proposed prayer chapel.

In an effort to calm the raging storm and soothe the charged emotions, I spoke with all factions, assuring them we cared as much as they did about the stark beauty of the Arizona desert. They refused to listen—they were so entrenched in their stand against the proposal.

I was devastated.

Then support began to come in. I got a call from an old friend of mine who then worked in the White House. He told me that he knew of private funds that would help me fight all the way to the Supreme Court if necessary.

Christian television hosts called me and offered airtime to take our case to the Christian community and to set straight the lies of the media. They were also preparing to raise a "war chest" to fight for the vision God had given me.

The public and the press had gathered for a bloody shootout. The scene was to be at the "Not-So-O.K. Corral," better known as city hall. I was the target, and my opponents already had my tombstone etched.

Whenever I get in a situation like this, at first I usually feel hurt. I tend to get discouraged, and I want to say, "Just forget it." My second reaction is a desire to hold my ground and fight if I have to. In this case, I seemed to have plenty of weapons—money, Christian media, lawyers, and thousands of people from my church who were ready and willing to march on city hall. After a period of time I finally get to the place where I give up my fighting and let go of my hurt. All I want then is what God wants. I have found that it's hard to find a miracle in the house until you get to this place.

When you're trying to fight the battle with your own strength, another danger arises: You are tempted to manufacture your own miracles. Remember Abraham trying to make his own miracle with his handmaiden Hagar? When Sarah couldn't give him a son, he tried to produce an heir through Hagar. The result of the union was Ishmael (Gen. 16). Later God caused Sarah to conceive, and she gave birth to Isaac (Gen. 21:2–3).

Applying that story to our situation made me realize that we could have fought and probably won—but we would have given birth to our own Ishmael. Just as the descendants of Ishmael and the descendants of Isaac were mortal enemies, we would have lived in strife from that time onward. Ishmael is a symbol of what we produce by our own efforts when we give up on our faith and patience to wait on God.

I knew further fighting would only destroy what God had brought us to Phoenix to build. This controversy would have to stop and stop quickly. Although I believed we could have fought and won this battle, we might have lost the *real* war. Our real battle and purpose were to win the lost. Anything that would divert my attention was the real enemy!

When all the parties were gathered together at city hall on the appointed day, I stood and asked for the floor. Before the first shot could be fired, I publicly apologized, saying, "I want you all to know that we had no intention to be anything but a blessing to the city. Whether we build on the side of the mountain has no bearing. We're going to keep doing what we are doing—feeding the hungry, clothing the naked. . . . "

The shootout fizzled when I refused to fight, and those whom I felt were "the bad guys" had to holster their loaded verbal weapons. The city council quickly agreed to the demands of the Phoenix Mountains Preservation Council, who had wanted our land all along. We later learned they had resented our buying the property because they fully expected the previous owner to give it to them. When he failed to make the gift, they took their wrath out on us.

Some city council members tried to mollify us by praising our church for its work with children, the elderly, the homeless, and the handicapped. Councilman Howard Adams even told the press, "It's nice to hear the pastor plans to continue his good works, just a little closer to sea level."[6] Assistant parks director L. B. Scacewater admitted, "I think it was just so emotional [that] it got out of hand."[7]

Things certainly had gotten out of hand, and it was no fun being caught in the vortex of public disapproval. Although this was not an altogether new position for me, it still stung and threw me off balance for some time. It was only on my knees that I found perspective and learned to rise above the squabble so I could keep my eyes on the real battle—the battle for the lost souls of dying men and women.

I had wanted to fight to the finish in order to claim our miracle. I had my faith in full gear for the prayer chapel. I hate accepting defeat, but something inside me was saying, "Give it up, Tommy."

It seemed at that time there was no miracle to be found in this situation. The only good to come out of it was perhaps the humbling of Tommy Barnett. But as I said earlier, the miracle that God wants to give you often comes in the most unexpected ways.

The first miracle that happened as a result of this altercation with the press and city officials was related to the sale of our property to the city council. This piece of land was on a very steep part of the mountain. It was really only valuable to us because we wanted to build on it. In addition, the cost of building on the property would have been high. But, because of all the furor the commission stirred up about it, the value of those eleven acres skyrocketed. We finally sold them for $1.2 million, four times the previous value. That was half of what we originally paid for the entire seventy acres of property!

There was another financial miracle that happened as a direct result of this controversy. One of our deacons had a retired friend named Scott Shady. Scott knew about the church and how many things were being done to help hurting and needy people from every segment of society in Phoenix. He was so upset about how the newspaper had misrepresented us that he decided to give the church a large sum of money, and he became a more dedicated Christian.

A third miracle that came out of this was favor with the media.

This miracle started with Mayor Terry Goddard, who was not pleased with what had happened. Before allowing the city hall meeting to adjourn, he took a swipe at those who opposed our plan. He criticized the park staff for not informing him that our land was considered to be a high-priority parcel for the preserve. He told the council and press of his meeting with me years before and how he had heartily endorsed the chapel plan because he was operating under the assumption the city did not want or need the land. The mayor felt the matter had not been handled properly and wanted the press, public, and council to know his position.

I was invited to many radio talk shows. We were exonerated, the dirty tricks of the commission were exposed, and we have enjoyed great favor with the media ever since.

Don't let troubles keep you from the making of a miracle! That doesn't necessarily mean you should forge ahead, bulldozing everything in your path. If we had done that, we would have missed God's miracle for us.

You will get offtrack if you think you know for sure exactly what kind of miracle God wants to give you. Remember that miracles come from surprising places in unexpected ways. You have to trust that God is working all things together for good according to His great plan. Do everything you can to flow with His plan rather than trying to force Him to bless yours.

"God loves you and offers a wonderful plan for your life!" That's law number one in Campus Crusade's *Four Spiritual Laws* tract. Part of that wonderful plan is to bring us to Christian maturity and to perfect our faith—but sometimes that process doesn't seem so wonderful.

The apostle Peter said we were "protected by the power of God through faith" (1 Pet. 1:5). You would think that protection would include the attacks of deceptive and antagonistic newspaper reporters. I've found that God watches over us more than we will ever know. But I've also discovered that His purposes are sometimes worked out through circumstances that we would rather avoid.

After saying we are protected by God, Peter continues with these words:

> In this you greatly rejoice, even though now for a little while, if necessary, you have been distressed by various trials, that the proof of your faith, being more precious than gold which is perishable, even though tested by fire, may be found to result in praise and glory and honor at the revelation of Jesus Christ.
>
> —1 PETER 1:6–7

In the final analysis we had won a great victory in the Phoenix prayer chapel controversy. One of the benefits of that agonizing experience was the proving and maturing of our faith. Perhaps, in God's eyes, that was the most valuable part of all, for He knew that our troubles with the media were not over.

Officials of my denomination called and asked that I cooperate with an article being written by the *Wall Street Journal* about the Assemblies of God. They assured me this was to be a good piece, which would help the denomination recover from the bad press after the disaster of the television scandals. They had been approached by the prestigious paper and promised that a major positive feature would bring into balance all the negative and unfair publicity the movement had been receiving. I hesitated because I knew firsthand what a prejudiced press could do. The officials persisted, however, so I reluctantly agreed to cooperate.

Reporter Robert Johnson soon showed up assuring me of his good intentions, underlining all that my denominational leaders had said. He was all smiles, and I was immediately drawn to this "open-minded" man.

Setting aside many hours from my demanding schedule, I took

the journalist for tours through our facilities and among our various outreaches in the city. He seemed genuinely impressed and often commented on what a wonderful work we were doing. The culmination of our time came when he attended our Sunday morning service and came to the altar in response to my call for conversion. When he left, he assured us we would be most pleased with the positive article the *Journal* would do.

I relaxed too soon, and it did not take me long to realize I, and many others, had been duped.

Featured on the front page of the *Wall Street Journal*, under the headline "Heavenly Gifts," were several subheads setting the tone of the slashing story. These journalistic hooks shouted, "Preaching a Gospel of Acquisitiveness, a Showy Sect Prospers" and "After TV-Minister Scandals, Assemblies of God Emerge Bigger, Richer Than Ever." The last pejorative subhead proclaimed, "Praying for a Honda Accord." Then the real attack started.

Ignoring other pastors and Assemblies of God officials, the story started with a cynical slam of me. The reporter then attacked the denomination, citing inaccurate statistics and suggesting that our worship style is more fluff than substance. An Assemblies of God spokesperson was misquoted as saying, "The image of a cosmic Santa Claus has crept into our church."

The *Wall Street Journal* article smelled more like a tabloid attack than a balanced report of a responsible newspaper. Nothing was said about all the good work our people do in touching the hurting and helpless of our city.

When the *Wall Street Journal* article came out, the calls and letters started to come in. Some suggested I sue the *Journal*. Others were angry because all our hard work among the homeless, hurting, and helpless was totally ignored by the article. Every day I had calls, letters, and faxes telling me what I should do in response.

The general superintendent of the Assemblies of God, G. Raymond Carlson, wrote, "I have tried to call you several times in recent days since the job the reporter did on us in the *Wall Street Journal*. He made every approach as being on the level, but in turn did a piece of dishonest journalism. Possibly Matthew 5:11–12 would be helpful at this point."

The Scripture passage that Superintendent Carlson called to my attention simply says:

> Blessed are you when men revile you, and persecute you, and say all kinds of evil against you falsely, on account of Me.

> Rejoice, and be glad, for your reward in heaven is great, for so they persecuted the prophets who were before you.
>
> —MATTHEW 5:11–12

Finally, I did do something. I wrote a letter to Robert Johnson. Here is what it said:

> Dear Rob:
>
> Choice Christian greetings!
>
> Although your article has brought me much distress, my real heartbreak is that I apparently failed to be a good witness of Jesus Christ to you.
>
> Rob, if my words and actions in any way offended you or were a bad example, I ask you to please forgive me. I have examined my heart before God in prayer and have asked Him to remove anything from my life that should not be there.
>
> I really did enjoy my time with you and found you to be a very likable, nice man. I do truly love you, Rob, and if at any time I can be a blessing in any way, please just contact me.
>
> Again, please forgive me! In our short day together I felt you are earnestly seeking for God and reality. And, although we might have turned you off by our methods, please keep your eyes on Him who never fails! I pray for you every day, and I would appreciate it if you would also pray for me.
>
> YOUR FRIEND,
> TOMMY BARNETT
>
> P.S. A reply is not necessary.

There is a simple and spiritual reason I wrote that letter and meant every word of it. I had to. I had to forgive because you can't move forward looking in the rearview mirror!

My church did not need a bitter pastor. They deserved better. The hurt I experienced was so small compared to the gaping wounds of our world. If I spend all my time licking my own wounds, I cannot help heal the wounds of others. Therefore, I had to make a conscious and determined decision to let go of my hurts and anger so I could get on with my reason for being. It was not important for the *Journal* reporter to apologize, ask forgiveness, or even acknowledge my letter. But it was important that I take my eyes off the rearview mirror and lift them to the whitened harvest all around me.

As I pondered how to respond to the unfairness dealt me, I was taken back to the cross and the example of our Lord in His last moments. There is a stirring and startling scene that grabs me and holds me in check when I am tempted to react too quickly. The Scripture says, "And when they had come to a place called Golgotha, which means Place of a Skull, they gave him wine to drink mingled with gall; and after tasting it, he was unwilling to drink it" (Matt. 27:33–34).

Christ tasted the gall, but He spit it out!

Gall was a poisonous herb growing spontaneously in the furrows of the fields in Israel. Frequently this wild weed, or gourd, was mixed with wine to make a stupefying drink powerful enough to shut off pain for a season. Gall was brutally bitter, and during Jeremiah's day sore punishment was likened to a drink of gall water. We are not told whether Jesus was offered the drink out of mercy or meanness. All we know is that when He tasted the wine mixed with gall, He spit it out.

Life is so structured that at times we will be handed wine mixed with gall. If we are to be like Jesus, we must spit out the bitterness, refusing to ingest it.

It is always tempting to drink wine mixed with gall when we are being "crucified." When we hurt so badly, anything that makes the pain stop for even a moment feels good. Self-pity and bitterness are like gall. It will ease pain momentarily as we justify our position and lash out at those who are hurting us. But bitterness will also kill us! The Bible warns, "Watch out that no bitterness takes root among you, for as it springs up it causes deep trouble, hurting many in their spiritual lives" (Heb. 12:14–15, TLB).

Tragically, many are like the lady living in the early part of this century who was bitten by a rabid dog. She immediately got a pad and pencil and started writing down a long list of names. When asked why she was doing this, she replied, "These are the people I plan to bite before I die."

Raymond Carlson gave the right advice: Rejoice and be glad when you are persecuted and lied about for His name's sake. But you can't rejoice unless you spit out the gall of bitterness.

The present pain will pass, but how we react and respond during these tense and testing times will follow forever. After I had written that letter to Rob Johnson, my spirits soared. I was free again!

There was a new spring to my step and a new note in my song. I enjoyed preaching, and my heart overflowed with love for the wonderful people God had given me. I saw sunshine everywhere I looked. I forgave and forgot for my own sake—and in doing so found fullness of life!

Making Trouble Become Your Servant

I WANT TO give you one principle that has changed my life and our church. Speaking through the prophet Jeremiah, God made this comment:

> Nebuchadnezzar king of Babylon, My servant. . . .
>
> —JEREMIAH 25:9

I can understand why Abraham, Moses, Job, Joshua, and others were called "My servant." But Nebuchadnezzar? This wicked, ruthless, vile, and merciless king?

Nebuchadnezzar hated everything about God. He hated the house of God. He destroyed Jerusalem, the temple, and the altar, and he carried the vessels used in worship to Babylon. He hated the people of God. Most were killed, and many were taken into captivity and treated as slaves.

It is as if God were saying, "This wicked king hates Me and is trying to destroy My work, My people, and My house. He would try to destroy Me if he could. He thinks he's trying to hurt My people, but I'll make him My servant instead. I'll confound his plans and use his evil intentions for good."

We can also cause our adversaries and our troubles to become our servants.

What you are, you have made yourself. By yielding to Satan and his pressures, you can allow adversities to break your spirit and destroy you. Your troubles can become a stumbling block, or they can become a stepping stone that lifts you to higher ground. They can become your master, or they can become your servant.

I have determined that I will use my adversity and opposition as my servants, and you can do the same thing.

Remember when the newspaper editor refused to hear my side of the story and declared that he could print anything he wanted? *The Arizona Republic* and *The Phoenix Gazette* determined to be my opponents, but God caused their unjustified criticism to be a servant to Phoenix First Assembly and to me.

There are people who experience what seems to be much more than their share of difficulties. The hard times make some bitter and others better. Some have allowed past problems to spoil their faith. Whenever they face a new challenge, all they can think of are the problems of the past. They sound like broken records reciting them. Consequently, they have little faith that anything will ever turn out good for them.

Gideon was like that. The Midianites had invaded and brutally dominated the children of Israel. Like many people today, Gideon had difficulty believing the God of miracles was with them because of all the troubles they had encountered.

> Then the angel of the LORD came and sat under the oak that was in Ophrah, which belonged to Joash the Abiezrite as his son Gideon was beating out wheat in the wine press in order to save it from the Midianites. And the angel of the LORD appeared to him and said to him, "The LORD is with you, O valiant warrior." Then Gideon said to him, "O my lord, if the LORD is with us, why then has all this happened to us? And where are all His miracles which our fathers told us about, saying, 'Did not the Lord bring us up from Egypt?' But now the Lord has abandoned us and given us into the hand of Midian." And the Lord looked at him and said, "Go in this your strength and deliver Israel from the hand of Midian. Have I not sent you?"
>
> —JUDGES 6:11–14

The occupation of the Midianites had its purpose in the discipline of the children of Israel. But it was also an opportunity for Gideon. If he was to be used by God in a historic dimension, Gideon would first have to forget what was behind and move ahead in faith. He had to quit nursing the problems of the past.

Troubles can be your servant, or they can keep you from the making of a miracle. They can be your stepping stone or your stumbling block. They can make you better or just bitter.

It's up to you.

9

Pass On to the Positive

WHEN THE CHURCH initially got into the conflict with the media and city officials over the prayer chapel, I felt some real anxiety. Only those very close to me knew how troubled I was.

One of the ten commandments for the making of a miracle is this: Don't be blinded by negativism, but pass on to the positive. (See chapter 2.)

When a crisis like this takes place, the first inclination is to worry. It sometimes takes me a couple of days to get back into a positive frame of mind. But after I get over those first few days, people ask how I can be so joyful in the midst of such a mess.

I always try to keep a good attitude. Certainly I have my moments when I'm not on top of things, but I'm always working on my frame of mind. If I didn't work on it so much, I wouldn't do as well as I do. We all need to know better how to fight the battle against negativism and pass on to the positive.

Creating a Monster in Your House

YOU NEVER COME to be something or someone you did not first become in your thoughts. The wise man said, "As he thinketh in his heart, so is he" (Prov. 23:7, KJV). Who you are is a direct result of what you think.

Jesus instructed us not to be worried or anxious about our lives, our clothing, or our food. We shouldn't waste time on worry because the things we worry about so rarely come to pass anyway.

Worry and anxiety won't do anything to help fix a real problem, either. That was Jesus' point when He asked, "Which of you by being anxious can add a single cubit to his life's span?" (Luke 12:25). His rhetorical question implies that no one can.

Worrying about Goliath's threats did nothing to help the Israelite army defeat him (1 Sam. 17). Worrying won't make your problems go away either. But there is one thing that meditating on and mulling over your predicament will do for you. It will create a monster inside you.

Like most monsters, this one is small when he is born, but he has a voracious appetite. Every time you entertain negative, fearful thoughts about the problem at hand, you feed the little monster. And, of course, he grows. He really loves those negative thoughts. Imagining the worst possible way a situation could end up is the sweetest treat of all for him.

He's never satisfied and always wants more. If you feed him enough, the thought monster inside you will become bigger, hungrier, and more difficult to kill. In fact, he will grow to be even bigger than the external problem that spawned him. He can also be more dangerous. The fear of losing your job can take on a more destructive aspect in your life than the actual consequences of being laid off.

Some people grow very fond of their monster and love to feed him. They don't really want their problems to go away. Then they'd have no negative thoughts with which to feed their pet. But if their problems do go away, they will quickly find more to take their place.

Are you feeding any pet monsters in your life? They are fun to play with for a little while, but be careful. They'll eat your dreams, your hopes, and your faith. They'll destroy your life.

The only way to get rid of these guys is to starve them. Paul gave the prescription for victory over anxiety and negativism.

> Be anxious for nothing, but in everything by prayer and supplication with thanksgiving let your requests be made known to God. And the peace of God, which surpasses all comprehension, shall guard your hearts and your minds in Christ Jesus. Finally, brethren, whatever is true, whatever is honorable, whatever is right, whatever is pure, whatever is lovely, whatever is of good repute, if there is any excellence and if anything worthy of praise, let your mind dwell on these things. The things you have learned and received and heard and seen in me, practice these things; and the God of peace shall be with you.
>
> —Philippians 4:6–9

One of the ways to stop feeding the monster is to think about something else. You may believe you are helping somebody by sitting with them hour after hour, day after day, talking about their problems. But, in effect, you are indirectly helping them feed their anxiety.

The most important thing both of you can do is get your minds back on God. If you release your problem to God and stop worrying about it, it becomes God's problem. But when you start worrying, it becomes your problem again.

Problems are perpetuated in direct proportion to the amount of thought you give them. You will discover that the problem loses its power over you as you stop meditating on it.

> You will keep him in perfect peace,
> Whose mind is stayed on You.
>
> —ISAIAH 26:3, NKJV

The Secret Chamber

EZEKIEL WAS SITTING in his house one day with the elders of Judah when "the hand of the LORD God fell" on him (Ezek. 8:1). He saw a brightly glowing heavenly figure that "stretched out the form of a hand," picked him up by the hair of his head and transported him in a vision to the temple in Jerusalem (Ezek. 8:3).

At the north gate of the inner court, Ezekiel saw people worshiping an idol that was called the "image of Lust" (Ezek. 8:5, NEB). The heavenly being said to him:

> Son of man, do you see what they are doing, the great abominations which the house of Israel are committing here, that I should be far from My sanctuary? But yet you will see still greater abominations.
>
> —EZEKIEL 8:6

As bad as the offense was in the court of the temple, there was still something more sinister taking place out of sight. Elijah was taken to a place near the entrance to the inner court and was shown a hole in the wall. Ezekiel was instructed to dig through the place in the wall, and, having done so, he found an entranceway and a passage that led to a secret chamber.

> And He [the heavenly being] said to me, "Go in and see the

> wicked abominations that they are committing here." So I entered and looked, and behold, every form of creeping things and beasts and detestable things, with all the idols of the house of Israel, were carved on the wall all around. And standing in front of them were seventy elders of the house of Israel, with Jaazaniah the son of Shaphan standing among them, each man with his censer in his hand, and the fragrance of the cloud of incense rising. Then He said to me, "Son of man, do you see what the elders of the house of Israel are committing in the dark, each man in the room of his carved images? For they say, 'The LORD does not see us; the LORD has forsaken the land.'"
>
> —EZEKIEL 8:9–12

The elders of Israel were having secret meetings in a hidden chamber where they burned incense to their images and idols. This was taking place in the temple, not far from the most holy place and from the court where the sacrifices were offered on the altar.

Ezekiel's vision provides a good illustration for us and challenges us to consider what is going on in our temple.

The New Testament teaches that we as Christians are the temple of God because the Holy Spirit lives in us. Think of the burning of incense as a person's meditations and thought life.

Among those things offered up as sacrifices in our temple are our thoughts. We are to offer up "a sacrifice of praise, the fruit of lips that give thanks to His name" (Heb. 13:15). David said, "Let the words of my mouth and the meditation of my heart be acceptable in Thy sight, O Lord, my rock and my redeemer" (Ps. 19:14).

Every person has a secret chamber in his heart. No one sees what it contains or what goes on in there. No one but the Lord, that is.

Are there dark, secret chambers in your temple where incense is burning to images it shouldn't be? Are there images or altars of lust, hatred, and jealousy? If so, you need to cleanse the dark closets because God sees even in the darkest and most hidden of places.

Another sin of the mind is represented here. The Scripture says that the elders were burning incense in the dark, "each man in the room of his carved images," because, they said, "the LORD does not see us; the LORD has forsaken the land" (Ezek. 8:12).

Apparently a series of trials and tribulations had caused them to give up on their faith in God. They assumed that He had forsaken them.

Going through difficult times will either make you bitter or better.

Unfortunately, the pain, discouragement, and disappointment of the past have gotten the best of some. In the secret chambers of their thoughts they continually burn incense to images of resentment, fear, and the pain of disappointment.

It's time for us to pull down the idols, rid ourselves of the images, and get back to offering the acceptable sacrifices of praise and worship. The apostle Paul said we should be "casting down imaginations, and every high thing that exalteth itself against the knowledge of God, and bringing into captivity every thought to the obedience of Christ" (2 Cor. 10:5, KJV).

Sometimes you have to think things through to come up with answers. You don't have to deny that difficulties exist, but *how* you think about them is what will make the difference. You should look at the problems in the light of this fact: For the unlimited God you serve, all things are possible.

God can solve a problem in a thousand ways. When you look at the obstacles in that frame of mind, He will reveal one of those solutions. My advice is that you don't consider your problems until you have the faith to see them from God's perspective. Try imagining ten different ways God could work things out for you.

You need to take your thoughts captive before they take you captive. Remember: Whatever you are, or will be, started with your thoughts. Don't grow a thought monster inside that you will have to feed forever. Don't burn incense on the altar of resentment, doubt, and fear. Don't be blinded by negativism.

Pass on to the positive.

10

The More You're Spilled, the More You're Filled

As pastor of Phoenix First Assembly of God, I spend much of my time trying to provide ways for people to pour—that is, ways for people to use what they have.

That's why we have 180 outreach ministries. Even if they did nothing for the people we are trying to reach, pouring out is essential for our own sakes. We are only happy and we only grow when we are pouring into empty vessels.

When you dam up streams of water, they become stagnant. Fish die in stagnant water. In that way, many churches have become dead seas rather than flowing rivers.

I have often heard people talking about how "Spirit-filled" a church or a person was. In our consumer-driven society I think we have twisted the meaning and purpose of being Spirit-filled.

Sometimes we describe Christian experiences like merit badges.

"Are you born again?"

"Have you been water baptized?"

"Are you filled with the Holy Spirit?"

These are not awards to be displayed like patches on your sleeve. They are parts of a dynamic and ongoing relationship with God.

"Oh, yes, I was filled with the Spirit back in 1972," I've heard people say. Sometimes I want to ask if it had occurred to them that they might have leaked a little since then.

Peter and John were dragged before the counsel of the scribes and Pharisees (the Sanhedrin) to give an account of how they had healed the lame man who sat outside the gate of the temple.

> And when they had placed them in the center, they began to inquire, "By what power, or in what name, have you done this?" Then Peter, filled with the Holy Spirit, said to them . . .
>
> —ACTS 4:7–8

The literal rendering of the text is noted in the margin of many translations. In the New American Standard it reads: " . . . having just been filled with the Holy Spirit." Peter was filled with the Holy Spirit, and then he spoke out in boldness.

The same phrase is used again referring to Paul in Cyprus when he confronted Elymas the magician.

> But Saul, who was also known as Paul, [having just been] filled with the Holy Spirit, fixed his gaze upon him.
>
> —ACTS 13:9

The text goes on to say that Paul proclaimed that Elymas would be blinded because of his opposition to the gospel. It happened as Paul declared, and as a result the proconsul believed.

When Peter and John returned from their confrontation with the scribes and Pharisees over the healing of the lame man, they reported to the rest the threats that had been issued; that is, that they should not preach anymore in the name of Jesus. All that were present lifted up their voices in prayer. As a result the place where they gathered was shaken, and they were "all filled with the Holy Spirit, and began to speak the word of God with boldness" (Acts 4:31).

Here were all these apostles and disciples being filled with the Holy Spirit again!

Some Pentecostals and evangelicals have differing ideas about the baptism of the Spirit as a second blessing. But regardless of your belief about theology and terminology, we all need to be filled with the Holy Spirit, continually, regularly, daily.

I pray for power every morning—even beg for God's power. I believe God likes to hear me dependent on Him! I have little signs I post in my car and office that read: "Pray for power." I had these little notes printed up for our church, too. Our people have them stuck up everywhere.

Paul exhorted the Ephesians to be filled with the Spirit (Eph. 5:18). The use of the present tense form of the Greek verb *plerousthe,* "be filled," signifies that being filled with the Spirit is a continuous and repetitive process.[1]

For the apostles, being filled with the Holy Spirit was not something that happened only once. It was an ongoing occurrence that always resulted in a demonstration of love and service to others.

No one has any need to be filled unless he or she intends to be poured. And the more you are poured, the more you are refilled.

The more appropriate question would be: Are you Spirit-spilled?

Getting blessed, being touched, or even "falling under the power" is not the same as being Spirit-filled. The measure of our spirituality should be not how much we get but how much we give—how much of the Spirit and grace of God flows through us, not just to us.

I have heard people talk about how much they love a particular church because they really get blessed there. You need to get blessed in church, but it is more important that you become a blessing and become someone else's miracle.

People argue about the biblical pattern of being filled with the Spirit and the corresponding theological implications. If the biblical pattern tells us anything, it is that being filled with God's Spirit turns you into a lover and a giver (1 John 4:12–13).

Every year at Christmastime I ask our people to go out and buy a present for a hurting, underprivileged child in our city. They can spend as much as they want, but it has to be worth five dollars or more. I also ask them to pray that God will lead them to the present He wants them to buy.

They bring their presents in and put them at the foot of our huge singing Christmas tree. Last year we brought in about eight thousand underprivileged kids to our church for a special Christmas program. At the end of the service, we led all the children into the auditorium.

The orchestra and the two hundred people standing on the forty-five-foot singing Christmas tree led the congregation in singing carols as the children came in to find two mountains of presents under the tree, one for the boys and one for the girls.

Every year when those children come down the aisle, the adults in our congregation weep and cry so much they can hardly sing.

Dear reader, please hear this: If it didn't bless any of those kids, I would continue to give away presents for the sake of our congregation. Every person who puts a present under that tree has the opportunity to pour into an empty vessel. They have found that the joy of the Lord comes from pouring.

One of the little boys asked his bus pastor to pray with him that he would get an electric train for Christmas.

"Do you think God would give me an electric train?" he asked.

The bus pastor really didn't know what to say as they prayed together. He was afraid that a disappointment could destroy the little boy's faith. He knew that someone in the church might buy a train. But the presents were wrapped and given out randomly. Nobody knew who would get what package. But, as you can guess, someone in the church was led to buy a Lionel electric train set. And, out of all the other presents, that's the one the little boy received.

That young man will never forget that, in the midst of eight thousand dirty, rambunctious little kids, he was so special to God that his prayer was heard and answered. But it was no less of a blessing for that family who had the privilege of seeing a miracle happen as they poured into an empty vessel.

The Kingdom Invisible Appears

TEMPERATURES WELL OVER 100 degrees in Phoenix are not as uncomfortable as 90-degree weather in other places. The reason is the low humidity in Arizona. There is very little moisture in the air.

Even in areas with low humidity, however, there is always some water in the air all around us. We breathe it, and sometimes we can feel it on a muggy day.

The *dew point* is the temperature at which that moisture in the air begins to form into water droplets. When that happens at high altitudes, the droplets fall as rain. The coolness of the evening causes dew drops to form on the ground.

It is at the dew point that the invisible reality of airborne water becomes visible.

God is like the moisture in the air: He's everywhere. Theologians use the word *omnipresent,* which means "present at all places at the same time." The power, glory, and love of God are all around us, but His kingdom is invisible to our eyes.

When the nature and character of God are displayed through His servants, the kingdom becomes a little more visible. When miracles occur, we begin to realize how close God really is. This was true with the feeding of the five thousand, the water turned to wine at Cana, the great catch of fish from the other side of the boat, and so on.

When we give in faith and pour into others, the invisible kingdom of God manifests itself. When the widow began to pour into the empty vessels, the kingdom invisible became the kingdom visible.

One of the kids at the Christmas party looked up and saw that huge singing Christmas tree, the lights, the presents. He turned to his bus pastor and said, "Is this heaven?"

In a way, yes, it was, not the place we go to spend eternal life, but a visible manifestation of the kingdom of God.

What made it happen? People gave.

It seemed like heaven for the little boy, but it seemed that way even more so for the members of our church, because by pouring into those empty vessels they felt the nearness of the presence of God.

The Giving-ness of God

GOD GIVES LIFE and breath to all mankind, He gives grace and mercy irrespective of our unworthiness, and He gave His only Son for us because He so loved the world. God is a giver!

When you look at the giving-ness of God, you peer right into His very heart and nature. It is the very essence of who He is. We are not offered forgiveness because we deserve it, nor do we live and breathe because we are worthy of it or go to heaven because we have earned it. God is love, and love gives freely.

There are two ways you can live: either as a giver who is becoming more and more like God, or as a taker preoccupied with self. The Bible says that no man can see God and live (Exod. 33:20). When you see the giving-ness in the heart of God, you will begin to die to your selfishness, your grasping, and your acquisitive nature. That, however, is when you really begin to live.

The Pouring Principle

A MAN CRIED out of the crowd, asking Jesus to settle an issue between his brother and him. Apparently, one of the brothers was hoarding the family inheritance.

> And He said to them, "Beware, and be on your guard against every form of greed; for not even when one has an abundance does his life consist of his possessions." And He told them a parable, saying, "The land of a certain rich man was very productive. And he began reasoning to himself, saying, 'What shall I do, since I have no place to store my crops?' And he said, 'This is what I will do: I will tear down my barns and build larger ones, and there I will store all my grain and my goods. And I will say to my soul, "Soul, you have many goods laid up for many years to come; take your ease, eat, drink and be merry."'
>
> "But God said to him, 'You fool! This very night your soul

> is required of you; and now who will own what you have prepared?' So is the man who lays up treasure for himself, and is not rich toward God."
>
> —LUKE 12:15–21

The rich man was not a fool because he was rich. God loves prosperous and successful people. But it had never occurred to this rich man that his prosperity was a gift from God for the purpose of pouring abundantly into others. One man in our church, whose business has been very productive, buys two hundred fifty brand-new bicycles each year at Christmas for the needy kids. But this rich man Jesus spoke of hoarded it all for himself.

One of the greatest hindrances to real joy is that we let our perceptions and behavior be determined by those who want to sell us something. American commercials tell us constantly that value, self-worth, and happiness come from what we can obtain. In other words, our lives consist of our possessions.

Wrong!

Our culture and the media driving it teach us what is contrary to the kingdom of God—that joy comes from abundant possessions rather than abundant giving.

This even finds its way into our churches. We are instructed to give so that we can get more. The operant words there are *so that*. . . . The misguided force behind this teaching is that life comes from abundant possessiveness.

To be a cheerful giver means that I'm not giving to get more, all along thinking that life is in the return. A cheerful giver pours because he believes that life is in the pouring.

Those who feign cheerfulness but in reality only rejoice in the thought of their "hundredfold return" will eventually hoard their blessings.

That kind of giving is like playing the stock market. You invest to get a greater return, to reinvest for even greater returns, and so on until you take the cash and run. The point all along was to hoard.

The miracle of multiplication continued as long as the widow continued to pour. The miracle of abundant life continues in our hearts as long as we continue to be "Spirit-spilled." If you stop giving, you will certainly dry up as a Christian, and your vessel will be empty. Always keep yourself in a position in which you are able to give.

The widow at Zarephath must have surely hesitated to give her last meal to Elijah. But having given it in faith, there was a miracle in her house. The oil and flour were not exhausted (1 Kings 17:16).

Taking the time, effort, and expense to pour into empty vessels is not a drain. Rather it is invigorating. I always receive back more than I give. That's why after so many years I'm not feeling burned out or exhausted.

So what are you looking for? Are you looking for what you can get out of life, or are you looking for what you can pour out in life? Are you going to be a giver or a taker? Make a decision right now: I am going to pour into empty vessels and be a Spirit-spilled Christian.

11

The Miracle's in the Bush

ONCE AGAIN EXHAUSTION overcame me. I pulled over to the side of the road and stopped the car. It was only seventeen miles from my church to my home, but I had to stop and sleep until I regained the strength to continue.

I had been feeling this way for about three or four months, and I was at my wit's end. I had always jogged five to seven miles a day and played basketball in the church basketball league. I was an extremely active person physically. Even my family noticed the difference. When we vacationed in Hawaii, I spent most of the two weeks in my hotel room. I would get up in the morning and be so tired that I didn't even want to go to the beach. We knew something was wrong.

I was puzzled, but I knew I was God's property and decided to leave it in His hands. If He wanted me to stay in the ministry, He would give me the strength to do it.

Finally I could hide it no longer. Because of the church building program, I was forced to go to the doctor. The bank had asked me to insure the loan; I had to take out a life insurance policy for $7 million to cover the cost of the church. If something happened to me and I couldn't guarantee the loan, the bank would get their money. For that kind of life insurance policy I needed to see several doctors.

I visited the first doctor and took the required test. The report came back, stating that I had a very serious heart condition and was not insurable. I went to two more doctors who gave the same report. We were planning to pursue treatment the following week.

I told George Zimmer, our business manager, what the doctors had said. "Don't tell the church," I cautioned him. "The church doesn't need a sick pastor."

Of all things that Sunday, after my visit to the doctors, I preached on healing.

After the service George came up to me and said, "Tommy, I believe God will heal you if you believe."

"Let's pray," I said.

George laid hands on me and prayed.

Two or three days later he came to me and said, "You look better."

I feel better, I thought.

"Have you been tired?" he asked me.

"No," I told him.

"I believe God healed you," he said.

"How about that?" I said. "I think He did."

We decided I should verify my healing with more medical tests. George said he was going to call Dr. Edward Diethrich to schedule an appointment for me. Dr. Diethrich is a world-renowned heart doctor. In fact, one of our board members, Allan Mayer, the owner of the Oscar Mayer company, was on Dr. Diethrich's board. He personally asked the doctor to test my heart.

At the doctor's office, we went through two days of extensive testing. At the end of those tests, he said to me, "You're the picture of health. There is nothing wrong with your heart. Your heart is great."

God healed me. Now I go every year for checkups for my insurance. After eight years they have never found anything wrong with my heart.

All the blessings Abraham had received meant nothing unless he had an heir to whom he could pass them on. Isaac was the miracle child, the miracle in Abraham's house. And it was through this miracle that all the promises of God to Abraham were going to be realized. Abraham had been promised that his descendants would be as numerous as the dust of the earth and the stars of the heavens (Gen. 13:16; 15:5).

Old Abe might not have been sure he would live to see those descendants, but in Isaac he saw them all. Without Isaac none of the promises of God to him would ever come to pass. Isaac was to Abraham and his promise what my voice was to me and my promise.

> Now it came about after these things, that God tested Abraham, and said to him, "Abraham!" And he said, "Here I am." And He said, "Take now your son, your only son, whom you love,

> Isaac, and go to the land of Moriah; and offer him there as a burnt offering on one of the mountains of which I will tell you."
>
> —GENESIS 22:1–2

You've got to learn to hold the promises of God lightly. Jesus didn't grasp at His rightful position (Phil. 2:6–7). He laid it aside and as a result was exalted by the Father to be the King of kings and Lord of lords.

If God has truly given you a promise, a vision, a gift, or a ministry, you don't have to grasp for it. It is in His hands to bring it to pass. If you hold it too tightly, the gift can eventually become more precious to you than God who gave it.

Though it surely made no sense to Abraham, he set about to do what God had commanded. He ascended the mountain, built the altar, and bound his son.

> And Abraham stretched out his hand, and took the knife to slay his son. But the angel of the LORD called to him from heaven, and said, "Abraham, Abraham!" And he said, "Here I am." And he said, "Do not stretch out your hand against the lad, and do nothing to him; for now I know that you fear God, since you have not withheld your son, your only son, from Me." Then Abraham raised his eyes and looked, and behold, behind him a ram caught in the thicket by his horns; and Abraham went and took the ram, and offered him up for a burnt offering in the place of his son.
>
> —GENESIS 22:10–13

To Abraham, following this God who first spoke to him in Ur certainly had a lot of emotional ups and downs. He left civilization to become a wanderer in the wilderness. He waited for his promised child to be born to his ninety-year-old wife. Now this. But he learned to walk the walk of faith, and it was because of this faith that he received the promises.

It is worth noting that Abraham didn't recognize that the ram was stuck in the bush until he had passed God's test. In the same way, you will often be unable to see that your miracle is also in the bush until you pass the test by putting your desire and your vision on the altar—even if those visions and desires are something you think God has given you.

Sometimes the key to finding your miracle is letting go and letting God fulfill His promise.

When God called me to go to Davenport, I thought, *Surely this offer is just a test.* But sometimes it's no test. God actually wanted something put on the altar. In that case, it was my desire for a big church. But if I had persisted in grasping my vision and what I thought was God's means of fulfilling His promise to me, I would have missed the greatest blessing of all.

Worshiping the Source of Your Miracle

PUTTING YOUR GIFTS, abilities, and even the promises God gives you on the altar is an act of worship to God. If you refuse to do so, it is because you have begun to worship the gift, the talent, or the vision God has given you.

It would be like the widow worshiping the bottle from which the oil continued to pour. When God moves on our behalf, we tend to try to pass on to the next generation the instrument or the method God uses to send us our miracle. Eventually we will make relics out of the instruments of God's blessings.

People have always had the tendency to forget that the source of their miracle is God.

Bronze Serpents Last a Long Time

WHEN THE CHILDREN of Israel were being led through the wilderness, they often complained and rebelled against the Lord and against Moses. On one occasion the Lord sent fiery serpents among the people. Many were bitten and died. They came to Moses repenting of their sin and asking him to intercede for them that God would remove the serpents.

> Then the LORD said to Moses, "Make a fiery serpent, and set it on a standard; and it shall come about, that everyone who is bitten, when he looks at it, he shall live." And Moses made a bronze serpent and set it on the standard; and it came about, that if a serpent bit any man, when he looked to the bronze serpent, he lived.
>
> —NUMBERS 21:8–9

It wasn't the serpent that healed the people; it was God. Yet who could ever forget the significance of that bronze serpent?

Of course, God told Moses to make the serpent, but Moses was the one who decided to make it out of bronze. He might have done better to have made the serpent out of something more perishable. Bronze serpents tend to last a very long time.

More than five hundred years later in the midst of the spiritually dark ages of Israel there arose a young king named Hezekiah. Though his father, King Ahaz, was thoroughly wicked, Hezekiah led a revival that brought Israel back from apostasy. The first order of revival business in those days was the destruction of the altars used for pagan idol worship.

> And he [Hezekiah] did right in the sight of the LORD, according to all that his father David had done. He removed the high places and broke down the sacred pillars and cut down the Asherah. He also broke in pieces the bronze serpent that Moses had made, for until those days the sons of Israel burned incense to it; and it was called Nehushtan.
>
> —2 KINGS 18:3–4

The bronze serpent, once the instrument of the miraculous power of God, was now worshiped as an idol.

Once a missionary came back to America from a country where the people were starving. What they needed more than anything else was a well and a pump to get the water out of the ground. They were Christians, and they needed help. So the missionary raised thousands of dollars to dig that well and put a pump on it. It was wonderful. The water flowed, and the crops began to grow, and they were saved from famine and starvation.

Soon after the well and irrigation system were installed, the missionary went home on furlough. When he returned, he was shocked to find the people had made a shrine and were worshiping the pump.

Being a Purpose-Driven Person

I SURPRISE PEOPLE when I say that I am not a goal-driven person. They wonder how we could have ever built such a church, started so many outreach ministries, and accomplished so much.

I certainly know where I'm going, but I don't dwell on the end goal. Purpose drives my life. It is my purpose to win lost people to Jesus Christ. That's what motivates me every day.

The vision and goal are clear, but they're put away and are seldom reviewed. You see, what you dwell on every day, what drives and motivates you, the thing that becomes the central focus of your life, can easily become something that you worship. And when we start to worship our dreams, visions, and goals, it's very hard to lay them on the altar.

For preachers the goal might be a large church. For others the vision might be for success in business or athletics or living in a more affluent neighborhood. We also have plans and goals for our children.

None of these things is wrong. But if you are looking for a miracle in your house to enable you to fulfill your dreams, you might not find it until you are willing to put those dreams on the altar.

Your vision cannot become your idol. As a young man I dreamed of pastoring a great church. Through the years I didn't ask every day when it was going to come to pass. I didn't think every day, *I'm working toward the vision.* It was just there in my subconscious. I didn't fret; I was enjoying the trip. I was happy abiding in the Lord. If it was His vision, He would bring it to pass.

One day I looked up at our church sanctuary and realized something. It was what I had envisioned when I was a young man. I marveled to myself: *Well, it did come to pass after all.*

I am amazed that I am living in the vision I had years ago. But it has not been an idol, and I have not been obsessed with it. The trip has been more enjoyable than the destination.

Ungrasping Assurance

One of the greatest feelings is to know that what you are doing is God's idea and not your own. If you're doing God's thing, then you have even more assurance that He is going to be with you to help you bring it to pass.

One of the questions most asked of pastors is this: How do you know if what you are wanting to do is just your desire or God's plan?

It's hard to have assurance that it's from God until you put those plans and dreams on the altar. But when the sense of God's guiding is still there after you've laid those things before Him repeatedly with a willing heart to let them go, then you begin to have that assurance.

You can say, "This is not my idea. I laid it on the altar many times. This is God's plan, and I feel it's my duty to obey."

At first you hold on to the vision. Eventually, the vision begins to hold on to you. You couldn't let it go if you wanted to. They say if you keep a vision for five years, it will come to pass. But most people cannot keep a vision for five years. They get discouraged and give up.

I could have grasped for my dream of a large church and missed the miracle of the tiny church in Davenport. I could have refused to leave Davenport and missed the miracle of Phoenix. I could have lost my ministry in that neck operation. Nevertheless, I laid all those plans and dreams on the altar and found that each time God had a miracle in store for me. The miracle was in the bush.

12

The Interval Between Promise and Miracle

GOD SPEAKS TO people in many ways—sometimes through the Bible; other times through people, through dreams, through visions, or through an inner intuition we know as the still, small voice.

However it comes, when a person receives a promise from God, there is usually an interval of time between the promise and the manifestation or fulfillment of that promise. Whether it is a day or years or a lifetime, waiting for God to come through with your miracle can be an agonizing struggle. God is not forgetful, and He's not too busy to attend to the things concerning you. He has a definite purpose for all that He does, even for the delays. So it is important that we know how to respond to God in the interval between promise and miracle. Here are a few things to remember:

1. There Is an Appointed Time for Everything

GOD'S CLOCK DOESN'T seem to operate like mine. I always want to see the answer immediately. Sometimes that happens, but it's not the norm. I've come to learn that there is a difference between what I mean when I say *now* and what God means when He says *now*. For God, *now* is the point He speaks or wills something to be done. It makes no difference whether it has happened in our realm of reality or not. If He wills it, it is so. It is as good as done. For us, *now* is not until we see the physical manifestation.

How God's foreknowledge and His predetermination factor into the outworking of His will in our lives is beyond our knowing. Some have said that, for us, it's as if we're watching a grand parade through a knothole in the fence. We see all the bands and floats go by one by one. But for God, it is as if He sits atop the highest point and looks over the fence to see the entire parade from beginning to end—all at once. For the eternal God, the whole parade of history is *now*.

It's difficult for me, one who lives totally within this world of time and sequence of events, to understand God and His timing. Yet I know there is an appointed time for all things.

Paul in his sermon to the philosophers at Mars Hill said that it was God who "determined their [the nations'] appointed times, and the boundaries of their habitation" (Acts 17:26). He also said, "He has *fixed a day* in which He will judge the world in righteousness through a Man whom He has appointed" (Acts 17:31, italics added).

Part of the reward for Christ's suffering was that He would be made Lord of heaven and earth and that at His judgment seat every knee would bow. That is without a doubt a promise from the Father that, from God's perspective, is already done. But God has *fixed a day* on which the actual event will take place and the fulfillment of the promise to the Son shall be manifest.

God also has a time appointed for the fulfillment of the promise He has made to you. If God has promised it, in a very real sense it is already done.

God had an appointed time for the fullness of Abraham's promise. When Abram was seventy-five years old, God gave him a promise—that from him would come a great nation (Gen. 12:1–3).

But time went by, and there was no child.

The promise was repeated again in more specific terms:

> Then behold, the word of the LORD came to him, saying, "This man [Abram's servant, Eliezer] will not be your heir; but one who shall come forth from your own body, he shall be your heir."
>
> —GENESIS 15:4

Perhaps at that time Abram was tired of believing for the child and was willing to settle for something else and rationalize that it was God's answer. The Lord said, "No, it's going to be a child of your own."

More time passed—twenty-four years to be exact—and still no child. "I am the God Almighty," the Lord said the next time He spoke to him.

Abram may have thought, *Yeah, I'm Abram, and I'm ninety-nine years old. I thought I was going to be a father.*

At this meeting God changed Abram's name to Abraham, which means "the father of a multitude" (Gen. 17:5). It was a strange name for a man almost one hundred years old with no children.

The people who knew Abram, who now called himself Abraham, must have been snickering in their tents, "The old man now calls himself the father of a great multitude." It would seem that the struggle of faith in the interval period had finally gotten to old Abe.

The Lord appeared to Abraham and repeated the promise for the third time. He said:

> Is anything too difficult for the LORD? At the appointed time I will return to you, at this time next year, and Sarah shall have a son.
>
> —GENESIS 18:14

The miracle had been for an appointed time all along. But as far as God was concerned, it was already done, because He had already willed it, spoken it, and even foreseen it. For God, Abraham had always been the father of a multitude.

God has His timetable, and His appointed times are probably not affected very much by our begging and pleading. Abraham, in his frustration over God's timing, tried to make the promise happen by conceiving a son with his maidservant Hagar. You would think that God would have speeded things up to keep Abraham from making such a mistake. No, God had His time, and His time had a purpose.

Solomon said it most beautifully:

> There is an appointed time for everything. And there is a time for every event under heaven—a time to give birth, and a time to die; a time to plant, and a time to uproot what is planted. . . . What profit is there to the worker from that in which he toils? I have seen the task which God has given the sons of men with which to occupy themselves. He has made everything appropriate in its time. He has also set eternity in their heart.
>
> —ECCLESIASTES 3:1–2, 9–11

2. God Is Preparing *You* for the Miracle

MOST OF US would like to run to heaven's bank to cash in on a promise before the day is done. Why does God make it so difficult? Why doesn't He make things happen sooner? Why must we struggle through this interval between promise and fulfillment?

There's a good answer to that, but you may not like it.

It is to perfect our faith and to give it endurance. (See James 1:2–4; 1 Peter 1:6–7.) If we all said what we thought, many of us would reply, "I don't care about having my faith perfected. I just need a miracle, and I need it right now!"

Most of the time when we struggle with God it is because we don't see things from His perspective. The quality and enduring nature of our faith is of relatively little value to us, compared to the supreme importance God places on it. It is to Him more valuable than our good works, our comfort, or even our lives. It was Abraham's faith that was counted as righteousness (Gen. 15:6). It is our faith that brings us salvation and all the promises of our inheritance.

We are always in a hurry to get on with God's plan for our lives, but God's first order of business is dealing with our faith. It is through these intervals, the periods between the promise and the miracle, that this "most holy faith" is perfected (Jude 20).

Abraham was not the only person in the Bible to have his faith operated upon. Jacob waited many years for the promised birthright. His efforts to speed up the process by stealing it from his brother accomplished nothing to speed up the process. He should have learned that from his grandfather's example.

Joseph had to wait and endure much as an Egyptian slave before his dreams came to pass.

Many years and a lot of troubles passed between the time David was anointed as king by Samuel and the day he actually came to sit on the throne.

Each of these biblical figures received a promise but went through a lot in the interval. They were all changed in the process and prepared to receive the promise. That may not be very important to you, but it's the highest order of business to God. In fact, it's the most important thing for you, too. It's just that often you don't realize it.

3. You Need to Prepare Yourself for the Miracle

KING SENNACHERIB OF Assyria invaded Judah during the fourteenth year of the reign of Hezekiah, king of Judah. Sennacherib's messenger, taunting Hezekiah, said:

> Now therefore, come make a bargain with my master the king

> of Assyria, and I will give you two thousand horses, if you are able on your part to set riders on them.
>
> —Isaiah 36:8

That Scripture passage has for years stuck in my mind because it reminds me of one of the first principles I learned concerning the kingdom of God. That principle is: If you just learn to ride, God will give you a horse. In other words, if you will prepare yourself for God's promise, He will bring it to pass.

When I was only four years old, God gloriously came into my heart and saved me. By the time I was ten years old, I knew that I was called to be a preacher. I began to prepare my life for that great event.

At the age of thirteen I would go out in the woods and preach from the tree stumps. I remember the time when I got my buddies together in one of the old buses at my dad's church and preached a sermon complete with an altar call. Some of my friends were saved that way.

I remember going into the church auditorium, locking the doors, turning on the public address system, and preaching to the empty pews. One day I forgot to lock the back door. A man who lived on the street saw the lights and walked in. He saw that no one was there listening to the preacher, but since he had nothing else to do, he sat down and listened to the message. When I gave the altar call, he raised his hand to be saved. So I said, "I want all of you who raised your hands to come forward, from the left to the right, from the front to the rear of this building." The man stood and came forward to receive Christ along with my multitude of imaginary converts.

I would often go down to the mission and preach to the alcoholics and transients. That's one of the reasons why I love those people so much today. I was just a kid, not a minister or a preacher. I was learning how to ride, even though I didn't have a horse.

When I was sixteen years of age, I held my first revival in Seminole, Texas. Some might say that is when my ministry began. Actually, it began at ten years of age when I received the promise. But during the interval between the promise and the manifestation, I was learning how to ride. Pretty soon God gave me a horse.

You may feel God has spoken to you about getting married. Even if you don't know who the lucky person is, prepare yourself. Read books; go to seminars; prepare your finances. Whatever the promise may be, do something to put your faith into action. Prepare yourself by learning how to ride.

4. Be Careful How You Claim the Promises

IT CAN BE terribly disappointing to spend years believing for a promise, only to find that it was not God's promise to you but something you just claimed for yourself. We must be careful how we claim promises.

The Scriptures record what God had to say to certain people in the context of their situations. Those words often contain promises that a Christian can claim and apply to his or her situation. But, it's helpful to get advice from pastors and other mature Christians concerning which verses or promises you should accept as a promise from God for yourself. In the end, however, you alone are going to have to discern what God is saying to you.

One of the ways the callings and promises of God are confirmed is in the process of learning to ride without the horse. If you think God has spoken to you and given you a promise, do something as an act of faith. If you believe He's told you that you will go to the mission field, in the interval while you are waiting for the open door, study foreign culture and language, reach out to the internationals in your city, and pray for the nations. If you go to the mission field, you know you'll have to clean out that sock drawer. So go ahead and clean it out.

It *would* be foolish to do something like quitting your job presumptuously. Many people have made mistakes because they got ahead of God's appointed time. But do what you can until God opens the door to take a further step.

Many people are waiting for a promise but not preparing for it to come to pass. The rudder on a ship does no good unless the ship is moving. It is in the process of doing what you can, stepping out in faith and learning to ride, that God's calling and promises are either confirmed or redirected in your heart.

The interval between the promise and the manifestation can be a difficult struggle. But remember that God has His appointed time, and if He has said it, it will surely come to pass. In this interval of time let God do His perfect work in your faith. As for you, get busy learning to ride.

13

Whatever He Says to You, Do It

IT SEEMS THAT almost everyone looks for a method—for healing, church growth, success in business, repairing broken relationships, and so on.

Many will travel to the ends of the earth to attend a conference that will show them step-by-step how to be successful in one area or another.

"I need a miracle, and I want to be able to put my finger on exactly how to make it happen for me."

I suppose it would be much easier to reduce everything to formulas, but that's not how it works with God. That's not how it works in life either. Methods and formulas enable us to calculate long-term strategies and manage risk. But they also offer the hope of results without the trouble of a relationship with God.

Good ideas, methods, and even the examples of others' successes by themselves are like a fine-tuned engine without any gasoline. It is God who fuels our efforts and turns our dreams into reality. This is the most important part of the making of miracles—it is God who is the miracle maker.

There are two more stories of miracles in the house that I want to talk about. The first took place at a wedding.

> And on the third day there was a wedding in Cana of Galilee, and the mother of Jesus was there; and Jesus also was invited, and His disciples, to the wedding. And when the wine gave out, the mother of Jesus said to Him, "They have no wine." And Jesus said to her, "Woman, what do I have to do with you? My hour has not yet come." His mother said to the

> servants, "Whatever He says to you, do it." Now there were six stone waterpots set there for the Jewish custom of purification, containing twenty or thirty gallons each. Jesus said to them, "Fill the waterpots with water." And they filled them up to the brim. And He said to them, "Draw some out now, and take it to the headwaiter." And they took it to him. And when the headwaiter tasted the water which had become wine, and did not know where it came from (but the servants who had drawn the water knew), the headwaiter called the bridegroom, and said to him, "Every man serves the good wine first, and when men have drunk freely, then that which is poorer; you have kept the good wine until now."
>
> —JOHN 2:1–10

As the years went by, no matter how many times they refilled those waterpots, the water would never again be turned to wine. No matter how many times the widow would try to reproduce the circumstance that led up to her miracle, she just couldn't get the oil to multiply in her little bottle.

It wasn't the type of waterpots they refilled or the arrangement of the borrowed vessels or time of day she poured the oil. In each case what caused the miracle to occur is that the people did what the Lord said. If there is any formula here at all, it is that obedience to the Lord is the essential ingredient for the making of miracles.

The angel Gabriel, after telling Mary she would conceive a child by the Holy Spirit, said to her, "For nothing will be impossible with God" (Luke 1:37). Literally, the verse reads, "No word shall be impossible with God." The Greek word *rhema* that is used in this verse refers to the spoken word. Whatever God speaks to you is possible.

There's always a miracle in the house somewhere, but it's not always in the same place, and it often does not occur in the same way twice. We must be careful how we presume upon God's directions.

On one occasion, Moses was commanded to take the staff in his hand and strike the rock. He did so, and water came out (Exod. 17:6). Later he was told to speak to the rock, but he just went ahead and struck it as he had done before. When Moses used his staff in disobedience, it cost him his trip to the Promised Land (Num. 20:7–13).

We can't operate on someone else's vision or methods. We have to get a firsthand revelation from God ourselves. At our conference each year over six thousand pastors and church leaders listen for days to us talk about our 180 different ministries, special event days, and hundreds of other ideas that have worked for us in Phoenix. But in the final session I tell them to go and get God's plan for themselves. They have to have a firsthand revelation of what God wants them to do.

On the last night we all go out to the mountain on the backside of our property, where we make a large cross out of hundreds of candles. The mountainside is filled with people singing and crying out to God for their own direction. You can hear it all night for miles.

To do it just the way I've done it, I tell them, might be like young David putting on Saul's armor. It just didn't fit. God was wanting to do something miraculous through David but in a totally different way.

Victory is not in methods but in miracles. Mary gave the best advice of all: Whatever He says to you, do it!

There is one final story in the Bible about miracles we need to consider. This time the miracle was in the boat.

The multitude pressed hard around Jesus to hear His every word. Seeing two boats at the edge of the lake of Gennesaret, He asked the fishermen who were washing their nets to put out a little way from the land so that He could preach from the boat. The boat belonged to Simon, who was also called Peter.

> And when He had finished speaking, He said to Simon, "Put out into the deep water and let down your nets for a catch." And Simon answered and said, "Master, we worked hard all night and caught nothing, but at Your bidding I will let down the nets." And when they had done this, they enclosed a great quantity of fish; and their nets began to break.
>
> —Luke 5:4–6

In the making of every miracle are faith, obedience, and the willingness to take a risk. These represent for you the three hurdles that you must overcome: doubt, fear, and thinking you know it all.

It would have been much easier to ignore Jesus' suggestion rather than to load the nets up again into the boat. Fishing all night tends to wear you out. Simon and his coworkers had no reason to believe they would catch anything—except that Jesus said to do it.

What did Jesus know about fishing anyway? They were the experts. Sometimes we become prisoners of our knowledge and expertise. I have heard so many people, church-growth authorities included, tell me at every juncture that what I was attempting to do wouldn't work. The miracle happened anyway—but not because I was so smart. I had no reason to believe it would work either. I had nothing on which to base my faith except that I felt God said to do it.

Some people are addicted to impossibility thinking. For them nothing is going to work—ever! All they can see are the problems, the obstacles, and every possible thing that could go wrong. Oftentimes such a negative, cynical perspective is rooted in a failure or a series of past failures.

Cynics are disillusioned idealists. Somewhere along the line something didn't work out for them. They became disillusioned and have been rehearsing their disappointment ever since. They have become shipwrecked with regard to their faith. Every promise of God and every hope and expectation for miracles are qualified or even discounted by the memory of their past disappointments.

It is as if they had fished all night and caught nothing. So why should they try anymore?

Paul, at the end of his ministry, said to his friends in Philippi:

> Brethren, I do not regard myself as having laid hold of it yet; but one thing I do: forgetting what lies behind and reaching forward to what lies ahead, I press on toward the goal for the prize of the upward call of God in Christ Jesus.
>
> —PHILIPPIANS 3:13–14

Paul said that forgetting what lies behind was the *one thing* he did. We need to see how important forgetting really is.

If you ponder the past, your life will be shaped by it. What you hold in your memory, you will see in your experience. But if you are going to start walking in victory and newness of life, you have to forget how you have lived a life of limitation, failure, and futility.

How do you know what it is you haven't forgotten? Tell me what you think about all the time, and I'll show you what you haven't forgotten. If it's constantly on your mind, it will constantly be in your experience. Let me tell you something. Attitude is everything. The world is full of people with wounded faith, and if you happen to be one of them, today is the day to stop living in the past. You need to forget your failure and go on.

Remembering the past is a habit. Habits take time to form and discipline to break. One of the best ways you can change is to cultivate new thoughts. You can't think about two things at once. So get a new thought to crowd out the old.

Paul was reaching for the ultimate, so he had to forget what lay behind and press on. God has a great purpose for your life, so don't sit back nursing your memories. Be like Simon Peter who said, "We worked hard all night and caught nothing, *but at Your bidding* I will let down the nets" (Luke 5:5, italics added).

Launch Out Into Deep Water

JESUS SAID TO Peter, "Put out into the deep water and let down your nets for a catch" (Luke 5:4). Though the depth of the water presented no danger at the time for the fishermen in the boat, remember that it was this same Simon Peter who later took a dangerous step out of the boat in the midst of a storm to walk on the water.

For us, deep water can be symbolic of taking a substantial risk. The greatest hindrance to walking by faith is trying to be fail-safe. Methods and formulas are for people who want to calculate their risk. But following God is totally unpredictable. Abraham left Ur of the Chaldees without a plan or a road map. He was just obeying the voice.

People are longing for God to work in their lives or perform miracles in their situations. The problem for many is that if He speaks, they won't do anything. If He challenges them, they will not take the risk.

When the challenge comes, they say, I just need one more sign and one more confirmation. Some have hundreds of words and confirmations. There's no sense talking about asking God for a miracle if you're not going to do anything when you hear from Him.

Every time I've found a miracle in the house, it's because I took the risk and obeyed the leading. Every time I've released people to take charge, it's a big risk. What if they fail? What if they are unfaithful? What if the water's too deep, and they're in over their heads? Well, we'll be in trouble. But I'll never know—and they'll never know—until they take the plunge. So many times as a pastor I just pray, lead the cheers, and hold on for the ride. Every time we plan a big event, try a new idea, or reach out to a new group of people, we take a risk. What if the miracles stop?

I believe in people, and I believe in miracles. As long as we have kept pouring, the fresh oil has kept multiplying. God will do that for you, too.

It's not just that God wants to give you a miracle; He wants to *make* you a miracle in someone else's life, too. That's where the greatest joy of all comes from. Remember: The more you're spilled, the more you are filled.

So make the decision to be a giver and a pourer. You may just discover that the miracle's in the house.

Forget what lies behind.

Step out into the deep.

Find some empty vessels and start pouring.

And whatever He says to you, do it.

NOTES

Chapter 3:
Being Led to Your Next Miracle

1. From the hymn "Trust and Obey," text by John H. Sammis, music by Daniel B. Towner. Public domain.

Chapter 5:
Finding the Miracle Within

1. Tom Peters and Robert Waterman, *In Search of Excellence: Lessons From America's Best Run Companies* (New York: Warner Books, 1982), 228.
2. *The New Strong's Exhaustive Concordance of the Bible* (Nashville, TN: Thomas Nelson, 1984), Greek Dictionary of the New Testament, #264.

Chapter 7:
Miracles on My Doorstep

1. From "The Shoes of Happiness" by Edwin Markham (1852–1940). Reprinted from the book *Giant Hours With Poet Preachers,* compiled by William L. Stidger (New York: Abingdon Press, 1918).

Chapter 8:
Don't Let Troubles Keep You From the Making of a Miracle

1. Editorial cartoon, *The Arizona Republic* (Phoenix), 18 September 1988.
2. Editorial, *The Arizona Republic* (Phoenix), 16 September 1988.
3. Ibid., 18 October 1988.
4. Editorial cartoon, *The Arizona Republic* (Phoenix), 18 October 1988.
5. Dee J. Hall, "Church's Chapel Plan Irks Neighbors," *The Arizona Republic* (Phoenix), 16 October 1988, section B.
6. Dee J. Hall, "Church's Tower Plan Is Derailed," *The Arizona Republic* (Phoenix), 19 October 1988, section A.
7. Ibid.

Chapter 10:
The More You're Spilled, the More You're Filled

1. John Rea, *The Holy Spirit in the Bible* (Lake Mary, FL: Creation House, 1990), 293–294.